Antifascism and the Avant-Garde

Antifascism and the Avant-Garde

RADICAL DOCUMENTARY IN THE 1960S

Julia Alekseyeva

UNIVERSITY OF CALIFORNIA PRESS

University of California Press
Oakland, California

© 2025 by Julia Alekseyeva

All right reserved.

Library of Congress Cataloging-in-Publication Data

Names: Alekseyeva, Julia, author.
Title: Antifascism and the avant-garde : radical documentary in the 1960s / Julia Alekseyeva.
Description: Oakand : University of California Press, 2025. | Includes bibliographical references and index.
Identifiers: LCCN 2024030503 (print) | LCCN 2024030504 (ebook) | ISBN 9780520415669 (cloth) | ISBN 9780520415676 (paperback) | ISBN 9780520415690 (ebook)
Subjects: LCSH: Documentary films—History and criticism. | Antifascist movements in motion pictures. | Motion pictures—Japan—History—20th century. | Motion pictures—France—History—20th century.
Classification: LCC PN1995.9.D6 A375 2025 (print) | LCC PN1995.9.D6 (ebook) | DDC 070.1/8—dc23/eng/20240917
LC record available at https://lccn.loc.gov/2024030503
LC ebook record available at https://lccn.loc.gov/2024030504

34 33 32 31 30 29 28 27 26 25
10 9 8 7 6 5 4 3 2 1

Pour tous mes compagnons de route

Contents

	Acknowledgments	ix
	Introduction	1
1.	1960 Japan: ANPO and Antifascism in the Neo-documentary	34
2.	1962 France: Dreamlike Communism and the Left Bank in a Decolonizing World	65
3.	1964 Japan: The Allegorical Semi-documentary in an Age of Neonationalism	97
4.	1969 France: Unpleasure and Radical Epistemology in Post-May Godard	130
5.	1969 Japan: Queer Self-Revolutions of the Art Theatre Guild	157
	Coda	193
	Notes	203
	Bibliography	231
	Index	247

Acknowledgments

This book would not have been possible without the efforts and kindness of more people than I could ever name. We are all an amalgamation of our disparate communities, and I am thankful to have been a part of so many, across so many eras and so many continents.

I am especially thankful to Justin Weir and Alexander Zahlten, who were instrumental in the book's first seedlings of conception and encouraged me through years of grueling dissertation research. Without any exaggeration, your courses and guidance changed my brain chemistry. I am also lucky to have been surrounded by so many brilliant thinkers while at Harvard: Tom Conley, who forever inspired me to look closer at every frame; Diane Wei Lewis, Franz Prichard, and Nick Kapur, for drawing me ever closer to Japanese film and history; and to my friends and comrades of the grad student proletariat—Ania Aizman, Lusia Zaitseva, Kate Rennebohm, Katie Kohn, Tatyana Gershkovich, Andrew Littlejohn, and Molly Klaisner.

My deep dive into Matsumoto would not have been possible without Ari Sato, who helped me crack the first intimidating round into *Discovery of the Image,* watched endlessly bizarre Japanese films to understand my research, and who, perhaps most importantly, taught me that Hulu in

Japanese is "Fooroo." My IUC friends in Japan kept me going through a very dark and difficult period, and I am so thankful to Kelly McCormick, Paride Stortini, Will Carroll, Kyle Peters, Nick Risteen, Erika Enomoto, and Lingling Ma for fun and joy and solidarity. Thank you to Kazu Watanabe at the Japan Society in NYC for providing a crucial screener for this volume. Enormous thank you, also, to Chelsea Szendi Scheider, Anne McKnight, Jennifer Coates, and Erin Schoneveld for being wonderful friends and compatriots and modeling strong feminist practices and mentorship in Japanese film studies.

I am grateful to John MacKay, Justin Jesty, and Erin Schlumpf for providing expert feedback as I tried to jigsaw a fractured dissertation into a cohesive book project. And to Alex Juhasz, whom I am so lucky to call a mentor, and who continues to be a source of inspiration.

Thanks to the Black Sheep Society and especially Rossen Djagalov and Djordje Popović, who invited me into a leftist community of scholar-comrades beyond my wildest dreams. To my Gdansk crew, Dominic Leppla, Andrew Philip, and Kamila Kuc: in my imagination we are always frolicking in the Baltic Sea. I am especially thankful to Jennifer Coates (again!) and Maria Corrigan for bringing me into their writing groups and helping me workshop early versions of several chapters in this volume. I am indebted to many librarians and archivists, especially Uesaki Sen at the Sōgetsu Art Center, Jason Sanders at the Pacific Film Archive in Berkeley, the many archivists at the Getty Research Institute, and Christoph Etzlsdorfer at the Austrian Film Museum. Huge thanks to Rebecca Mendelson and Charles Cobine for expert archival and copyright guidance. Thanks to my many colleagues in Penn English, cinema and media studies, Russian and Eastern European studies, East Asian languages and civilizations, and art history, and at the Center for Experimental Ethnography, especially Heather Love, Peter Decherney, Chi-ming Yang, Kristen Ghodsee, Brian Kim, Whitney Trettien, So-Rim Lee, Emily Steiner, Kevin Platt, Ayako Kano, Ian Fleishman, Rahul Mukherjee, Meta Mazaj, Chenshu Zhou, Jolyon Thomas, Jennifer Ponce de Leon, Ashley Brock, Ricardo Bracho, Margo Crawford, Suvir Kaul, Ania Loomba, Sukaina Hirji, and Deb Thomas. Enormous thanks to Karen Redrobe and Lilya Kaganovsky for providing extensive feedback on an earlier version of the draft and for their belief in my project. Masha Salazkina and Miryam Sas provided incredibly helpful and thorough feedback and helped ultimately midwife this book to its final stage. I am so honored to call these scholars and thinkers my friends and comrades.

This book is also dedicated to the memory of those who have since passed on: Phil Watts and Svetlana Boym both contributed immeasurably to my ability to think critically about art and film. This book would not have been possible without them.

I am eternally thankful to Aileen Cornbleet, Patti Rain, and Dan Gonzalez, who nurtured an early love of learning; to my family, especially my mother, grandparents, great-uncle Leonid, and my late great-grandmother Lola, for bearing with my stubborn artsy and academic caprices; to my Brooklyn pals Tin Acosta, Ben Freeman, Melissa Chua, Lena Chandhok, Paul Swartz, Lane Sell, Madeleine Boucher, Erich Erving, Shawn Groce, Rivka Mitnik-Kostanyan, Faria Chaudry, and Tony Fu; to my beloved LA community, especially Alex Billet, Kelsey Goldberg, Alex Wolinetz, Sobaata Chaudry, Natalie Holt, Jenn Nguyen, Rachael Zambias, Jake Fertig, and Peter Labuza; to Melissa Schade, all members of Queer Run Club, and What the Float for keeping me sane through doses of weekly collective joy; to the Philly crew, especially Ruby Chen, Thaddeus Echevarria, Howard Chen, Brian (again!), Joy Ding, 8 Gianfortini (cookbook club 4 ever), DSA pals Patrick Wargo, Daisy Confoy, Chris Romano, and Kelsey Romano; to Arielle Cohen, Rafael Khachaturian, Laura Bucci, and all the members of the unnamed (but forever appreciated) weekly Philosophy Book Club: Dave Mesing, Claire Griffin, Colbert Root, David Lee, Kelsey Baack, Ben Webster, and Jacob Greenstine; to my globally dispersed but beloved college friends Nikitha Reddy, Maxine Paul, Laura Weldon, Evx Gonzalez-Ruskiewicz, and Megan Eardley; to my dear Chicago friends Jenny Lam, Mareva Lindo, Jesse Lopez-Cepero, Louis Sachs, and especially Katie Robinson and Kirsten Layer, my forever travel-mates and concert buddies. You are my soul-friends, and I'm so lucky to know you.

Thank you to Brandon Wolfeld, who sat through many an arcane academic rant and was a rock of support in the grueling early years of academia, to Eva Boodman, for inspiring the heart of this project, and to Jon Danforth-Appell, for endless microfascist discourse and our yearslong collaboration. And to Leopold Bloom and Akiva the Wise, neither of whom could read, but who reminded me of the importance of play and rest, and a good scratch behind the ears.

May the struggle continue.

Introduction

On July 27, 2022, I attended a concert by the Ukrainian "ethno-chaos" band Dakhabrakha in Ardmore, Pennsylvania. Dakhabrakha, whose name means "give and take" in Ukrainian, is known for mixing Ukrainian (and occasionally Russian- and other Slavic-language) folk songs with avant-gardist flair, also interweaving a mechanical drone, the sound of animals (produced by human mouths), unusual harmonies, and a frequently syncopated beat. Symbolizing the band's avant-folk aesthetics are the enormous black furry hats worn by all band members, reminiscent of the *papakha* hat worn in the Caucasus region but elongated so much that they appear more absurdist than traditional. I had been a fan of Dakhabrakha since first seeing them in 2014 and looked forward to the performance in Ardmore, which I knew would be full of much more solemnity and gravitas because of the Ukrainian war. Just as at previous times I had seen them, attendees gathered around the stage, many dressed in the traditional embroidered shirt called a *vyshyvanka*.

Here is where the story becomes more complicated. Behind the band members a screen was erected, projecting a blend of animated and photographic visuals representing the trauma of war. Escherian birds slowly morphed into war planes. A collage of photographs depicted grotesque imagery of shelled and bombed-out buildings in Ukraine, strewn with blood and corpses. An animated film loop in a naïve, almost twee, children's storybook style showed a hip young white couple holding their children in a folkloric house, which grew roots that stretched into the ground and seemed to protect the family from rockets overhead. Perhaps most horrifying were the abstracted women with flower crowns, flowing with ribbons on both sides—a common symbol of Ukrainian nationhood—hovering on the screen like ghosts, their bodies patterned in white lace. The women had shields instead of faces, and on these shields were crosses—specifically reminiscent of the cross of St. George, the crusader and warrior saint, used by many ultranationalist political parties in present-day Europe. Even more crosses hovered in the air around the shield-women.

Confusion, and then horror, set in. I was born in Kyiv and emigrated to the United States in childhood, with the second wave of Jewish refugees from the USSR, now leaving a newly independent country embroiled in political chaos and swift economic collapse. Seeing the animated visuals behind my favorite band, I realized with growing horror that my ethnicity—euphemistically titled the *piatyi punkt*, or "fifth point" on the Soviet identification card, on which "Jew" was unceremoniously written—continued, even in the twenty-first century, to render me a perpetual Other: *I* could never be one of *them*. To be Ukrainian did not mean to live and breathe in a region, but to share a bloodline rooted in the soil. The Russian word for peasant is *Christian*.

There was more: in that moment of shock, I momentarily forgot my own complicity in this endeavor. Indeed, I attended the concert as a longtime fan, and like many, I assumed Dakhabrakha's art was antifascist. I had brought eight friends with me, not knowing the show would devolve into a dangerous ethnonationalism masquerading as left-wing politics. I did not stop the screening; I did not grab my loved ones by the hand and walk out; I did not stage a protest. I stood petrified, unable to reconcile the contradictions in aesthetics and politics that I was witnessing on the stage.

I did not expect to confront these concerns at the concert of an experimental folk band on the outskirts of Philadelphia. As the odd blood-and-soil rhetoric of this avant-folk concert demonstrated, the media of a state battling imperialism is not de facto antifascist in nature. Nor, indeed, is artistic experimentation antifascist in itself. What, then, is antifascism?

What kind of media and art could conceivably be called antifascist? At the Dakhabrakha show, I could feel myself powerfully swayed by the visuals—indeed, I noticed several strangers wipe away tears—just as a deeper, far more traumatized part of my psyche rang distant alarm bells. As media scholars we are trained to notice when techniques of editing and cinematography affect our mental states. Why use a jump cut (à la Agnès Varda), or superimposition (à la Sky Hopinka), or an unbearably long tracking shot (à la Abbas Kiarostami) if not to affect the way we think, feel, and perceive the world? Dakhabrakha's show concluded with the audience forming a circle to sing the Ukrainian national anthem; I noticed several off-duty cops sporting Blue Lives Matter T-shirts and hung back. Whatever antifascist media was, this was not it.

I do not use this anecdote to stir up support for Russia's vehement claims about Ukraine's antisemitism; far from it. Russia continues to be the fascist aggressor in this (and many) scenarios, and Russia's anti-American sentiments do not make the country any more anti-capitalist or anti-imperialist. Nor do I use this anecdote to criticize Dakhabrakha, a band I still admire greatly. I use this anecdote to highlight a sticking point in our understanding of political aesthetics, and specifically, the affects and effects of experimental documentary filmmaking.

At first I was fascinated by the band's decision to use animated documentary for political purpose, especially a style so unusual, so painterly and whimsical in nature. Yet experimentation in documentary does not in itself make antifascism, any more than the Ukrainian Jewish director Dziga Vertov and the unapologetic Nazi Leni Riefenstahl are aligned politically in their tendency to use canted angles in documentary. As Andrew Hewitt argues, leftist movements do not lay claim to the aesthetics of the modern, as exemplified by Italian futurist and protofascist F. T. Marinetti. Hewitt argues: "We must first desist from painting fascism as statis, standardization, and regimentation if we are to unsettle our sense of having done with fascism."[1] He aligns with Georges Bataille, who views fascism as a concentration of "heterogeneous elements" that provoke intense affective reactions.[2]

One cannot, then, derive an artwork's fascist or antifascist nature from aesthetics alone. Nor can we derive it from explicitly militant intent. Bataille argues that although socialism is integral to countering the "revolution" of fascism, its only truly effective opposition is not a rejection of affect through the upholding of rational positivism, but through the mobilization of "unproductive" and "heterogeneous" irrational forces: "violence, excess, delirium, madness . . . breaking the laws of social homogeneity."[3] To be effective, antifascism must not attempt to tie up the mysterious and poetic, the unknown and unseen neatly into a rational and scientific bow. In the field of documentary, a medium so frequently, and perhaps singularly, complicit in the upholding of fascistic power relations, antifascist work should not aim to inoculate the viewer with the ideology of Truth, but should aim to unveil, estrange, and reenchant; it should inspire and empower the viewer to perform the analytical work themselves.

As I will demonstrate, this idea was shared among many radical, unorthodox communist documentary filmmakers of the 1960s. This book answers the question, "What is antifascist documentary?" by arguing that the project of antifascist media entails a critical, questioning lens—a challenging of knowledge production and the status quo via what film theorists Annette Michelson and D. N. Rodowick term *epistemological struggle*. Experimental filmmaking and editing techniques are usually essential to induce this rupture of consciousness, one that joins difficulty and sometimes violent discomfort—what Japanese theorist and filmmaker Matsumoto Toshio calls the "sadomasochistic aesthetic"—with affects of liveliness, play, and even pleasure.[4] The goal of this struggle is personal and political emancipation through a revitalization of perception, both an estrangement (Russian: *ostranenie*) and a surrealist *reenchantment* that makes life, in Svetlana Boym's words, "lively and worth living."[5]

This book traces its argument to antifascist documentary theorists and filmmakers in France and Japan during the 1960s; it charts a trajectory of interrelated movements that respond to their specific historical and national context yet are fiercely and consciously intertwined in transnational debates around Marxist political aesthetics. While the Soviet avant-garde, especially Dziga Vertov and his contemporaries, is not the object of my analysis, I use it as a conceptual and aesthetic horizon. The 1920s avant-gardes continue to be a perennial point of reference for radical filmmakers as well as radical critics, from Annette Michelson to Susan Buck-Morss to Karatani Kōjin. This book echoes the polyvanent 1960s in its international approach. It is methodologically and theoretically capacious, occasionally drawing connections to Latin America, the United States, and Southeast Asia in addition to the USSR, while restricting its historical and geographical contours to France and Japan. Its case studies, crucially, are not niche, but are often frequently discussed in journalistic accounts from the period; I mobilize them as paradigmatic examples of aesthetic antifascism and of the highly unorthodox communist politics that are representative of the 1960s Left milieu.

My conception of antifascist aesthetics joins the political with the psychological. It is inspired by Gilles Deleuze and Félix Guattari's theory of "microfascism," which, as media theorist Jack Z. Bratich argues, does not mean small in scale "but something multiple and molecular rather than coherent and uniform—a proliferation of resonances, practices, and relations that can cohere into operative bodies and collective agencies."[6] I mobilize their conception of fascism alongside Matsumoto Toshio's in considering fascism a state of mind, before its manifestation into organized ultraright ethnonationalism. In Bratich's words, microfascism thinks through fascism's *"emergent dimensions*—the subtle dynamics in play before historical expressions manifest."[7] Antifascist documentary, then, aims to disrupt and transform a fascist consciousness and provide a model of personal and political liberation that joins pain ("discomfort," "sadomasochism," "estrangement")—frequently connected to the work of self-criticism and to a reckoning with one's own complicity—with liveliness ("ecstasy," "reenchantment") and with strange and heretofore unknown pleasures.

JAPAN AND FRANCE IN THE 1960S: ART, CRISIS, COMPLICITY

This study employs pitoval examples of Japanese and French film in the 1960s to illustrate how the theory and practice of antifascist documentary responded to crucial and *critical*—in the sense of responding to a crisis—eras within the 1960s in both countries. Yet *critical* also refers to scholarly analysis and investigation, and both France and Japan were immersed in a veritable flourishing of the *critical*, in both senses of the term. Key for this volume's theoretical paradigm is the aforementioned filmmaker-critic

Matsumoto Toshio, a paragon of antifascist aesthetics within a new generation of artists who grappled with the trauma of the Pacific War. Although the application of the term *fascism* to Japanese wartime ideology is controversial, when applied, it usually refers to Japan's ultranationalist, militarist, and expansionist era during the early Showa years, from 1926 to the end of World War II in 1945.[8] Many communist critics and artists of the 1960s, including Matsumoto as well as Nagano Chiaki, Sasaki Hajime, Matsukawa Yasuo, Hariu Ichiro, and Kuroki Kazuo, explicitly connected fascism to Japanese wartime politics and discussed the need to prevent the reawakening of fascism within Japan. The term *fashizumu* crops up especially frequently in writings of the early 1960s, becoming less common after the early 1970s.

Sadly and disturbingly, the connection between "fascism" and Japanese wartime atrocities is even less common today. Unlike in Germany, there is little public acknowledgment of Japan's fascist past in contemporary discourse—a reality present-day Japan shares with France, in its culture of silence surrounding both its wartime collaboration with the fascist Vichy government and its general refusal to discuss the war in Algeria, which many contemporaneous (especially communist) critics saw as a continuation of wartime fascism—despite the culture of France as "the Resistance," embodied in President Charles de Gaulle. My decision to label both French and Japanese political and military maneuvers during the wartime period *fascist* responds explicitly to a contemporary culture of silencing extant in both countries today.

I use *fascism* in this book to refer not just to its origin in Benito Mussolini's Italy, but also to an ideology that is interwoven with racist ethnonationalism and the drive to eradicate "unproductive" elements of society, what Bataille describes, according to Robyn Marasco, as "the mobilization of the masses against its own difference and disorder."[9] Importantly, as Jennifer Barker describes in *The Aesthetics of Anti-Fascist Film*, fascism "demanded public unity" and "an erasure of private life and individual taste."[10] This understanding of fascism as an erasure of the private and personal, of the complete subduing of the individual into the will of the collective, was especially important in both French and Japanese understanding of fascistic ideology in the 1960s.

But why look at (anti)fascism in the 1960s? In this turbulent era, many artists in France and Japan fought against an increasingly conservative political atmosphere that appeared to hurl those countries back inexorably toward wartime fascism.[11] This was an era in which extreme economic growth and a renewed sense of postwar stability were part and parcel of participation in American imperialist hegemony and of a cultural forgetting of individual and nationwide complicity with terror. World War II was not yet a distant memory, and Japan, especially, became a battleground in which the newly "peacekeeping" nation saw a neonationalist resurgency—this time with a peculiar American Cold War flavor.

Yet the reasons for choosing France and Japan for this book's analysis are more film industrial than geopolitical. I concentrate on France and Japan in this book because of three overarching industrial factors: their temporally overlapping New Wave movements, the parallel richness of their explicitly leftist film journalistic output, and the importance of documentary in their ecologies of media criticism. First, the "new wave" movements of both France and Japan were buoyed by unprecedented economic growth and cultural support. The French and Japanese new waves were the earliest in the world—as Daniel Fairfax aptly notes, Japan was actually "in advance of its French 'model'"—and the most cataclysmic.[12] Both French and Japanese political avant-garde filmmakers felt stymied by "Golden Age" era film and rejected what they interpreted as staid formal conservatism. Their film cultures were very much aligned, with both seeing an apex of audience patronage between 1959 and 1961.

By all accounts, in 1960 France and Japan were the leading producers of arthouse film in the entire world. France reached a peak of homegrown films winning national and international awards in 1961, with 218 *films primés* (prize-winning films) released that year. Although in 1957 France only had 40 *films primés*, between 1958 and 1963—the heyday of the French New Wave, between the release of the (debatable) first New Wave film, Claude Chabrol's *Le Beau Serge* (1958), and Jean-Luc Godard's *Le Mépris* (*Contempt*, 1963)—these years saw an average of 156 *films primés* per annum.[13] Japan, likewise, saw film attendance peak precisely in those years. It might surprise readers that in the same era more films were produced in Japan than in France, with more than 500 films produced in both 1960 and 1961 (547 and 535, respectively) in Japan, compared to 352 and 377 films produced in France in those same years.[14] Admissions to Japanese theaters began to decline after peaking in 1959 (after an astronomical 1.088 billion theater tickets were sold that year), and there was a palpable sense of an industry in crisis as audience members continued to wane; cinemas screened several feature films per screening in an attempt to recover numbers.[15] Japan and France were on top of the world as the decade began to turn but shortly thereafter plummeted. Yet both countries remained *the* producers of global arthouse productions, with their film cultures retaining a buzz of critical respectability and irreverently cool *je ne sais quoi*, arguably, to this very day.

Second, both France and Japan maintained a strong leftist critical tradition during this period. The geopolitical situation of both countries created the conditions for a vehement opposition to American-derived imperialism. Both France and Japan were decimated during World War II, but by 1960 they were economic and cultural powerhouses. In *Fast Cars, Clean Bodies*, Kristin Ross notes that in France, modernization was eerily swift—"headlong, dramatic, and breathless"—transforming France from a rural, Catholic empire into an urban, fully industrialized, and, allegedly, decolonized nation. Within ten years, a rural woman in France might witness the acquisition of electricity, running water, a stove, a refrigerator, a television, and finally, a car.[16]

In Japan this rapid modernization was equally, and perhaps even more keenly felt. Nick Kapur writes that from 1950 to 1973, Japan's GDP grew at a staggering rate of nearly 10 percent per year, a rate unparalleled globally until China's extreme growth rates in the early 2000s.[17] Everyday citizens appeared to emerge from utmost poverty into the appliance-filled world of the urban middle class, seemingly overnight. By 1968 the Japanese economy overtook West Germany's to become second in the capitalist world, after the United States.[18] This was, and continues to be, frequently described as an economic miracle. Yet the massive advances in economic viability and quality of life in Japan and France were inextricably bound to their ties with racist and imperialist policies, particularly with the United States.

Third, leading from their sordid wartime history—with the Vichy collaborators in France, and with more obvious forces of fascism in Japan through the Greater East Asia Co-Prosperity Sphere—leftists in both countries shared a skepticism of official truth telling and reportage. Many communists described a desire to unveil hidden atrocities, including one's own complicity. It is meaningful, indeed, that any French film that suggested national complicity was likely to be the target of rather severe censorship, especially until the end of the Algerian War in 1962. The French history of wartime complicity was a taboo topic nonpareil in postwar French society.[19] Communist film historian Georges Sadoul denounced censorship as the most important issue of the age in the early 1960s; an entire issue of the arts and cultural communist-aligned weekly *Les Lettres françaises*, led by surrealist Louis Aragon, was devoted to censorship in France—a censorship that prevented Alain Resnais, Chris Marker, and Jean-Luc Godard from screening several of their films from 1955 until late 1962.[20]

Similarly, discussions about Algeria were heavily censored within film and media; the slightest mention led to extraordinary controversy. In even the most politically leaning of early 1960s French films, such as Agnès Varda's *Cléo de 5 à 7* or Edgar Morin and Jean Rouch's *Chronique d'un été*, the debacle in Algeria looms in the background but cannot be treated outright. Other films that attempted to take the subject of Algeria head on, such as Godard's *Le petit soldat* (1963), originally filmed in 1960, were banned and not released until after the conflict had ended. This might appear extreme, but with the gift of hindsight, it is important to remember that censorship in France and Japan was relatively slight compared to other countries in the same era. Viewers of the Argentinian experimental documentary *La hora de los ornos* (*Hour of the Furnaces*, Fernando Solanas and Octavio Getino, 1968) risked life and limb to attend its underground screenings; several shows led to military confrontations. Indeed, as an Algerian stated in the preface to the 1962 *cinéma-vérité* documentary *Octobre à Paris*: "*dans notre pays seul pouvait se réaliser un tel film pendant, et non après*" (it is only in our country where one can make a film *during* and not *after*).[21]

Given the interest in preventing a fascist uprising and investigating imperialist power relations, it is not surprising that both France and Japan were fully immersed in the interrogation of documentary. This investigation was crucially tied to the importance of arts, cultural, and film-specific journalism of this period. Most scholars of film and media are no doubt familiar with the cultural provenance of *Cahiers du cinéma*, but alongside *Cahiers* France also had the popular surrealist-inclined leftist film magazine *Positif*, more aligned with the "Left Bank" of Agnès Varda, Chris Marker, and Alain Resnais, and *Les Lettres françaises*, for which

Georges Sadoul was an editor and regular columnist. I have found that this latter journal was actually cited in Japanese film journals as frequently as, if not more than, *Cahiers*. There were also many smaller grassroots publications such as *Miroir du cinéma*, which came out of the Aubervilliers commune and is treated in chapter 2.[22]

Japan, likewise, had its mainstays of film criticism, *Eiga hyōron* (Film criticism) and *Kinema Junpō* (Seasonal cinema news), and the short-lived but highly influential *Kiroku eiga* (Documentary film).[23] In the wake of the late 1960s countercultural movements and protests, the "ultraleft" *Cinéthique* emerged in France, while the similarly ultraleft *Eiga hihyō II* (Film review II) was revitalized in Japan and included the participation of Japanese political avant-garde filmmakers Ōshima Nagisa, Wakamatsu Kōji, Adachi Masao, Matsuda Masao, and Matsumoto Toshio. *Eiga hihyō II* was embroiled in *shutaiseiron*, or debates on "subjectivity." Both this journal and *Cinéthique*, notably, published many articles extolling the virtues of Godard's Dziga Vertov Group (DVG). Both France and Japan thus had extremely rich and prolific film criticism, with a special interest in documentary during the 1960s. Japan and France were also fervent intellectual and cinematic interlocutors; in Japan, articles on global cinema were more likely to be translated from French than any other language. Likewise, French filmmakers and theorists were engaged in a veritable quasi-obsessive cinematic *japonisme* in the 1960s; the decade began with special issues devoted to the realist of Japan's "Golden Age" Mizoguchi Kenji and ended with many articles on the experimental iconoclast Ōshima Nagisa and special issues focused on Japan.

Yet I offer a different model of the relationship between France and Japan, one that is not based on the slippery notion of "influence" but instead speaks to reponses to similar yet distinct political and aesthetic pressures and historical conditions. As Japanese filmmaker Hani Susumu stated in the pages of *Cahiers du cinéma*, Japanese "new wave" cinema attempted, like France's *nouvelle vague*, to find a radical alternative to the dominance of American cinema, even if its aesthetic influence was more easily traced to Italy.[24] The overlapping film cultures of France and Japan resulted in the existence of an unprecedented number of wildly experimental and arthouse films with a strong connection to political documentary. Their directors enjoyed relative freedom and even at times extraordinary international prestige. The moviegoing public had enough time and income to attend film screenings, and the enormous baby boomer generation of youth in both countries, alongside leftists and humanists of all ages, drew great attention to works of political and avant-garde documentary.

Thus, France and Japan were both primed for a rich and widely varied film tradition that still had the relative freedom to screen highly controversial and even rather politically militant works. Crucially, both French and Japanese documentary traditions during this time questioned the role of documentary as a "truth-telling" device, consciously rupturing a false binary between fiction and nonfiction and between the popular and experimental. This was a privilege and a luxury. The money poured into their film industries, and the relative freedom that both enjoyed led to an immense amount of experimental documentary output during the 1960s. The theoretical writings on these film experiments, such as by Sadoul, Hanada Kiyoteru, or Edgar Morin, often had seismological influence on later film cultures, nationally, regionally, and globally.

Communist artists in France and Japan were united in their rejection of American politics and aesthetics. In the post-Stalinist era of the 1960s, they were also united in their rejection of Soviet hegemony and conservatism, although with considerably less vitriol than their rejection of the former. In the 1960s, fascination with the early years of the Soviet Union, especially the experiments of the 1920s, was emblematic of a turn toward socialism's (thwarted) revolutionary potential. Although French and Japanese theorists varied with regard to access to early Soviet texts, one filmmaker stands out as integral to the development of avant-garde documentary: Dziga Vertov.

Vertov's work provides a crucial, and prophetic, introduction to the avant-garde documentary as an aesthetics of liberation. France especially was immersed in heated debates about Vertov's filmmaking. Although this was less the case in Japan, Ōishi Masahiko sees a Vertovian quality in certain avant-garde documentaries of the Japanese 1960s, especially Matsumoto Toshio's *Bara no sōretsu* (*Funeral Parade of Roses*, 1969).[25] And Hanada Kiyoteru, first theorist of the avant-garde documentary in Japan, held Dziga Vertov in exceptionally high regard among European filmmakers.[26] Hanada, and the philosopher Nakai Masakazu, whose works are often compared to Walter Benjamin's for their engagement with the politics of aesthetics, used the Soviet avant-garde to inform their own theoretical work.

Although I leave an extensive analysis of Vertov's influence in the 1960s to another study, it is important to point to the important but little-discussed antifascist dimensions of the Soviet avant-gardist's filmography. As we will see, Vertov's filmmaking persistently denies viewers the passive pleasure of the suspension of disbelief; the disorienting pleasure of Vertov's antifascist avant-garde is of another breed entirely.

DZIGA VERTOV AND THE ANTIFASCIST AVANT-GARDE

In the last ten minutes of Soviet filmmaker Dziga Vertov's 1929 avant-garde documentary *Chelovek s kinoapparatom* (*Man with a Movie Camera*, 1929), the eponymous cameraman shows the viewer a woman wielding a rifle during target practice. Her target is a rather silly looking cardboard cutout of a man in a top hat, emblazoned with a swastika. In other words, a fascist. Vertov cuts from fascist to woman twelve times, each shot with decreasing length and accelerated rhythm, until finally the woman pulls the trigger and, after she successfully hits her target, a hidden mechanism reveals a sign; in Ukrainian, it reads Bat'ko Fashysmu, translated as Father of Fascism. More accurately, the term is a diminutive, "Father Fascism" or "Daddy Fascism"—implying silliness alongside evil.

The scene follows one set in a beer hall in which Vertov's dizzying camerawork, with the camera careening from side to side, induces something akin to drunkenness in the viewer. Cuts become increasingly quick, exploding into cacophony, until suddenly the frame pauses on an image of Vladimir Lenin on the façade of a building. As if finally able to take a breath, the camera pans over to a placard: the Lenin's Worker Club. The camera enters the space, and we see several feats of stop-motion and reverse-reel: hands sweep over first a checkerboard and then a chessboard, setting the game for play as if by magic. In between these sequences, Vertov shows us images of solitary men and women reading newspapers. The aforementioned scene of fascist killing follows. The slower, deliberate montage in this Worker's Club sequence, seemingly worlds apart from the drunken camera a mere twenty seconds prior, indicates tacit approval of the events

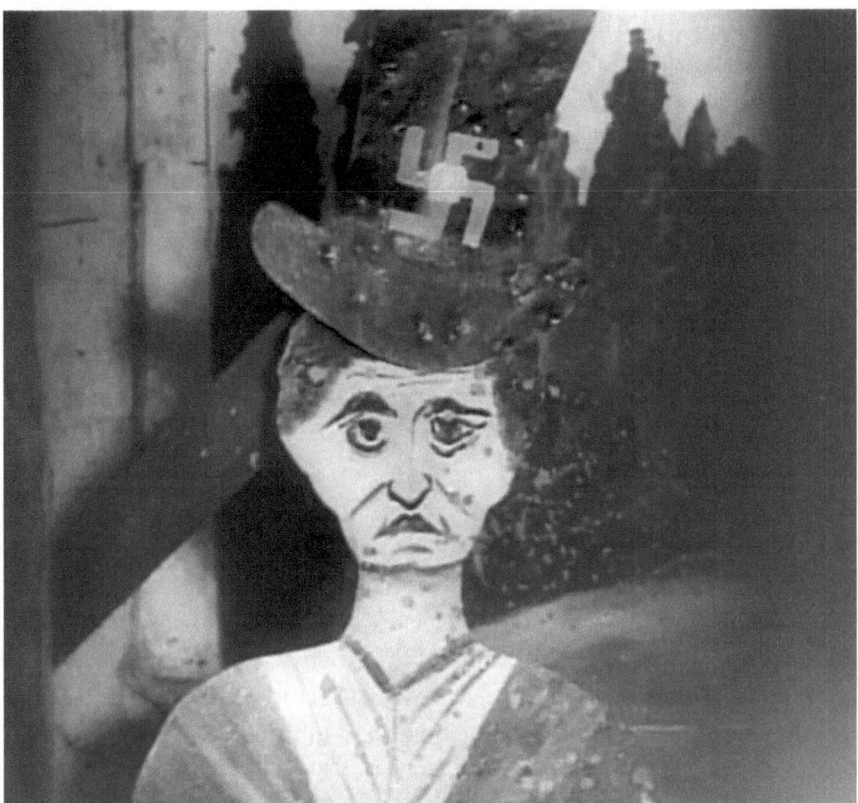

Figure 1. "Daddy Fascism" target at Soviet shooting range, in Dziga Vertov's *Chelovek s kinoapparatom*, 1929.

presented. Despite its lack of intertitles, this concluding scene guides us in an interpretation of events presented through tricks of editing and cinematography.

Given the film's canonical status, it is curious that this part (to my knowledge) has never been addressed outright. It appears oddly prescient: more than twelve years before the Soviet Union's entry into what will be called the Great Patriotic War, Vertov's Kino-Eye warns against fascism and presents us, with the aid of the rifle-shooting woman, a corrective to the fascist threat. The scene appears especially, even eerily, poignant given Vertov's Jewish heritage: he was born David Abelevich Kaufman in

Bialystok in the Pale of Settlement, the only territory in which Jews were allowed to live until the Bolshevik Revolution; Vertov's parents would die in the Holocaust before the end of the war. While Vertov did not tend to discuss his Jewishness, Aleksandr Pronin argues that Vertov sustained significant trauma from the memory of the Bialystok pogroms he experienced as a ten-year old child. This was centered in a screenplay he wrote called *V rodnom gorode* (In my hometown) in 1939, coterminous with the Nazi invasion of Poland.[27] While I do not want to dwell too long on the biographical, the visceral importance of antifascism in connection to Vertov's upbringing is fairly undeniable.

The scene of Nazi killing in *Chelovek s kinoapparatom* presents us with several layers of meaning and several methods of combating the fascist threat. The first is literal: work on your aim, Soviet women, and you too can kill a fascist in battle! However, the film emphasizes another antifascist corrective: Vertov's *triuki*, or tricks, of editing and cinematography. Not only do his *triuki* show the viewer the power of filmmaking, but they also have another inherently antifascist function: they expose the fundamental createdness and artificiality of the cinematic medium.

In 1972 Annette Michelson described Vertov as an epistemologist in the pages of *Artforum*, in an article that John MacKay claims, half a century later, is "still the most important essay ever written on the filmmaker": "Vertov questions the most immediately powerful and sacred aspect of cinematic experience, disrupting systematically the process of identification and participation, generating at each moment of the film's experience, a *crisis of belief*."[28] Michelson sees in Vertov the generation of "a crisis of belief": a "systematic disruption" of our perceptual capacities. I highlight Vertov and Michelson here not to point to Vertov's unique version of what D. N. Rodowick describes as political modernism; as he notes, following Michelson, "The deeper theme involves ... the critique of illusionism": "its central rhetorical feature" is "the idea of the epistemological break."[29] While Vertov's participation within the canon of political modernism is well-trodden territory, I instead emphasize Vertov's use of modernist formal experimentation as epistemological inquiry because I believe this to be central to antifascism in documentary. In Michelson's words, Vertov's films operate "through the systematic subversion of the certitudes of illusion—a threshold in the development of consciousness."[30] By engaging in constant epistemological questioning, Vertov's films teach us how to see.

I argue that a central goal of avant-garde documentary filmmaking in the vein of Vertov is pedagogical and epistemological, as these films fundamentally train viewers in the practice of what might be called *radical media literacy*, a concept to which we will return. Joshua Malitsky notes that films from Vertov's most avant-gardist period are "designed to instantiate not just a new vision of the Soviet collective but a new conceptual apparatus for making sense of [their] role in revolutionary society."[31] Crucially, his films function at the level of the individual: "[Vertov's films] educate citizens in the proper way of behaving *as individuals* in postrevolutionary society. And they provide the tools necessary to begin transforming the self."[32] This fervently Marxist individualism contrasts, then, with the self-obliteration required by fascistic ideology. Yet this individualism would increasingly get Vertov in trouble with a collectively minded Soviet state, especially as the 1920s progressed. Vertov, however, knew that the existence of the Soviet Union did not in itself magically transform every citizen into a freethinker. Avant-garde documentary films, starting with but not limited to Vertov's, question the seemingly infallible nature of reality. In so doing, such films use disorientation to train the viewer's mind in the liberatory and antifascist practice of questioning, whether it is questioning those in power, one's place in society, or life itself.

Vertov's "systematic disruption" is not limited, of course, to his own filmmaking. And here his (pseudonymic) name is less representative of a singular individual than an aggregate of his collaborators and comrades, such as his brothers Boris and Mikhail, and his editor and partner, Elizaveta Svilova, primarily responsible for disseminating Vertov's theories abroad, alongside Georges Sadoul, after the death of Joseph Stalin. The concept of a "systematic disruption" goes far beyond Vertov in the 1920s; it is also crucially tied to formalist Viktor Shklovsky's concept of *ostranenie* (estrangement) and, to a lesser extent, to Bertolt Brecht's *Verfremdungseffekt*, known as the Alienation Effect—more familiar to the French and Japanese filmmakers I discuss here than the work of Shklovsky. Arguably, however, the latter is equally important as, if not more so, than Brecht for his belief in the ethical and political power of art's *formal* qualities *in themselves*.[33]

In addition, Walter Benjamin forms another pivotal star in this antifascist constellation. Miriam Hansen notes that for Benjamin, the task of any truly political art is "critical" and "cognitive": it must unveil the fundamental illusory quality of so-called reality, "that mythical chain of mirrors."[34] It is not an accident that almost every existing volume on antifascism and art—by figures such as Jennifer Barker, Mark Bray, Jack Z. Bratich, and Patrick Nathan—deploy Benjamin crucially in their work.[35] While this book primarily looks at France and Japan in the 1960s, these figures of the European avant-gardist 1920s, including Shklovsky and Benjamin but especially Vertov, are woven throughout; indeed, Vertov especially becomes a communist specter haunting the ghost of the 1960s—especially in France, where Godard named his post-May 1968 radical filmmaking collective the Dziga Vertov Group, and his *Kino-Pravda* (Cinema-truth) newsreels (1922–1925) lent their name to the revolutionary documentary genre of *cinéma-vérité*, enormously influential for documentary to this day.

Art, for Vertov as well as for Benjamin and Shklovsky, must be a critique and a challenge. As Vertov claimed, the dizzying range of experimental editing techniques in his films "[challenge] the human eye's visual representation of the world" and declare its own, distinct, defamiliarizing "I see!" (in Russian: *svoe "vizhu"*).[36] Vertov's camera wrests the viewer away from their status quo, reorganizing images of the everyday and placing them in an unexpected, montaged stage. The perfection of the camera's vision exists less for itself and more for human beings to recover their perceptive abilities, training the eye to regard the world anew. Its gaze lies in the interstices of subjectivity and objectivity—neither scientifically precise nor full of human fallibility. However, this avant-garde distancing effect is profoundly sensorial and affective; Vertov's films exemplify a new type of direct, unmediated sensuality (*chuvstvennost'*), opposed to a cold and restrictive bourgeois art. As he declared: "We need conscious men, not an unconscious mass . . . submissive to any passive suggestion."[37] This drive for what Vertov called *kinooshchushchenie*, or cinematic sensation, can be analyzed as a communist mobilization of affect in the Soviet 1920s.[38] Vertov aimed for his films to *activate* their viewers; their techniques were meant to inspire a reengagement with life and feeling, resulting, at best, in an awakening of political consciousness.

Yet this feeling is not a passive reception; it guides the viewer to an active questioning of truth-telling devices. Vertov's tricks lead to a clarified understanding of the fundamental created-ness of so-called documentality. For Michelson, this "result, articulated most powerfully through the presentation of the filmmaking editing and projection process, is a revelation, an exposure of the terms and dynamics of cinematic illusionism."[39] As Vertov described it, his goal was the "preparation of the viewers" for "the reception (*vospriiatie*) of new things."[40] This drive for a renewed perception was connected to the untranslateable Soviet concept of *byt*, the humdrum, mind-dulling habits and the increasing complacency of quotidian life.[41] The playfulness of tricks, whether it is through printing, montage, or other editing techniques, leads to a more robust, entirely new Soviet mental activity and mode of perception—one that rejuvenates the senses.

The tagline of Vertov's first feature-length film, the manifesto *Kino-Glaz* (*Kino-Eye*, 1924), is *zhizn' v rasplokh*, usually translated as "life caught unawares." This concept was frequently discussed in 1960s France by the early proponents of *cinéma-vérité*, but its Russian etymology contains an added hint of discomfort; it is semantically related to *polokh*, which means fear or fright. To "catch life unawares" is indeed meant to be an uncomfortable experience, at least at first, as this discomfort is essential to see the world in a new way. In this book I describe this experience, shared by many antifascist experimental filmmakers of the 1960s, as *revolutionary phenomenology*. Indeed, for Vertov the ideal Soviet mind is not only one that shoots a fascist with a rifle. Perhaps more importantly, it is also a mind that is capable of perceiving other moments featured in his oeuvre: a chessboard, arranged with a single sweep of a hand; lobsters dancing on a plate; a cameraman emerging from a mug of beer; a tripod bowing coyly to its audience. For it is this mind—liberated from the shackles of habit, scientifically rigorous in its questioning of reality, but simultaneously, and perhaps paradoxically, *reenchanted* by a "life caught-unawares," that is capable of recognizing fascism in the first place. And then, armed with the tools of revolutionary phenomenology, it might be able to defeat fascism in oneself.

THE AGONY AND THE ECSTASY OF EVERYDAY ANTIFASCISM

My use of fascism as a conceptual framework is closely tied to Deleuze and Guattari's expansive notion of fascism; their study of the concept in relation to what they term schizoanalysis (as opposed to psychoanalysis) in their 1972 *Anti-Oedipus: Capitalism and Schizophrenia* might, as Michel Foucault postulates, alternately be titled *An Introduction to a Nonfascist Life*. In his preface to *Anti-Oedipus*, Foucault writes that Deleuze and Guattari's concept of fascism is "not only historical fascism, the fascism of Hitler and Mussolini . . . but also the fascism in us all, in our heads and in our everyday behavior, the fascism that causes us to love power, to desire the very thing that dominates us and exploits us."[42] The fascism in this book likewise expands beyond a fascism witnessed in actually existing ultraright-wing parties (although it certainly, and necessarily, includes them). It argues, with Deleuze and Guattari in *A Thousand Plateaus*, that "fascism is inseparable from a proliferation of molecular focuses in interaction, which skip from point to point, before beginning to resonate together in the National Socialist State"; but first, they are "a molecular and supple segmentarity, flows capable of suffusing every kind of cell."[43]

Deleuze and Guattari premise their analysis of fascism on reconciling Karl Marx and Friedrich Nietzsche with a critique of Sigmund Freud.[44] Deleuze and Guattari were not alone in this combined Marxist-Nietzschean analysis. Bataille, for instance, attempted to wrest Nietzsche away from the German fascists, who misappropriated his writings. In the 1960s Herbert Marcuse, perhaps the most emblematic figure of the May 1968 generation and one of the "Three M's" of "Marx, Mao, Marcuse" (even if the majority of student radicals could not really comprehend his arguments), employed a similar reconciliation of Marx and Nietzsche in *One-Dimensional Man* in 1964. Eugene Holland explains that while Marx and Nietzsche are both historical materialists critical of contemporary society, their objects of analysis are quite different, and their conclusions are "practically opposite: emancipation from capitalism . . . through collective social transformation" (Marx), or "emancipation from nihilism . . . through personal self-transformation" (Nietzsche), referring to Nietzsche's concept of the "transvaluation of values."[45] Holland focuses especially on Deleuze and Guattari, but one can argue that all of these thinkers understand that both Marx and Nietzsche are required to resolve the problems of contemporary life, that exploitation and alienation are as socioeconomic as they are individual and libidinal.

Here, also, is where pleasure comes in—and indeed Foucault reminds us that Deleuze and Guattari "do not think that one has to be sad in order to be militant."⁴⁶ The often-pleasurable affects of the films discussed in this book are embodied in the personal as well as the political and follow Lauren Berlant's description of "affective atmospheres" in *Cruel Optimism*, which "are shared, not solitary." Borrowing Raymond Williams's concept of the "structures of feeling," Berlant argues that "affective responses may be said significantly to exemplify shared *historical* time."⁴⁷ Berlant writes alongside Brian Massumi's conceptualization of affect as protopolitical transversality; it is a "process [that] cannot be characterized as exclusively subjective or objective."⁴⁸ Miryam Sas uses the term "affective scale" to describe the work of Japanese media theorist Matsumoto Toshio, as his work is a "continuum ... between subjective/personal and larger structures."⁴⁹ Sas, Berlant, Massumi, Matsumoto, Deleuze, and Guattari, among others such as Sianne Ngai and Sara Ahmed, "demonstrate" (in the words of Ngai) "how feeling can be used to expand the project of criticism and theory."⁵⁰ This book considers how a certain quality of affect can be "mobilized" (Ngai), and how we can consider it, in tandem with a radical epistemology, as integral to the project of revolutionary becoming.

Affect, pleasure, and antifascism are not usually discussed alongside one another. And most analyses of antifascism writ large come from explicitly militant presses such as Haymarket, Common Notions, Verso, or Counterpoint. Writing for the latter, Patrick Nathan, in *Image Control: Art, Fascism, and the Right to Resist*, posits a certain pleasure in antifascist artwork that resists ease, passivity, and commodification. While certain filmmakers—namely Godard—balk at the idea of a pleasurable antifascism, Nathan singles out films by David Lynch and Krzysztof Kieslowski that shock, disrupt, and estrange but do not reject affect. Nathan writes: "There are people—me included—who find great pleasure in being so changed, so destroyed."⁵¹

This interest in pleasure alongside affects of destruction, violence, and difficulty finds significant resonance with Matsumoto Toshio's concept of "aesthetic sadomasochism," which he claimed to be integral to the project of antifascist artmaking, especially in documentary. Matsumoto is best known today in the anglophone context for the queer experimental quasi-documentary *Bara no sōretsu*, which transplanted the story of Oedipus

Rex to the "gayboy" culture of Tokyo at the end of the 1960s; it is analyzed in chapter 5. Although Deleuze and Guattari did not publish *Anti-Oedipus* until 1972, Matsumoto's use, and critique, of the Oedipus myth is a fascinating coincidence—and one taken up explicitly by James Phillips, who analyzes the film through Deleuze as "an oppositional strategy for the disabling of Oedipus."[52] It might not be a coincidence at all that both *Anti-Oedipus* and *Bara no sōretsu* respond to the global insurrections of 1968 by presenting a critique of Oedipus Rex. Both represented what Julian Bourg describes as the "antinomian spirit" and radical internationalist anti-psychiatric movement surrounding May 1968.[53]

Matsumoto and Deleuze/Guattari were deeply interested in psychology. Matsumoto intended to pursue a career in psychology at the prestigious University of Tokyo before secretly abandoning those plans and joining the department of French literature.[54] His work continued to think through the psychological in relation to film, frequently responding to Freud. Matsumoto also believed in the power of film to, as Jonathan M. Hall notes, "produc[e] an optic corporeality, a force upon the body that corroborates fantasy and the real within the body of the spectator."[55] Its potential force is striking and able to destabilize our conceptions of truth and fantasy. Experimental documentary is essential for this rupture.

In "Consciousness of the Aesthetic Sadomasochist: or, On the Internal Process of Creation and Its Artistic Utility," an article published in *Kiroku eiga* in February 1960, he criticizes educational documentary by noting that the artist must not be a "teacher," merely inoculating the viewer with Truth. Matsumoto criticizes the majority of documentary films for being either "educational" or "instructional," taking their cues from Enlightenment era positivism; he also criticizes them for being regressive, for "continu[ing] to fetishize the previous century's tailbones." Instead, these regressive and reactionary qualities of contemporary documentary "must be denied by an artistic propaganda," "which strikes within oneself, is knocked back, and transforms itself as well as others spontaneously."[56] This is what Matsumoto means when he describes an "aesthetic sadomasochism" in the article's title: it is a leftist auto-critique which marries political ideology to self-analysis.

For Matsumoto, neither "fetish" nor "education" in filmmaking can suit what he terms the "revolutionary era of the 20th century" and its "political catastrophe," undoubtedly referring to the Asia-Pacific War. Investigations of the wartime past were extremely common at the specific time of Matsumoto's writing: protests had started to ramp up against the controversial US-Japan Treaty of Mutual Cooperation and Security, known as ANPO (from Nichibei Anzen Hoshō Jōyaku), which allowed the United States to maintain military bases on Japanese soil. As the Cold War progressed, the United States attempted to strategically use the unique geographic position of Japan to keep communism at bay. The US leadership reinstated former war criminals in positions of power; one of these war criminals, Kishi Nobusuke, eventually became prime minister.[57]

Just a few months after the publication of Matsumoto's article, on June 15, 1960, Japan would see, as Nick Kapur writes, "the climax of what were, by almost any measure, the largest and longest series of popular protests in Japan's history.... For a period of fifteen months, from March 1959 through June 1960, an estimated 30 million people from across the archipelago—approximately one-third of Japan's population of 92.5 million—participated in protest activities."[58]

Matsumoto was writing near the climax of a highly politicized era—one in which everyday citizens, who still remembered the trauma of war, saw collaboration with the warmongering Americans as a potential return to a fascist past. Although Article IX of the 1945 Japanese constitution, drafted at the behest of the United States, prevented Japan from participating in military endeavors, Japanese leftists knew that although Japan had a global image as a "peaceful nation" in the wake of the catastrophe of World War II, in reality it was nothing of the sort.[59]

The context of Matsumoto's writing, then, is a criticism of an alleged claim to knowledge when confronted with political hypocrisy, as well as the terror of potential imperial remilitarization. For Matsumoto, film needed to confront "the consciousness of those who had to face the execution of criminal war leaders with complicated feelings, and the consciousness of those who are trying to reflect on their own experiences." Matsumoto notes that Prime Minister Kishi Nobusuke "was a war-criminal fascist, and continues to be a war-criminal fascist," and that "the Japanese monopoly capital and its government are now becoming newly imperialist." There is thus a particular need to address wartime experiences and war responsibility in the contemporary moment.

For Matsumoto, in order for documentary to overcome its roots in an outdated positivism, it must include elements of the irrational; it must "become an artistic propaganda that internally generates the destructive effects of everyday consciousness beyond the category of recognition." Here is where sadomasochism comes in: film must "sadistically reveal the irrationality of the external world and penetrate deep with the scalpel of criticism" while masochistically "dismantling the artist's consciousness." This, importantly, "is nothing less than a daily conversion"; without it, "the distance from here to war propaganda movies is not far." What Matsumoto calls "aesthetic sadomasochism," then, is nothing less than antifascism as a daily practice.

Matsumoto was not the only writer in *Kiroku eiga* who shared such thoughts, but he was certainly the most vocal. He unleashed his most vehement vitriol against works of socialist realism, such as the 1960 film *Buki naki tatakai (Fight without Weapons)* by Yamamoto Satsuo, a fervent member of the Japanese Communist Party (JCP).[60] Matsumoto's concept of auto-critique, of looking inward to transform the external world, has much in common with the project of surrealism—what Donald LaCross describes, following Michael Löwy, as a "romantic anticapitalism," an "independent, revolutionary Hegelo-Marxist dialectics barbed with strikingly original libertarian impulses" that "underscores the internal necessity of binding internal revolts of consciousness to outburst of insurgent collective action."[61] Like Deleuze and Guattari, Matsumoto's Marxism aimed to cleave individual, "internal revolt" to the project of revolution. In fact, it is revolt's prerequisite.

Individual creativity is key for the project of revolution. In a June 1958 article in the introductory issue of *Kiroku eiga*, Matsumoto explicitly ties imperialism and fascism to the suppression of creativity witnessed by generic public relations (PR) films:

> We can say that: the outside world is that which suppresses my artistic creativity and seeks to dismantle me through the murderous mechanism of making vulgar PR films, labor intensification and low wages, exploitation and oppression, the resurrected sound of military boots, the rapid resurgence of monopoly capital dreaming of imperial independence, Okinawa, Tunisia, the dangers of Wall Street and the atomic and hydrogen bomb wars, the emasculated and fetishized many.... A true avant-garde fights

uncompromisingly with this sick part, the energy of the masses is like a dormant volcano, it is interlocked with the self-aware organization centered on the proletariat class. It is a history of struggle, revolution, the progress of the peace movement on an international scale, the struggle for freedom and independence, and the conviction of human liberation. The inner world is my anger, sorrow, suffering, joy, etc. towards the outer world.... It is an ideology and a passion that seeks to achieve the emancipation of the self and the transformation of the external world, by engaging itself to the avant-garde of history.... When I say that I perceive and express reality subjectively, I must perceive both the outside and the interior holistically.[62]

This is emblematic of the Marxist Japanese postwar documentary sensibility. Matsumoto ties together world and self-emancipation, noting that both are necessary for the struggle of liberation. He argues that an artist must be an avant-gardist who "fights uncompromisingly" with the "sick part" of society, in contrast to the "emasculated and fetishized many." Elsewhere in *Kiroku eiga* Matsumoto criticizes the fetishization of the masses—"For the most part," Matsumoto writes, "the masses ... have absolutely no self.... They are closely tied to dogmatism, blindly enforcing the policies of authoritative leaders"—and, as we have just seen, sees documentary filmmakers "fetishizing ... tailbones."[63] Yet Matsumoto's distrust of the "masses" should not be read as a procapitalist sentiment of the individual against the collective. For Matsumoto, the "masses" do not exist as a uniform organizational body. Each citizen must perform an internal transformation that is then carried out into the external world through revolutionary acts.

Matsumoto privileges the avant-garde documentary as the sole form of film that aids the transformation of consciousness and "the emancipation of the self." It is not mere form but "an ideology and a passion" that "fights uncompromisingly" with militarization and protofascism. Matsumoto analyzes all of film history as a Hegelian dialectic: the nonfictional "discovery" of the Lumière brothers was a thesis to the fictive, avant-garde "creation" antithesis of Georges Méliès, "the dialectic of the discovery and creation of the moving image" (*ugoku eizō ni yoru hakken to sōzō no benshōhō*). As he writes: "[The Lumières'] camera 'finds' from among existing things, while Méliès 'creates' from those that do not exist." The outcome of their synthesis is what Matsumoto describes as a "neo-documentary" or "documentary-like avant-garde film" (*kirokuteki zen'ei eiga*).[64]

Matsumoto was not the first to view film history in this light; in the 1960s, this "dialectic between Lumière and Mèlies" was a common thread between many global cinematic traditions, described not only by Matsumoto but also by Georges Sadoul, Siegfried Kracauer, Jean-Luc Godard, Joris Ivens, Nakahara Yūsuke, Pascal Bonitzer, Sergei Yutkevich, and Edgar Morin, among surely many others.[65] Some of these figures, namely Godard and Ivens, also, like Matsumoto, provide their own filmmaking as examples of the merging of these two traditions into their version of experimental documentary. Matsumoto goes further, however, in arguing for avant-garde documentary as *the only antifascist documentary style* of the postwar period, and the only one that responds accurately to current historical conditions.

By centering Matsumoto, this book subverts a common tendency of scholarship that uses European- and North American–derived texts to analyze primary source material from Asia, Africa, or Latin America. This is often framed as an inevitability, given the seeming scarcity of homegrown film history and theory. Instead, here I use Japanese documentary film theory of the postwar period—almost none of which is currently available in English translation—as its framing device. I center my argument on analyses of primary source documents from understudied journals in Japanese (especially *Kiroku eiga*, but also others such as *Eiga hyōron*) as well as French (especially the criminally underappreciated *Lettres françaises* and *Miroir du cinéma*). I balance this investigation of primary documents with a thorough and capacious analysis of filmic texts. Such a turn allows us to look at French and Japanese avant-garde documentary with fresh eyes. One finds, in fact, that the critiques Matsumoto Toshio formulated anticipate many of the concerns of our contemporary moment, especially its concern with what we now call media literacy. These concerns were also shared in France, especially around and after May 1968.

RADICAL MEDIA LITERACY AND ANTIFASCIST LIVELINESS

In the first issue of the post–May 1968 "Red Years" of *Cahiers du cinéma*, the majority of the editorial staff—Pascal Bonitzer, Jean-Louis Comolli, Serge Daney, Jean Narboni, and Jean-Pierre Oudart—collectively wrote a highly detailed, almost Talmudic exegesis on Jean Renoir's Popular Front film *La vie est à nous* (*Life Belongs to Us*, 1936). This article, published in March 1970, appeared after a four-month hiatus in which the politics of the journal were seriously reevaluated. Fairfax argues that this film provided *Cahiers* an "ideal opportunity . . . to combine its cinephilic heritage with its new political strategy of liaising with the PCF (*Parti communiste français*)."[66] I claim that this exegesis argued for a specifically communist practice of film as pedagogical tool for radical media literacy—thus tying Renoir's film to epistemological struggle and to antifascist aesthetics as a whole.

La vie est à nous has no single plot; it mixes actuality footage and newsreels with acted sequences and reenactments, a common practice in many of the films discussed in this book, films that ceaselessly question the fiction/nonfiction binary. In Renoir's film, a significant portion of the fictional scenes depict a successful factory strike following the firing of an elderly worker, and another plotline follows an unemployed mechanic who joins the Communist Party.[67] Its surprisingly lighthearted tone and collage-like, somewhat slapdash mix of fiction and nonfiction counter the solemnity and what Bratich, following David Neiwert, describes as the "eliminationist" and dehumanizing narratives of Nazism with slapstick, humor, and song.[68]

For the post-May *Cahiers* editors, the film "fulfills exactly the condition of any militant film: to propagate a unique political meaning, an unambiguous message"—specifying "militant both in the political and cinematographic sense" (*cette unité duelle, cinématographique et politique*); however, the film also includes "an interference (*l'interférence*) in the filmic process of the production of meaning."[69] *Cahiers* then spends much time analyzing the introductory scene of the film: first, the audience sees newsreel footage of the countryside and factory workers, while a bombastic male voice-over pontificates on the beauty and productivity of the French nation. This is expressed as rather conventional documentary exposition, one with which the French public would be quite familiar. However, the film then reveals the audio to be coming not from the "voice of god" narrator but from a fictional schoolteacher, played by Jean Dasté (who also appears in Alain Resnais's 1966 antifascist film *La guerre est finie,* or *The War Is Over*). The camera first cuts to the schoolteacher, then pans to his young students rapt in attention. Documentary is revealed to have been fiction all along.

For Bonitzer et al., *La vie est à nous* is a militant film not just for its semidocumentary nature, but also because this dialectic between fiction and nonfiction teaches the audience to view the work *as* propaganda. It is a propaganda that bares its own device—an epistemological break and what the *Cahiers* editors describe as a fundamentally communist unveiling. The schoolteacher is revealed to be deceitful—"*décalés, mensongers*"—rather than a source of knowledge.[70] Dasté's dogmatic Francophilic messaging reveals itself to lack all credibility. It is especially notable that the bombastic voice-over aligns with nationalist and fascist ideology, and that the film, in its process of unveiling, does not need to argue the reverse explicitly. The film does not inoculate the viewer with an opposing ideology, but liberates the audience to conduct the critical work themselves. Fairfax highlights that indeed "it is the fiction sequences that have a greater epistemological credibility," since similar newsreels of the period would have been all too familiar for the viewer, representing the dominant bourgeois ideology of the period.[71] Critiquing the very form of the documentary is thus essential in a truly "militant" documentary, as the form, as Matsumoto also noted, is most culpable in fascist indoctrination.

Importantly, the *Cahiers* article makes a particular point to highlight Vertov as a progenitor of this film, as the first creator of a *montage du documents*; it likewise pairs Vertov with Brecht, who also "used fiction and representation for political analysis."[72] Yet I would like to expand the argument of the *Cahiers* editors by arguing that these fictional elements are also used for pleasure, giving the film a distinct sense of *liveliness*. And it is here that we must take Renoir's title at its word: Life Belongs to Us, with the "Us" referring to antifascist communists. The title is spoken diegetically by a group of communists late in the film, who enjoin the fictional unemployed worker (and audience) to "return to life." As if reminding us of the leftist adage, frequently attributed to the socialist leader Salvador Allende (assassinated by the US Central Intelligence Agency), that there can be no revolution without song—*no hay revolución sin canciones*—the film ends with these workers singing "The Internationale" while walking directly into the camera. The gathering of several groups of workers in long shot, with the horizon line cutting across the frame and bodies moving from the periphery to the center of the composition, revisits the ending sequence of Sergei Eisenstein's *Stachka* (*Strike*)

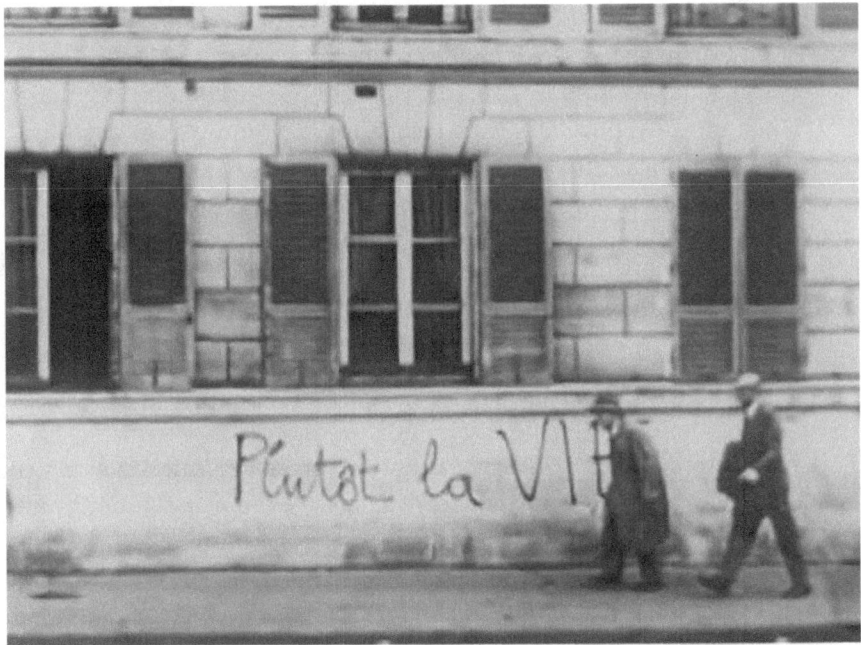

Figure 2. Graffiti in Paris in May 1968, featured in Jean-Luc Godard's *Un film comme les autres*, 1968.

from 1925. *Stachka* is best remembered for its famous use of dialectical montage, in which Eisenstein crosscuts the murder of striking workers with the slitting of a cow's throat. In Renoir's communist film, however, the striking workers live.

Antifascist filmmaking has long known the revolutionary potential of a filmmaking that is as affective and sensorial as it is critical. While the filmmakers I discuss vary in how pleasurable they view their art to be, all see the antifascist avant-garde documentary as a critical mode of *activation* and *enlivening*. The emphasis on "life" contrasts with what Bratich describes as "deathstyle fascism," what Deleuze and Guattari describe, on capitalism, and following Nietzsche, as "the ascetic ideal . . . the cultural extract, judging life, belitting life"; "everything labors for death, everything wishes for death."

I am reminded of a famous May 1968 graffito, also featured in Godard's first film after May, *Un film comme les autres* (*A Film Like Any Other*,

1968). The graffito reads "Plutôt la VIE," a reference to committed communist and surrealist André Breton's poem of the same name, from 1923, usually translated as "Choose Life Instead." This dictum, which might also be translated "Life above all," "Life rather," or "Life more than anything," might serve as a beautiful summary of the aesthetics of antifascism, tying the arguments of the 1920s and early 1930s to the revolutionary era of the 1960s. It contends that, fundamentally, the battle for the antifascist mind is a battle for life as we know it.

FORM, CONTENT, AND FORMAT

This book orients each of its five chapters around significant years in French and Japanese history that serve as pivotal moments, junctures in which an evolution in aesthetic form emerged from communist responses to specific cultural and geopolitical events: 1960 (the ANPO struggle), 1962 (the end of the Algerian War), 1964 (the Tokyo Olympics), 1969 (after revolutionary 1968; two chapters). In the films described here, the form does not passively *react* to social and political change but actively seeks to transform the world—especially through the crafting of an engaged, liberated, enlivened, and actively antifascist viewing public. This book's title, *Antifascism and the Avant-Garde*, recognizes that although the bulk of the filmmakers in this book actively desired their films to be antifascist, at times other qualities might render these films more complex and even contradictory. Jean-Luc Godard, for instance, rejected audience pleasure in favor of a certain asceticism during his DVG period, and Imamura Shōhei's films exude a certain ethnonationalist concern, such as in *Nippon konchūki* (*Insect Woman*, 1963), that sits somewhat uneasily in the formulations I've described here. Antifascist avant-garde documentary cannot be painted over with the same broad swath.

Likewise, the films described vary in the extent to which they use the term *documentary* to describe their work. Part of my argument rests on the fact that the antifascist avant-garde documentary explicitly questions the divide between fiction and reality. Chapter 3, especially, is unusual in this regard, for including films such as Kuroki Kazuo's *Tobenai chinmoku* (*Silence Has No Wings*, 1966), which appear fictional at first glance, although I argue that they belong to a specifically mid-decade genre I term *allegorical documentary*. Many of the films in this chapter are also quite popular and rest uneasily in an avant-gardist formulation that usually spurns mass appeal. I include these examples, however, because I see them all participating in a wider ecology of experimental documentary filmmaking with powerfully antifascist exigencies. Despite their differences, their similarities are exciting, rich, and increasingly relevant to our contemporary age. Across the book, I choose films that were heavily discussed at the time of release, are oriented toward transnational leftism, and speak to a variation of styles within the antifascist avant-garde documentary framework.

These chapters are chronological, and the French and Japanese chapters weave among each other, showing how the development of their respective film cultures was often interconnected and mutually determining. The story of French and Japanese radical documentary of the 1960s is, as I will show, one of neither simple influence nor a nebulous "simultaneity" or "synchronicity." They were responding explicitly to the local with an eye perpetually turned to the global, and often, and especially, to each other. This book is especially interested in engagements, in the ways individual filmmakers interacted with one another and with filmmaking cultures worldwide, as well as in communities and groups of organizing comrades—as in my analysis of Agnès Varda, Alain Resnais, and Georges Sadoul's "roundtable of friends" in 1961. My investigation of individual work cannot be separated from its participation in the social.

Chapter 1 begins with a more thorough investigation of Matsumoto Toshio's antifascism in form and how this emerged as a response to the ANPO struggle of 1960. It first summarizes the many theoretical writings on the avant-garde documentary published in journals in the early 1950s, tracing Matsumoto's theory to Hanada Kiyoteru, and then takes a deep dive into several "neo-documentary" films by Matsumoto himself that provide the most paradigmatic representations of these theories in 1960s Japanese cinema.

Chapter 2 turns to France in 1962, at the end of the Algerian War. It also draws a decolonial connection between France and Cuba and to an optimistic spirit in its early postrevolutionary era. The chapter traces an antifascist ecology through the Left Bank of the New Wave, as witnessed through early 1960s productions by Agnès Varda and Chris Marker. I center much of my analysis on the antifascist journal *Miroir du cinéma*, closely tied to Marker, Varda, and Alain Resnais, and the communist cultural weekly *Les Lettres françaises*. The chapter unveils, especially, the tie between decolonialism and the need to "engage" the spectator through processes of perceptual dehabituation—yet one that is often, for Marker and Varda, lively, playful, and affective.

Next, chapter 3 returns to Japan, explicating the origin of what I term the *allegorical semidocumentary*, emerging with the Tokyo Olympics in 1964: an era of great, even vertiginous, economic improvement. I argue that this movement away from militant activism around the 1960 ANPO protests and toward middle-classification and feverish consumption of consumer goods caused a reevaluation of anti-imperialist and antifascist artistic practice. It resulted in an explicit turn toward the fictional, and occasionally even toward a strange, uneasy complicity with certain nationalist concerns around "Japaneseness" conveyed through myth and the folkloric.

A few years later, the worldwide 1968 protests returned leftist militancy to center stage. Chapter 4 looks at several quasi-fictional, quasi-documentary, "anti-cinematic" productions by famous iconoclast Jean-Luc Godard during the DVG period, alongside the contemporaneous writing of the "ultraleft" film journal *Cinéthique*. The chapter interrogates pleasure and affect in Godard and questions the denial of pleasure as political praxis by integrating intersectional feminist and Black studies.

Finally, chapter 5 investigates the same period in Japan, focusing on the fervently experimental films of the Art Theatre Guild (ATG) of the late 1960s and early 1970s. In contrast to Godard's rejection of pleasure, I argue that these films embraced the affective and ecstatic as inextricable from the project of revolution, pointing to the countercultural New Left project of a "self-revolution of everyday life." These films, less tied to the Soviet avant-garde, introduce a new emancipatory aesthetics and ethics—importantly, one that is both formally and diegetically queer. Here I grapple with the queer content of these films, investigating how on-screen homosexual relationships, trans and nonbinary personhood, and other unusual or "aberrant" portrayals of gender and sexuality served as both literal *and* metaphorical representations of "self-revolution," yet without optimistic or easy solutions.

My work argues that these experimental aesthetics in documentary cannot be extricated from, and are in fact deeply intertwined with, economic, political, and social factors. Form and content are not two separate entities, but rely on one another, existing in a productive and endlessly fascinating dialectic without synthesis (to quote Naoki Yamamoto's formulation of Hanada Kiyoteru's philosophy).[73] As already witnessed by these introductory pages, my analyses cross between macro and micro levels. As Matsumoto would have it, the internal and external worlds weave and collide in complex ways. The form of this book might thus feel somewhat vertiginous in its tendency to zoom into minute specificities of film form—a close-up, an ultraspecific reference to an earlier film, a sudden jump cut— and then zoom out into an establishing shot that presents larger historical, cultural, political, and philosophical questions.

In addition, in this book I choose to look at French and Japanese film traditions on their own terms, with each chapter as a disparate unit, although I introduce comparative frameworks throughout. A different book might choose to analyze their many overlaps more explicitly. Indeed, just looking at all the Japanophilic and East Asia–based films of Chris Marker and Agnès Varda would provide material for an entire book; likewise, the discussion of Alain Resnais and Jean-Luc Godard by Japanese film theorists, critics, and filmmakers would itself make for an excellent and worthy publication. However, here I generally choose to highlight the specificity of each movement in its country of origin, occasionally gesturing to fascinating transnational entanglements.

My scholarship is greatly informed by Yuriko Furuhata's pioneering work on the "cinema of actuality" of the Japanese 1960s—the "common strategies of appropriating and recycling current, topical, and often sensational materials culled from the realm of journalism" in 1960s and early 1970s Japan.[74] My work is also buttressed by Naoki Yamamoto's analysis of theories of realism in prewar and postwar Japan through Hanada's concept of a "dialectics without synthesis." Miryam Sas's analyses of media theory and art in connection to the "affective scale" in the Japanese context are likewise greatly influential. Before these, Markus Nornes's histories of Japanese documentary paved the way for all future Japanese film scholars in illuminating a previously little-discussed yet immensely important aspect of Japanese media ecology.

On the Soviet side of things, Masha Salazkina's work on connections between the Soviet Union and the "third world" showed the radical possibility of scholarship tracking what Salazkina terms "The inextricability... the relationship beween the global cultures of modernity and film."[75] Likewise, Joshua Malitsky's work documents the connection between postrevolutionary film in the USSR and Cuba and demonstrates the transformative possibilities of comparison across continents and eras. I am greatly influenced by the connections John MacKay draws between Vertov and French postwar film culture; his analyses are unparalleled in rigor and care. Finally, Daniel Fairfax's *Red Years of Cahiers* provided massively important context to a complicated and, frankly, intimidating time in global film history and theoretical discourse.

Fundamental to my argument is the belief that film history theories can be better understood through their comparison. Their juxtaposition allows new perspectives to emerge that would be difficult through a more myopic gaze. I bring together works from numerous disciplines that include area studies fields as well as comparative literature, film and media studies, art history, and philosophy. I aim for this book to be accessible to many, across and beyond the humanities and social sciences. I share the sentiment of Sara Ahmed when she states, "I was 'brought up' between disciplines and I have never quite felt comfortable in the homes they provide."[76] However, this book is based on previously untranslated primary source research. In an age of broad categorizations, it argues for the importance of slow, thorough understandings of national contexts and the subtle connective threads unearthed by reading sources in their original languages.

This book also draws upon both traditional academic scholarship and more outward-facing public humanities scholarship on the Left. I believe we are in an era of leftist journalistic flourishing, and if the increasing numbers of independent, explicitly communist presses are any indication, our current moment rhymes uncannily with both the 1920s and the 1960s. I integrate works of contemporary theory that are published by communist presses in a (perhaps quixotic) attempt to bridge the gap between academia and public-facing work.

As Noh scholar Tom Hare once said to me, comparative work inevitably has an air of intellectual promiscuity. For this, I beg forgiveness, while nonetheless believing, like Ahmed, that "the promise of interdisciplinary scholarship is that the failure to return texts to their histories will do something."[77] For this project, the avant-garde documentary may not provide a sole solution to global fascism and imperialism, but it might provoke a method to think and perceive otherwise. Estranging, confounding, but also pleasurable and wonder inducing, the antifascist avant-garde documentary becomes an alternative framework for political engagement in art. At stake is my sincere belief in the power of the avant-garde documentary to serve a vital role in revolution—that, in the words of Matsumoto, the "emancipation of the self" is integral to "the transformation of the external world." This is the central claim of the book, and it extends beyond the cinematic and into the sphere of daily life. It is my hope to offer this book to a larger conversation within the history of world cinema and political aesthetics, indebted to the many thinkers and filmmakers whose theories have buttressed much of the research within its pages.

1 1960 Japan

ANPO AND ANTIFASCISM IN THE NEO-DOCUMENTARY

EXPERIMENTAL DOCUMENTARY
AS ANTIFASCIST UNVEILING

The title sequence of Matsumoto Toshio's short film *ANPO Jōyaku* (ANPO treaty), released at the end of 1959, begins with several photographs depicting the rubble of a war-torn region, while the soundtrack joins occasional percussion with an unsettling electronic drone. As the unmistakeable face of the Showa emperor (Hirohito) is superimposed, cartoon-like, on the images of rubble and slowly grows larger, the background darkens and the voice-over begins: "War's footsteps (*sensō no ashiato*) approach again. Japan, to take self-defense measures, and to prevent armed attacks on Japan, hopes the United States of America keeps its military in and around Japan: the US-Japan Treaty of Mutual Cooperation and Security: ANPO." We are meant to read "hope" ironically. Just as the narrator delivers the last word, "ANPO"—a term with massive psychological and historical pathos in the context of 1960s Japan, with enormous, generation-defining protests against its ratification—the image is reversed into a film negative. A beat later the viewer sees, and hears, the explosion of a bomb, followed by archival footage of war and destruction. The unsettling stasis of the first few seconds of still photographs is violently exploded.

The juxtaposition of Hirohito with the bomb is not surprising: Hirohito ruled Japan both during the Pacific War and in "peacetime," until his death in January 1989. Criticizing Hirohito was fairly ubiquitous in leftist circles, as the emperor represented Japan's unrepentant relation to its own imperial and fascist history. Importantly, the emperor also represented American Cold War hypocrisy through his retention by General Douglas MacArthur: the choice to treat the emperor as a "powerless figurehead" rather than a highly powerful (indeed, godlike) character directly responsible for the deaths and suffering of untold millions across East and Southeast Asia. This act demonstrated American prioritization of anti-communism over democracy. Japan was, and continues to be, used as a powerful economic and military stronghold against the Soviet Union (now Russia), and later, China. Hirohito symbolized Japan's bloody history in its lack of postwar self-criticism and atonement for war atrocities and its complicity in American military aggression.

ANPO Jōyaku uses tricks of editing and cinematography to unsettle the viewer and support its virulently anti-war and anti-ANPO message: a broken windowpane flickers on screen, juxtaposed with an image of a US soldier accused of killing a Japanese citizen; India ink flows across still images of women, symbolic of sexual violence; a photograph of Class A war criminal turned prime minister Kishi Nobusuke breaks like porcelain into nine pieces, revealing a caricature of Kishi in a military helmet; and a clawlike hand unfolds, Nosferatu like, over a map of the world, symbolizing the evils of American imperial hegemony, and indeed, the vampiric nature of Cold War capitalism. The last example evokes Soviet propaganda imagery during World War II and earlier, in which Hitler's army was represented by a variety of anthropomorphized monsters, from baboon to tarantula.

Indeed, Matsumoto's film explicitly attempts a form of propaganda influenced by Soviet filmmaking from the 1920s but updated for the postwar era. As director Nagano Chiaki wrote in the pages of *Kiroku eiga*, *ANPO Jōyaku* witnesses "the process of making the unknown known" and "orients itself towards a method of transforming reality.... [T]he work has the potential to evoke new meanings and qualities in propaganda."[1] The term *propaganda* did not have a negative connotation in the context of a left-leaning journal such as *Kiroku eiga*, helmed by Matsumoto Toshio

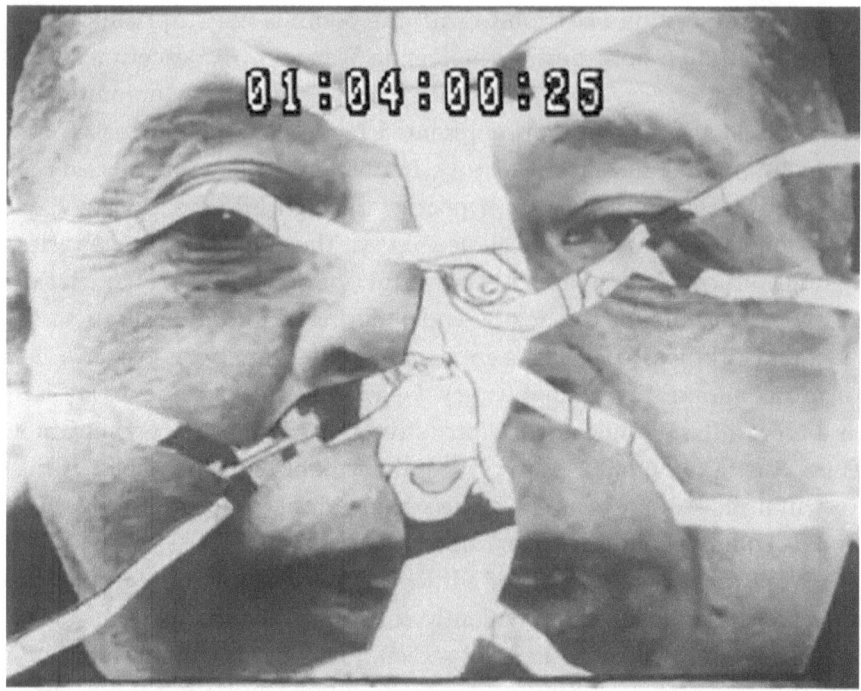

Figure 3. Caricature of Prime Minister (and former Class A war criminal) Kishi Nobusuke in a military helmet, in Matsumoto Toshio's *ANPO Jōyaku*, 1959.

himself, and here it is easily applied to Matsumoto's avowedly experimental short film. Likewise, the use of editing techniques to "evoke new meanings and qualities" elicits the methods of the prewar avant-garde, especially in France and the former USSR. Nagano also notes that the film was in the tradition of Prokino (the Proleterian Film League of Japan, or Nihon Proretaria Eiga Dōmei), thus connecting the film to communist-aligned organizations. The film's connection to the Soviet Union is also evident in sequences that uplift the communist nation, in which the film's voice-over intones, alongside idyllic images of agitational propaganda (agitprop)-inspired Soviet life (at the beach, happily working in the factory, celebratory parades): "In the country they call their enemy, the worker is the protagonist. The world was made by this working class. Capitalists don't make a single nail. They just exploit workers as their slaves. If

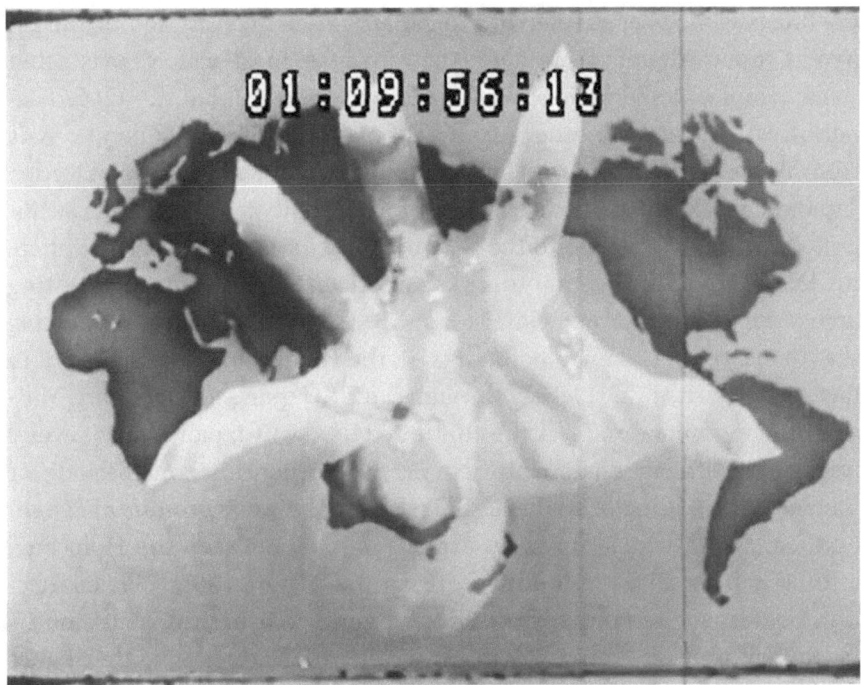

Figure 4. Claws of American imperial hegemony, in Matsumoto Toshio's *ANPO Jōyaku*, 1959.

the world didn't have capitalists, there'd be no war. Advancements in calculation decrease labor time. Everyone enjoys life more." *They* refers to the United States, and it is *they* that represent wanton death and destruction, in contrast to Soviet enjoyment. Death is connected to imperialism, as the voice-over narrates: "Imperial ashes of death envelop the world. Ashes of death (*shi no hai*).... They will envelop the world as an invisible fear.... Death creeps closer. Anxiety envelops the world." The contrast is thus between American death and Soviet life, between the "anxiety" (*fuan*) of capitalist imperialism and the pleasures of socialism.

In an intriguing turn, the film also maps American imperialist aggression in the postwar era directly onto Japanese imperial aggression during World War II. In the last few minutes of the film, the voice-over directs the viewer to "repeated unexplained bombings on the Greater East Asia

Co-Prosperity Sphere," referring to Japan's fascist conception of the inherent superiority of the Yamato (the Japanese "master race") over other Asian peoples. Imperialist Japanese ideology dictated that the alleged superiority of Japan over other Asian nations would thereby "liberate" Asia from Western imperial powers by installing Japan as Asia's natural leader. Japanese fascism is powerful precisely for its ability to masquerade as liberatory. In this reference to the Greater East Asia Co-Prosperity Sphere in *ANPO Jōyaku*, Matsumoto links American nuclear weapons testing across the Pacific to Japan's fascist history: Japan, by passively supporting the "repeated unexplained bombings" in the Pacific, does not reject but in fact *continues* its fascist legacy through the US-Japan security treaty. Matsumoto's insistence on fascism's continued legacy in Japan echoes several works of antifascist documentary in France during this same period: for instance, the ending of Alain Resnais's seminal *Nuit et brouillard* (Night and fog, 1956), which draws an explicit parallel between the Holocaust and French atrocities committed during the Algerian War. The connection to Resnais is especially meaningful given that he was Matsumoto's favorite filmmaker, appearing in his writing more than any other figure during this period.

Matsumoto's controversial film demonstrated his belief in the power of experimental techniques in documentary to reveal the normally hidden; while avowedly a work of propaganda, *ANPO Jōyaku* uses its myriad editing experiments to destabilize common conceptions and drum up support for the struggle against ANPO. As Nagano wrote in his review of *ANPO Jōyaku*, the film "creates new ways of expression" and "crystallizes [his] theory of documentary creation." These formal methods, though, have an avowedly political purpose: "Matsumoto draws out the helpless and oppressive consciousness that has been buried deep in our bodies in the fourteen years since the end of World War II, and confronts it with historical reality. It's meant to be transformed into something real. He is trying to approach the complexity of everyday reality by stripping the subject [*taishō*] of images of the everyday, using powers unique to film."[2] Rather than a style of propaganda that supports widely understood notions and deeply held beliefs, Matsumoto's film "strips"—the Japanese is literally "strip off the veil," or *vēru o hagitori*—commonly seen images, confronting them with a historical reality that had been "buried deep." This unveiling, however, can only occur "using powers unique to film." Following Matsumoto and Nagano, I argue that experimental documentaries such as *ANPO Jōyaku* perform this antifascist unveiling process through instigating an affective shock to the senses. The rapid-fire and wide-ranging editing tricks associated with the surrealist avant-garde is meant to confront the viewer directly, implicating them in the current political situation of Japan. While this directly shocking mechanism would change slightly over the next several years, in the early 1960s short political documentary used disorientation as an affective strategy to render the viewer complicit in the continuation of fascist policies, in the hope of instigating radicalization, self-critique, and then political action. What Matsumoto will soon call the "neo-documentary" answers the call for a documentary filmmaking that breaks with wartime ideology in content *and* in form.

The writers of *Kiroku eiga* frequently discussed fascism and imperialism in its pages, especially during the heyday of the ANPO struggle. Nazi Germany was a constant reference point, largely due to a strong understanding of documentary film as a medium complicit in, and in fact inextricable from, wartime propaganda. Yamamoto notes that film critics such as the Marxist Iwasaki Akira, central theorist for proletarian film, spoke of the need for Japan to come to terms with its complicity during the Pacific War. For Iwasaki, because so many contemporary critics shared responsibility for horrors committed during wartime, engaging in ethical and enlightened film criticism required a coming to terms with one's past—with what the voice-over of *ANPO Jōyaku* terms the "traces on their skin."[3]

This language of surreal, uncanny embodiment, in which fascism and imperialism continued to leave quasi-supernatural "traces on skin," is echoed by many theoretical texts of the era. As critic Sasaki Hajime wrote in September 1959, just a few months before the release of *ANPO Jōyaku*: "Japan's documentary film showed unprecedented prosperity due to the war, and the policy of forced screening of cultural films in the war . . . still haunts [our contemporary methods]. Although the ideologies of wartime and postwar films seem to be diametrically opposed at first glance, there is an extremely close relationship between them."[4] Here, as in Iwasaki, supernaturally imbued terms like *ghost* (*yūrei*) and *haunt* (*shutsubotsu suru*) proliferate, and we will see more instances of what one might call the antifascist supernatural recur later in this chapter. Sasaki here argues that the task of the postwar documentarian, especially in the wake of the ANPO struggle, is to shine a light on the ghosts of fascism within the contemporary landscape.

Yet critics such as Nagano, Matsumoto, and Sasaki constantly reiterate that this task is both external and internal: fascism cannot only be confronted externally, in protests or penned proclamations; it must also be vanquished at the level of individual psychology. The stage for the defeat of fascism is both the public square and the psychoanalyst's couch—or more precisely, the mirror. As Matsumoto argues, in an article written approximately coterminous with the creation of *ANPO Jōyaku*: "It is through postwar responsibility that we unabashedly examine the negative ideological structure that permeates our war and post-war experiences, recognizing the somber truth."[5] A revolution experienced on the ground must necessarily interweave dialectically with a revolution experienced internally, with an examination of "the somber truth" of "post-war responsibility."

This chapter theorizes the avant-garde documentary in Japan through its engagement with antifascism in the late 1950s and early 1960s. The crux of this chapter is the pivotal juncture of June 1960, during which Japan saw the largest protest movement in its history, and when the treaty was forcibly ratified against the will of most politicians and the majority of the citizenry. The chapter builds upon crucial work on Matsumoto Toshio by Yuriko Furuhata, Michael Raine, and Miryam Sas, as well as documentary history on Japan more broadly by Naoki Yamamoto and Markus Nornes. It interweaves crucial and rarely discussed archival evidence on documentary ethics and history from journals such as *Kiroku eiga* and *Eiga hyōron*. Taken together, this evidence demonstrates that Matsumoto's neo-documentary aimed to use its shocking, surrealist form and antifascist content to battle against imperialist ideology and reactionary politics in the Japanese postwar. Thinkers from art historian and theorist Hanada Kiyoteru to theorist-filmmakers Matsumoto Toshio and Noda Shinkichi saw surrealistic experimental nonfiction as the only style of filmmaking responding adequately to the aftermath of World War II. As we shall see, Matsumoto's approach integrated an "aesthetic sadomasochism," combining a "Sadean eye" that battles against fascism in the external world with a "masochism" of self-criticism that constantly thinks through one's own complicity in personal and political fascism.

First, however, it is important to demonstrate the rich theoretical groundwork that had already existed in Japan for several decades through an investigation of the politics and aesthetics of documentary that stretched from the prewar to the postwar eras, especially through theorists Imamura Taihei, Nakai Masakazu, and especially Hanada Kiyoteru.

JAPANESE AVANT-GARDE DOCUMENTARY THEORY BEFORE MATSUMOTO

In the prewar period, film theorists such as Nakai and Imamura were laying the groundwork for a particularly Japanese flavor of art and film theory, one that rejects claims to objectivity and invites comparisons to creative repurposings of the cinematic medium—even to animation. What we would call the avant-garde documentary was an integral component of Japanese film theoretical ecology early on. As Thomas Lamarre argues, Imamura's 1940 essay "A Theory of Documentary Cinema" emphasizes "documentation [as] a form of subjective expression, not objective recording."[6] The priority of objectivity in documentary is always called into question. Imamura's film theory is indispensable in recognizing what one might call the *animated* qualities of documentary and the surprisingly documentarian qualities of animation. Contrary to the commonplace understanding that documentary is "objective" while cartoons are "fantastical," Lamarre argues that "Imamura's film theory ... stresses subjective expression in the context of documentary, while his cartoon theory lingers on the realism stemming from photographic methods."[7] The prioritization of subjective expression and a rejection of seemingly objective documentary methods would lay the groundwork for Hanada—and later, for Matsumoto Toshio's film critical practice and his integration of surrealism within nonfiction.

For many Marxist theorists in prewar Japan, especially Hanada and Nakai, the Soviet avant-garde represented an era that symbolized new formal as well as political possibilities. Yet by the early 1930s the changing political climate in both Japan and the USSR—fascism in the former and Stalinism in the latter—made future transmission even more difficult.[8] Yet we know that certain Soviet avant-garde films were well-received in the 1930s, especially by leftist critics such as the young Nakai Masakazu, attentive reader of Vladimir Lenin, Karl Marx, and György Lukács, and whose aesthetic philosophy and Marxian politics frequently draw comparisons to Walter Benjamin.[9] Nakai was famously impressed by avant-garde documentary *Vesnoi* (*In Spring*), a 1929 film by Mikhail Kaufman—Vertov's brother, *kinok* cinematographer, and the eponymous cameraman of Vertov's *Chelovek s kinoapparatom*. Nakai, who loved Kaufman's quick edits so much that he brought a stopwatch to the screening, used the film to develop his burgeoning ideas of technology as the revelation of a noninstrumental, more imaginative time.[10] He described the film ecstatically as an "aesthetics of abandon, something that flows in a crystalline way," with all the strange and beautiful contradictions the terms entailed.[11] Nakai, however, was arrested in 1937—one of the many victims of a regime that banned all overt criticism.[12] He was eventually released and continued to publish after the war—importantly, praising the form of the semi-documentary in the postwar period, as the third chapter discusses. His writings therefore profoundly align with a Japanese media theoretical ecology that emphasized documentary subjectivity and experiment.

Most integral to Matsumoto's theory and oeuvre, though, were the postwar writings of Hanada Kiyoteru. As a part of the earlier generation of leftist critics, in January 1948 Hanada founded the postwar artist collective Yoru no Kai (The Night Society) with avant-garde artist Okamoto Tarō.[13] Hanada would go on to inspire many filmmakers of the Japanese political avant-garde of the 1960s, including Ōshima Nagisa, Hani Susumu, Teshigahara Hiroshi, "documentary" novelist Abe Kōbō, and importantly, Matsumoto himself, whose film theory most clearly evinced a connection to, and evolution from, Hanada's writings. Importantly, this literary group explicitly sought to integrate surrealism with Marxist social and political ideals as an alternative to socialist realism. Although the group disbanded in February 1949 because of political differences, Margaret Key notes that its debates laid the groundwork for a surrealism-informed avant-garde practice that would directly influence the avant-garde documentaries of the 1960s.[14]

Hanada was inspired by Okamoto's concept of "bipolarism"—*taikyoku shugi*—which argued for a juxtaposition of rational and irrational elements in art. Hanada proposed a similar dialectic within postwar documentary film: between "concreteness" (*gutai*) and "abstraction" (*chūshō*). As we will see, this dialectic continued to evolve with the theories of Matsumoto Toshio, who posited the "rational" world of documentary against the "irrational" world of experimental and avant-garde filmmaking practices. In the early 1950s Hanada developed a theory of sur-documentary (a name meant to evoke surrealism), a dialectical form that was meant to contrast with the conventions of socialist realism. For the literary and artistic avant-garde groups of the postwar period, as Key notes, surrealism was the primary aesthetic, and Marxism was the primary political influence. Surrealism did not see art as subordinate to politics and viewed the relation between the two as more complex and symbiotic than hierarchical. As Michael Löwy attests, "Revolutionary aspiration is at the very source of Surrealism—it is not by accident that one of the movement's first collective texts, written in 1925, is called 'Revolution Now and Forever.'"[15] Surrealism was seen as an art that would force societal change, and it was especially appealing in the wartime period for its antiauthoritarian nature.[16]

Like the writers of *Kiroku eiga* a decade later, Hanada believed avant-garde documentary was key for the development of new possibilities—both internally and externally, leading to new political futures. As Margaret Key writes:

> [Hanada] viewed art as a tool for changing society's value system and argued that in the postwar era, in which Japan's traditional values have proven hollow, old forms of realism must be abandoned and a new method of representing reality must be devised. He declared that this revolutionary, new form of realism must integrate realism and what had previously been considered non-realism while maintaining the tension between them.... This principle of Hanada, *tairitsubutsu o tairitsu no mama toitsu suru*, or "unification while maintaining opposition," was a development of an argument advanced in his 1940 work *Sakuran no ronri* (The Logic of Derangement), in which he calls for a synthesis of inner, psychological reality and external, objective reality.[17]

Hanada thus saw surrealism as a crucial methodology, combined with and inseparable from revolutionary thought, that must be developed in the Japanese postwar period. Terms like *sakuran*, meaning confusion or derangement, might be productively compared with the Russian formalist concept of *ostranenie*, or estrangement; although the two cannot be exactly equated, both serve as an artistic *technique* that has great ethical and political importance. Yet Hanada's conception of "derangement" certainly evolved directly from surrealist discourse, and although I do not address this at length, it might be productively compared to the French *dépaysement*.

Connected to this interest in surrealism were debates on the nature of subject-hood, or *shutaisei*, in documentary. These debates attempted to develop a mode of filmmaking that highlighted the relationship between filmmaker and object inherent in documentary production, rather than presenting the object through a seemingly objective approach (the latter would mean alienation from one's labor, in the language of Marxism). For many Japanese theorists, documentary entailed the coexistence of both subjectivity and objectivity; likewise, the documentary image also necessarily documented the relationship between the filmmaker and their object (*taishō*) of filmmaking.[18] While both *taishō* and *kyakutai* are translated as *l'objet* in French or "object" in English, *kyakutai* emphasizes the thing-creation of documentary film, while *taishō* emphasizes the object as a target of analysis (or the "subject" of a documentary film, in English). Nonetheless, both are differentiated from the *shutai* (subject) and emphasize the relation between the filmmaker and their object of study. The English translations of *shutai* (subject) and *kyakutai* (object) do not do these loaded terms justice, as "subject" here connotes a more thoughtful and less scientifically rigid subjectivity.

Several dialectics are at play in Hanada's thought: interiority and exteriority, psychological reality and sociopolitical reality, subjectivity and objectivity. Avant-garde documentary became, for Hanada and Matsumoto, the filmmaking style that integrated the complex dialectics of the filmmaker-subject relationship. It is also important that Hanada was critical of many modes of standard proletarian realism since the early 1950s, and that avant-garde documentary filmmaking practices emerged as an alternative to aesthetic practices tinged with Stalinism and the Old Left, especially socialist realism. These modes were considered old-fashioned and crept even outside of official communist-aligned works. As Nick Kapur claims, at the same time that humanism, "reportage," and socialist realism prevailed in the JCP, similar modes of realism, rationalism, and humanism prevailed in the studio system as well, coupled with uplifting stories celebrating the triumph of the human spirit.[19] For both Hanada and Matsumoto, such an emphasis on rationalism and what Matsumoto claimed as "positivism" led to complacency.²⁰ Although it might sound a bit extreme today, for Matsumoto, their simplified politics and overly optimistic, uncritical form even brought such films closer to wartime propaganda than to antifascism. Instead, the neo-documentary, directly drawn from Hanada's sur-documentary, avoided such pitfalls, becoming Matsumoto's privileged form for antifascist documentary.

MATSUMOTO TOSHIO'S NEO-DOCUMENTARY DIALECTICS

For Matsumoto, film form was not apolitical but in fact interwoven with ideological meaning. His ideal filmmaking style threaded interiority into exteriority and saw individual and collective struggles as fundamentally linked. As Sas writes, "Matsumoto is a creative theorist of that space and scale of artistic/mediatic potentiality located above the individual and below the larger system (whether the latter is conceived, as it might be today, as infrastructure or platform)."²¹ His media theory joins the importance of a personal, psychoanalytical grappling with antifascism alongside a cultural and societal reckoning.

Matsumoto described the neo-documentary, his own dialectic of fiction and nonfiction, by analyzing the early years of film history in the late nineteenth and early twentieth centuries. In *Eizō no hakken*, he linked this dialectic to the politics of surrealism and connected it to earlier film, art, and literary works, notably listing Alain Resnais's ekphrastic short documentary *Guernica* (1950) as an important precursor to his own work.²² The fact that Picasso's artwork is resolutely anti-war and antifascist is of vital importance. Equally important, though, is Resnais's adjoining documentation and experiment: Resnais's film is noteworthy for never showing a single shot of Picasso's work in its entirety; the film fragments the painting, adding a myriad of cinematographic and editing effects that produce a distinctly surrealist sense of abject horror. As Matsumoto writes, Resnais's method is one "of skepticism toward the external world"—an important prerequisite for political art. As he writes, "Contemporary art must... set itself to finding ways to destroy that naïve faith in the object, the too-classical understanding of the human that is based on a conciliatory attitude toward the object."²³

For Matsumoto, films like *Guernica* embody a dialectic inherent to film history since its inception. Matsumoto claimed that early cinema saw two competing tendencies: "discovery," or nonfiction, on the one hand, and "creation," or fiction, on the other. These existed in a quintessential Hegelian dialectic: the fictional, avant-garde "creation" of the fantastical films of Georges Méliès, such as *Le Voyage dans la lune* (A trip to the moon, 1902), became the antithesis to the "thesis" of the nonfictional "discovery" of the Lumière brothers' actuality films. Matsumoto names the tension between Méliès and Lumière "the dialectic of the discovery and creation of the moving image" (*ugoku eizō ni yoru hakken to sōzō no benshōhō*). Such writing immediately, and consciously, echoes Hanada's "dialectics without synthesis," which he also called an "elliptical imagination." As Matsumoto explains: "[The Lumières'] camera 'finds' from among existing things, while Méliès 'creates' from those that do not exist."[24] The enfolding and interweaving of these is what Matsumoto describes as a neo-documentary—or "documentary-like avant-garde film" (*kirokuteki zen'ei eiga*). This resulted in a productive and curious folding of nonfictional elements into fictional film, and fictional elements into nonfictional film, in a variety of uncanny ways. Fiction and documentary are not entirely subsumed into one another, and both elements result in a productive and dialectical tension.

While Matsumoto's avant-garde documentary or neo-documentary theory is somewhat distinguished from Hanada's conceptions of the sur-documentary and the more explicitly fictional style called the semi-documentary, there are significant overlaps between them. As Miryam Sas describes: "The problems of intrapsychic and extrapsychic structures refracting one another already formed a fundamental part of his theoretical frame. Writing about avant-garde work, he brings the experimental, antinarrative, or antilogical visions one would associate with experimental filmmaking—sometimes said to reflect the workings of the interior of the psyche, the unconscious, and so on—together with the documentary impulse, as the necessity to see and refract the real or larger world. Both terrains are crucial for the filmmaker's search, and they have a necessary relation to one another."[25] Both the documentary and experimental impulses, then, are central to filmmaking for Matsumoto, with the "intrapsychic and extrapsychic structures refracting one another." Sas echoes

Michael Raine, who notes that Matsumoto envisioned the subjective and objective worlds to be in dialectical relation, orbiting around each other, rather than a self-contained subject describing a stable object.[26] In addition, Matsumoto clarifies Hanada's dialectical formulation and interest in surrealism, connecting it to a dialectic inherent in all film history. This must then be reconciled with the political landscape: the "antinarrative, or antilogical visions" must be brought together with "the necessity to see or refract the real or larger world." To utilize both in a productive tension is the central task of political filmmaking.

It is important to specify that Matsumoto did not desire to blend art with the political indiscriminately; rather, he was extremely wary of an art that claimed to be political, arguing that this would subsume the artwork under mainline political opinion. Matsumoto criticized the lack of self-criticism witnessed by the Japanese documentary industry, switching first from fascism to collaboration and then to an artistic subservience to socialist realism and the JCP. This switch, seemingly overnight, was deeply suspect. As Matsumoto wrote: "During the war, [documentary filmmakers] uncritically produced films collaborating with the war, changing course because of absolutely external power and transitively switching directions (*tenkō*) without any serious internal criticism. In that period of political promotion they quickly and hysterically, in the manner of a rapidly spreading disease among children, engaged in a biased practice that subordinated art to politics. Lacking principles, they subsequently adapted to the PR film industry in a period of retreat. Here, consistent from start to finish, there are only slavish craftsmen lacking subjectivity. One might say that, from the beginning, there were no artists here."[27]

Lacking "any serious internal criticism," documentary filmmakers went from "a biased practice" during wartime propaganda to the PR films in the postwar period. Such a rapid switch in ideology, seemingly overnight, with no analysis or atonement, was "lacking principles," and thus directors were "consistent" in being "slavish craftsmen"—not artists. Like Iwasaki and Hanada before him, Matsumoto described the necessity for techniques of self-criticism within leftist political organizing. Indeed, Matsumoto even likened the mindless subordination of art to politics to an infectious disease. Such an uncritical enmeshing, predicated on extant ideologies, rids the work of the political potential inherent in aesthetic form.

Key to the work of art, however, is the individuality and subjectivity of the artist, which necessarily separates them from "the people" at large. Matsumoto Toshio explicitly argued against a "fetishization of the masses" linked with Stalinism, writing in 1962: "Stalin's basic thought structure [is a] fetishism of the masses.... True art sometimes has to stubbornly refuse the more direct demands of the public."[28] Matsumoto was critical of an aesthetic form subordinated to party policy and instead desired to investigate the politics inherent in art itself. Films seemingly geared toward the proletariat were viewed as akin to socialist realism, and Japanese filmmakers turned to avant-garde experiment to reawaken the political vanguard in cinema, to revitalize both cinema as a medium and cinema in its ability to cause seismographic changes in the political landscape.

Both Hanada Kiyoteru and Matsumoto therefore claimed that documentary filmmaking must necessarily undergo an aesthetic revolution to reflect the changing climate of the postwar period. Art itself must necessarily be transformed in light of the trauma of war. It is notable, then, that Matsumoto's neo-documentaries after *ANPO Jōyaku* are tinged with the perceived failure of the ANPO struggle. The collective trauma of the experience of fighting alongside students as well as workers, and the turn of the media against the protesters after the death of young student Kanba Michiko on June 15, 1960, would be replayed in the May 1968 protests in Paris eight years later. The collective trauma of the post-ANPO period entailed a change in form for Matsumoto's neo-documentaries, and indeed here one sees Matsumoto more fervently investigating the uncanny and surreal aspects of film form; his films increasingly limit the use of expository voice-over, and the already copious editing techniques were even more heightened and unusual. The supernatural and ghostly, extant in *ANPO Jōyaku* and in other shorts such as the dreamlike bike advertisement/PR film *Ginrin* (treated extensively by Miryam Sas), became an even more prevalent part of his filmmaking practice.

SURREALISM AND THE SUPERNATURAL IN THE NEO-DOCUMENTARY

Yamamoto notes that although Hanada did not write of this extensively, he suggested the creative adoption of ghost or supernatural creature stories written and circulated in Japan since the Edo period. For Hanada, such stories are rife with surrealistic elements and can be successfully merged with realistic techniques.[29] Many Japanese avant-garde filmmakers of this period, from Matsumoto to Imamura Shōhei, Hani Susumu, and Terayama Shūji, appear to have fulfilled this prophecy and included significant surrealistic "ghost story"–like elements into their own work. In such films, supernatural elements are not a simple trope but reveal meaningful undercurrents in Japanese society.

As if responding to the need to "unveil" the trauma of war, the ANPO protests, and the intended viewer's own wartime complicity, Matsumoto's films are full of ghosts, demons, and mysterious forces outside of a narrator's control. His neo-documentaries find many counterparts in the work of Abe Kōbō, who also participated in groups such as the Association for Documentary Art, and whose connection to documentary forms is extensively treated by Yuriko Furuhata and Margaret Key. Key argues that documentary was a way for Abe to intervene in social and political life, while also challenging familiar conceptions of reality, truthfulness, and objectivity. Indeed, Abe believed his work to have creative origins in documentary as much as in fiction, and like many of the figures analyzed in these chapters, did not see the imagination as antithetical to the documentary mode.[30] Furuhata, meanwhile, posits that Matsumoto and Abe both argue for an irrational, dreamlike inflection to the documentary form. For both artists, a true documentary must leave room for the uncanny and illogical; it cannot assume total knowledge. Abe writes, following Hanada, that the "spirit of documentary" entails respecting "the accidental elements that fall outside of our consciousness." Quintessentially surrealist, Abe claimed that the "interior worlds" of surrealism needed to aim toward the "exterior world" in order to produce a new realism.[31]

Matsumoto's films for television in the 1960s seem to faithfully follow Hanada's earlier sur-documentary suggestion, as well as Abe's claim. In both his texts and films, Matsumoto emphasizes a synthesis of the "interior world" with the "exterior world," thus arguing against the suppression of subjectivity over a perceived political objectivity. For Matsumoto, films must express both things that we see in reality, as well as the *mienai mono*: the "unseeable things." Films that ignore the world of the *mienai mono* assume that the *mono*, or thing, apparent in the director's field of vision is the same reality experienced by all others. The claim that documentary filmmaking must render visible the otherwise unseen or unseeable resonates profoundly with French documentary filmmaker Chris Marker, who aimed for his films to *donner à voir*—to make visible, to literally "give to sight."

This surrealistic interest in the unshown and unseen, as well as his synthesis of avant-garde and documentary, interior and exterior worlds, is especially notable in three of Matsumoto's short films made for television: *Nishijin* (Weavers of Nishijin) from 1961, *Ishi no uta* (Song of the Stone) from 1963, and *Haha-tachi* (Mothers) from 1967. In *Nishijin* Matsumoto shows the viewer the Kyoto-based workplace of the weavers of stunning kimono fabrics dear to Japanese tradition, but in a far more uncanny light. This is a far cry from a patriotic extolling of the traditional arts. In the bulk of the twenty-six-minute long film, Matsumoto shows these weavers behind their enormous contraptions of wood, string, and fabric while a deep, omnipresent voice narrates in verselike phrases. The weavers are dwarfed by these gargantuan geometrical structures, and Matsumoto hides the faces of these workers behind the shadow of their tools. Likewise, the soundtrack by Miyoshi Akira emphasizes the eerie mechanical sounds of the loom; another director might have included the chatter of elderly weavers, but Matsumoto opts for a more destabilizing and dehumanizing effect.

In a review in *Eiga hyōron*, the critic Satō Tadao notes that "the workers are not described in a 'humanlike' (*ningenteki*) manner" although they exist merely as a means of production.[32] Meanwhile, the voice-over uses a constant refrain, which transforms into an ersatz Buddhist mantra: *Rekishi o mamoru / Nishijin o mamoru* (Protect history / protect Nishijin). The voice-over includes several overlapping meanings: if interpreted as a "voice of God" (or here, "voice of government") narration, it might represent the nationalist drive to maintain traditional arts during a time of resurgent nationalism. Such a voice is robotic and uninterested in the larger questions of artmaking, and the film is evidently critical of this ethnonationalist belief system. Yet if interpreted as the voice of the filmmaker, the phrase signifies an attempt to protect laboring workers from continued exploitation. As Matsumoto's film clearly indicates, these workers are martyred for the sake of a historical art form. The laborers of Nishijin operate both as the Marxist proletariat—alienated and, indeed, overshadowed by the products of their labor—and as venerated religious figures. Both voice-over meanings operate simultaneously and dialectically. Matsumoto's film

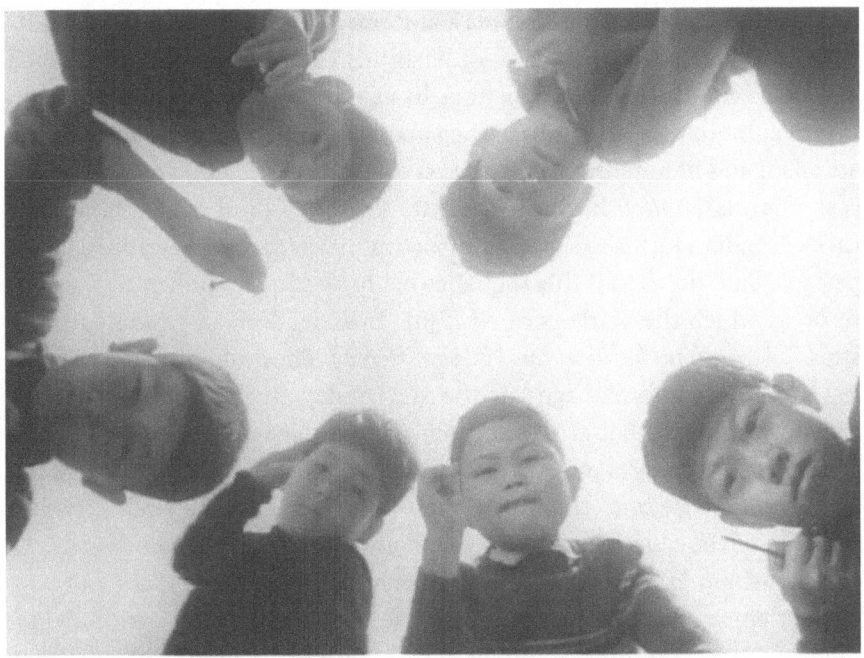

Figure 5. Boys throwing nails at the camera, in Matsumoto Toshio's *Nishijin*, 1961.

does not provide a simple solution, and viewer complicity is brought to the fore. How, in our participation within the capitalist market, are we adding to worker pain and exploitation? And how is the support for traditions complicit in an ethnonationalism associated with Japan's fascist past?

Matsumoto's surrealism digs inward, eliciting a "masochistic" self-confrontation. It manifests visually in an uncanny light and again juxtaposes the modernist with the traditional: in one particularly chilling sequence near the end of the film, lacking any diegetic explication, clumps of dried mugwort powder are burned onto the skin of a woman's back in the ancient art of moxibustion. Then the camera is placed at a low angle, showing us a group of young boys staring down at the lens. In a sequence of shots barely a second long, they throw nails onto the ground. When the nails stick in the ground, this image is juxtaposed with the ominous whizzing, clacking sound of a loom. Then the camera returns to the shot of the back and burning powder. Then a form wearing a demon mask appears, dances a sequence from a Noh play, and promptly disappears, while Matsumoto resumes the discussion of Nishijin. The audience is left shocked and haunted—but all this, of course, has a purpose.

Matsumoto wanted to reveal the subconscious of Japanese society: the animism and hauntedness that persist even among capitalist gain and excess, the *unheimlich* hiding among the *heimlich* (and it is notable that these Freudian terms are quoted verbatim in Matsumoto's writings of the period). Satō notes that this sequence echoes a phrase spoken by the narrator, in which the workers of Nishijin "live in a body in which nails are stuck" (*karada no naka ni kugi ga sasatteiru*). The ever-present nails persist from the primordial age into the present day, stuck regardless of modernist invention: a haunted tradition. As one voice-over states, while the screen depicts images of elderly Japanese people in kimonos blowing the smoke of incense onto their eyes, their bodies "within the smoke, within the eyes of the elderly . . . within my body, things unable to be seen (*me ni mienai mono*) enter into our nightmares." This, then, is the purpose of the demon mask, the children with nails, and the body with burning mugwort powder: things "unable to be seen" persist in the subconscious of the Japanese worker, disregarding the dream of economic growth and prosperity. Although a blend of fact and fiction, subjectivity and objectivity, characterizes much of the Japanese political avant-garde, Matsumoto's version blends the aesthetics of Japanese religion, both Buddhist and Shinto, within a larger political and economic context.

Continuing the critique of capitalism, in a slightly later sequence Matsumoto films a group of businessmen discussing, allegedly, profits over a dinner table. He shoots them from above, describing a set of vaguely humanoid abstract geometrical figures, then films them from behind, masking their faces in shadow, or behind papers.

They are given voices, but all dialogue is post-dubbed, creating a diegetic rift between sound and image. Matsumoto also scratches the audio recording purposefully, so the businessmen repeat themselves like a broken record; sometimes even their coughs are repeated eerily, placing old Japanese salarymen within the selfsame animistic context of their exploited Nishijin workers. Matsumoto's filmmaking thus actualizes his call to blend the documentary with avant-garde, to represent both the "visible" and "invisible" worlds. The unnerving quality of his films differs

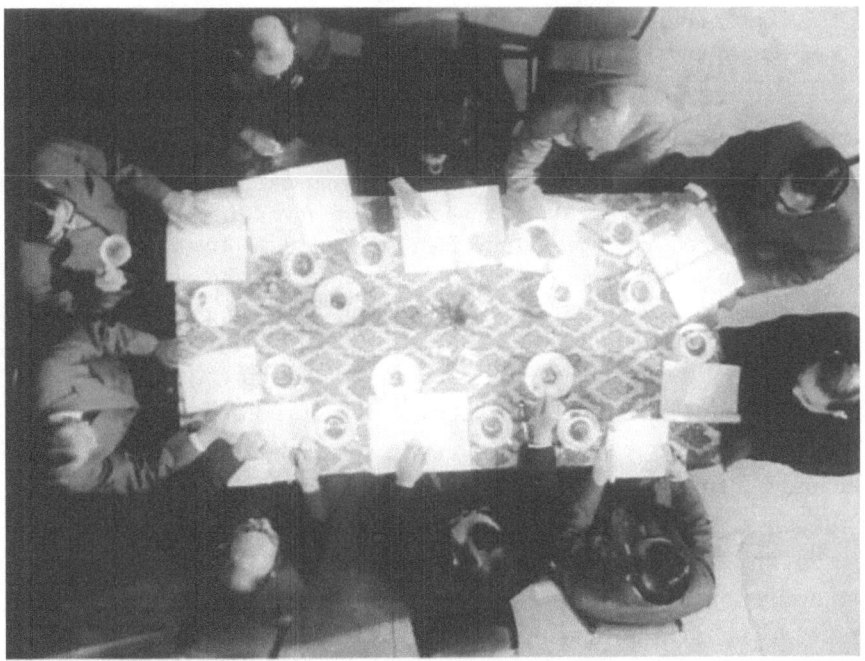

Figure 6. Japanese businessmen around a table, shot from above, in Matsumoto Toshio's *Nishijin*, 1961.

significantly from a documentarist revealing their own subjective worldview explicitly, in the manner of Agnès Varda's *Les Glaneurs et la glaneuse* (*The Gleaners and I*, 2001) or Chris Marker's *Sans soleil* (*Sunless*, 1983). Matsumoto's films deny easy access to the subjectivity of the filmmaker or an objective account of a political situation and result in an investigation of contemporary Japanese society through the methods of the Freudian uncanny, with a decidedly Marxist twist.

Nishijin was discussed widely in the pages of *Kiroku eiga*, with the bulk of the entire September 1961 issue devoted to its analysis. While many articles praised the film, a few vehemently criticized it; translator Ozawa Toshio, for instance, said it "felt like reading a social studies textbook," and would have preferred a more humanitarian take, as in Hani's *Furyō shōnen* (*Bad Boys*, 1961).[33] Film editor Watanabe Masami praised the film, noting that it "conveys a physical rawness":

> The film . . . did not attempt to appeal to general objectivity, and this is the most meaningful part of the film. . . . The traditional consciousness created by solitary labor is pushed into a corner of the modernized machine industry; the manufacturers are thrown out of the era. The low wages, labor unions for better treatment of craftsmen . . . various aspects are fragmented through montage. The insane repetition of words and the one-sided, illogical conversation must have been an attempt to reveal the turbulent social structure of Nishijin from within [their] consciousness. The novelty of this film lies in the fact that everything is narrowed down to the relationship between humans and the gripper loom, and the dimension of consciousness defined by that relationship.[34]

Watanabe thus links the film's effectiveness to its editing techniques—the emphasis on fragmentation symbolizing the alienation of labor. He again echoes Matsumoto's dialectic between "the traditional consciousness" and "the modernized machine industry," seeing it manifested in "insane repetition" and "the illogical." The fundamental drive in Matsumoto's films is an awakening of *consciousness*—an attempt to integrate self-analysis and self-criticism within the sphere of political liberation through Marxism. Watanabe thus echoes the personal aspect of the antifascism structuring the argument of this book and the unique ability of emotional "turbulen[ce]" and "the . . . illogical," expressed through montage and fragmentation, to unveil the normally hidden within documentary.

Several filmmakers and critics connected the film to Alain Resnais, unsurprising given *Kiroku eiga*'s fascination with the director. Noda Shinkichi, known to adhere quite closely to Matsumoto's film theory, connected the film to the fragmentation of memory and consciousness in *Hiroshima mon amour* (1959, horribly translated as *24 Hour Love Affair* in Japanese). Normally quite supportive of Matsumoto's works, here Noda is a tad more cautious, writing that Matsumoto did not sufficiently include his own personal viewpoint (perhaps he hoped for more voice-over, in the vein of Marker and later Varda, or the previously discussed *ANPO Jōyaku*). He did, however, wholeheartedly support how the film showed the "alienated and objectified" Nishijin weavers:

> "Nishijin" is Matsumoto's attempt to pursue the consciousnessness of the people who live there. . . . [T]he hands and movement, and the monotonous repetition of the group weaving, create an unusual tension due to its

monotony. Through scenes of rags, the face of the weathered *Jizo* stone, whose eyes and nose are scratched with ink, the smoke of incense, the face rubbed with a large nail scraper... entangling all of these, we see an alienated, lonely, closed image. These are the best parts of "Nishijin.". . . In all Matsumoto's works, he tries to depict a world that is like a cage, a stagnant world that is inherent in everyday life . . . in so doing, he is inspired by the "Nishijin" within himself, which becomes an image of emotion, an image of pain, an image of resentment.[35]

Matsumoto's film thus depicts the alienated existence of contemporary Japan through "monotonous repetition," creating a "lonely, closed image." The world in Matsumoto's film appears "like a cage, a stagnant world." The images convey "pain" and "resentment," necessarily connected to the socioeconomic conditions of Japan in the early years of the 1960s—years that symbolized the beginning of tremendous economic growth, yet one that left many workers behind in the process. Yet it is important that *what* the fragmentation means is complex and open-ended. Its lack of voice-over compared to *ANPO Jōyaku*, its overlapping meanings and emphasis on what Matsumoto termed an "aesthetic sadomasochism," refuse a single, stable meaning, creating "an unusual tension."

Matsumoto's next film after *Nishijin* was the 1963 television documentary *Ishi no uta*, or *Song of the Stone*; this film is treated extensively by Sas and Furuhata, so I will only touch on it briefly. In this extraordinary film, still images of stones and stonecutters in the Aji village in Shikoku, shot by *Life* photographer Ernest Satow, are constantly manipulated, reversed, spun, zoomed into, abstracted, and made into film negatives—an ecstatic work of editing seemingly aligned with Vertov's frenetic manipulation of images in *Chelovek s kinoapparatom*, but with a distinctly eerier touch. Indeed, Vertov scholar Georges Sadoul praised *Ishi* when it was featured in the Tours film festival: "This cine-poem beats like a human heart under stone," he writes, noting the film as one of the freshest and most exciting shorts of the festival.[36] Fresh indeed; the film's use of in-camera editing is so wide-ranging that the viewer has the distinct sense of Matsumoto taking these techniques to their farthest limits, sometimes creating forms that approach total abstraction: for instance, shots in which photo negatives of stones, shot from above, flicker, producing forms akin to cubism and constructivism. Matsumoto also uses a superimposition of animate

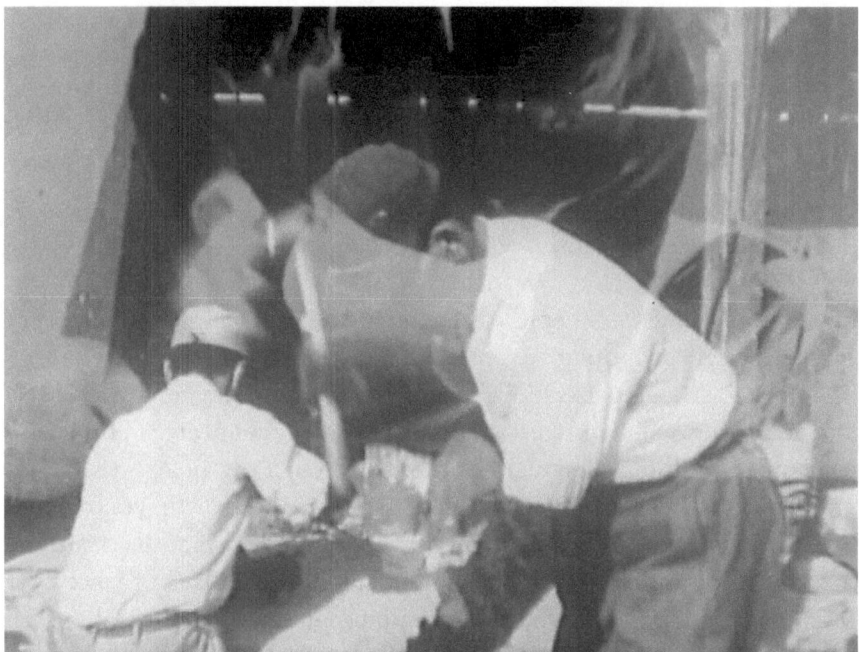

Figure 7. Ghostlike superimposition of men working in stone quarry, in Matsumoto Toshio's *Ishi no uta*, 1963.

and inanimate objects, as the narrator discusses the stonecutters' treatment of stones as living things. The narrator states that the act of excavating and cutting stone is an act of killing—lending a decidedly eerie and mournful quality to the work, in which stones are imbued with liveness (or rather, ghostliness). Likewise, sound and image often repeat, resulting in a mantra-like depiction of forms—no accident given that these rocks would one day become Buddhist sculptures.

The film's soundtrack was composed by Akiyama Kuniharu, a member of the avant-garde group Jikken Kōbō (Experimental Workshop), from the sounds directly recorded at the quarry. The *musique concrète* work also has a connection to the broader *musique concrète* movement at the Sōgetsu Art Center, a vibrant and crucial space for the avant-garde documentary movement, as well as animation. For Miryam Sas, the eerie music of the film, in which the striking of stones is ever present, punctuates the work's concrete "construction," while the images are placed in "ghostly superimposition": "making what cannot speak be nonetheless alive, and yet also resistant to capture either by language's significations or by human consciousness."[37] For Sas, the images and sounds of *Ishi no uta* emphasize both intrastructural and intrapsychic landscapes, subjectivity as well as objectivity: elements of the concrete materiality of the world (in the Marxist sense) that can also become irrational.[38] Matsumoto's film thus becomes an ideal encapsulation of a work that reveals a hidden truth that nonetheless exists: a *me ni mienai mono*, or "unseeable thing." Both Marxist and Freudian, Matsumoto uses the form of his film to bestow new meanings on Satow's photographs, especially meanings that a modernized, capitalist landscape tends to obscure.

The film's experimental form also draws a clear connection to French avant-garde documentarists of the era. Indeed, the film immediately recalls Chris Marker's *La jetée* (1962), a short science fiction film—one of the very few explicitly fictional films created by the French documentarist—also composed of still images. While Matsumoto had not seen Marker's film, both Marker and Matsumoto were inspired by Alain Resnais's *Guernica*. Furuhata notes that Marker saw *Ishi no uta* when he visited Japan in 1964 and was so impressed that he sent Matsumoto a copy of *La jetée*.[39] Thus, while Matsumoto's film is tied to its Japanese context, its form indicates a transnational movement working between fictional and documentary forms, invested in the potential of the image to transform thought and consciousness. It is therefore not surprising that a few years later, as Sas notes, the script of *La jetée* would be published alongside Ōshima Nagisa's *Ninja bugeichō* (*Tales of the Ninja*, 1967), speaking again to the resonances between Marker's film and the Japanese avant-garde documentary movement.[40]

Matsumoto was often (unfairly) criticized for putting formal experiments ahead of content. Satō Tadao's otherwise rave review of *Nishijin* chides Matsumoto for "the importance of the pursuit of precise details," although he praises Matsumoto for taking a step in the right direction for documentary filmmaking that "emphasizes abnormal events."[41] One must admit that Satō's analysis is quite astute: Matsumoto's films, from his abstract and highly conceptual video projections of the 1970s and 1980s, to his neo-documentaries of the mid-1960s, to the frenetic, epic comedy-drama of *Bara no sōretsu*, and even to his *jidaigeki* (Japanese historical drama film) *Shura* (translated either as *Demons* or *Pandemonium*) in 1971, are all defined by an extremely precise attention to detail. This hypersensitivity to aesthetic form is especially evident in his film editing technique and composition of shots. Although filmmakers such as Ozu Yasujirō are known for their obsessively composed mise-en-scène, Matsumoto's version strove to dehabituate—and thus his films, from the most commercial to the most abstract, focus on mirrors, doubling, and illusion. The irrational always presides over the rational, the subconscious always holding court.

This does not, however, mean that Matsumoto's films all exhibit the same formula of irrationality, abstraction, and uncanniness. One finds that as the 1960s progressed, Matsumoto's neo-documentary style grew less "sadomasochistic" and more emotive. The film *Haha-tachi* (Mothers, 1967) signified this turn toward the emotional, although the film still derives its potential for estrangement from its element of hidden darkness. The film, a short documentary made for television, spends the first half juxtaposing mothers and their children in Paris and New York City. Meanwhile, a poem by Terayama Shūji, fellow multihyphenate and avant-garde documentarist, is recited in the background. The poem itself incorporates Matsumoto's much-beloved trope of repetition: each line has the same poetic construction ("A mother is a [noun] only a child can [verb]"), a play on difference and repetition. This first half has a soft, nostalgic quality and functions as several city symphonies in miniature. The tone suddenly shifts drastically, however, in the film's portrayal of mothers in Vietnam, in the middle of a bloody war. The music skips, creating a sound akin to gunfire. At other moments, the music stops entirely, while the camera pans over a woman's napalm-scarred back. Another scene refuses the pan entirely and is composed of a collection of photographs of victims of the Vietnam War.

Matsumoto's emphasis on the brutality in Vietnam must be contextualized within the larger history of ANPO and the Japanese public. His film is a criticism not only of the ill-fated American war but of the Japanese people and especially their government, which continued (and continues) to implicitly support military endeavors due to the continuance of the US-Japan security treaty. By juxtaposing an extremely emotive and sensual

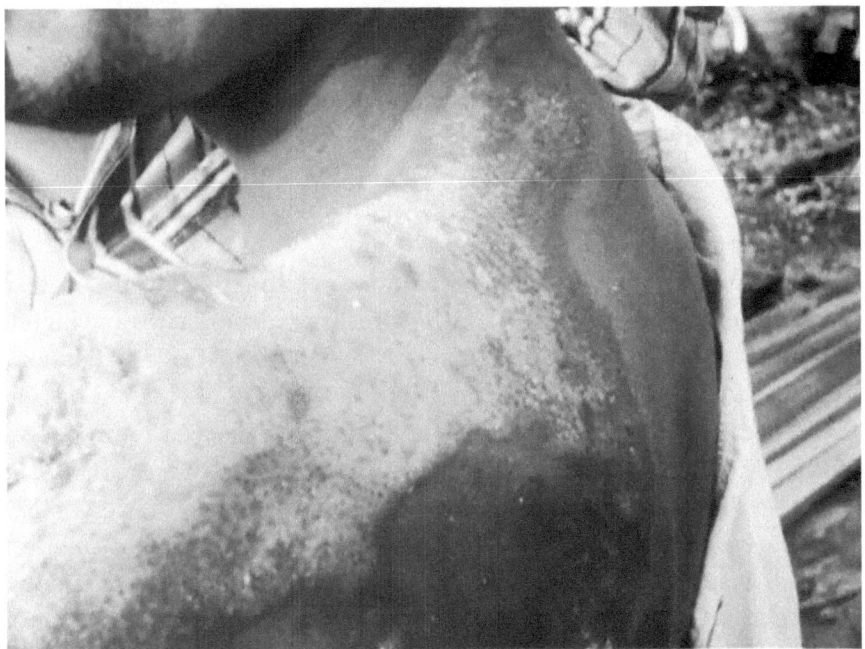

Figure 8. Woman's napalm-scarred back, in Matsumoto Toshio's *Haha-tachi*, 1967.

mode of filmmaking in the earlier section of the film, Matsumoto's criticism of Japan's role in the violence in Vietnam during the second half becomes much more effective, and affective. Matsumoto thus actualizes Russian formalist Viktor Shklovsky's claim of the implicit violence in habituation: one becomes increasingly habituated to war and violent imagery the more one is exposed to it. Furuhata similarly compares Matsumoto to Shklovsky in *Cinema of Actuality*, noting that his conceptualization of documentary echoes the Russian formalist "in his insistence on breaking down perceptual habits."[42] In the vein of Russian formalism, then, Matsumoto returns the inherent violence of war to images by juxtaposing them with other, softer images. In other words, by comparing violence with love. Indeed, the last few scenes of the film, this time depicting mothers in the Ibo tribe of Nigeria, become a manifesto for a return to love: a pregnant woman is shown standing at a beach, flanked by children.[43] As the narrator concludes, "Now is the time to think about love (*Ai ni tsuite kangaeta hi no yo*)." In the context of the beach scene depicted, the "time to think about love" is juxtaposed with scenes of Vietnam only minutes earlier, scenes in which a mother wails while holding a child presumed to be dead. Such juxtapositions and variations in filmmaking style retain the estranging qualities present in even the most disparate of Matsumoto's films, although *Haha-tachi* remains one of the most embodied and emotive films in his repertoire.

Matsumoto's films serve to dehabituate reality and unveil political meaning behind the everyday through surrealist stylistic devices and highly destabilizing editing techniques. A 1967 article penned by Matsumoto in the *Gendai eiga jiten* (Contemporary encyclopedia of cinema) details the importance of cinematographic and editing tricks as a rejuvenation of thought and consciousness and as a form of subjective expression. He praises "experiments that go beyond the established form of expression," *kisei no hyōgen keishiki ohamidasu jikken*, listing them as fast-motion or "high speed" photography (*kōsokudo satsuei*), time-lapse photography (*bisokudo satsuei*), reverse rotation photography (*gyaku kaiten satsuei*), jump cuts or frame skipping (*koma tobashi*), stop motion, unusual montage, repetition of frames, double (and triple/multiple) exposure, utilization of photo negatives, and transforming a frame using a distorted glass or mirror (as in Abel Gance's *La Folie du Docteur Tube*, 1915).[44] Such an exhaustive list of editing tricks recalls the rapid-fire editing of the Soviet avant-garde, especially Dziga Vertov, and the importance of "tricks and a maximum of invention during all kinds of filmmaking"—answer number one to the question "What must and can be done now in Russia" in 1922.[45] The unusual manipulation of newsreel footage "prepared viewers for the reception of new things"—a mantra aligned with that of Matsumoto, who wanted his tricks to "rebel against the reproducible character of images" and "stimulate the imagination."[46] For Matsumoto, such experiments—and he named his own *Ishi no uta* as an example—provide meaning to images that mere documentation cannot allow. Both Matsumoto and Vertov share, despite their geographic and temporal distance, a belief in the ability of film form to transform human perception, creating space for new imagined possibilities.

Matsumoto believed surrealistic and experimental film techniques had a strong liberatory and antifascist potential. As Markus Nornes describes,

Matsumoto saw the suppression of subjective procedures at the heart of filmmaking to be "fundamentally irresponsible and dangerous because it inevitably involved a veiling of politics as well. The realist agendas of nonfiction filmmaking 'for the people' hid an authoritarianism . . ."[47] Such techniques were strategies for self-reflection and self-criticism in the wake of the Pacific War. For Hanada, as well as for Iwasaki and their contemporaries, such a confrontation with the past was the goal for postwar forms of filmmaking and film criticism. Yet Matsumoto was often criticized for these selfsame techniques; as the composer Kawachi Kaname chided in *Kiroku eiga* after the release of *Nishijin*, "Montage is not a good tool for sharp *weapons*, but a technique for making *movies*."[48] Ironically, Matsumoto would argue the exact opposite: that it is precisely montage, and editing more generally, that should be utilized as a highly effective cinematic weapon to unveil the problems facing contemporary existence.

CONCLUSION: UNVEILING "REALITY"

This chapter has discussed Matsumoto's neo-documentary and its connection to antifascism. This style of documentary was launched around the most vehement protests against ANPO in 1960, yet became decreasingly surrealistic and less forcefully shocking after 1963. *Haha-tachi*, indeed, has quite a different tone from Matsumoto's earlier films. Yet this was not a definitive ending point, and by way of conclusion, I argue that Matsumoto's surrealistic inclinations in the neo-documentary were shared by other filmmakers even later in the decade. While Imamura Shōhei's allegorical semi-documentary is discussed in chapter 3, his more explicitly documentarian *Ningen jōhatsu* (*A Man Vanishes*, 1967) shares several elements with Matsumoto's neo-documentaries of the early 1960s.

In this film, the uncanny and even the supernatural intermingle with footage recorded with hidden cameras and sound recording equipment.[49] The film at times appears to be a relatively conventional documentary about a woman looking for her missing husband—a common occurrence in the postwar period, as many men left families in rural villages to work in Tokyo and other megalopolises, never to be heard from again. In between interviews, unexplained still images of decomposing human bones appear. Likewise, an eerie female figure wearing ceremonial robes, spotlit and surrounded by total darkness, appears in very brief snapshots—an image evoking a Noh performance and immediately recalling the image of the Noh performer in Matsumoto's *Nishijin*. Near the end of Imamura's documentary, the performer is shown to be a medium: what was thought to be a surrealistic interlude is revealed to be nonfictional and diegetic, although this does not make her presence any less nightmarish. As Terayama Shūji once said of Imamura, "[In his films,] nobody understands what is real and what is fantasy. Imamura's crime for the Japanese critics and pundits is that he mixes the two indistinguishably."[50]

Likewise, the end of the film embodies the importance of "unveiling" as an ethos of documentary, as the film begins to bare the device of its documentary form, revealing itself to be a quasi-fictional project. And here, Imamura shocks the viewer by entering into his own film for the first time. In the film's diegesis, the woman known as "the Rat" has been trying to locate her fiancé, who vanished two years before; she accuses her sister, "the Rabbit," of having an affair with him. The scene begins with the camera placed outside of a window, voyeuristically surveying the conversation within: Rat on the left, Rabbit on the right, and the Detective in center frame. In a drastic move several minutes into the interrogation, Imamura's camera does what filmmakers refer to as "crossing the line": the camera shifts perspective 180 degrees and is now placed on the opposite side of the room, facing the Rabbit. The effect is disorienting, jolting the viewer to attention. The uncanniness of this reversal increases a few moments later; unable to come to an agreement about what occurred between the characters, the Rat asks, looking off-screen: "So, director, what is truth?" (*Shinjitsu te nan deshō?*). The camera pans back, revealing Imamura himself, sitting cross-legged in the corner. He states, "I don't know, either. That's why I want to probe for the real truth. I don't know what the truth is." (*Nani ga hontō no koto, kangae sagashitaindesu. Wakaranai desu.*)

It is a shocking moment within what has previously appeared a fairly conventional documentary about a missing person, replete with interviews, evidence, and actuality footage. Yet fictionality is blatantly woven throughout; for instance, the "detective" helping them with the case is the actor Tsuyuguchi Shigeru, whom Imamura cast in his fiction film *Akai satsui* (*Intentions of Murder*) three years before. The fictive world of

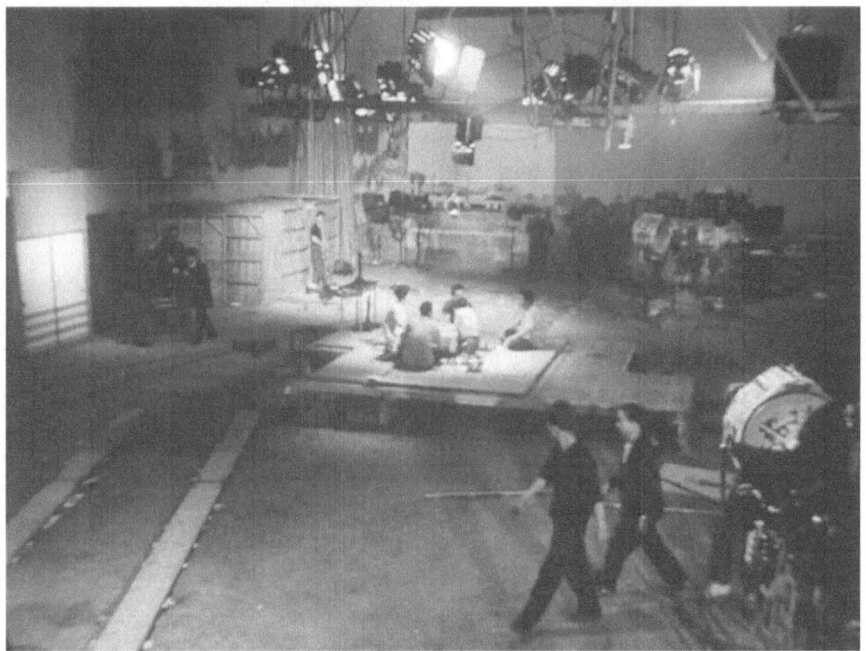

Figure 9. Set revealed, in Imamura Shōhei's *Ningen jōhatsu*, 1967.

Imamura's earlier films crawls into a stern documentary space, while the hidden camera awaits the results of this avant-garde documentary experiment. Responding to Imamura's claim that he doesn't know the truth, the Rabbit answers that only she knows the truth, since she experienced it. Imamura retorts, "Nobody knows the truth, not even you." Then, in a radical move, Imamura decides to lay bare his project, revealing the conceit behind the documentary: he yells "Pull down the set!" to a figure off-camera, while the camera pans back, revealing not a room within a house but a stage set borrowed from the Nikkatsu studio. Imamura ends the film with a monologue emphasizing the unknowability of objectivity: "One's feelings cannot be trusted. This is fiction.... This story has developed among somewhat unnatural lines. It developed as we intended."

In Imamura's case, the presence of the camera creates fiction from what one assumes to be nonfiction: after all, there are actors, a director, the call "action," and a clapperboard. Writing about this scene many decades later, Imamura claimed: "To call something a documentary, you cannot avoid artificiality. While some believe it to be truth, in reality it is likely a virtual image (*kyōzō*)."[51] The virtual image reveals itself as artificiality; it is inherent in cinema itself— even, and especially, in a documentary. In this moment, Imamura reveals, like Matsumoto, what Deleuze would call a "crystal image": a coalescence between the virtual and actual worlds. Or simply, a stage: a duplication of reality.

As Diane Wei Lewis argues, "Imamura's film is self-conscious and self-reflexive in a way that Curtis's and Flaherty's films are not."[52] Instead of a strict documentary, Imamura's film reveals, in his words, "the betwixt of drama and documentary."[53] In essays on *Ningen jōhatsu* in the journals *Kinema Junpō* and *Eiga hyōron*, critic and novelist Osabe Hideo argued that Imamura's films put into practice Hanada's concept of "sur-documentarism," thus drawing a line from Hanada through Matsumoto's neo-documentaries to Imamura's surreal avant-garde documentary.[54] These filmmakers looked to Hanada's theoretical writings to imagine a filmmaking that uncovers the uncanny truths about modern existence and to create space for self-reflection and self-criticism in the wake of World War II. Their focus on radical media literacy and formalist estrangement was intended as a tool for political criticism of the status quo and a fundamentally antifascist unveiling.

In France, documentary films similarly attempted a process of unveiling fascist legacies and complacency, especially through the filmmaking of those associated with the New Wave Left Bank: Agnès Varda, Chris Marker, and Alain Resnais. Although France's documentaries from the period were perhaps less formally shocking than Matsumoto's somewhat abrasive "sadomasochistic" style, they share much of his interest in surrealism and his probing inquiry into the nature of subjectivity in documentary. Oriented generally around the end of the Algerian War in 1962, these films attempted to join the critical and the pleasurable, what Georges Sadoul would call the "potato" and the "flower" of political filmmaking.

2 1962 France

DREAMLIKE COMMUNISM AND THE LEFT BANK
IN A DECOLONIZING WORLD

RÊVE ET RÉVOLUTION

In Alain Resnais's 1966 feature film *La guerre est fini* (The war is over), the communist spy Diego Mora, played by Yves Montand, states: "*Rêve et Révolution commencent par la même lettre*" (Dream and revolution begin with the same letter). This phrase serves as a *mot d'ordre* for Resnais's circle of filmmakers, the group now commonly associated with the Left Bank of the French New Wave. Resnais himself restates the phrase in an interview with journalist Yvonne Baby (stepdaughter of Georges Sadoul), and it is reprinted in a glowing review of the film by Sadoul in the cultural weekly *Les Lettres françaises*, edited by communist-surrealist poet Louis Aragon and funded by the PCF (Parti communiste français). Sadoul, whose own life as an underground communist and resistance fighter mirrors the shapeshifting Mora's, writes: "In this film, as in all the others by Resnais, the dream mixes with reality, the fantastic with the quotidian."[1] Resnais shares this tendency with other filmmakers of the Left Bank, especially Agnès Varda and Chris Marker, who likewise join fictionality and documentary, dream and reality, "the fantastic and the quotidian."

They are also bound together by a little-discussed aspect of their filmmaking trajectories: Marker, Varda, and Resnais are all closely associated with antifascism and communism, especially through their connection to Georges Sadoul and *Les Lettres françaises*; Marker and Resnais, in addition, were the most prized filmmakers, alongside their compatriot, filmmaker and playwright Armand Gatti, of the explicitly antifascist and *gauchiste* film publication *Miroir du cinéma* (1962–1965). The founding of *Miroir du cinéma* in 1962 is meaningful, given the end of the Algerian War in the same year. The year 1962 was pivotal for antifascist activism in France, and filmmakers from this group embarked on a number of experimental documentary projects during this period that attempted to unveil French complicity within global imperialism, colonialism, and fascism. As in Japan, this unveiling had a particularly surrealist flavor—one that is more subtle and dreamlike than Matsumoto's "aesthetic sadomasochism."

This chapter demonstrates that filmmakers Agnès Varda and Chris Marker, buttressed by the anti-imperialist arena of communist journalism and film criticism, privileged the avant-garde documentary as an ideal form for an engaged and critical political aesthetics around the end of the Algerian War. What this book calls the avant-garde documentary is broadly interpreted; in Japan a semi-documentary includes works with an almost exclusively fictional conceit, but that might use untrained actors and bits and pieces of archival footage. In this chapter, the avant-garde documentary encompasses works described *as* documentary films by Marker and Varda, yet which maintain and even emphasize the subjectivity of their creator. Yet compared to Japanese works by filmmakers such as Matsumoto Toshio, with whom Marker can be productively compared, the French filmmakers emphasize pleasure, affect, and whimsical playfulness; this results in a somewhat more lighthearted flavor than the Japanese "neo-documentary" and its aesthetic of "sadomasochism." Both, however, crucially tie the practice of antifascism to decolonialism, as communist filmmakers grappled with the memory of French complicity during World War II and France's continued fascist legacy through the end of the Algerian War.

Marker's work has been more extensively tied to his leftist commitment, especially through texts by Tim Corrigan, Nora Alter, and Catherine Roudé. His interest in surrealism is also well known; as Alter notes: "For Marker . . . it is often in the imaginary that reality reveals itself," echoing Resnais's *rêve et révolution* dictum.[2] This surrealism is fundamentally tied to politics, for, as Alter reminds us: "Like Bazin and others in his circle, Marker was interested in fusing existentialism and surrealism. Yet what distinguishes him is his steadfast refusal to diminish the importance of Marxism in this mix."[3] However, the specific manner in which Marker's politics is actualized by the dreamlike and affectively charged form of his films, and the mobilization of his filmmaking by the communist press of the period, are largely left unaddressed by film historians. Yet it is this commitment that isolates Marker from more mainstream film journals such as *Cahiers du cinéma*, in which his films were often met with ambivalence and even sharply criticized; one article by Louis Marcorelles even described Marker as "a craftsman making the same exact basket a thousand times."[4]

Although Marker is famously elusive, "catlike" in his refusal to give many interviews, both his films and the film journalism responding to them, especially in the early 1960s, show a strong connection between Marker, communism, and antifascism (and in fact, *Miroir du cinéma* published more interviews with the director than any other journal). This connection between Marker and the radical Left is especially evident through his collaboration with the former antifascist fighter Gatti. Interviews with Gatti and Marker in *Miroir* show an especially strong tie between Marker, Gatti, and antifascism writ large. Importantly, *Miroir du cinéma* ties this antifascism to the importance of crafting an "engaged" and "active" spectator; in 1963, the journal's tagline became "Democratic Revue for an Active Spectator" *(un spectateur agissant)*. This latter phrase is important: *spectateur agissant* connotes an "active" spectator, but also one that enjoins readers to act (*agissant* derives from the French verb *agir*, "to act"). *Agissant* shares a Latin root, *ago*, with the English *agitate*—to disturb, to stir up, to arouse the feelings of; its association with Soviet agitprop is not coincidental.

For Varda, who is similar to Marker in her catlike elusivity, this connection to communism is less clear, but nonetheless evident. In particular, Marker, Resnais, and Varda all share close ties with Aragon's *Les Lettres françaises*, and their interest in surrealism is coupled with engagement with socialist ideology. Varda's filmmaking might not be as explicitly militant as Marker's, whose *Le fond de l'air est rouge* (*Grin without a Cat*, 1977) is perhaps the best known of his political films and serves as a reflection on the May 1968 protests. However, Varda's filmmaking, such as the short documentary *Elsa la rose* (1965), shows a clear engagement with the communist figures of her time. This film centers the longtime love between Soviet expatriot and writer Elsa Triolet and Louis Aragon and investigates the continued legacy of the Soviet avant-garde in 1960s France—with special attention paid to Vladimir Mayakovsky, beloved and privileged poet of *Les Lettres françaises*.

In fact, Varda's connection to communist journalism of the period is as strong as, or even stronger than, Marker's—not only through her ties with "the mythic couple" of Aragon and Triolet, but also, and especially, through her close personal relationship to Georges Sadoul. In her ode to Sadoul for a commemorative issue of *Les Lettres françaises*, she writes:

> I love Georges Sadoul, his pleated smile, his debonair pipe and his tweed jackets.
> I love his very long articles, and the seriousness with which he uses his sense of history and his taste for justice, to define rather than to judge a film . . .
> I love that he defends freedom of expression and the right to this freedom everywhere in the world.
> Should we really talk about Georges Sadoul in the past tense?
> This death that upsets conjugations, this death that upsets our habits, because we read him and loved him, this death pains me.[5]

Varda noted that Sadoul was one of her "film godfathers" alongside André Bazin. This intimate, indeed paternal, connection between Varda and Sadoul—she calls it an *intimité* in her eulogy—also resulted in Sadoul being Varda's loudest advocate in the French film ecology of the 1960s. This did not mean absolute and uncritical support: Sadoul was somewhat less enamored of her early documentary travelogues such as *Ô saisons, ô chateaux* (1958) and favored her more experimental works that blended fantasy and reality, such as her first feature *La Pointe Courte* (1955) and the whimsical yet biting documentary *l'Opéra-Mouffe* (1958): half a fantasy-imbued landscape of the markets of Paris's rue Mouffetard, half document and diary of Varda's own pregnancy.[6] But Sadoul was especially drawn to *Cléo de 5 à 7* (1962), which he called "revelatory": "Few films moved me so profoundly. . . . The reality of the film is the reality of our time. . . . [T]his film *opened a wound in my heart*."[7]

Beyond her personal connection to Sadoul, Varda's films were generally far more connected to the leftist film journals, which also included the surrealist non-PCF *Positif*, than to the "formalist" *Cahiers du cinéma*.[8] In fact, a comparison between *Cahiers du cinéma* and *Les Lettres françaises* finds that there are *more than twice* as many reviews of Varda's films in the communist journal within the same ten-year period. This is especially notable because Aragon's journal, although published weekly, only contains two or three pages on cinema at any given time (the rest is taken up by literature, theater, pop culture, and scientific reports). *Cahiers*, published monthly, contains at least fifty to one hundred pages on cinema. This connection to communist journalism might be the reason it took far more time for Varda's films to receive international recognition than Godard's or François Truffaut's—even later than Chris Marker's. Despite her general elusivity when it came to questions of politics, both Varda's and Marker's films and interviews denote a clear participation in the project of engaged filmmaking, one that challenges and confronts the spectator, providing tools for the viewer's liberation. Neither Varda nor Marker rejects the emotional, but instead they moblize affect and pleasure alongside techniques of disorientation. As such, they provide a committed leftist and antifascist formal framework that serves as an alternative to the rejection of the pleasurable in political modernism—especially what I describe as the asceticism of Godard's DVG, analyzed later in this book. Yet in Marker and Varda, this engagement of the affective is always combined with radical, liberatory epistemology that rejects claims to documentary objectivity.

Before launching into an analysis of Varda's and Marker's films from this period, however, it is important to highlight Alain Resnais, a paterfamilias for committed filmmaking of the 1950s and 1960s, despite his relatively young age compared to the rest of those considered here (Varda was only six years younger, and Marker in fact was a year older). The work of Resnais similarly marries the affective with the critical—as we will see, Sadoul calls this his "Potato-Flower Cinema" in a roundtable *des amis* in *Les Lettres françaises*—and his oeuvre becomes a lodestar for much of Marker's and Varda's work.

ALAIN RESNAIS, *SES AMIS*, AND POTATO-FLOWER CINEMA

In a 1962 interview with *Miroir du cinéma*, Marker called Resnais "without any doubt" the greatest French filmmaker.[9] Resnais inspired antifascist documentary in regions as far-flung as Japan, where the leftist documentary film journal *Kiroku eiga* spent more pages analyzing the films of Resnais than those of any other filmmaker, with Luis Buñuel at a close second. Its editor in chief Matsumoto Toshio even used Resnais as inspiration for his neo-documentary ethos. In both France and Japan, Resnais was the prototypical representative (along with Buñuel and, later, Vertov) of a cinema that was *engaged* formally as well as politically, one in which the form and the content of film was a complex, mutually determining dialectic. Franck Tourret recently published a book-length analysis of Resnais's "formalism" that connects fundamentally to the Soviet definition, but without the original derogatory connotation of the term, derived from Socialist Realist attacks on literary critics and intellectuals in Viktor Shklovsky and Boris Eikhenbaum's circle. Tourret highlights, specifically, a taste for reflexivity and transparency in Resnais, which aligns with his tendency to imbue documentary with fiction and theatricality.[10]

Resnais, filmmaker of the documentary *Nuit et brouillard* (Night and fog, 1956)—one of the first films about the Holocaust, and still, with Claude Lanzmann's *Shoah* (1985), the most theoretically rigorous in its attempt to craft a film form that denies the mind any habituation to horror—and of the multiply censored *Les Statues meurent aussi* (Statues also die, codirected with Chris Marker, 1953), a fervently anti-colonial, anti-imperialist critique of Europe through an analysis of African art holdings—never tried to hide his antifascist and anti-racist commitment.[11] He is also a filmmaker who reflects on the contemporary moment. Emily Wilson points to the connection between *Nuit et brouillard* and the Algerian War, arguing that the film is "a response to the present as much as the past." As she notes, the film was "about France, France under the Occupation *and* France in its colonial wars."[12] For Resnais, film should serve not just to unveil a society's past misdeeds but to prevent future horror. When questioned in the Soviet journal *Isskustvo Kino* on the antifascist and ekphrastic *Guernica*, Resnais replied, "This film should have been made not ten years after the destruction of the city, but ten years before." For this reason, for Jean Wagner in *Cahiers*, Resnais is a filmmaker who strives "to make films not after the disaster, but before, to prevent it."[13]

Preventing horror entails not jailing potential malefactors (carceral capitalism being truly the opposite of abolition and antifascism), but fundamentally shifting the way people think and feel, to liberate the mind and create an engaged spectator. This often means *more* thinking, and *more* feeling; in the words of Russian formalist Viktor Shklovsky, it would entail recovering the "fear of war" "devoured" by "habitualization."[14] Active political engagement requires such a return to feeling. For *Miroir du cinéma*, Resnais was the ultimate representative of a filmmaking that inculcates this *spectateur actif*, enjoined to act politically. *Miroir du cinéma* was a unique film journal in its near-exclusive focus on antifascist filmmaking—the theme of the first issue (released, notably, in 1962) is *fascisme ne passera pas*, or fascism will not pass—yet it was independent of the PCF, while still maintaining ties to other journals, especially *Positif*. The second issue of *Miroir du cinéma* centers on Marker and Gatti and presents Resnais as a philosophical figurehead for their filmmaking. Anticipating much discourse post-1968, in this 1962 article Albert Cervoni, who would later become one of the editors of the PCF-funded *La Nouvelle Critique* in 1967,[15] praises Resnais for making the viewer complicit in their act of viewing:

> Too many directors show constant commercial caution—an eternal flight from audacity—for Resnais' courage not to be, from the outset, regarded as the most commendable. For this courage to be rewarded, it is probably enough for the spectator to be attentive, to be an active spectator, that he is not content to just see but that he admits to watching, to be in some way responsible for the film which is proposed and not to passively undergo an intrigue struck according to the classic recipes. The only ambiguity lies in this sector; we are all, one and the other, subjected to the drug of a cinema of ease which, by dint of putting the things shown in "dramatic" order, never again finds the fluidity of concrete reality, its apparent disorder, its absence of categories inventoried in the catalog of the good little screenwriter on duty.[16]

In this complex and literary encomium, we can see that the filmmaking of Resnais is useful, and "commendable," for its ability to inculcate a feeling of *responsibility* in the viewer. This is aligned with a sense of *complicity*—that the spectator must not only critique the world around them but recognize those aspects of the self that might align with nonrevolutionary attitudes. Taking this argument a step further, for Resnais the French spectator must also feel themselves at least partially responsible for the horrors perpetrated by their own government. This is a cinema that aims to cause not ease but unease, or *dis*-ease. Importantly, this unease emerges through formal experimentation. Resnais is courageous for rejecting "constant commercial caution"—perhaps leading him, inevitably, to complete films that are banned by censors, such as *Les Statues meurent aussi* and *Nuit et brouillard*. Thus Resnais's films activate the viewer, preventing the "passive" experience of the "classic recipes" associated with Hollywood-derived filmmaking, "the good little screenwriter on duty"—the "dramatic" formulas to which we are all susceptible, cinema as a "drug."[17] For Cervoni, Resnais's films retain the "fluidity" of so-called concrete reality, its "disorder" and "absence of categories."

Just a few months before Cervoni's article, Resnais, in a roundtable with Varda, Sadoul, Gatti, and Henri Colpi that was published in *Les Lettres françaises* in December 1961, described his filmmaking in much the same way: a cinema prioritizing thought and engagement. All filmmakers present spoke to the importance of film that was both beautiful and useful, pleasurable yet agitational. Resnais, in particular, also cautioned against what he termed an "opium cinema," resonating with the "drug" described by Cervoni. As we shall see, the filmmakers use the metaphor of the "potato" and the "flower" and refer to the leftist adage "we want bread, but we want roses, too." This *"Rendez-vous* of Friends," as it was titled, also shows the amity shared by the filmmakers and film historian Sadoul, as well as their shared political commitment. While Marker did not attend the roundtable—by this point, he had ceased to give many interviews, preferring the sheen of mystery surrounding his personage—he was frequently invoked by the participants, which also included Gatti, his assistant on *Lettre de Sibérie* (*Letter from Siberia*, 1957), and Colpi, editor of Resnais's *Hiroshima mon amour* (1959) and *L'Année dernière à Marienbad* (*Last Year at Marienbad*, 1961). The fervently militant and outspoken Gatti and Colpi are both certainly antifascist filmmakers in their own right—Gatti's *El otro cristóbal* (*The Other Cristopher*, 1963) is a fervently surrealist and militantly anti-colonial Cuban film whose style prefigures the work of Alejandro Jorodowsky, and Colpi's *Une aussi longue absence* (*The Long Absence*, 1961) delved deeply into the trauma of World War II—but their less explicitly documentarian work falls outside of the purview of this project. They did, however, aid Varda early in her career. As Varda notes at the beginning of the roundtable, "Marker, Resnais, Colpi, then Gatti were first of all the first people I knew in the cinema and for a very long time I didn't know any others.... [I]t is true that, in terms of sentiment, I agree with them."[18]

In the roundtable *des amis*, all figures agree vehemently that their work is tied fundamentally to documentary, even if certain filmmakers, like Colpi and Gatti, work primarily in fiction. Sadoul brings Marker into this conversation as well, as the creator of what Sadoul terms "literary documentary," or *documentaire littéraire*. The roundtable spends significant time arguing about committed cinema (*cinéma engagé*) and whether their films can be considered militant. While all agree each respective filmmaker's works are *political*, they differ in their understanding of what engagement and militancy entail. The exchange is incredibly illuminating and deserves to be cited at length—not only for its insight into the filmmakers' oeuvres and connections to politics, but also for its jovial and playful humor:

GEORGES SADOUL [GS]: I'd like to talk about potatoes. This refers to Resnais. Someone asked him in an interview, I don't remember where: "You, who have made *Nuit et brouillard*, who have made *Les Statues meurent aussi* (prohibited by censorship), who have made *Guernica, Hiroshima*, why did you make a non-committed film this time?" [referring to the release of his film *L'Année dernière à Marienbad*] Then Resnais responded—(the terms might not have been exact, but they express his thought process)—"Well! In my country, as Breton says, one plants flowers and one plants potatoes too!"

ALAIN RESNAIS [AR]: It's possible that I could have said this, I don't remember.

GS: If I understood correctly—and it's for him to say if I commented poorly on his thinking—maybe Resnais considers *Marienbad* (and certainly not *Hiroshima*) as a flower and his other films as potatoes (but there is also a potato side to *Marienbad*, which is not mentioned enough). What is everyone's attitude in this group *vis-à-vis* potatoes and flowers?

AR: Poppies in wheat fields, yes, but poppies are also poppies and so, *voilà*, now we're in opium cinema.

GS: If I understood the metaphor, the potato signifies a cinema which is directly useful for man, an everyday food, and the flowers are something useful for man in another way.

AR: But man doesn't live on bread alone.

GS: Bread and roses, as I heard somewhere.

AR: But we need them both.

HENRI COLPI [HC]: I myself essentially consider all of cinema as a flower—that is to say, to go back to our twenties, that cinema is an art. All well and good! But apart from that, it's a potato-flower.... The most crucial point for me, is that a film, in the language of potatoes, has flowers because if I start from my axiom, according to which cinema must be of an artistic order and, let's say, just to exaggerate if nothing else, that the other must have flowers and marvelous flowers at that—variegated, colorful flowers growing on a potato ... [He goes on, a bit pedantically.]

GS: Are you concerned with bringing potatoes into your films, yes or no.

HC: With Resnais it's quite clear.

AR: It's not for us filmmakers to say, it's for others.... One might have ambition, one might have hope, but they can't know if they succeeded or not. One would want to, of course, all the time.

AGNÈS VARDA [AV]: In the case of Resnais, one easily sees that he wants to create a useful cinema *(cinéma utile)* in the same sense that it's a very beautiful cinema, it's a cinema that, in general, brings something ... another way of thinking and seeing ...

ARMAND GATTI [AG]: ... The spectator may or may not receive it, but in any case he offers it. When *La Pointe Courte* was released, I remember the reactions very well precisely because *La Pointe Courte* brought a different way of seeing. I saw an interview with Agnès on TV in Brussels where she said it very succinctly: "I wanted this because it was wrong."

AV: Noted.

AG: It was very valuable insofar as it was not an approved truth, a truth that had been true for thirty years of cinema, because the valuable elements for you were different from the usual way of seeing. There's a sentence that strikes me often—I think it was [Soviet writer] Ilya Ehrenburg who uttered it in Lyon. He was harassed on all sides by journalists, and he said this admirable sentence: "When an apple tree blossoms in the USSR, it is a political event." (*laughs*) When a valuable film exists, it is a cinematic event. It doesn't matter what you put into it.

GS: Yes, but in *La Pointe Courte*, there was a sought-after and desired dissonance between a very literary dialogue, especially for the time, and a quasi-documentary reality of one of the poorest neighborhoods of Sète, if I remember well. So, undoubtedly this film also had a potato side . . .

AV: Yes, but it is precisely a bad example because in my mind at the time of making *La Pointe Courte*, I wanted to try to find a junction between the two worlds: that of the flower and that of the vegetable.

Besides the cleverness of the exchange, in which the participants jostle and adroitly navigate playful references to Soviet and Marxist thought, the use of potatoes as a metaphor is important and prescient—not least because Varda became associated with the vegetable forty years after this exchange, during the release of her documentary *Les glaneurs et la glaneuse* (*The Gleaners and I*, 2001).[19] Her career thus actualizes her claim, at the conclusion of the roundtable, that her films "try to find a junction between the two worlds": "of flower" and "of vegetable," of leftist utility and ephemeral formal beauty. Yet beyond their "potato-flower" filmmaking, both Marker's and Varda's films share a "desired dissonance" (Sadoul) that ruptures "the usual way of seeing" (Gatti), creating what Cervoni termed an "active" spectator.

This chapter dives deeply into two films, a feature-length documentary by Marker and a short film by Varda, both of which were made in 1962 (and released, in Varda's case, in 1963). These films emphasize the "potato-flower" aspects described by Sadoul and Resnais, although, notably, the roundtable participants themselves admitted that it was a false dichotomy. Yet I claim that when compared to other films discussed in this book, Marker's and Varda's films lean much more heavily on the "flower" side of the equation, emphasizing artistic engagement, animal life, camaraderie, and the ludic without compromising their antifascist and Marxist commitments. These films also emphasize the sphere of the *everyday* as a locus of struggle, speaking to the 1960s zeitgeist that was greatly informed by Henri Lefebvre's *Critique of Everyday Life*, the first volume of which was published in 1947.

In Marker's case, I delve into *Le Joli Mai* (*The Beautiful Month of May*, 1963), which emphasizes subjectivity in documentary and is in dialogue with the first film of *cinéma-vérité*, Jean Rouch and Edgar Morin's *Chronique d'un été*. I argue that Marker's film engages ambivalently with the rise of *cinéma-vérité* as a new documentary genre by always emphasizing the camera's inherent subjectivity. The film, however, is resolutely political and criticizes French political complacency and a certain historical amnesia in the wake of the end of the Algerian War. For Varda, I analyze *Salut les Cubains* (1963), the first documentary she created after the release of her much-praised *Cléo de 5 à 7*, which Varda herself described as signifying a maturity and confidence in her filmmaking style, and which solidifies her ability to enjoin the fictional with the documentarian. While *Cléo* could itself be included in this book as an example of what the Japanese term *semi-documentary*, I utilize *Salut les Cubains* because it is considerably less addressed in the anglophone context, more directly engages with Marker's work, and is imbued with the strongly decolonial spirit of 1962. Both films investigate the way political systems manifest in everyday activities and behavior; as we will see, Marker's Paris in 1962 expresses an aura of anxiety through a continued complicity with imperialist and carceral aggression, while Havana in the same year exudes, for Varda, liberation and play.

PLAY OF *VÉRITÉ* AND SUBJECTIVITY IN *LE JOLI MAI*

Marker's films frequently uproot dangerous and difficult themes in French society, from Mai '68 to the Algerian War. *Le Joli Mai* is rather unique in Marker's filmography, however, as the bulk of the film is composed of interviews, rather than impressionistic voice-over accompanying observational and archival footage. At first glance, it appears more similar to *Chronique d'un été* than Marker's earlier films, especially when compared with Marker's much-lauded short science fiction film *La jetée*, also released that same year. And *Chronique* and *Joli Mai* do seem to have much in common: both include on-the-street interviews with passersby, attempt to document a very specific moment in French history (summer 1960 for the former and May 1962 for the latter), and are resolute in their leftist commitments. Antoine de Baecque even lists *Joli Mai* as the second film in a trilogy that began with *Chronique* and concluded with Godard's *Masculin Féminin* (1966).[20]

While the films are certainly in conversation, *Le Joli Mai* goes further than Rouch and Morin's film by laying bare its own subjective elements. This is especially notable for the period, as by May 1962 *cinéma-vérité* had ceased to be an "experimental" genre and the loose structure of *Chronique* was replaced by an increasing concern with access to "the real" through technological breakthroughs, especially the Nagra magnetophone recorder and the Coutant-Malthot-Éclaire camera. *Cinéma-vérité* began to blur into Direct Cinema in North America, especially through the filmmaking of Robert Drew and Richard Leacock. Indeed, in October 1962, a few months after shooting wrapped on *Le Joli Mai* and just a few months before its release, *Miroir du cinéma* published an entire issue criticizing this technologically determined (and more resolutely capitalist) offshoot of *cinéma-vérité*.[21]

As Chris Marker pithily stated in 1962: "*Truth is artifice.*"[22] Although the film is mostly composed of interviews, by using Marker's characteristic voice-over technique—poetic and meandering, diametrically opposite a "voice of God" exposition—*Le Joli Mai* is instead fervently, unrepentantly subjective. As Chang-min Yu argues, where Morin's and Rouch's *cinéma-vérité* allows human dramas to unfold before the camera lens, in Marker's film, fictionality manifests itself differently. Where *Chronique* emphasizes the performative quality of each subject's participation, magnified through the camera lens through a collaborative process between subject and camera, in *Le Joli Mai*, the cinematic medium is able to reconfigure daily life.[23] Sadoul writes that in contrast to other *cinéma-vérité* films, Marker's does not aim to "seize life à *l'improviste*"—referring to the language of Edgar Morin's article "For a new *cinéma-vérité*," which gave the genre its name.[24] Sadoul attempts to place *Le Joli Mai* into the *cinéma-vérité* canon, but insists on the film being in fact *better* than *Chronique* and other works of the genre. For Sadoul, Marker's film "opens up new paths to French cinema and to *cinéma-vérité*"; he suggests that "after *Joli Mai*, *cinéma-vérité* will not be what it had been before." For Sadoul, "This is what '*cinéma-vérité* is"—or perhaps, more accurately, *should* be, for the French historian: "a man who takes sides, not a machine recording the best and the worst indiscriminately." Sadoul sings the praises of this film precisely for its "tak[ing] sides"—what he calls Marker's "constant militant ardor." Sadoul's ideal *cinéma-vérité* never hides its bias and is suffused with communist fervor. Unfortunately, today we know that *cinéma-vérité* as a genre was already declining during this period, and from the hindsight of the twenty-first century, *Le Joli Mai* is indeed quite a unique work and genre altogether.[25] As Roger Tailleur claims in his 1963 review of *Joli Mai*, Marker replaced *cinéma-vérité* with *ciné ma vérité*: cinema, my own truth.[26]

Sadoul informs us that the film was made with forty-eight recorded hours of film, which was then edited down to six, then to three, and finally to 150 minutes.[27] *Le Joli Mai* attempts to chronicle the city of Paris during a particularly meaningful time in its history: it was the first May after the end of the Algerian War, which had dragged on with devastation, chaos, and bloodshed for much of the postwar period, from 1954 to 1962. Marker documents a city at once relieved and yet, somehow, extremely anxious. Peace does not immediately result in liberation, and Marker's film suggests that an insidious oppressiveness remains within the capital. *Joli Mai* likewise unveils a Paris that shows severe racism and economic inequality. While France at the time was embarking on a vast middle-classification and an unprecedented growth in consumer culture, Marker's film depicts a Paris in which the *Lumpenproletariat* and proletariat are still extant, even if conveniently hidden from view. These members of the underclass are frequently Algerian. One extended interview—one of the longest in the film—is with a young Algerian man living in a shantytown, called a *bidonville*, outside of Paris. Ross writes that during the Algerian war, the population of Algerians in France grew exponentially, from 211,675 in 1954 to 350,484 in 1962. Many of these migrants settled in *bidonvilles* exactly like the one depicted in the film, in which poverty and racial violence were rampant.[28]

The film details another interview with a large family living in extremely small living quarters in what are called the *îlots insalubres* or "unhealthy blocks" inside of Paris; these were densely populated city blocks that received their name in the 1930s due to the high tuberculosis mortality rate in the region. As Ross details, in 1954 these were still largely intact, and more than one hundred thousand people lived in them, although tuberculosis was no longer a problem. Yet these tightly packed, visibly impoverished areas created rather poor marketing for the image of Paris as a fashionable, modern powerhouse. Regardless of the actual existence, or rather inexistence, of disease in these regions, sanitation and hygiene was used as the major justification for launching urban renewal operations, which fundamentally destroyed the homes of a large percentage of Parisians.[29] Given the attempt to eradicate such visible poverty from the center of Paris, Marker's film is especially notable for the grace and tenderness with which his crew interviews several of the extant dwellers within these slowly disappearing vestiges of prewar French existence. It is this intensely political aspect of the film that makes it, in Sadoul's eyes, a weapon: "Handled by Marker and Jean [*sic*] Lhomme, the living camera is a weapon, and not a hall of mirrors in which all of Paris looks at itself with narcissistic complacency. The cinema witnessing a pretty May is not a gossip, a socialite chronicler, a boulevardier of the Champs-Elysées, an onlooker; it engages in battle. This film is thus a new description of a fight (*description d'un combat*)."[30] The latter phrase, "*description d'un combat*," refers to Chris Marker's 1960 short film of the same name, on Israel. Chris Marker later disowned this film, pulling it from circulation after the Six-Day War in 1967 in support of Palestine. At the time, however, *Description d'un combat* exemplified Marker's ideology as a communist and antifascist and included the socialist potential of kibbutzim, community-oriented agricultural collectives. For Sadoul, *Joli Mai* continues Marker's ever-present militancy. Yet in this film, which "engages in battle," which becomes "a new description of a combat," which shows tenderness in its interviews with lower-class Parisian citizens—all these contrast greatly with the camera's often haughty, critical gaze at other, especially wealthier, Parisians. In fact, the film's interviews are all filmed somehow differently; the camera angles and mise-en-scène vary significantly, and the camera tends to rove, almost moving on impulse.

Sometimes the juxtaposition between the camera technique and interview dialogue has a great sense of humor; for instance, in one sequence the filmmakers are speaking to an arrogant businessman who speaks against feminism and instead praises "great men" and "inventors" (perhaps reminding the twenty-first-century viewer of prototypical Silicon Valley "disrupters"). The camera, however, obviously reflects the cameraman's distaste for this subject's perspective. As the "disrupter" is speaking, the camera, as if restless from boredom, notices a long-legged spider crawling over the man's sportcoat. The camera zooms in, and the man continues his monologue, entirely unaware. The spider now takes up the majority of the screen, and as if noticing the camera's attention, retreats inside the man's sportcoat. As he speaks of inventors being "all a little crazy"—*tous un peu dingue*—the interviewer asks, "*une araignée au plafond?*," to which the man replies, "exactly." However, unbeknownst to the man, the interviewer just made the viewer laugh at his expense: to have *une araignée au plafond* means the French colloquial equivalent of "to have a screw loose," but literally, it means a spider on the ceiling. The camera zooms in and out of scenes and has its own humorous, occasionally mocking voice—always "punching up" rather than down, always refusing any notion of unbiased objectivity.[31]

Camera operator Pierre Lhomme is credited as codirector of the film because of his central role in creating the film's idiosyncratic visual images. As in *Chronique d'un été*, the camera is extremely mobile: Lhomme used an early Coutant handheld camera, connected to a Nagra tape recorder; these two technologies combined to create what critics referred to as the *caméra-vivante*, or "living camera." Yet in contrast to Rouch and Morin's film using the *caméra-vivante*, here the camera shifts positions following what is spoken. And again, Marker's individuality emerges in the film's voice-over. In one sequence, the film depicts images of doves being caressed by women, and Marker laments that the dove is the symbol of beauty. He then cuts to a woman gently caressing a small owl (one of Marker's familiars, alongside cats) as the voice-over praises the small bird for being "beautiful, pleasant, and deep." There is no diegetic necessity for this sequence in the documentary—no interviews mention owls, and the bird serves seemingly no purpose in Parisian life in 1962—but it expresses authorial voice and feeling. The owl is used to bemoan a certain superficiality in French society and to provide a possible alternative.

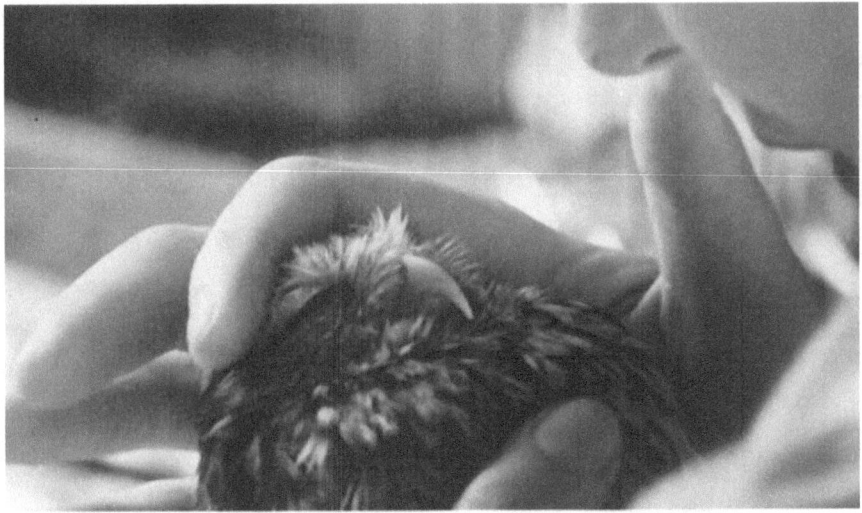

Figure 10. Woman petting an owl, in Chris Marker's *Le Joli Mai*, 1963.

Such elements proliferate in the film, which is infused with far more outright subjectivity than *Chronique d'un été*. Likewise, the film contrasts with the chronological advancement of Morin and Rouch's film; instead, Marker offers a kaleidoscopic view of Paris, in which scenes are chained by associations: a bird, a car, or a spider might echo in subsequent scenes, and reveal, as Yu claims, greater meanings.[32] The interviews and voice-over do not necessarily merge but orbit around each other in a dialectical fashion. Interviews complement the subjectivity of the voice-over, and Marker's film extends its focus to embrace the myriad ways in which Parisians choose to express themselves. The film is framed and guided by a free association created by the camera, and the ordinary frequently merges into the surreal.

Yet this surrealism is always communist in flavor. This is best exemplified in the film's conclusion, which puts aside the interview format and relies on dizzying aesthetics and politically militant voice-over. We are shown several minutes of stunning time-lapse footage of iconic regions in Paris such as the Arc de Triomphe as the narrator lists seemingly innocuous statistics about the city: how much Parisians have consumed in the month and how many deaths and births have occurred.

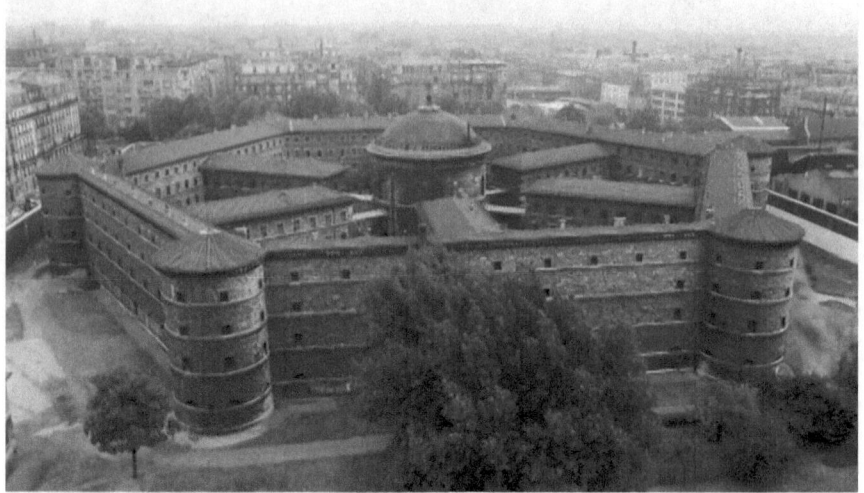

Figure 11. La Roquette prison, in Chris Marker's *Le Joli Mai*, 1963.

The upbeat jazz score contributes to the scene's frenetic pace as the voice of narrator Yves Montand begins to fade. When the music crescendos and then abruptly stops several minutes later, the rushing imagery stops as well, and Marker presents us with a single, still image: the hexagon-shaped Parisian prison known as La Roquette, the shape inspired by Jeremy Bentham's panopticon.

After the rushing cinematography of the time-lapse footage, the film ends with a melancholy reminder of the darkness behind quotidian Parisian existence: that, in contrast to the previous interviewees of the film, for the inmates of this prison, "each day is exactly the same." As Montand's voice-over concludes after an audio-only interview with an inmate and after several close-ups of Parisians on the street: "As long as poverty exists, you are not rich. As long as despair exists, you are not happy. As long as prisons exist, you are not free." Such a conclusion places Marker's authorial voice firmly in the sphere of antifascism and abolition (and as I continue to argue in this book, the two are intimately connected). The conclusion of *Joli Mai* is a rare moment of militantly political exposition and jolts the audience suddenly to attention. Yet even here, truth is revealed through camera tricks—zooms, time-lapse, frenetic pacing, tonal shifts—as well as through a literary and memoiristic voice-over, which joins disparate elements into a single, leftist whole.

Marker presents us with a Paris not glamorized by its appliances and wealth or by the everyday life of Parisian youths. His documentary can only end with the prison, tied inevitably to the imperialist circumstances of the film's production. Like Matsumoto's sobering discussion of exploited workers in *Nishijin*, Marker's antifascist affects reveal the hidden within plain sight: the prison standing in the middle of Paris, a vision with which its citizens have grown familiar. In such a way the film criticizes the emphasis on material wealth, the carceral system, and and the silence and forced forgetting following the end of the Algerian War.

Yet for some critics, like Jacques Doniol-Valcroze, one of the founders of *Cahiers du cinéma*, the very subjectivity of *Le Joli Mai* is fundamentally disturbing: "From an objective document on the Parisians in the month of May, the work metamorphoses into subjective chronicle of the author's impressions."[33] Doniol-Valcroze particularly reviles the end of the film, which takes "a leap into the absurd, where the images accelerate and destroy their immediate meaning," recalling, for the critic, the "panic reaction" at the end of Michelangelo Antonioni's 1962 *L'Eclisse* (*The Eclipse*). At the famously mysterious end of Antonioni's romance starring Alain Delon and Monica Vitti, the couple disappears, and for a long seven minutes, the film gives way to abstract shots of cold suburban housing developments, soulless landscapes, and the steely faces of strangers, accompanied by a tense soundtrack. However, what appears disturbing to Doniol-Valcroze is exactly the point, for *L'Eclisse* and *Le Joli Mai* are intimately connected through their ruthless critique of capitalism (in Antonioni's film, Delon's chacter Piero is a cold-hearted but attractive stockbroker, a 1960s precursor of the modern "finance bro"). In Antonioni as in Marker, formal abstraction and absurdity provide a shock and estrangement essential for the process of political awakening.

Joli Mai is also a film that, like Marker's earlier *Lettre de Sibérie*, explicitly recalls Dziga Vertov; in fact, Marker's film engages with Vertov more emphatically and explicitly than the *cinéma-vérité* films that claim Vertov's influence. Jean Rouch, who was somewhat ambivalent about Marker's film in a *Cahiers* interview, compared *Joli Mai* to Vertov directly. For Rouch, Vertov might be "too dangerous. We are playing with fire. . . . *Le Joli Mai* is a film which, indeed, may make the French think, increase their anxiety or trigger phenomena that we do not know."[34] For Jean-Louis Pays, editor in chief of *Miroir du cinéma*, this danger of *Joli Mai* is precisely the point: "[Marker] leaves the spectator the freedom and the responsibility to recognize himself and to draw conclusions."[35] Through the combination of interviews, commentary, clever editing, and cinematographic effects, the film attempts to "trigger phenomena" while "leav[ing] the spectator" their "freedom"; it utilizes the *caméra-vivante* for the service of subjectivity, play, "militancy" (Sadoul), and liberation.

FROM MARKER TO VARDA

Critic Steve MacFarlane writes that Marker's films "represented a bridge between the worlds of activism and the art gallery, or between direct action and polemical documentary: playful, self-aware, humanist, maddening, and always aware of their inherent contradictions."[36] Yet Marker's activism always attempts to go against the grain of contemporary culure and the status quo. In the roundtable *des amis* cited earlier, Gatti notes that his filmmaking is grounded on rejecting the conventional.[37] In a combined interview with his friend Marker, Gatti equates nonconformism with antifascism and anti-imperialism: "As long as there is injustice in the world, a certain conformism which is always obligatorily established, if I had to make an affirmation, it is in terms of combat."[38] Gatti also claims that while working with Marker on *Dimanche à Pékin* and *Lettre de Sibérie*, "I saw how one makes cinema: one has a little box-like thing (*une espèce de petite boîte*) and one fights against the wind all the time."[39]

Marker, indeed, would continue "fighting against the wind"—both in the form and content of his films, as well as in their strategies of production. After creating the experimental documentaries described in this chapter, Marker would embark upon a series of collective filmmaking experiments in the wake of May 1968. Unlike Godard's DVG, these experiments, according to Catherine Roudé, were truly collaborative, allowing Marker to withdraw into the backround although his influence was inevitably felt. In November 1968 he founded SLON (the *Société pour le lancement des oeuvres nouvelles*, or Society for Launching New Works), also the Russian word for elephant. SLON had ten other members, including many of the directors, technicians, or administrators involved with his 1967 anthology film *Loin du Vietnam* (which also included the participation of Varda and Godard), the earlier Medvedkin group, and his "Ciné-tracts" (a silent militant filmmaking experiment realized during May 1968), and sometimes all three. This cooperative included Alain Resnais as well.[40]

Yet Marker was not the sole filmmaker in France who "fought against the wind" of conventional documentary strategies. Even when Varda created an explicitly fictional film like *Cléo de 5 à 7*, her work was compared to documentarists of the same period, with Varda usually emerging the victor. As Sadoul argued: "[Varda's] *caméra-stylo* is ten times more sophisticated than the mechanical primitives still used by Leacock or Jean Rouch."[41] And as a glowing review of *Cléo* in *Cahiers* attests: "Who better than [Varda] to give us an exact description—without malice, almost objectively?"[42] Yet this sense of "objectivity" in fiction and of "subjectivity" and playful fictionality within documentary, also carries with it a profoundly affective sensibility: "Varda's camera . . . gladly takes pleasure. . . . [I]ts nature is whimsical and appreciates, first and foremost, all the proceeds offered by the cinematograph, the seesaw games of editing and parallel actions . . . quite simply: modesty, lyricism . . . amazed lucidity, unvarnished youth, tenderness—for all that exists is in this world refers to this unique thing: sensation. Agnès Varda is profoundly realistic, yes, but she is—let's allow (*homologuons*) this bizarre plant (*plante bizarre*)—a sensitive realist."[43] Varda's world, as the review notes a few paragraphs later, "beats to the rhythm of her heart." Even when "almost objective," her works are suffused with sensitivity and "tenderness." Yet such tenderness is the result of quite vertiginous editing: "the seesaw games of editing and parallel actions," all the possible techniques offered by cinematic technique. These seemingly contradictory elements combine to create "this bizarre plant" of potato-flower cinema.

This chapter now turns to Varda's *Salut les Cubains*, a rarely addressed but prototypically Vardaian film that speaks to her idiosyncratic documentarian lens, created and released in the same year as *Le Joli Mai* and directly following the events of 1962—or rather the nonevents, the emergent peace even with its anxieties. Alongside her other short documentaries from the period, such as *L'Opéra-Mouffe*, *Elsa la rose*, and

Oncle Yanco (1967), *Salut les Cubains* merges the autobiographical and the political, documentary and fiction, in playful and meaningful ways. The films give to documentary a strong flavor of fiction, echoing the documentarian flavor imbued in the ostensibly fictional *Cléo de 5 à 7*—the first time, according to Varda, when she "succeeded in reconciling the two aspects of reality that interest me: the very premeditated and reconstructed aspect, and the documentary style (*le reportage*), things caught in the moment."[44] Her first post-*Cléo* film, *Salut les Cubains* accomplishes the same. Here, Varda merges her drive toward the personal with a critique of the consumer culture rampant in both France and the United States. Most importantly, this film speaks directly to her immersion into the sphere of global anti-imperialism, decolonialism, and communism.

THE DANCING CAMERA OF *SALUT LES CUBAINS*

While this chapter has so far focused on the end of the Algerian War as emblematic of the decolonial spirit of 1962, it is important to recognize Cuba's role in this important cultural moment. Cuba had only become communist in 1959, and the failed Bay of Pigs invasion in April 1961 signified a moment of optimism and potential for the new revolutionary state. Thus, in the early 1960s Cuba was an extremely popular subject for budding communist European filmmakers, and many coproductions ensued in this exciting moment, from the Soviet Mikhail Kalatozov's *Soy Cuba* (*I Am Cuba*, 1964) to Chris Marker's *¡Cuba Sí!* (1961, banned in France for being an alleged "apologia for Cuba" with "ideological propaganda" elements), to Soviet documentarist Roman Karmen's *Pilayushchii ostrov* (*Blazing Island*, 1961, on the Bay of Pigs invasion), to Armand Gatti's aforementioned wickedly surrealist and proto-Jodorowskian *El Otro Cristóbal*, to Joris Ivens's *Carnet de viaje* (Travel notebook, 1961) and *Cuba pueblo armado* (A people armed, 1961).[45] ICAIC, the Instituto Cubano del Arte e Industria Cinematográficos, Cuba's institute for the film industry, was led by the Vertov-like "pamphleteer" Santiago Álvarez. ICAIC was the first cultural body created in postrevolutionary Cuba. Malitsky notes that in this period ICAIC invited numerous filmmakers to Cuba, as the institute sought to become a center for Latin American and Caribbean leftist film culture.[46]

Cuba, then, explicitly sought the participation of international communist and communist-sympathetic filmmakers in its program of revolutionary agitprop. The Cuban-based films emerging from these collaborations were highly varied in nature, but the majority clearly echo the early Soviet drive that joins formal experimentation with radical political practice. Of these, Varda's *Salut les Cubains* most clearly comments on everyday life and cultural production in Cuba, the world of art, culture, dance, and music; it best exemplifies her often uncanny admixture of joyful exuberance and the solemnity of the historical. It shares with Marker's *¡Cuba Sí!* a strong concern for, and critique of, the usual media representations of Cuba, yet compared with Marker's film, as well as the bulk of other films set in Cuba in the early 1960s, *Salut les Cubains* focuses on what Varda described as the *savor* of contemporary Cuban life.[47] More than any other film on Cuba during this period, it highlights the change in the *everyday* in Cuban life—reminding one of Lefebvre's argument from the *Critique of Everyday Life*: "Socialism (the new society, the new life) can only be defined *concretely* on the level of everyday life, as a system of changes in what can be called lived experience."[48] Thus Varda defines Cuban socialism as *savor*, to unearth socialism in its (mostly) joyful effects on everyday life.

Yet such *savor* is not detached from revolutionary history. Art and revolution here go hand in hand. The film's exclamatory title, bidding hello to Cuba, crafts the film to be a gift to the young revolutionary nation—Varda calls it an "homage"—and indeed the film shares many qualities with agitprop.[49] It is, in many ways, an advertisement for this nation, one that does not shirk from its troubled history, emphasizing the role of Black people in the struggle and the painful history of slavery and colonialism. It also emphasizes Cuba's connection to France, through the immigrants to Cuba arriving from the Haitian revolution—thus implying that the French viewers of the film are complicit in the island's troubled history. The message is meant to be confrontational and provocative for French viewers.

In addition, the film's attention to revolution in narrative is coupled by a revolutionary form. *Salut les Cubains* is a cinematic photomontage. In it photographs appear to jump from the frame and come to life; in certain sections, they are even animated. Varda uses every tool at her disposal to edit the four thousand photographs she took during a visit to Cuba. In the end Varda's film took six months and used fifteen hundred photographs.[50]

The film also includes illustrative drawings and postcards and thus immediately recalls Chris Marker's films using still photographs and drawings, which include *¡Cuba Sí!*, *Dimanche à Pekin*, *Vive la Baleine* (1972), and of course *La jetée*; it also recalls Matsumoto Toshio's *Ishi no uta*, filmed in the same year and likewise an experimental work of avant-garde photomontage as documentary. The fact that *Salut les Cubains*, *La jetée*, and *Ishi no uta* were released within the same two-year period is intriguing: all three films—made, importantly, by communist directors—use strategies of disorientation to engage audience affect in various ways. Yet rather than what Matsumoto called his "sadomasochistic" surreality, which mobilizes the Freudian uncanny (indeed, Matsumoto frequently cited Freud directly) and is meant to incite a palpable discomfort and unease in its audience, Marker's and Varda's films are more narrative oriented than abstract. Varda's version, even in contrast to Marker's science fiction tale, is characterized by joyful exuberance and pleasure. In fact, Varda calls it a *film de plaisir* in an interview with *Cahiers*.[51]

Salut les Cubains is far more than a history lesson, and the vast majority of the film is spent highlighting Cuban music, dance, art, and poetry. This emphasis on the literary and artistic is quite common for Varda and very well known as an aspect of her work (see, e.g., Rebecca DeRoo's *Agnes Varda: Between Film, Photography, and Art*). Her emphasis on the ekphrastic, as in Resnais's own ekphrastic works, is integral to her filmmaking. In the same period of the mid-1960s, her film *Elsa la rose* highlighted the career of communist writer Elsa Triolet, and *Oncle Yanco* looked at a long-lost relative who became an artist. In addition, later films such as the feature-length documentary *Mur murs* (1981) looked with awe and admiration at the murals of Los Angeles, especially in its Chicano neighborhoods. *Mur murs*, like *Salut les Cubains*, sees the history of colonialism, imperialism, and disenfranchisement as integrated in the artworks she discusses. Yet importantly, no artwork is reduced to politics alone. As Varda notes, "I really found the Cubans extraordinary and the forms of their socialism surprising and joyful."[52]

There are a few profiles of famous figures—for instance, the singer Benny Moré, who passed away between the film's production and its release and receives a dedication. Images of Moré dancing and singing are timed precisely to the beat of his music, creating a stop-motion effect in which the film itself appears to be dancing. Such exuberance proliferates: in one sequence, Varda includes several photographs of men with beards which look similar to Fidel Castro's, "but the most popular *barbe* (beard)," Varda recites, as the image cuts to a photo of a child happily munching on fairground treats, "is a *barbe de papa* (cotton candy). It's an island of sugar." There is an emphasis on leisure and excess—not as debauchery, but as the inevitable products of a communist form of government, uniquely able to provide citizens time for rest, joy, volunteer work, and cultural activity.

Perhaps it is not surprising that this film, the only one directed by a woman in the Cuban international coproductions, is more focused on women's experience than any of the others. As Varda exclaims in the voice-over, paired with an image of a woman Cuban soldier: "Here's to Marxism-Leninism in the beret of a female militant." Indeed, the film takes great pleasure in depicting women as laborers and soldiers, rather than as glamorous dancers, singers, or housewives (although these also abound). The film's militancy highlights military uniforms but delights in *photogénie*; women are officials and diplomats, as Michel Piccoli's voice-over notes during a photograph depicting a *cuerpo diplomatico*, or "diplomatic body." Riffing on the image, he notes, "*mais c'est un corps mélodique*" (but it's a melodic body), emphasizing the S shape of a woman's curvature. These frames and voice-over in any other hands might appear misogynistic, but Varda's touch is more sensuous than objectifying. In Varda, in contrast to Godard during his DVG period, the sexual is not aligned with nonpolitical or anti-political evasion; it is not a distraction from politics but an embodiment of communist liberation, of communism as manifested in the everyday. Varda's dancing bodies on screen are equivalent to the lighthearted communist sex jokes of Vertov's films: for example, the third moment of time reversal in *Kino-Glaz*, showing divers emerging from the water and returning to their diving boards. In Vertov, the camera engages the haptic mode, passing its lens directly through the diver's legs: a cinematographic sex joke. So too do Varda's films engage such cheeky metaphors—especially when supporting, as Vertov was, a newly communist state.

The film is oriented around dancing; it bookends the film, begins and ends with it. But this dancing is also imbued in the film's form, and it has a powerfully reflexive quality: the film crew, including Varda herself,

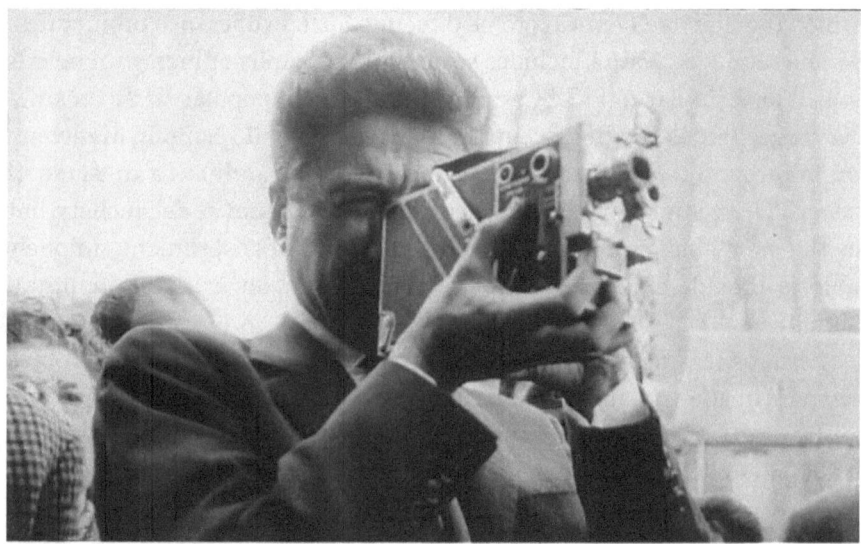

Figure 12. Cameo by Alain Resnais, in Agnès Varda's *Salut les Cubains*, 1963.

appear in the opening credits, wielding cameras among dancing Cubans. This is one of the few moments of live action footage rather than still photography. Alain Resnais even briefly appears holding a Bolex camera. The communist avant-garde participates in the celebrations, but primarily to document.

Then the camera turns its lens to the viewer and the frame freezes; the title of the film appears, with Varda's name: A Vardaian Kino-Eye. It also refers explicitly to *¡Cuba Sí!*, Marker's own film about Cuba. At times, Varda comments on the film's creation during her half of the voice-over, and the voice-overs even reflexively comment on one another. Her commentary often describes her personal experience, for instance: "I noticed a particularly Cuban gesture of a man putting his possessive hand on a woman's shoulder." Although Varda includes more "I" statements than does Marker's *Joli Mai*, both imbue their films with an unapologetic subjectivity. *Salut les Cubains* balances a joyful, celebratory tone with extreme self-reflexivity and self-consciousness; the camera always appears to be thinking about its own technique and mechanism and revels in the varied, explicitly musical nature of its shots. At times the film appears to

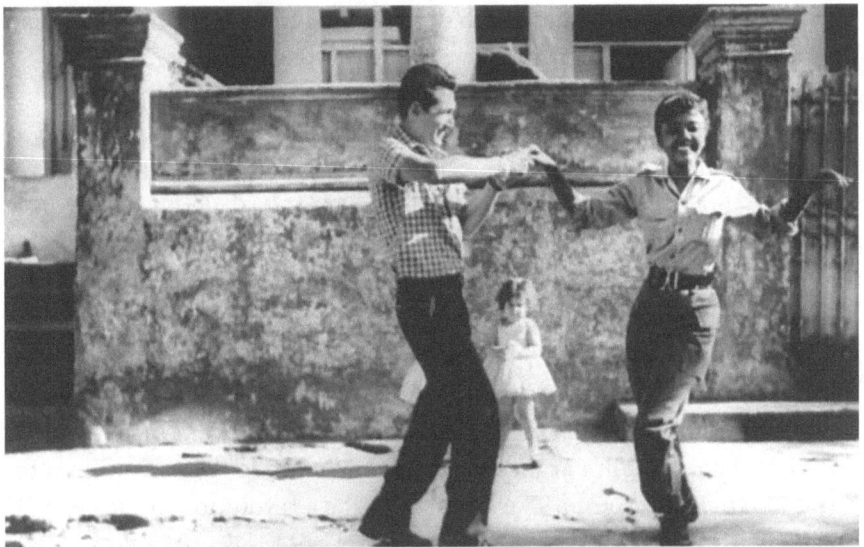

Figure 13. Sara (Sarita) Gómez dancing, in Agnès Varda's *Salut les Cubains*, 1963.

be Mickey Mousing, as objects appear to move in stop-motion to the exact beat of the music.

The film ends in an apotheosis of joy and self-reflexivity during a concluding discussion on ICAIC. The film shows the then-young film student "Sarita Gómez" dancing joyfully, encouraging others to dance the cha-cha-cha with her. This is Sara Gómez, the most influential woman filmmaker in Cuba's history and the director of the much-lauded *De cierta manera (One Way or Another,* 1977). *De cierta manera* itself would fit exceptionally well in the formal framework of this book: it is a semi-documentary that combines actuality footage and an illustration of Cuban history with a mostly fictional story and typically "new wave" techniques (jump cuts, experimental editing that brings attention to its own craftedness). The film, meaningfully, is likewise located in the arena of the everyday—yet with an ironic twist. As opposed to Varda's film from a much more optimistic revolutionary moment, Gómez's film (mostly shot in 1973–1974) argues that the everyday has not yet been sufficiently transformed. Machismo, racism, sexism, and classism continue to pervade Cuban society. As Gómez playfully argues—decidedly in the antifascist avant-garde documentary vein—people are sometimes much more willing to transform society than they are to transform their mindsets and everyday behavior.[53]

Gómez would die tragically at the age of thirty-one, during postproduction of *De cierta manera* and just shortly after shooting wrapped. Yet at the time of Varda's filming Gómez was merely twenty years old. This sequence of shots of young "Sarita" dancing in *Salut les Cubains* has recently turned into a viral GIF. The coincidence of Gómez's appearance concluding Varda's film, the juxtaposition of the two women luminaries of global new wave cinema, and the knowledge of Gómez's tragic death make the GIF a veritable hauntology—but one that unites two communist women filmmakers on opposite sides of the Atlantic. Indeed, Gómez and Varda share significant overlaps; as Annie Geng notes in a recent analysis of *De Cierta Manera*, the film argues "that there is more to revolution than reforms and political action. There must, too, be a revolution in the heart."[54] So, too, with Varda.

ANTIFASCISM, AFFECT, AND THE INTELLIGENCE OF THE SPECTATOR

While Marker only places himself in his films through various avatars, from Sandor Krasna to Chris Villeneuve and Fritz Markassin, and removes his physical presence from the camera, Varda begins to place herself center stage after *Salut les Cubains*. Prior to *Oncle Yanco*, her most personal documentary had been *L'Opéra-Mouffe*, which included abstracted imagery of her pregnant body. Despite the inclusion of such personal, and evidently embodied, details, the film avoids her unique voice, which is reserved for travelogues and biographies. After *Oncle Yanco*, Varda more emphatically embarked on the project of her most mature and well-known documentaries, "to film one hand with the other," as she describes it in *Les Glaneurs et la glaneuse*, three decades later.

According to Geneviève Van Cauwenberge, Varda's documentary form does not consist in a reproduction of reality; it is an interpretation of the real, filtered through individual experience, and the cultural context of Varda herself, the cinéaste.[55] Varda always insists on the role of individual and collective imagination. Thus, for Rebecca DeRoo, Varda positions herself less like a didactic political theorist than like a magician. DeRoo analyzes the short film *Daguerrotypes*, in which a magician stands before the Eiffel Tower in the opening scene, delivering a performative address. DeRoo argues that the magician here refers to Georges Méliès, cinematic "inventor" and director, who frequently appeared as a magician in his own films.[56] By including a reference to Méliès in the opening scene, Varda announces to the audience the fabricated, artificial nature of even this "documentary" production. Varda's filmmaking style is, in fact, very controlled in its formal elements: the composition, the music, the mise-en-scène. For this reason, both Varda and Marker are "magicians of the real" according to Georges Sadoul.[57] Varda, like Vertov and like Marker, aligns with the playful and pleasurable aspects of the political. As Varda has noted, "I don't want to be *serious*. I want to say that I *enjoy* doing it [making films]. I want to come in curious."[58]

Yet Varda's films are no less "shocking" for their playful affects. In fact, as she noted in a 1964 interview, "I think the mechanism of shock triggers a more acute sensitivity" (*déclenche une sensibilité un peu vive*). As she notes: "*On doit conditionné les gens.*"[59] A direct translation of this latter phrase is "we must condition the people"—a phrase that might sound dystopian to contemporary audiences used to perceiving Varda's films as merely whimsical. For Varda, the purpose of "shock" is to increase sensitivity, rather than dull it; it is an attempt return viewers to liveliness (imbued in the term *vive*). This is the "conditioning" she describes—a communist reengagement and revitalization that is, for Viktor Shklovsky's *ostranenie*, the project of art itself. Paradoxically, it is conditioning as *de*habitualization.

There is a dry, biting quality to Varda's filmmaking from this period, and her interviews from the 1960s are likewise full of wit and candor. (When asked whether the "generation 1960" is similar to the "generation 1930" in a survey, Varda answered, "See astrological forecasts.")[60] In this earlier era of her career, Varda conceived of herself as a fundamentally Brechtian filmmaker. While film theorists like Peter Wollen connected Godard's DVG especially to Brecht by being "suspicious of the power of the arts—and the cinema, above all—to 'capture' its audience without apparently making it think, or changing it," Varda's films embody a more approachable Brechtianism that does not deny the pleasure of the audience.[61] In

Varda's films, the audience enjoys the difficult rupture of their perceptual capacities, their own processes of shock and dehabitualization; they are made to "think," to "change," but the process deployed is youthful, exciting. As Varda states: "Brechtian distancing does not necessarily mean aggressiveness.... [I]t's not about banging people on the head and yelling: *wake up!*"[62] Varda prefigures Thomas Elsaesser, who pithily stated three decades later: "Not all the Brechtianisms in postwar cinema... are true to the spirit of Brecht, and among those who have claimed him for their work, fewer inherited his questions than copied his answers, which, of course, were by then no longer answers."[63]

Given the connection to Brecht, it is important to remember that both Marker and Varda treat the spectator with respect, believing them to be capable of the difficult work of media literacy. As Nelly Kaplan writes in a review of *Déscription d'un combat*: "*Chris Marker nous crois intelligents (il a raison, d'ailleurs)*" (Chris Marker believes us to be intelligent [and he's right, by the way]).[64] Such respect toward the viewer is echoed by other Left Bank filmmakers, as evidenced in the roundtable *des amis* cited at the beginning of the chapter. Henri Colpi describes this as "a certain attitude towards cinema audienes, an attitude of, let's say, non-contempt... a way of seeking to interest the public through films, through a form that is not what is current or usual; and, on the other hand, by going even further afield, seeking not a leveling down but a leveling up." Varda agrees, replying, "You [must] treat the public as equals."[65] It is not surprising, then, that Varda uses the same phrasing as Marker—*donner à voir*—when describing her filmmaking. As she explains in an interview with communist critic Michel Capdenac in *Les Lettres françaises:* "It was for me to give to see (*donner à voir*), to allow the spectator to keep their distance and to judge. I did not seek to play on the emotion of the spectator, but to ensure that the emotion at the same time arouses reflection: there is sharing of emotion with the spectator."[66] Affect, then, becomes integrated into the concept of distancing and of a respect for the spectator's intelligence. Varda's films do not play on (*jouer sur*) the spectator's emotion, but emotion is not rejected wholesale. "Emotion... arouses reflection," resulting in a "sharing of emotion" that is as affective as it is intellectual.

Emotion is not passive, but a methodology for active audience engagement. This engagement was seen as especially important in the postwar, as leftist journals continued to warn against a fascist mindset. The year 1962, which centers this chapter, was defined by a certain measured victory for the communist Left, but one that still carried with it significant anxieties. The Algerian War finally ended; Cuba appeared, however briefly, to be at peace; but French citizens must still continuously wage battle against passivity and complacency. As Albert Cervoni concludes in his article "Resnais: For an Active Spectator":

> It is through political struggle that we will obtain from the cinema an art truly in the image of the man of our times. It is for this reason that we cannot dissociate our fight as cinephiles from our fight for public political awareness. Not to admit this is to deny the objective reality of the facts. We live in anguish: momentarily caught up in the greatest social and human achievements, we are subjected to the threats of war and fascism which jeopardize the very existence of man, which slow down his development in all areas. We also have the firm resolution to put an end to this aberrant torpor, we want to live to build a new history of humanity in which a Chris Marker, paid by the year, could at leisure travel the world with a camera in his hand. This moment, however, can be the most sublime if it participates in the construction of this becoming. An Armand Gatti, an Alain Resnais, a Chris Marker—these filmmakers of human dignity participate in the realization of this future.[67]

For Cervoni, during an era when "threats of war and fascism" "jeopardize the very existence of man," film must "fight for public political awareness." In the same issue, Francis Gendron draws a firm connection between Marker and antifascism: "Marker's philosophy is essentially antifascist.... [I]t is always good to remember that some filmmakers are antifascists, first and foremost."[68] This antifascism is explicitly tied to the rejection of "cheap propaganda"; instead, "his genius ... lets our mind take the form of consciousness it desires."[69] For communist journalists of the era, Resnais, Gatti, and Marker are exactly the filmmakers capable of crafting an active and engaged spectator—to which, I believe, we should add Varda as well, for Varda's films, though not always as explicitly militant as Marker's, nonetheless participate in a drive to unveil, shock, and dehabituate.

As we will see, Japanese filmmakers from this same period of the early to mid-1960s similarly engage the affective. Both Japanese and French communist filmmakers responded to an allegedly "peaceful" era with reminders of their respective country's complicity in geopolitical terror—indeed, of their fascist or fascist-collaborationist pasts. Looking at both together, we see, then, the connection between avant-gardist form and geopolitics. However, as we will see, the Japanese moment of the 1964 Olympics revitalized nationalism, leading to a documentary style that was far less militant than it had been previously. Japanese documentary blended increasingly into the fictional, and even the allegorical, in its attempt to remain legible.

3 1964 Japan

THE ALLEGORICAL SEMI-DOCUMENTARY
IN AN AGE OF NEONATIONALISM

DOCUMENTARY FICTIONS, OR TRUTHS FROM A LIE

The title card at the beginning of Luis Buñuel's *Los Olvidados* (*The Young and the Damned*, 1950) reads: "This film is based entirely on true facts and no character is fictional." This would seem to place the film within the documentary canon, yet today the film is usually considered narrative fiction, inspired by both neo-realism and 1920s surrealism. The film's claim to documentary would be taken up by filmmakers of the 1960s such as Hani Susumu and Matsumoto Toshio, the latter of whom even cites *Los Olvidados* as a precursor for his own "neo-documentaries." A similar claim is made in the introductory titles of Hani's first feature film, *Furyō shōnen* (*Bad Boys*, 1961), which reads: "This is a documentary film, but its characters and events are fictitious." A more literal translation of the Japanese is: "This film uses documentary methods, but all of the creation and composition are the responsibility of the artist/creator." The film, like Buñuel's, actively blends fictional narrative with nonprofessional actors and documentarian research: "a work at the limits of reality and fiction," according to Marcos Centeno Martín.[1] Such a disclaimer could accompany many documentary films in the Japanese 1960s and early 1970s, as Japan had a much more expansive view of the term *documentary*. This included the nebulous, Japanese-specific category semi-documentary, of which *Furyō shōnen* is a pitoval example.

In this book, I argue for the inclusion of semi-documentary within the avant-garde documentary constellation in the 1960s. However, with its focus on films usually considered narrative feature films in the contemporary context, it appears to take us further away from a comparison to the Soviet avant-garde. The European avant-gardist inspiration remains; however, I argue that Buñuel becomes a clear reference point rather than Vertov—with Buñuel's *Los Olvidados* emerging as the victor over his earlier and infamous *Un chien andalou* (1929). Rather than pointing to documentary films from Japan's mid-decade, this chapter demonstrates how some of Japan's most famous documentary filmmakers turned consciously *away* from documentary and toward fiction, ever disputing what they claimed to be the superficial divide between the two. Thematically, it explores a new evolution in the genre of avant-garde documentary that is specific to Japan's historical and economic moment, yet whose antifascism is no less fervent for its embrace of fictional conceits.

In this chapter, I argue that not only should the semi-documentary be considered an integral part of the avant-garde documentary movement in 1960s Japan, but it was *the* privileged style of documentary in the middle of the decade, when 1964 Olympic fervor and a resurgent neonationalism swept the nation. I argue that the *allegorical semi-documentary* emerged during this seemingly apolitical period to render fierce anti-capitalist and antifascist critique visible—albeit often subtler and in more symbolic registers. Films like Imamura Shōhei's *Nippon konchūki* (*Insect Woman*, 1963) and Kuroki Kazuo's *Tobenai chinmoku* (*Silence Has No Wings*, 1966) were enjoyable narrative films tailored to the middle-class viewer but also insisted on their nonfictional components and addressed oppression, inequality, and imperialism by crafting their central characters as symbolic of national and geopolitical problems. My use of the term *allegory* to encompass these films is unusual; as we will see, the films do not necessarily hide their politics under the veil of spiritual or religious symbolism. And yet the films' poetic structure and folkloric dimensions—perhaps, as we will see, even imbuing these anti-establishment films with a certain nationalist complicity they claim to reject—draw them closer to a traditional meaning of allegory than we may be led to suspect.

The term *semi-documentary*, however, is not my own. Theorist Hanada Kiyoteru praises the semi-documentary in a 1958 article entitled "Documentary's Future Prospects." Here, he lays out his desire for a merging of surrealist fictionality and documentarian sensibilities that combines fictional and nonfictional modes in a more overt manner.[2] Naoki Yamamoto argues that the semi-documentary genre was also supported by other figures in Hanada's intellectual milieu, such as film theorist Imamura Taihei.[3] These figures tied the genre to similar works in Western Europe and the United States that served as important precursors, such as the Italian neorealists (Robert Rossellini, Luchino Visconti) or Jules Dassin, frequently discussed in Japanese film outlets through the early 1960s. By then, Dassin had been blacklisted because of suspected communist affiliations and prevented from working in Hollywood. In January 1960, directors Ōshima Nagisa and Iwasa Hisaya described Dassin's films as *the* documentary aesthetic of the period; as Iwasa noted, "If a studio uses the word 'documentary,' the image that comes to their mind is Dassin's [1948 noir] *The Naked Town*," with Ōshima agreeing that it would also look something like Italian neorealism.[4] Semi-documentary, then, was a pivotal term for Japan, often indicative of a *noir*-ish and pessimistic leftism, a drier tone and more materialist politics—as distinguished from an "easy" (from the perspectives of Japanese avant-garde filmmakers) humanist realism associated with the JCP.

Philosopher Nakai Masakazu likewise praised semi-documentary as enlivening postwar cinema without compromising its political critique, writing in 1950 "that British and Italian cinema are opening up new, living faces as a form of semi-documentary film bodes well for a grand awakening."[5] Nakai then states that this hybrid medium "will provide new directions for aesthetics ... leading it to new, living form."[6] The invocation of life, living, and liveliness is important, as this "return to life" has an intensely antifascist function. For Hanada and Nakai, semi-documentaries open up new, lively pathways within film history, pathways considered most crucial for the present political moment and the most fitting of the cultural and intellectual zeitgeist. It is meaningful, also, that Nakai's work is frequently compared to Walter Benjamin, a central figure for the analysis of allegory. Both Nakai and Benjamin were also vocal antifascists heavily oppressed by their respective regimes. Although Benjamin did not have the luxury of even conceptualizing a "postwar period," Nakai's post–Pacific War writings returned to an interest in the ability of new cinematic forms to revitalize the experience of cinema. Semi-documentary was privileged in this regard.

The term *documentary* here might subvert the expectations of anglophone audiences. Naoki Yamamoto notes that the term had an "unusual and indirect" importation into Japan, through Paul Rotha rather than John Grierson; thus, instead of the Griersonian definition of documentary as a "creative treatment of actuality," Japanese filmmakers saw *dokyumentarī* as a "creative *dramatization* of actuality"; inherent in the medium is a dialectic between fiction and nonfiction.[7] As Nornes argues, Rotha's writing was fiercely discussed: "No other theorist had more impact on actual film practice or underwent as much 'processing.'"[8] The result was a rich theoretical landscape in which fiction was folded into conceptions of documentary in Japan from the start. So capacious was this term, in fact, that *Kiroku eiga* seems to center at least half of its articles on films considered "fictional" by contemporary standards, including many on Buñuel's *Los Olvidados*.

In fact, *Los Olvidados* might be mentioned more frequently than any other film in the journal's run. *Los Olvidados* follows the young delinquent Pedro, a preteen boy in the slums outside Mexico City, in the wake of rapid industrialization; despite attempts to escape the misery of his existence, Pedro is unable to escape a tragic fate, and he represents those left behind by Mexico's modernization projects in the postwar period. The film was lauded by theorists of documentary for its surrealist dream sequence with highly Freudian overtones: Pedro dreams of the forgiveness of his mother, who is cruel to him during waking hours. In the dream, she appears angelic, dressed in white, and her distorted speech does not match the dubbing; she hands Pedro a rotting meat carcass while a dead boy crawls out from beneath his bed. Characters move in slow motion while chicken feathers float mysteriously across the frame.

Japanese critics saw the film as documenting an internal postwar reality by depicting moments of absurdity and surrealism externally. They were quick to see reflections of Buñuel's tragic and nightmarish film in the rapid modernization of postwar Tokyo. In *Kiroku eiga*, art critic Hariu Ichirō wrote, "The visible external absurdity is decomposed into an

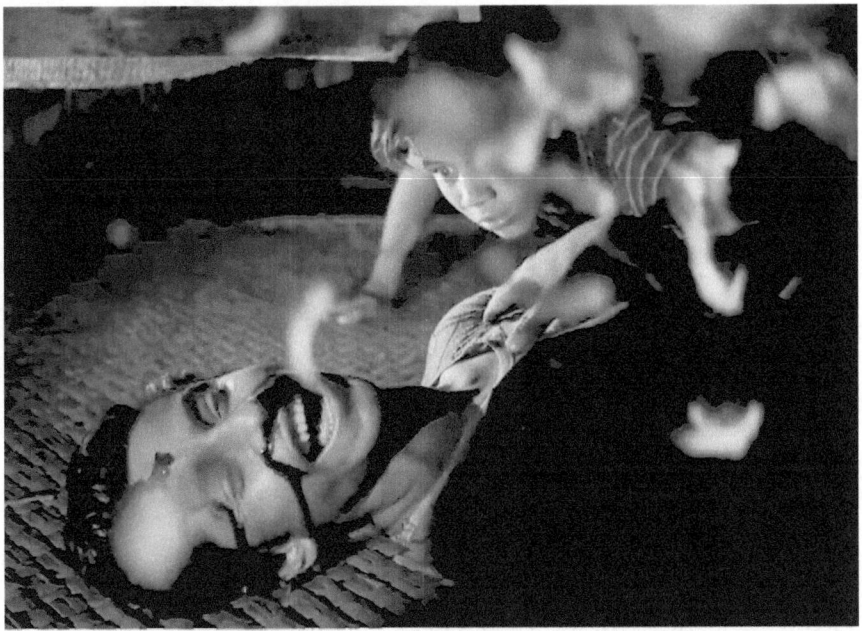

Figure 14. Surrealist dream sequence, in Luis Buñuel's *Los Olvidados*, 1950.

internal absurdity, which is transformed once again into the invisible absurdity of society. This unique work goes beyond surrealism's attempt to expand the gap between objects and consciousness, by depicting the gap between society and human beings. . . . *Los Olvidados* renews the method of montage through surrealism."[9] *Los Olvidados* thus exemplified a narrative filmmaking practice that used its obviously crafted, experiment-laden fictionality to document the "absurdity" of the postwar condition, the "gap between objects and consciousness," as well as the "gap between society and human beings." For Japanese critics, its surrealist qualities were central to its ability to document the current destabilizing condition. This connects *Los Olvidados*, also, to Matsumoto's neo-documentary dialectics of the "interior world" (subjectivity) with the "exterior world" (objectivity). Film needed to express aspects of life and society that we cannot see (*me ni mienai mono*), yet for many filmmakers, in contrast to Matsumoto, these normally "unseen" aspects of everyday experience could only be communicated through explicitly *fictional* rhetorical stragegies.

As Hani Susumu notes, "There is not a clear difference between fiction and documentary," thus embodying the zeitgeist of this productive and highly theoretically informed era.[10] His films revel in what Justin Jesty calls an "unpredictable intersubjective process" between camera, filmmaker, and subject. Such a tension—between "the motion of the world" and "the internal motion of the filmmaker (and audience)"—makes his semi-documentary *Furyō shōnen*, in Hani's words, a "firm joint (*kansetsu*) between human beings and reality," which he calls a "dynamic balance."[11] Hani embraced unpredictability and intersubjectivity, the "dynamic balance" within the filmmaking process itself. While Hani's film is less explicitly allegorical than later 1960s productions, it serves as an important precursor and entryway into a peculiar genre dominant in political avant-garde filmmaking in the middle of the decade and deserves our attention in this context.

FROM *FURYŌ SHŌNEN* TO THE ALLEGORICAL SEMI-DOCUMENTARY

Hani's film follows a teenage delinquent named Asai Hiroshi as he attempts to steal jewelry, is apprehended, and is finally sent to a correctional school with other young rebellious teens. The film's connection to Buñuel's much-discussed *Los Olvidados* is fairly obvious. First, like *Los Olvidados*, Hani's film uses nonprofessional actors and on-location shooting. Hani also claims that the film only cost the equivalent of $15,000—a very cheap production and comparable to the cost of short nonfiction films rather than full-length features.[12] Many of the characters in the film, as in Buñuel's, performed versions of their real-life selves. Both *Furyō shōnen* and *Los Olvidados* feature a young protagonist living at the borderland of a modernizing city—Tokyo and Mexico City, respectively—in constant view of the city's growing wealth, but unable to tap into its riches without resorting to petty crime. In both, the teenage protagonist gets caught up in a gang and, after being apprehended, is ensnared in a reform process. *Los Olvidados* ends tragically, but in both films, the reformers are presented positively.

The film is also reminiscent of François Truffaut's *400 Coups* (*400 Blows*), which screened in France in June 1959 and in Japan in March

1960 (as *Otona wa wakatte kurenai*, or Adults Don't Understand Us), ostensibly while Hani was working on *Furyō shōnen*; notably, *Cahiers du cinéma* film critic Luc Moullet explicitly compared Hani's filmmaking to Truffaut's in 1962.[13] Yet Hani's film is more documentaristic than Truffaut's and employs grittier techniques associated with nonfiction, such as choppier cinematography, the inclusion of real graffiti scratched onto a wall at a reform school, or the documentation of unsuspecting passersby on the street. However, this footage is also juxtaposed with several highly crafted and surrealistic point-of-view shots that reject a "fly-on-the-wall" technique, such as the inclusion of Asai's annoyed, mumbling thoughts in voice-over during a scene in which an administrator in the reform school faces the camera directly, pontificating while sitting at a desk.

In another example of experimental subjectivity, Asai reminisces about his youth, wearing sunglasses; meanwhile, a close-up of his face fades into a close-up of a very young boy wearing similar sunglasses, followed by another close-up of teenage Asai, dark with expressionist tones, which fades into a shot of an ocean (echoing the famous last shot of *400 Coups*: a freeze-frame of Jean-Pierre Léaud standing before the sea). This surrealist-inflected sequence emphasizes dreams and memory, thus merging moments of avant-garde surrealism with neorealist grit. Compared with Truffaut's film, Hani's is both *more* documentarian and *more* avant-garde, aligning the film more easily with Buñuel's earlier production.[14]

Compared with Truffaut, Hani also has far more extensive history working with the documentary form. Five years before *Furyō shōnen*, Hani created a series of documentary shorts for Iwanami Productions, such as *E o kaku kodomotachi* (Children who draw, 1956) and *Kyōshitsu no kodomotachi* (Children in the classroom, 1955).[15] These shorts were so impressive that Nornes describes them, echoing Bazin, as "seismographic" in their ability to change the very foundations of film history, as an earthquake shakes the earth.[16] Takuya Tsunoda even argues that Iwanami fostered the development of "cinematic modernism" in postwar Japan and rightfully claims that Hani's Iwanami films are the earliest examples of *cinéma-vérité* in the world, a half decade before the term was even invented.[17] They were well known for their empathetic and natural connection to the lives of children, joining observation with a tender humanism. Briciu terms Hani's early documentaries "ethical filmmaking," noting that

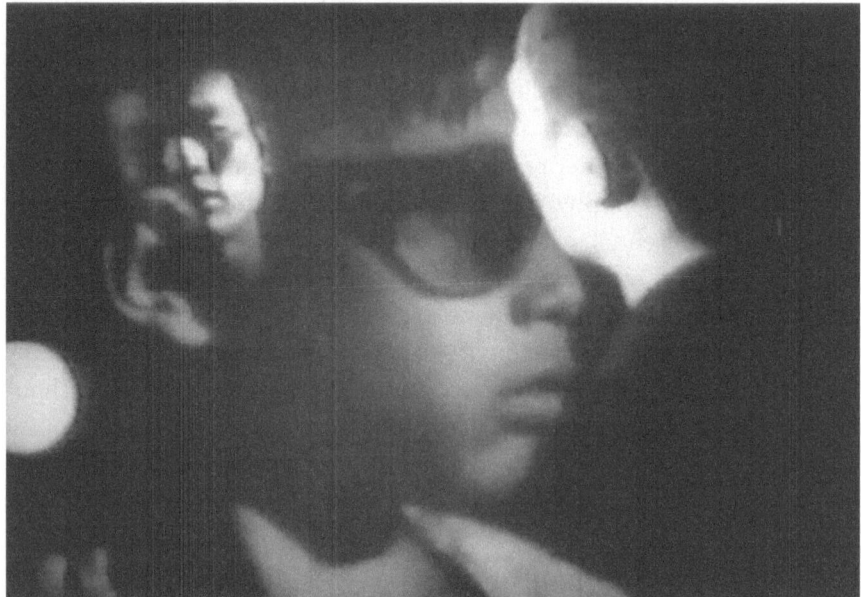

Figure 15. Superimposition of different ages of Asai, in Hani Susumu's *Furyō shōnen*, 1961.

"Hani believes in the filming as a human, taking into account the intersubjective engagement of the director and the filmed persons (objects) in a mutual encounter."[18]

Yet this humanistic quality also drew some criticism in *Kiroku eiga*, especially from Matsumoto Toshio, who compared it unfavorably to *Los Olvidados* precisely for these qualities. For Matsumoto, Hani's film was too concerned with observation, too focused on character and psychology. He writes, "Buñuel had the eyes to see the delinquent boy inside himself, whereas Hani saw him as an object of observation, in a position that had nothing to do with his own insides."[19] Matsumoto thus distinguishes Hani's semi-documentary humanism from the "sadomasochistic" aesthetic of his neo-documentaries from this same period, such as *Nishijin*.

Ōtani Shinpei describes how Hani's approach entailed a sympathetic gaze from the director toward his subject, while Matsumoto preferred a more analytical and self-critical approach that reflected back more explicitly on the director's subconscious.[20] Their approaches to leftist documentary thus inevitably made them rivals. Yet one should take Matsumoto's criticism with a grain of salt; he and Hani were comrades in leftist struggle and fellow avant-garde documentarists, although their approaches were not entirely aligned. Both, importantly, apply a surrealistic approach to the avant-garde documentary form.

Furyō shōnen appeared to define a new era in the Japanese semi-documentary, and despite being Hani's debut feature—and his first work with explicit fictional inflections—it clearly responded to the needs of the zeitgeist. It was voted the best Japanese film of 1961 in *Kinema Junpō* (*The Movie Times*), winning out even over *Yōjinbō* by Kurosawa Akira.[21] As Hani wrote in the pages of *Eiga hyōron* in 1958, "A new era seeks new content, and a new content requires new modes of representation."[22] For Japanese documentarists of this era, Annette Michelson writes, "questioning the system of production, rethinking spectatorship, meant ... a certain flexibility with respect to established genres."[23]

Furyō shōnen signified the beginning of a new era of Japanese avant-garde documentary, as it coincided with the sense of failure, or *zasetsukan*, surrounding ANPO. I argue that as this continued and a previously dormant nationalism began to resurface in the wake of the Tokyo 1964 Olympics, filmmakers began to use allegorical modes alongside semi-documentary as a more effective strategy to critique Japanese contemporary politics. Such use of allegory evokes J. Hillis Miller's claim that allegory implies making public, and available to profane ears, something that would otherwise remain secret. The mode of allegory thus allows this *something other* to be made public, visible, and audible—in other words, "theatrical," in the root sense of open to seeing, by such means.[24] By catering to a less militantly political audience and retaining a certain amount of big budget studio support, films by leftist filmmakers thus continued to exhibit a profound and even vicious critique of consumerism, American imperialism, and Japan's own fascist past. This allegorical quality would slowly metamorphose, with growing student unrest and growing interest in radical avant-garde experimentation, into the films characteristic of the ATG productions in the late 1960s and early 1970s.

For many, the mid-1960s seemed to be a time of calm and prosperity. Hannah Airriess notes that in much mainstream media of the time period, such as the Tōhō Studio's wildly popular *Shachō* (*Company President*,

1956–1970) series, had a "modern and bright" identity; these films, "salarymen producing salaryman films for salaryman audiences," were high-growth productions that treated "immaterial labor and management not as sources of alienation but comedy."[25] During such a seemingly "modern and bright" period, allegorical films allowed the New Left filmmaker to direct social and political realities, but filtered through somewhat more palatable means. This does not mean that the films entail the "Aesop-language" common to politically oppressive regimes; even though the country was trending in a conservative direction, the press remained relatively free to exhibit dissenting opinions. Instead, the allegories of Japanese films from the period are not dull and systemic but are rooted in what Angus Fletcher calls symbolic power struggles. As he notes, at the heart of any allegory is a conflict of authorities.[26]

The term *allegory*, however, is not frequently used in Japanese critical circuits, whether the English-derived *aregorī*, *gūwa* ("fable," a compound created from "implying" and "tale"), or *fūyu* ("allegory," created from "manner/wind" and "rebuke/admonishment"). This lack of a media theoretical tie to allegory may be a bit surprising; I believe this is partially due to the work of Walter Benjamin, now well known for his analysis of allegory, not yet being ubiquitous in Japan. Kyle Peters notes that Benjamin's work was not translated in the prewar antifascist cultural magazine *Sekai Bunka* (*World Culture*), to which Nakai also contributed articles. Yet the magazine was familiar with the Frankfurt School, as it translated Max Horkheimer, and Benjamin's "The Work of Art in the Age of Mechanical Reproducibility" was briefly mentioned in a list of articles for a general introduction to the Frankfurt School's *Zeitschrift für Sozialforschung* (*Journal of Social Research*).[27] I apply the term allegory, however, with Benjamin in mind—not because the films evinced a connection to Benjamin's texts as a reference point, but because the term productively implies a double-layered "masking" that many of the films from this period demonstrate. Many films, even those outside of the purview of the "avant-garde" like Imamura's popular films, reach out into entertainment categories. Thus a conflict emerges between two national ideologies, one depicting Japan as a rapidly growing economic powerhouse in the midst of modernization and another depicting the country as a continuing war-torn state in the midst of collective amnesia, burdened by inequality, patriarchy, and primitive superstition, extant since the early Showa period and earlier.

However, the beauty of Japanese allegorical semi-documentaries is that they do not make these competing ideologies obvious. The films can be, and have been, enjoyed without their additional allegorical readings. As Fletcher notes, "The whole point of allegory is that it does not *need* to be read exegetically; it often has a literal level that makes good enough sense all by itself."[28] Imamura's *Nippon konchūki* can be read as a simple narrative about an unlucky "bug-like" woman; Kuroki's *Tobenai chinmoku*, about a caterpillar's journey across Japan. Both surface-level readings make sense on their own, but the symbolism of the two insects is enriched when also understood as an embodiment of the Japanese geopolitical experience, a kind of affective biopolitics. This secondary reading enriches their analysis and makes them infinitely stronger and more interesting.

Allegorical semi-documentaries mirror Margaret Key's assertion that Abe Kōbō's novels represent "truth" through the "lies" of fiction, creating a space for complex metatextual ideas that were not readily acknowledged in their era and recalling communist-surrealist Louis Aragon's concept of the 'lying-truth,' or *mentir-vrai*—important for the communists of the New Wave Left Bank (it is explicitly mentioned in Agnès Varda's 1965 short documentary *Elsa la rose*).[29] The timeliness of "lying-truth" is important: Abe Kōbō claimed to reinvigorate realism by making "truth from a lie" in 1963, the year during which more allegorical films were released in Japan than any other, with the Tokyo Olympics in 1964 as a pivotal crux around which the films revolve.[30] Abe was not a filmmaker, although he did view his fiction novels as fundamentally documentarian; however, his frequent affiliation with film critical and avant-gardist circles proves that, indeed, there was something in the air in Japanese intellectual life that aimed to create allegorical productions that produced "truth from a lie."

This chapter builds on crucial work on Imamura Shōhei by Michael Raine and Diane Wei Lewis and unearths new archival information about the criminally undertheorized socialist filmmaker Kuroki Kazuo, in thinking through two enigmatic allegorical semi-documentary films that revolve around an insect metaphor. But before discussing the films themselves, however, it is important to properly investigate allegory as a potential rhetorical mode in documentary.

THE POLITICS OF ALLEGORY

As Benjamin writes, allegory invests work with "higher meanings not otherwise accessible."[31] In other words, a politically militant documentary portrayal of the pitfalls of postwar Japanese economics and social structure—in the agitprop manner of Matsumoto's 1959 *ANPO Jōyaku*, for instance—would not be similarly accessible to the viewing public just a few years later. The mid-1960s was a period of intense and dizzyingly rapid economic growth. In 1964, a shocking 90 percent of all Japanese households owned the "three sacred treasures" of postwar Japan: refrigerators, televisions, and washing machines.[32] As the majority of the population was swept up in the neonationalist fervor of the Tokyo Olympics, the idea of a strict leftist critique of Japanese culture and society seemed far less effective than it had earlier. It is not a coincidence that the leftist journal *Kiroku eiga* ceased publication in early 1964.

Yet as Watanabe Hiroshi notes, as this postwar political and economic chaos transitioned into a situation of "relative stability" (*sōtai-teki antei*), this stability was in fact indebted to the wars in Korea and Indochina.[33] Japan's economic boom was therefore complicit in American and French imperialism. The allegorical semi-documentary rendered an incipient critique of capitalism accessible to citizens who were more ambivalent about the sudden rise in Japanese consumer culture. It was also equally important that the film be enjoyable to watch for the message to be received: emotionally resonant, but promoting active, engaged thought rather than passive viewership. Brainard Cowan describes Benjamin's conception of allegory as possibility or potentiality of transformation, expressing "a constantly potential vision in the alienated world of capitalist economy."[34] In the face of "relative stability," then, allegorical films guide the individual to think *otherwise*—a *bouleversement* that Benjamin conceived as both intellectual and affective. Allegory strikes notes in the depth of one's being.[35] Allegorical structures are thus singularly capable of conveying radical leftist ideology to the average viewer—especially during the image-saturated 1960s.

Elsewhere, Benjamin equates the allegory with the ruin, laid bare in a landscape, in the middle of a flourishing city: "In the ruin, history has merged sensuously with the setting. And so configured, history finds expression not as a process of eternal life, but rather as one of unstoppable decline. Allegory thereby proclaims itself beyond beauty. Allegories are, in the realm of thought, what ruins are in the realm of things."[36] For Benjamin, a ruin reminds the passive surveyor that the grand cityscape in which they stand is not "a process of eternal life, but rather ... one of unstoppable decline." Miller reads this as Benjamin's sly critique of Hegel's teleological understanding of history: rather than an ever-perfecting *Geist*, here the ruin reminds the viewer of the inevitability of death.[37] Allegory is thus "beyond beauty"—a reminder that a life of wealth and leisure might hold more than meets the eye.

Allegorical works emerge not only in periods of political oppression; they may also find their potency in an era when the bulk of the population appears rather content. In a roundtable for the penultimate January 1964 issue of *Kiroku eiga*, Ōshima Nagisa and Matsumoto Toshio both agreed that Japanese film was experiencing a crisis, in which solidarity and collaboration were distrusted. Matsumoto linked this explicitly to the Japanese economic boom: "The rapid growth of the Japanese economy after the Security Treaty created a mass social phenomenon that has already become generalized and established; for the time being there will be no so-called extreme conditions. Mass change won't come about right now."[38] Similarly, just a few months earlier, Matsumoto wrote: "The situation is bad. Terribly bad.... [A]ll movements have suddenly turned into mere shells.... [T]he movement has plunged into a quagmire of unfathomable stagnation and confusion."[39] Filmmakers thus turned to allegorical documentaries in light of this strong sense of "crisis," "unfathomable stagnation," and "confusion" in which "mass change won't come."

Within this historical context of political stagnation in which revolution appears impossible, allegory arises as "the dwelling-place of truth," which, as Benjamin notes, is then "bodied forth ... in the dance of represented ideas."[40] Allegory, then, is able to *embody* a truth normally withheld from the viewing public. The viewer, after seeing their own experiences represented on screen, can draw radical conclusions about contemporary Japanese life. As Jameson notes, political class consciousness is only figurable—that is, visible, and accessible to our imaginations—when a class becomes a character in its own right; in an era largely devoid of working-class consciousness, allegory thus becomes a useful tool in making class struggle both figurative and visible.[41] For leftist Japanese filmmakers of the mid-1960s, the allegorical semi-documentary allowed both an affective and intellectual alignment between audience and the character depicted on screen—an alignment whose goal was a utopian class consciousness. Although some of these filmmakers were more explicitly Marxist than others (Kuroki was more notoriously radical in his politics than Imamura), I claim that the allegorical semi-documentary can utilize, and even weaponize, allegory in the pursuit of antifascism.

David Desser's claim that Imamura's *Nippon konchūki* serves as a microcosm of Japan's modern era applies to each of these films in turn.[42] This chapter therefore views the antifascist avant-garde documentary through the fraternal twin definitions of the French word *histoire* and thinks through Godard's formulation in his *Histoire(s) du cinéma* series (1988–1998): of *histoire* as both story (*monogatari*, in Japanese) and history (*rekishi*). History is both something fictive, aesthetically crafted into being (*monogatari*), and something nonfictive, documenting a historical fact (*rekishi*). We will find that the Japanese filmmakers of this period self-consciously aimed to merge these twin meanings of *histoire* within their films; nonfiction is blended with fiction to produce highly crafted, and highly varied, allegorical semi-documentary productions. Yet like Matsumoto's *Nishijin*, which claimed to "protect history" and "protect Nishijin," the films in this chapter align, at times, too closely to ethnonationalist discourse; through their persistent interest in the "Japanese condition," they find themselves complicit in a fascism they otherwise claim to critique.

ALTERNATIVE JAPANESENESS IN *NIPPON KONCHŪKI*

The films of Imamura Shōhei follow Hani's interest in intersubjectivity, yet like the films of Matsumoto Toshio, they have a surreal and somewhat sinister twist. Even though his films are now discussed as fiction, their documentarian nature was constantly evoked. As Coleman and Desser write, "Imamura's clear-eyed examinations seem almost documentary-like, and indeed, many are documentaries."[43] One issue of *Kiroku eiga* devoted three entire articles of its January 1964 issue to the allegorical works of Imamura Shōhei, especially *Nippon konchūki*. This was no small feat for a rather modestly sized journal of a few dozen pages per issue.

Diane Wei Lewis argues that Imamura's work was discussed in terms of "truth" and "actuality" as early as 1962.[44] While this film was arguably Imamura's most successful from the period, his other films from the mid-1960s are paradigmatic examples of the allegorical semi-documentary: for example, the 1961 *Buta to gunkan* (*Pigs and Battleships*), the 1964 *Akai satsui* (*Intentions of Murder*), and the 1966 *"Erogotoshitachi' yori jinruigaku nyūmon* (*The Pornographers*). Like Hani and Kuroki, who were also known for "stricter" documentary productions, Imamura did not distinguish between fiction and nonfictional forms. His difficult and highly allegorical films uncomfortably straddle leftist theory and the ethnonationalist inquiry of the period. His oeuvre appears to react to the nascent reemergence of *nihonjinron*, or theories of Japanese people, a largely nationalist study of Japanese cultural identity with a long and complex history, which has had several waves of increasing popularity and evolution reacting to the cultural zeitgeist. Indeed, Imamura's films tend to be marked by an anthropological inquiry into a "Japaneseness" that is neither praised nor vilified. Rather, his films tend to investigate a core root of Japanese culture and thus become ethically ambiguous.

His films are unique in their incorporation of myth, fable, and folklore, producing complex and disorienting works that uncomfortably straddle the line between fantasy and reality. The supernatural is enmeshed within modernity, recalling Benjamin's famous dictum that "it is precisely the modern which conjures up prehistory."[45] Around the time of the ANPO student protests, Imamura spent several years studying the research of native ethnologist Yanagita Kunio.[46] Although not entirely absent from political movements, Imamura turned inward during this formative period in Japanese postwar history. He was more interested in the research into Japan's past, in the search for clues into the formation of Japan's contemporary society and values. Yanagita had long since become a household name for his *Tōno monogatari* (*Legends of Tono*, 1910), a literary retelling of oral histories and myths akin to the Grimm Brothers in Europe. He was one of many Japanese intellectuals who turned away from a "progressive" narrative that saw Japan on a path to economic and cultural modernity. Instead, as Michael Raine notes, figures like Yanagita emphasized the indigenous (*dochaku*) aspects of Japanese culture—not as residual but as ongoing and formative qualities in the experience of Japanese life.[47]

However, there is a darker side to this interest in indigeneity. Concurrently, the cultural and anthropological inquiry into *nihonjinron* was becoming extremely popular. This coincided with the end of the official postwar period and was fueled by a desire to explain Japan's dizzying economic growth. This sudden appeal to native culture, as well as a similar movement in the 1920s, was therefore embedded with capitalist discourse, rather than necessarily fomenting a resistance to it.[48] The interest in "Japaneseness" as a national culture was distinct from a quest for what Frantz Fanon termed the people's "true nature" and was implicit in the modernizing ideological program of the postwar period—a program of capitalist gain, decreasingly attached to the ever-present reality of the people and daily life.

In contrast to this optimistic outlook fueled by Japan's huge economic growth, Imamura looked to folklore and traditional culture for the roots of a "Japaneseness" far messier and far more complicated than the slick, industrious image most media outlets would have one believe. Imamura echoes Yanagita Kunio and Hanada Kiyoteru in their strategy of "using the premodern as a negative mediation to overcome modernity."[49] His interest in Japaneseness is fundamentally anti-capitalist in nature, but therefore not immune to a certain ethnonationalist complicity. Imamura praised the allegedly "uncivilized" elements in Japanese society, writing that within them he saw a "liberated zone" (*kaihōkū*) that exposes "true intentions" (*honne*): "Regardless of age or hierarchy, I saw a liberated zone in one type of human being which lives and exposes a true intention: tough women, skillful in business; slovenly war veterans; the beckoning cop secretly seeking a bribe."[50] These alleged dregs of society are in fact the people who "expose a true intention"—the aspect of "Japaneseness" ignored by the vision of Japan as slick, salaryman-filled, economic powerhouse.

Importantly, these outcasts exposing Japan's "true intentions" were often real acquaintances and friends beloved by Imamura's crew: prostitutes, brothel madams, excommunicated priests, and prodigal sons. These real-life characters, whom some of Imamura's compatriots sardonically named, in an archaic fashion, *Chimimōryō* (魑魅魍魎), the "evil spirits of rivers and mountains," frequently dropped by his studio in Tokyo.[51] These figures, "thrown aside" by what Imamura termed "the shadow of a postwar Japan chasing wealth," would inspire many of the protagonists in his films.⁵² Although the "evil spirits of rivers and mountains" are generally "thrown aside" by a modernizing culture of capitalist accumulation, these spirits are nonetheless ever present, and their assumed "evil" nature is, if not entirely good, resolutely ambiguous and deeply fascinating.

Yet this interest in *nihonjinron* or "Japaneseness" can only fit uncomfortably into leftist thought in the 1960s. The proximity of Ōshima Nagisa, Matsumoto Toshio, and Terayama Shūji to ethnonationalist doctrine aligns them with similarly anti-capitalist theorists and writers on the Far Right of the political spectrum. This is best personified by such problematic figures as Mishima Yukio, whose nationalist texts and theories were often adored by the same students who protested against ANPO. Unlike figures such as Mishima, however, Imamura tended to idealize the tougher and more slovenly aspects of "Japaneseness"—a far cry from a clean-cut ideal. This near obsession with the dirtier versions of "Japaneseness" is reflected in his choice of characters and in his many allegories for Japanese society. *Nippon konchūki* is usually translated as *Insect Woman*, but its literal meaning is *Japanese Entomology*; as in the film, this "Japaneseness" is allegorized by a mere insect. In fact, one might even say that Imamura's filmmaking can be called "insect-like" in its obsession with lower forms, in contrast to the filmmaking of Ozu Yasujirō, for whom Imamura worked as assistant director. Raine recalls that Ozu once asked Imamura: "Why do you always write maggots (*ujiushi*)? Why not write a decent character for a change?"⁵³ As if to anger Ozu even further, the first shot sequence of the film is an insect in close-up, trudging up a dirt hill.

The allegory refers to an insect undergoing numerous trials and repeating the same mistakes over and over. The long-suffering insect is aligned with the life of the protagonist Tome, who endures one hardship after another. Tome, however, is also an allegory for Japan itself, and the cycles of exploitation it endures and then uses maliciously against others. The film weaves Tome's hard life into Japanese history by labeling years (importantly, by the Japanese calendar) and incorporating archival footage such as the American occupation, "Bloody May Day," in 1952, and the ANPO protests of June 1960.

Although this double allegory might seem a tedious rehearsal of Japanese history, it is nothing of the sort. The result is a tumultuous account in which characters are at the mercy of their own flawed wiring, trapped in a

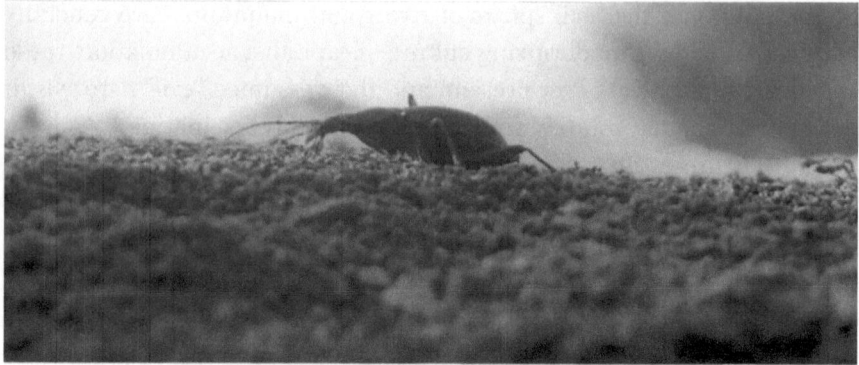

Figure 16. Allegorical insect in first scene, in Imamura Shōhei's *Nippon konchūki*, 1963.

system of exploitation outside of their control. We see Tome as a poor child, raised by her father and a community of tenant farmers. She is then sold to her landlord, has a child out of wedlock, and works in a factory during wartime. After this, she becomes a union leader, then moves to Tokyo for work, but can only find work as a maid and then as a prostitute. Exploited by some and sexually abused by all others, Tome finds solace in the Sōka Gakkai, a new religious sect, and manipulates her situation to become a brothel madam, only for the tides to turn and for herself to be exploited in return, continuing the insect's Sisyphean climb up its endless dirt hill.

The film was an amalgamation of many common postwar experiences; in fact, Imamura's film *Nippon sengoshi—Madamu Onboro no seikatsu* (*History of Postwar Japan as Told by a Bar Hostess*, 1970), which is an extensive interview and thus more explicit in its use of the documentary medium, mirrors the plot of *Nippon konchūki* almost perfectly. Thus, although Imamura was not as politically engaged as his contemporaries, his research attempted to find anthropological roots for the struggles of postwar Japanese existence, and he used this research to craft his characters. Indeed, film reviewers understood the characters in *Nippon konchūki* to represent larger cultural archetypes. Another important symbolic figure in the film is the character Nobuko, Tome's young daughter, who falls prey to many of Tome's schemes, including sex work and reliance on older men, yet at the film's conclusion, in a fascinating quasi-Soviet twist, Nobuko leaves for the countryside to work with young revolutionaries on an agricultural commune. Sekine Hiroshi, who cowrote Matsumoto Toshio's neo-documentary *Nishijin* (1961), describes Nobuko as living a "symbolic existence," a stand-in for Imamura himself, as she is a "critic of the old generation who cannot escape" from its power, while also being "a sprout of democracy that took root after the war."[54] Nobuko's future and role are ambiguous—at the conclusion of the film, she might be pregnant with her mother's erstwhile lover's child—yet she presents, at the very least, the *potential* of an escape from the inherited *akujunkan* (vicious cycle) of trauma and oppression.

The clear relationship between the film's characters and a larger conception of Japaneseness is aided by the film's extensive use of documentary footage: Tokyo streets bustling with people are almost entirely unstaged, and there is also a great amount of newsreel footage, including crowds of people rioting during the "Bloody May" of 1952, the vast crowd protesting ANPO in 1960, and the infamous(ly incomprehensible) audio recording of Emperor Hirohito's speech (not quite) admitting defeat and ending World War II. Weaving this footage throughout the fictional film, Imamura creates a style of filmmaking that allows the viewer to regard these loaded historical images—often mediated through news reports and propaganda, to which Japanese citizens had become extremely habituated—with a fresher eye and a renewed perception.

Michael Raine analyzes the explicitly documentarian nature of *Nippon konchūki*; he argues that the film broke the rules of studio filmmaking by being the first Nikkatsu film to be shot entirely on location, using long lenses and in long takes, with almost no built sets or postrecorded sound, and extremely minimal artificial lighting. These are, of course, choices: Imamura pointedly chose to use equipment and techniques common in the world of documentary filmmaking, not studio fiction film. The choice to use black-and-white stock also added to the documentarian effect and allowed him to shoot in mostly natural light. Cinematographer Himeda Shinsaka claimed to use two cameras with long (150 mm) lenses to further flatten the space, creating a documentary-like effect, rather than the centered, highlighted image and often postrecorded speech of the typical studio film. Instead, in *Nippon konchūki*, hidden cameras with long lenses and wireless microphones were used to create scenes that must be scanned by the viewer to find the speaker.[55]

However, the film also includes highly experimental and surrealist qualities alongside its documentary-like filmmaking. Continuing Imamura's interest in Yanagita Kunio's beliefs, the film is full of otherworldly superstitions and surrealist flourishes. Imamura knowingly set this film in northern Japan, in the least modernized area of Honshū, Japan's largest island. Also the setting for Yanagita's *Tōno monogatari*, it symbolizes the area of mainland Japan most connected to its primordial, Jōmon-period "Japaneseness," considered by Yanagita to be the root of Japanese culture. This adds a somewhat haunted dimension to the rural scenes in the film—a hauntedness that exists in the form of the film as well as the content. Alongside the use of long takes typical of documentary film, *Nippon konchūki* introduces sudden moments of uncanny, surrealist disruption, reveling in an occasionally radical break from its actuality-based footage and seemingly straightforward plot.

For example, one of Imamura's cinematographic trademarks is to blur the character speaking in the foreground, while the camera focuses on a relic or icon in the back of the shot. In *Nippon konchūki*, Imamura does this with an altar to a mountain god, which becomes a leitmotif in the film. The Greek origin of the English word icon is *eikon*, or "akin to"; similarly, when Imamura's camera focuses on these ritual objects, the camera identifies the character with her past and the roots of "Japaneseness" within her. Such examples of ritual objects abound in Imamura films, even after the 1960s. For example, in the highly praised *Kuroi ame* (*Black Rain*) of 1989, based on an Ibuse Masuji story, Imamura inserts a character entirely of his creation, not present in the original: Yuichi, a deranged Jizō stonecutter with extreme post-traumatic stress disorder. The inclusion of this new character is not examined at length here, although one may productively relate him to Matsumoto's own film about Jizō stonecutters, *Ishi no uta*, released the same year as *Nippon konchūki*; Yuichi is used, like ritual objects in *Nippon konchūki*, to create a liminal space between mythological, folkloric origins and our present world. In so doing, Imamura reminds the viewer of their own messy, chaotic reality, as well as their inherited, and unaddressed, trauma.

Another important method Imamura uses to weave the ancient within the modern is through the use of music and sound editing. The aforementioned introductory scene of *Nippon konchūki*, in which an insect climbs a dirt hill, is paired with the sound of a woman reciting an ancient poem, coupled with the twang of a *mukkuri*, or Jew's harp. One of the oldest instruments in Japan, the *mukkuri* derives from the Ainu indigenous group of Hokkaido, annexed during the imperial conquests of the Meiji Restoration; this iconic sound places the film alongside animistic and ancient roots in the North, thus actually supplying a sonic alternative to the fascist supremacy of the Yamato race in Japanese culture. This sound is used in pivotal moments in many of Imamura's films from the 1960s, especially *Akai satsui*, and functions similarly to an icon or ritual object: when the sound is heard, the protagonist is transported to a primordial state of being—interestingly, one that is often sexual. In *Akai*, the *mukkuri* is used in a flashback to a young man attempting to climb into the protagonist's window, or when she succumbs to desire despite herself. It is an aural indicator of primal sexual drive and signals the existence between a liminal space between ancestral origin and present life. In both content and form, Imamura's films parade the slatternly and earthly aspects of Japanese life, less friendly to Japan's self-image as a modern economic powerhouse.

Director Matsukawa Yasuo, who also cowrote Kuroki's *Tobenai chinmoku*, praised *Nippon konchūki* for uncovering the messy dregs of Japaneseness. He used the metaphor of an "album" (*arubamu*) or "baby book" that is carried "on the back" of individual people and passed down through generations: "Albums always hide under roofs, including our housing complexes (*danchi*), and cover the surface of Japan with mycelia-like slime seedlings. Japanese thought and expression grew out of the mycelia of this 'house,' so to speak. It's like a sour, slimy (*nume nume*), wet mushroom. The more you try to cut it off, the more the sticky substance clings to it like rice cakes."[56] Japaneseness here is a "sour, slimy, wet mushroom," representing an inherited, epigenetic trauma. The reference to *danchi* here is also important and aligns with common criticisms of the alienated life found in these massive suburban complexes.[57] Matsukawa then continues: "After you've finished watching [*Nippon konchūki*], the ancestors in the album will suddenly look like something out of a *bunraku* puppet performance, with their mouths open up to their ears, and golden horns growing out. This film stares clearly at the root of our decline—in other words, at Japanese alienation."

For Matsukawa, *Nippon konchūki* is capable of unveiling the horrors of the ancestral line. Images are estranged and destabilized, turned from human to puppets, and to demons with "golden horns" and "mouths open to the ears." The reference to Freud's theory of the uncanny is conscious and explicit (it was frequently discussed in Japanese film journals of the period and is especially connected to Matsumoto's work). Such unveiling is only possible through Imamura's tricks of surrealism, from the *mukkuri*'s twang to the uncanny icons, to ironic freeze-frames with Tome reciting her (terrible) poetry in voice-over. Such extensive surrealist methods recall Hanada Kiyoteru's early conception of the "sur-documentary" described in the first chapter. Combined with the film's explicitly documentarian techniques, the use of surreal objects such as religious icons and the *mukkuri* contrast in a dialectical fashion, creating a striking result.

Evidently, audiences agreed, and *Nippon konchūki* became the first of Imamura's five *Kinema Junpō* award winning films, also taking best director and best screenplay.[58] It was by far the most financially successful film of Imamura's career up to this point and a critical triumph, bringing in more than 350 million yen over a record four-week run. The film was the third-highest-grossing film of 1963 and returned at least ten times its production budget; in fact, the film was among the top twenty-five most successful films of the twenty years after World War II.[59] Much of this success, I argue, is due to its fundamentally documentarian style and mythic, allegorical framework, which unveils the dirt and lowlife messiness of Japan in its dizzying stages of transformation. Yet there is still political potential in this vision of Japan. As Matsukawa writes, "Imamura connects the uterus of the endless past to the umbilical cord of the eternal future."[60]

POETIC NATIONAL ALLEGORY IN *TOBENAI CHINMOKU*

In Kuroki Kazuo's allegorical semi-documentary *Tobenai chinmoku*, it is not a dung beetle that serves as an allegory for postwar Japan, but a butterfly. Kuroki Kazuo's lyrical film traces the path of a butterfly as it migrates from the scarred urban landscape of Hiroshima to the rural Ainu lands of Hokkaido. The butterfly's flight touches upon many highly contested issues in the 1960s, especially the haunted memories of the Pacific War. Like Imamura's dung beetle, Kuroki's butterfly—which spends the vast majority of the film as a caterpillar—is exploited by others, its impending beauty simultaneously feared and revered. Occasionally the butterfly is personified as a beautiful wide-eyed girl, played by Kaga Mariko, who weaves through the film's plot as a secondary character, her face eventually printed on enormous billboards in Osaka and Tokyo. But where Imamura's film allegorizes Japan within poor, drudge-like Tome, who is only rhetorically associated with the dung beetle in the film's opening credits, Kuroki's caterpillar is also physically present as such—a frail yet surprisingly omniscient character able to infiltrate the most private of Japanese spaces in its unassuming smallness. The slow, even graceful movements of Kuroki's caterpillar, echoed in the ballet-like motions of the poetic cinematography, worm through daily life in postwar Japan, reminding the viewer of insidious elements and unprocessed trauma that remain.

The film was produced by Nippon Eiga Shinsha, a subsidiary of Tōhō studios created out of the main wartime producer of propaganda documentaries. Kuroki Kazuo began his career in the Iwanami documentary film company alongside documentary legends such as Hani, but left Iwanami because, as Michael Raine notes, he "did not want to make PR films for Japanese capitalists." Although filmed not long after Imamura's *Nippon konchūki*, *Tobenai chinmoku* was shelved for a year because it became more experimental than the studios intended. Raine notes that the film was finally screened in the art film powerhouse ATG in February 1966.[61] I believe that the film's production during the height of Tokyo Olympic fever is important and linked to the film's allegorical nature.

In her article on Kuroki's later films, Carol Hayes argues that Kuroki was fueled by an investigation of wartime militarism: "One of the difficulties for Kuroki, and many of his generation, was the dramatic about-face from the jingoistic militarism of Japanese war propaganda, to the postwar rhetoric of democracy and pacifism. Although an advocate of pacifism, Kuroki was left questioning this sudden change, which made it difficult for him and others of his generation to trust the nation's leaders. It also prompted him to reflect with embarrassment on his own failure, despite strongly held personal views, to resist or at least speak up against the militarism of his age."[62]

Hayes analyzes Kuroki's incessant investigation of Japanese history as a type of collective and individual analysis and criticism, as he attempted to "speak up," belatedly, against fascism. Through this context, Kuroki's decision to craft this allegorical semi-documentary at the height of Olympic fever is significant, as the mid-1960s saw a reversion to a certain kind of "jingoistic militarism" that would have been familiar to Kuroki and others of the *yakeato* ("scorched ruins," a name for the postwar generation). Scholars such as Rio Otomo have linked Olympic fever to "the dominant discourses of the 1930s that effectively mobilized the nation for military expansion."[63] Yoshikuni Igarashi writes, on the massive reconstructions of Tokyo during the period, that "Japan's attempt in the 1960s to construct a more modern, rational space in Tokyo . . . could be materialied only through completing unfinished projects of the prewar regime."[64] Indeed, the resurgence of national pride during the Olympic period had a fascistic flavor that joined the perfection of a "modern, rational space" with the perfection of hygienic and athletic bodies. Witnessing such a return to wartime rhetoric led Kuroki to investigate Japanese history through techniques of cinema, in an attempt to counter this unnerving recurrence of fascist ideology.

Kuroki's experience with the creation of PR films, however, led to a rejection of this genre and the limitations of a strict documentary format. For Kuroki, a joining of the experimental/fictional and the documentarian was essential. Kuroki was critical of the state of documentary in the early 1960s and considered PR cinema a monopoly; he concluded one 1962 article with the mic-drop-worthy line: "The arteriosclerosis (*dōmyakukōka*) and hysteria that envelop the film world is by no means temporary."[65] He writes in *Kiroku eiga*: "I believe that documentaries are now weakened by PR films, and that documentary is debilitated and further exacerbated by alienation if we simply think of [fictional] films as unrelated to documentaries." In this same article, he lambasts "the situation of documentary" for its "uniform empiricism," writing that "documentary . . . does not stop at this stage"; indeed, Kuroki knows well that the labels "documentary" and "fiction" are inevitably contextually based: "The fact that documentary is established in reality, or cinema established in art, has always been determined on the basis of historical circumstances." Polemically, he even writes, "a documentary can be called a pseudo-truth," and "PR movies should be denounced because most of them are movies that sell false images." Kuroki criticizes the genres of documentary and PR film precisely because of their false claims to truth and objectivity. As if responding to the message of the Soviet avant-garde, Kuroki notes, "Our only method is to use new vision as our weapon."[66]

For Kuroki, the "flame" of documentary cinema—its most interesting and riveting aspects of the medium—lay in its willingness to use experimental and avant-garde elements.[67] While at Iwanami, Kuroki was a member of the experimental Blue Group (Ao no Kai) alongside other documentary pioneers such as Tsuchimoto Noriaki, Ogawa Shinsuke, and Matsumoto Toshio. Members of this group would meet to discuss the contemporaneous issues of documentary production. Nornes writes that it is within this group of filmmakers, who frequently drank, read, and discussed films late into the night, that the idea for *Tobenai chinmoku* was born.[68]

Even with Kuroki's documentarist roots, however, the plot of *Tobenai chinmoku* is very fable-like: a butterfly, eventually caught by a young boy in Hokkaido, travels sixteen hundred kilometers as a caterpillar from its Nagasaki origin; indeed, the butterfly's species is the Nagasaki ageha, or Nagasaki swallowtail. After the boy shows the butterfly to his schoolteachers, who refuse to believe he caught it in the wild, the film shows us its fictional journey, traveling from the petals of flowers sold to passersby, to a woman's ornate hat, to a newspaper, to the back of a shirt. By a string of implausible coincidences, the butterfly travels on the lapels and suitcases and hats of human beings, onto cars, trains, and airplanes, from Nagasaki to Hagi, Hiroshima, Kyoto, Osaka, Hong Kong, Yokohama, Tokyo, and Hokkaido. The citizens through whom and on which the caterpillar travels are given their own short vignettes and incorporate a great variety of cinematic genres: romantic intrigue and murder mystery in Hagi; war memory in Kyoto; the overworked and status-obsessed salaryman in Osaka; an action-packed yakuza chase; and government corruption in Hong Kong, Yokohama, and Tokyo. The result is an aesthetic that veers from poetic allegory to a number of different film genres, playfully navigating their similarities and differences. Yet while this aspect of the film is deeply, even exaggeratedly, fictional, the film incorporates a vast amount of documentary footage, which emerges between cuts as if revealing the

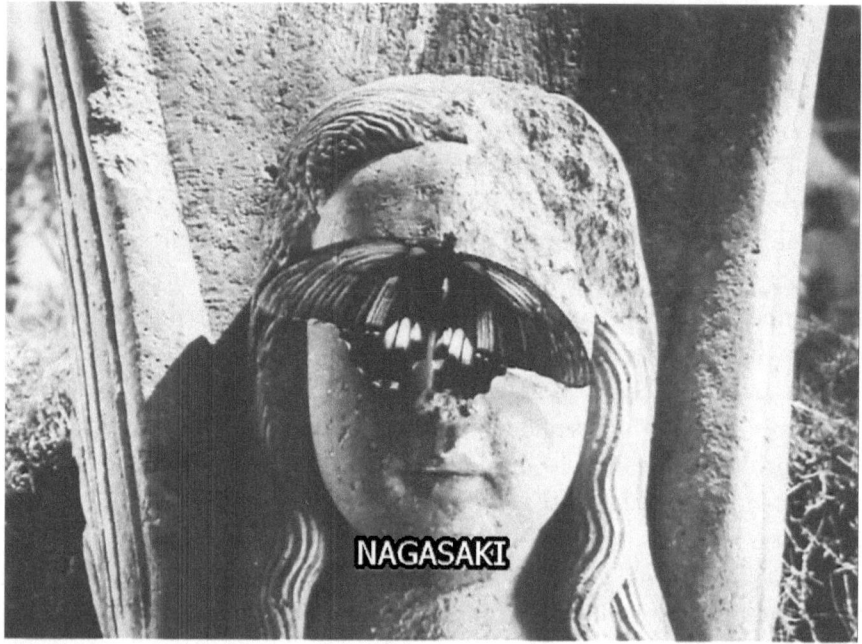

Figure 17. Nagasaki ageha butterfly in city of Nagasaki, in Kuroki Kazuo's *Tobenai chinmoku*, 1966.

id between ego and super-ego. History in its quotidian, disturbing reality creeps forth between fiction, giving it new breath.

For instance, each location of the fictional butterfly has great historical importance. The town Hagi, for example, was a hotbed of the 1868 revolution, and Nagasaki and Hiroshima still embody the aftermath of the world war. Compared with Imamura's *Nippon konchūki*, *Tobenai chinmoku* includes more purely aesthetic rhetorical flourishes, as well as more direct newsreel footage: although Kaga chews leaves, twirls a parasol, and sings melodies with very little diegetic tie to the "realistic" plot of the physical butterfly, an extraordinary array of documentary footage is used, especially in those moments related to the caterpillar's current location. In Hagi, for example, a romance and murder intrigue plot is cut with strange zooms onto samurai armor, and the camera pans alongside the crags and ivy of overgrown castle walls from the 1800s. In Hiroshima, a man chases

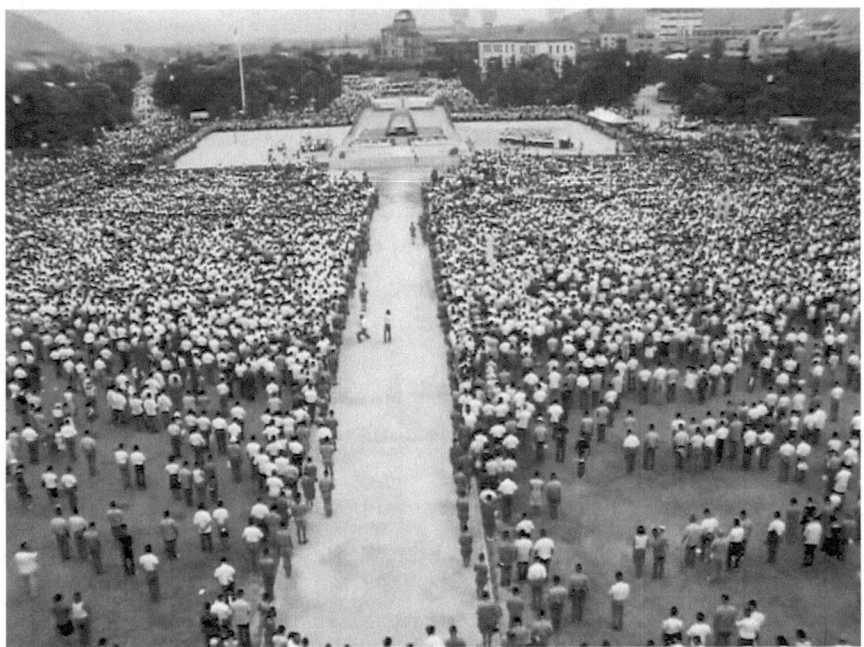

Figure 18. Archival footage of 1960 ANPO protest, in Kuroki Kazuo's *Tobenai chinmoku*, 1966.

the butterfly girl, now manifesting as a *hibakusha* (victim of nuclear radiation sickness), fearful of the bomb's eventual physical toll on her body; this plot is interwoven with shots of an anti-nuclear protest and includes documentary footage of visitors to the Hiroshima Peace Memorial Museum, as well as audio interview recordings of the experience of six *hibakusha* victims. He also includes the newsreel footage of Hiroshima in the immediate aftermath of the bomb. The result is harrowing and uncanny, and when the girl picks up the caterpillar, gently letting it crawl over her palm while she says to herself, "my mother's bones"—*haha no hone*—her words take on a deeper and more resonant meaning. As we will see, the film's allegorical structure allows for an emotional depth to which strict documentaries are not often privy.

Perhaps the most shocking documentary image used in *Tobenai chinmoku* occurs during a high-intensity yakuza chase, which also highlights contemporary government corruption: Prime Minister Kishi Nobusuke in 1960, forcing through the Diet the vote to ratify the ANPO treaty amidst commotion and chaos. This image is then repeated several scenes later, with a great amount of postprocessing and overexposure, and with the speed drastically reduced. This momentary surrealistic procedure creates a deeply unsettling effect and echoes experimental short films such as Matsumoto Toshio's *Ectasis* (1969), in which shots are estranged by endless repetition and overprocessing. In *Tobenai chinmoku*, iconic images of ANPO filter into the film's imagined space and are juxtaposed with scenes of a yakuza member escaping in a helicopter and dystopian imagery of marching Japanese Self-Defense Forces. These images thus provide a distinct sociopolitical context to the film's fictional diegetic world.

Kuroki's film allegorizes Japan as a caterpillar, and then butterfly: an iconic, even cliché, example of ephemeral beauty that is nonetheless easily exploited. When the butterfly-girl has loveless sex for money in Kyoto, Japan finds itself similarly exploited by the wartime propaganda of those in power. Like Imamura's Tome, the caterpillar finds itself unable to craft its own destiny: it is carried on hats, newspapers, and flowers throughout the country and exploited throughout. Thus, although Kuroki's allegorical film is extremely crafted, the rhetoric of its semi-documentary structure allows for a great amount of insight into the contemporary Japanese political landscape. Matsumoto Toshio, who wrote at length on the film after its first screening in 1966 at ATG, understood the film's semi-documentary sensibility perfectly, writing that although the film is ostensibly a fictional account, "In reality, the imagery of *Tobenai chinmoku* is clearly created within the field of anti-theatrical film."[69] The film's "anti-theatricality" was thus evident to its contemporaneous viewers; an allegory, after all, can be deeply realistic and even have documentarian tendencies.

In the same article, Matsumoto, following his concept of a dialectic of the "discovered" (qua Lumière) and "created" image (qua Meliès), writes that "film . . . is an art of 'encounter' (*deai*) and 'choice' (*sentaku*)," and notes that "these are film's 'terms and conditions.'"[70] Matsumoto defines Kuroki's film as a synthesis of chance discovery and aesthetically driven editing techniques. Perhaps most importantly, Matsumoto notes that the film can be a documentary despite the lack of actuality footage and even if nothing in the film actually represents "reality" as it is usually defined:

"Of course, common sense denies that this is reality. But a thing that does not exist is not the same thing as a thing that cannot exist. Rather, a thing may exist without actually being present."[71] Thus, *Tobenai chinmoku* represents reality despite its fictional structure, since it represents the thing that *may* exist instead of the thing that *does* exist. The specific semi-documentary structure of Kuroki's film posits a possible, existing world punctuated by present reality, rather than a fantastical space that *cannot* exist. This documentary of the *"may* exist" easily lends itself to allegorical procedures; as Benjamin describes, allegory is the affirmation of the existence of truth.[72] While this is a wholly different truth than one exemplified by observational documentary techniques, this more allegorical truth, found in films by Kuroki, Imamura, Hani, and others, affirms a deeper "existence of truth" beyond what the rigid constraints of documentary film would normally allow.

Matsumoto continues his analysis by comparing Kuroki to Alain Resnais and to the themes of memory, existence, and ontological questioning shared by the two directors. The films of Resnais were extremely influential for Japanese documentarists of the era, who saw in his early ekphrastic documentaries especially a dialectical synthesis of fiction and nonfiction. And certainly *Tobenai chinmoku's* immediate comparison is the 1959 *Hiroshima mon amour* (Japanese title, *Nijūyojikan no jōji*, translated as *24 Hour Love Affair*), which shares the theme of the aftermath of the atomic bombs dropped on Hiroshima and Nagasaki, as well as a poetic and dreamlike quality. *Hiroshima mon amour,* along with the aforementioned *Los Olvidados,* was the most frequently discussed work in *Kiroku eiga*—despite, like Buñuel's film, its having an allegedly fictional form. Kuroki, like Alain Resnais and Marguerite Duras's script, delves into a commonly taboo political space through allegory and includes accounts of personal trauma. Fiction becomes a newer, more uncanny way of approaching a subject too prone to habituation.

Matsumoto also sees *Tobenai chinmoku* as an extraordinary continuation of the themes present in Kuroki's earlier documentary films, as well as certain short documentaries by Tsuchimoto Noriaki. The juxtaposition of Tsuchimoto, best known for his stunning series of documentary films on Minamata disease, and Kuroki is not accidental, and points to a concern with anti-capitalism shared between these two filmmakers, although expressed in varying ways. For instance, Kuroki's films, whether documentary or semi-documentary, examine war memory and the regions that economic growth left behind; similarly, Tsuchimoto's films examine the dark side of the Japanese economic miracle, the rapidly changing topographical landscape of Tokyo, and the devastating effects of capitalist growth on the environment and on the most impoverished of human bodies. Although Tsuchimoto's works are more classically documentarian in the strict sense of the term, Tsuchimoto and Kuroki share a desire to reveal the dark underbelly of capitalist accumulation.

In a controversial article in *Kiroku eiga* titled "On Nothingness" (*mu ni tsuite*) Kuroki argues that film must respond to a nihilistic tendency in contemporary Japanese society, and he views his filmmaking as an explicit attempt to counter fascism. For Kuroki, "fascism has a certain historical experience in overcoming nihilism"; "it is a historical situation that eliminates our anxieties and our fears."[73] In order to counter a potential resurgence of fascism, true creativity is necessary that pushes the boundaries of the possible. For Kuroki, this entailed the inclusion of a fictional, highly allegorical frame narrative that weaves through newsreel footage, which is able to revitalize documentary filmmaking and rescue it from "alienation." Yet Kuroki, importantly, notes—in an intriguing echo of Benjamin—that documentary must not subordinate itself to "politics" (and Kuroki places the term in quotation marks in his own essay). Yet for the openly communist Kuroki, *politics* here refers to the political establishment, especially the JCP, and to what were called "sponsored" documentary films. Independence and individuation are key to effective revolutionary filmmaking: to counter fascism, the artists's consciousness must be made apparent and its criticism and theory be made explicit.

Kuroki's butterfly moves on a relatively linear journey through Japan, traversing space where Imamura's dung beetle traverses time. The caterpillar, as personified by the human girl, appears to desire freedom. Here the literal Japanese meaning of the title, *Flightless Silence*, might be actualized by the narrative: first the caterpillar, unable to fly, finds itself carried to and fro, exploited by others as it silently observes them; yet the moment the caterpillar acquires the capacity for flight and turns into a butterfly, it is captured by the boy from Hokkaido and killed—silenced, its wings forcibly removed. Yet the title also refers to the "silence" of unaddressed war criticism. Without addressing the experience of history in all its taboo, the butterfly remains flightless. Carol Hayes argues that Kuroki's films express "deeply felt antiwar sentiments" and "encourag[e] us all to reassess the cultural and historical impact of World War II on the Japanese contemporary psyche and the broader impact for the world as a whole."[74] In *Tobenai chinmoku*, Kuroki accomplishes this investigation of World War II and the postwar period by negating conventional documentary structure, instead utilizing allegory to craft an emotionally resonant and fiercely activist narrative.

THE PLACE OF WOMEN IN THE ALLEGORICAL MODE

It is important, however, to confront the elephant in the room: that despite the antifascist and anti-capitalist messaging of the allegorical semi-documentary, with very few exceptions, these films allegorize Japan through a woman's body. The issue of gender, then, needs to be confronted directly. The suffering, violation, or even death of the diegetic woman is regarded not as personal suffering but as the suffering of a nation at large. This use of the body of a woman is at the very best ambiguous. On the one hand, one can argue that such films use a woman to symbolize the trials of an oppressed group or subaltern, subjected by a rigid hierarchical structure rigged against her. This body thus reveals Japan's suppressed tensions and contradictions. This mobilization of the woman as metaphor thus might be productively compared to the films of Jean-Luc Godard during the same period, such as Anna Karina's melodramatic heroine Nana in *Vivre sa vie* (*My Life to Live*, 1962), although Godard becomes increasingly critical of his protagonists as the decade progresses (see his viciously critical gaze toward women in *Luttes en Italie* from 1971, discussed in the next chapter). On the other hand, the all-too-common trope of the woman, uniquely used to play out these complex metaphors in postwar society, can tend toward misogyny—a crucial problem for Godard as well. This objectifying gaze is especially clear in Kuroki's butterfly girl, who flits about as a human, apparently content to be a personification of grace and beauty.

Likewise, just as actresses such as Jane Fonda criticized Godard's misogyny on set, Raine notes that several of the filmmakers described in this chapter had rather problematic and unethical interactions with their female stars. For instance, Imamura was known to bully the pregnant Hidari Sachiko. As Raine notes, although Hidari was part of the New Left generation and shared the anger of Imamura's activist compatriots, she also regarded him as a male chauvinist.[75] Similarly, political filmmakers adjacent to this grouping, such as Ogawa's filmmaking collective Ogawa Pro, were known to use women in their filmmaking collectives almost exclusively as personal assistants, maids, and secretaries. This misogyny was even explicitly addressed by the documentary filmmaker Hara Kazuo, who criticized Ogawa Pro for their unequal treatment of women.[76]

This chauvinism, however, is somewhat complicated by the certain published works of documentary film theory during this period. Works that might appear sexist were often intended as the reverse: the aforementioned Matsukawa Yasuo, who titled his review of Imamura's film "A Masculine Reflection (*danseiteki hansei*) on *Nippon konchūki*," fills his review with vast and problematic generalizations about masculinity and femininity, but ends up praising Imamura's film for showing us "women with a crotch," by which he means powerful and even abrasive women such as Tome.[77] Matsumoto Toshio likewise heaps praises upon Simone de Beauvoir's feminist treatise *The Second Sex* (1949) before using women's emancipation as a metaphor for the "easy and uncreative slavery" of vulgar "prostitute craftsmen" of cinema—entirely ignoring, seemingly, the plight of actual women.[78]

Indeed, the lived experience of women, rather than a symbolic Japan as woman, often seems to evade many of the theorists and filmmakers associated with the allegorical semi-documentary. And of course one cannot forget that the directors of this genre have all been men—albeit men such as Kuroki and Hani, whose rather tender films strive toward humanitarian and political concerns. Thus, although the films are firmly situated within leftist cinema, one must acknowledge that their gender politics leaves much to be desired. Furuhata discusses this tension between revolutionary politics and gender with regard to the Japanese sexploitation genre of pink film, noting, with feminist film scholar Saito Ayako, that women's bodies in the work of pink film auteur Wakamatsu Kōji "are frequently put on screen simply to provide a blank canvas on which to paint vivid pictures of social contradictions."[79]

Yet many of these social contradictions can also be seen in France, as the earlier comparisons to Jean-Luc Godard can attest. Thus the next chapter brings the issue of gender directly into play by analyzing the role of pleasure and sexuality in the films of Jean-Luc Godard after May 1968—a period that saw a shift away from what Godard called "bourgeois modes of representation" and into more experimental territory, emblematic of antifascist avant-garde.

4 1969 France

UNPLEASURE AND RADICAL EPISTEMOLOGY
IN POST-MAY GODARD

FORM AGAINST FEELING

In 1970, *nouvelle vague* director and *enfant terrible* Jean-Luc Godard visited the Berkeley campus. The then forty-year old was on a tour with the twenty-nine-year old Jean-Pierre Gorin, a militant Marxist-Leninist and supporter of the Union de la Jeunesse Communiste Marxiste-Léniniste (Young Marxist-Leninist Communist League, or UJCML). Godard had fallen out with the journal *Cahiers du cinéma*, the bastion of auteur theory and arthouse cinema where he and many other New Wave filmmakers started their careers with film criticism—including François Truffaut, with whom he had also cut ties. For Godard, *Cahiers* was insufficiently militant and overly reliant on "bourgeois" cinematic forms. After the revolution of May 1968, Godard sought a more radical and destabilizing mode of filmmaking and a rupture from his previous work. Where Godard saw in the militant Gorin a "good" political collaborator in order to continue his work in cinema, Gorin needed the cinema to pursue his revolutionary practice.[1] The two joined forces in 1969 to start the DVG, a collaborative filmmaking experiment. Although other contributors certainly existed—for instance, Gérard Martin, Armand Marco, Nathalie Billard, and Jean-Henri Roger— the "group," as many attested, was essentially Godard and Gorin.

The two comrades were on a whirlwind tour of the United States to raise funds for the next batch of DVG films. The mood of their visit, however, was sour, and mired in controversy. Film critic Michael Goodwin wrote the following on Godard's historic visit, in an unpublished draft of an article that would eventually be printed in the journal *Take One*:

> The first session with Godard and Gorin took place in New York City, at the time when the astronauts were circling back around the moon with the air running out. "I hope they die," said Godard. It shocked me—since I was essentially a flower child, and wished ill to no man—but I tried to suppress the reaction. Godard was, after all, a Revolutionary, and furthermore a man who I thought (and think) one of the greatest film makers alive. I didn't want to come on in a counter-revolutionary manner (I mean, I have long hair, I call cops "pigs" sometimes, I know the rap) so I said, "Right on!"[2]

This paragraph did not find itself into the published article, as the editors were understandably wary of associating the famous *nouvelle vague* director with wishing death onto astronauts, bourgeois or not. Although this anecdote does not comment on Godard's filmmaking practice, it unveils a rejection of affect, feeling, and pleasure that stands at odds with a certain strand of revolutionary counterculture in the wake of May 1968. A "flower child" would find little in the DVG films to latch onto; so too would a "free love" partisan. Raphaël Jaudon, in his study of the "politics of the erotic" in the DVG films, argues that these films equate capitalism with fascism, and fascism with pornography: the objectification of bodies, and women's bodies in particular.[3] As he notes, Godard finds himself "stretched between the necessary (Marxist) denunciation of the commodification of the body, and the hope of a (revolutionary) reinvention of cinematographic eroticism."[4] Yet I go further than Jaudon in arguing that Godard's Marxist critique of the pornographic also coincided with a rejection of sensorial affect, and placed Godard in opposition to the *jouissance*-oriented pleasure politics in the wake of May 1968. The result is films that are resolutely anti-pleasurable, and their "politics of the erotic" become a sticking point in our understanding of revolutionary filmmaking. If the "free love" "flower child" ideology of the late 1960s needed to be questioned, the DVG films do not provide the viewer with a viable alternative.

In his attempt to throw himself into leftist struggle and shrug off the "bourgeois" films of the early 1960s, Godard crafted films that were often misunderstood in their abrasive quality. The revolutionary upheavals surrounding May 1968 demanded a complete reorganization of life as well as art and created an impetus for the development of a radical film practice. Journals such as *Cinéthique* and *Cahiers du cinéma* responded to this challenge by critically examining all aspects of existing film production through the lens of revolutionary anti-capitalism. *Cinéthique* especially was founded directly in opposition to the "bourgeois" filmmaking symbolized by *Cahiers* and was dominated by a "culture of virulent polemic."[5] As Paul Thomas Grant writes in reference to statements by *Cinéthique* cofounder Jean-Paul Fargier, "*Cinéthique* wished to think of itself as the cultural branch of a future Marxist-Leninist communist party."[6] The editors reexamined many debates conducted in the immediate postrevolutionary period in the USSR: about questions of the proletariat versus the intelligentsia, attitudes to "classical" (i.e., bourgeois) art, and the necessity to develop new aesthetic forms. The French critics were also engaged with other radical writings of Europe in the 1930s, especially Bertolt Brecht and Walter Benjamin.[7]

Godard and Gorin's DVG was the prototypical representative of revolution in practice for these critics. However, despite the moniker, the group's films seem extremely unlike Vertov's own filmmaking. MacKay notes that filmmakers Elizaveta Svilova and Sergei Yutkevich and scholar Sergei Drobashenko severely criticized Godard's use of Vertov's name, labeling Godard overly individualistic. Vertov's brother Boris Kaufman even considered suing Godard for misuing Vertov's name.[8] At the time, Vertov was most associated with Jean Rouch and Edgar Morin, who coined the term *cinéma-vérité* after *Kino-Pravda*, and communist film critic Georges Sadoul, singularly responsible for disseminating discussion of Vertov's films in France in the early to mid-1960s. Yet the ultraleft *Cinéthique* would lampoon any connection between Vertov and Sadoul as "*les pires sadouleries*" or "the worst *Sadouleries*"—a pun on Sadoul's name with *saleries*, or filth.[9]

Vertov was obsessively invoked in the film journalism of post–May 1968. *Cinéthique* editors Jean-Paul Fargier and Gérard Leblanc even cotaught a class on Vertov at the experimental "Paris 8" university in 1971—only their second, and despite having no academic credentials.[10] Neither *cinéma-vérité* nor *Cinéthique*, however, analyzed the affective aspects of Vertovian filmmaking, what Vertov and other early Soviets described as *kinooshchushchenie*. As Vertov writes: "The main and essential thing: CINEMATIC SENSATION (*KINOOSHCHUSHCHENIE*) OF THE WORLD."[11] Although this chapter does not contrast *Cinéthique* and Godard's work with Vertov's own at length, pairing them uncovers a crucial Achilles heel in the post-May ultraleft in France, which also aligned with the discomfort described by Goodwin's aforementioned anecdote at Berkeley: a rejection of affect and pleasure as mere spectacle and bourgeois ideology. What Godard and *Cinéthique* did share with Vertov, however, was a deep concern with epistemological inquiry. In Godard as in Vertov, access to a single objective truth is constantly thwarted, resulting in what D. N. Rodowick, following Annette Michelson, describes as the "critique of illusionism" and the "epistemological break" in political modernism.[12] This aligns with what Michelson calls Vertov's "speed, complexity, formal virtuosity, 'obscurity'—that produced the shock, the scandal, the bewilderment in its beholders . . . disrupting systematically the process of identification and participation."[13]

This chapter analyzes the sexual politics and critique of "truth"-telling reportage in rarely addressed films in Godard's oeuvre from the DVG period, stretching from 1969 to 1972: *British Sounds* (1969), *Luttes en Italie* (*Struggle in Italy*, 1971), and *Vladimir et Rosa* (1971). One might imagine this chapter a counterpart to Daniel Fairfax's *Red Years of Cahiers*, which examined these turbulent years in the journal's run; here, I focus more exclusively on *Cinéthique*, rival "ultraleftist" (and avowedly Marxist) film journal. *Cinéthique* identified strongly with Godard's filmmaking during the DVG period; in issue 5, its first truly Marxist issue, editor Gérard Leblanc labeled Godard's post-1968 films "the representation of the Revolution in cinema."[14] Fairfax notes *Cinéthique* continued to be the recipient of Godard's favor after his fallout with *Cahiers*, as the ultraleftist journal screened his films at public events and published his statements; the journal even frequently discussed its own *contradiction groupe Dziga Vertov-Cinéthique*, referring to itself in the third person in a Maoist self-critical vein.[15] In fact, the journal identified with the DVG so strongly that it saw in Godard's work a corrective to perceived faults in Vertov's filmmaking.[16] This chapter thus looks at the film theorist Godard and the film theory journal *Cinéthique* in tandem; it is informed by the film-philosophy work of D. N. Rodowick and Nico Baumbach and buttressed by Godard scholarship by Marc Cerisuelo, Tim Corrigan, Raphaël Jaudon, and Paul Douglas Grant. However, this chapter offers a contemporary perspective informed by intersectional feminist and anti-racist scholarship. It does not seek to "cancel" Godard but to work *with* his filmmaking and film theory to untangle its strategies and find alternative possibilities and futures of reception.

What resulted from Godard's interaction with Vertov's oeuvre after May 1968 is a series of highly, and increasingly, insular theoretical (*Cinéthique*) and film texts (Godard) that rejected audience pleasure (lest they be labeled "spectacle"—and indeed Godard claimed, "I more or less agree with the situationists. . . . [I]t gets integrated in spectacle; it's all spectacle").[17] Indeed, *Cinéthique* was so critical of any inkling of spectacle that the journal was entirely devoid of art or imagery, despite ostensibly being a film journal. After *Cinéthique* lambasted *Cahiers* issue 217 for its "decorative" qualities—"laid out not to be read, but skimmed, leafed through (*feuilleté*)"—*Cahiers* pared back the illustrative qualities of the journal in issue 218 after a four-month gap, the first run of its "Red Years."[18] According to Grant, this rejection of the decorative was the journal's main signal for its Marxist-Leninist political and theoretical development.[19]

The rejection of photography and illustrative design by both Marxist film publications as mere "dressing up" ("*s'habiller*") is directly related to its rejection of (feminized) spectacle.[20] This chapter occasionally returns to, and concludes with, the concept of "dressing up" in the DVG films, as one finds a veritable fixation on the critique of, specifically, women's clothing as emblematic of bourgeois ideology. This is connected to the strong masculinist (and at times explicitly misogynistic) air assumed by DVG-*Cinéthique* during this period; even in Raphaël Jaudon's generally optimistic take on the "innovative" "politics of the erotic" in the DVG, he admits they "exclude the woman's gaze."[21] And as far back as 1980, Laura Mulvey and Colin MacCabe famously criticized Godard's portrayal of woman as sexuality, noting that "her image does not relate to women but is a phantasm of the male unconscious."[22] Mulvey, MacCabe, and Jaudon tend to skirt around the issue of pleasure in Godard's filmmaking, but as the films, interviews, and theoretical texts demonstrate, the DVG and their compatriots were extremely antagonistic—if not outright belligerent—toward an affect-driven experience of spectatorship.

In "Godard and Counter-Cinema," Peter Wollen famously names the central characteristics of Godard's "counter-cinematic" approach in the DVG film *Le Vent d'est* (*Wind from the East*, 1970). He lists seven "deadly sins" and then presents their negation as expressed in Godard's DVG filmmaking, creating instead a "virtue": aperture (an open plot construction) instead of closure, foregrounding (obfuscation with literary quotations) instead of transparency, narrative intransitivity (difficult-to-follow plot lines) instead of narrative transitivity.[23] Having myself taught Vertov's filmmaking for over a decade, however, I need only remark on *Chelovek s kinoapparatom*'s role as a perennial classroom favorite to argue that, for Vertov, such disruptions did not necessarily result in "unpleasure"—yet Wollen lists "unpleasure" as a counter-cinematic virtue, with "pleasure" as a sin. Given recent work on "pleasure activism" by adrienne marée brown, drawn from Audre Lorde's writings on the erotic, and Lynne Segal's work on "collective joy" and "radical happiness" within the context of leftist organizing, one might argue that this rejection of pleasure and affect compromises the effectiveness of the DVG's avowedly antifascist and anti-imperialist message.

One might also reasonably argue that there has been quite enough work done on the films of Jean-Luc Godard, in and outside of the academy. Yet the death of the famous iconoclast in September 2022 invites us to a reinvestigation of his filmmaking legacy—one that does not throw out the proverbial baby with the bathwater but also resists the hagiographic impulse. Indeed, the contemporary attention to intersectional feminism, queer studies, and Black studies has much to teach us as we reexamine revolutionary movements of yore, especially a movement that skewed, at least in its public perception, so heavily white, male, and bourgeois. The comparison to Black studies is also especially apropos for Godard, who aimed to collaborate with, and provide a platform for, the Black Panthers in his DVG films; plus, the last completed DVG film, *Vladimir et Rosa*, explicitly addresses and critiques American racism in connection to fascism. One imagines, optimistically, given the DVG-*Cinéthique*'s investment in auto-critique, that the late director might even welcome such a comparison despite the evident discomfort it might entail.

It is not all doom and gloom, however; as I will show, even with the clear difference between Vertov's films and those of the DVG, both are invested in a fundamentally anti-imperialist and antifascist mode of filmmaking that is basically epistemological through its disruption of conventional filmmaking techniques—even if the films fail at the level of audience affective mobilization and engagement. These are not fun films, nor are they meant to be. In Irmgard Emmelhainz's words, the films of the DVG "address the viewer didactically and in a Brechtian vein, and consider him or her an active agent in the decodification of the movie."[24] To watch a DVG film is to engage in *work*. In their ability to challenge seemingly objective political and historical truths, the DVG films perform a Marxist-Leninist pedagogy of media literacy—of "active decodification"—that emerged explicitly out of the post-May '68 moment.

GODARD BETWEEN DOCUMENTARY AND THE AVANT-GARDE

To a certain extent, the media portrayals surrounding Godard and the DVG overshadowed the long history of militant Left filmmaking already underway for many years by the Left Bank of the *nouvelle vague*, including Chris Marker, Agnès Varda, and Alain Resnais. Godard spoke little of Varda and Resnais during his DVG period, but he admired Marker greatly, although always bemoaning his ties to the French Communist Party. As Godard exclaimed in 1970: "We are trying to make a real Marxist-Leninist out of [Chris Marker], and get him to stop working for the French Communist Party. It is very difficult."[25] One can argue that DVG films, all of which can be interpreted as avant-garde documentaries, share with Marker and Varda a questioning of "truth telling" within cinema and media and a reflexive unveiling of the cinematic apparatus. Yet Godard's avant-garde documentaries go further in the sphere of experimentation and abstraction than Marker and Varda by explicitly approaching the strategy of Situationist *détournement*—an untranslatable term meaning something akin to "rerouting" or "hijacking." As Baumbach writes, these strategies, such as repetition and stoppage, intend to interrupt—to reorient or reroute—the contemporary circulation of information and advertising that philosopher Alain Badiou called "the ideological indicators of our epoch."[26] Godard's complex and difficult works from the late 1960s to the early 1970s interrupt the dominant societal narrative of the era through aesthetic strategies such as quotation, perceptual rupture, and constant self-analysis and self-criticism.

Key to this rupture is a refusal to treat fiction and nonfiction as strict binaries, and Godard was heavily invested in this concept even early in his career. In an interview with *Cahiers* in December 1962, shortly before the official release of his most explicitly political film to date—*Le petit soldat*, on the use of torture during the Algerian War—he stated: "I believe that I generally start from the documentary to give it the truth of fiction (*pour lui donner la vérité de la fiction*)."[27] This phrasing is more complicated than it might at first seem and is almost an oxymoron: one expects a filmmaker to use documentary to give truth *to* fiction (*pour donner la vérité à la fiction*), but the use of *de* rather than *à* declares truth to be a trait inherent in the fictional. This is a typical Godardian rhetorical strategy in which he declares the seeming opposite to be true of our habitual responses; the rug is always pulled out from below.

In the same interview he notes the oft-repeated statement that film has two sides: the "*côté spectacle*" of Méliès and the "*côté recherche*" of Lumière. This statement echoes Matsumoto Toshio, who saw his "neo-documentary" works of the early 1960s as a dialectic between the "thesis" of Lumière and the "antithesis" of Méliès. Godard, however, claims he wants to make a film "*de recherche sous forme de spectacle*"—research in the form of a spectacle.[28] In other words, a documentary in the form of a fictional film. Godard's *nouvelle vague* films from the early to mid-1960s might be productively compared with the "semi-documentaries" of Japanese mid-1960s filmmakers such as Imamura Shōhei and Hani Susumu. As Michel Delahaye wrote in 1966, "The truth that Godard extracts from beings is that of a truth stretched between document and fiction."[29]

Godard's trajectory, however, skewed increasingly toward documentary—a fact noted in film journalism of the period. Antoine de Baecque even considers *Masculin Féminin* from 1966 the last film of a *cinéma-vérité* "trilogy," with Rouch and Morin's *Chronique d'un été* from 1961 and Chris Marker's *Le Joli Mai* from 1963 as the first two components.[30] In terms of Godard's film form, the rejection of "bourgeois filmmaking" after May 1968 was less a stark rupture than a slow progression from the exuberant (yet conservative-leaning, what Fairfax calls "quasi-fascistic")

Hollywood-obsessed cinephilia of the early *Cahiers* years, to the wholesale rejection of classic narrative film form in *Le Vent d'est*.[31]

Importantly, Godard's increasing engagement with contemporary sociopolitical affairs modes aligned with a more experimental narrative structure. As Sylvain Godet noted in *Cahiers* upon the release of *2 ou 3 choses que je sais d'elle* (*2 or 3 Things I Know About Her*) in 1967, his most documentarian film to date: "The more Godard interests himself in the most immediate social reality, the less realistic his films become."[32] This avant-gardism coincides with an increasingly marginal status: as the *Cahiers* editors explain in a 1972 exegesis of the DVG films, compared to the films that came before, they are radically on the fringes of both the market and leftist organizations. They do not follow any specific political line, nor do they serve as the mouthpiece for any specific political organization—neither Gorin's UJCML nor the PCMLF (*Parti communiste marxiste-léniniste de France*), although their "Marxist-Leninism" skews heavily Maoist. As the editors of *Cahiers* write, "The marked autonomy of the Dziga Vertov Group is of course no coincidence."[33] This emphasis on individual autonomy is both their strength and downfall, and a certain political purity and asceticism would lead to films that, alas, are chronically underseen and little appreciated.

The rest of this chapter analyzes (un)pleasure and the avant-garde documentary form in post-May Godard and the DVG productions. I focus here on three films associated with Godard's DVG period that are more explicitly oriented around the question of gender and (un)pleasure: *British Sounds*, *Luttes en Italie*, and *Vladimir et Rosa*. Taken together, these three films demonstrate a rejection of "feelings" and a domesticity associated with women's concerns. Such a rejection, however, is juxtaposed with a strong antifascism expressed diegetically in each film. The result is a contradiction: on the one hand, the films echo a "sadomasochistic aesthetic" described by Matsumoto Toshio, which joins external with internal self-criticism in content as in form. On the other hand, in denying the audience the complex affective pleasure produced by Matsumoto's experimental editing, Godard's version of "sadomasochism" rejects desire and results in a formal asceticism. This asceticism, as we will see, is largely the source of the sense of "failure" that surrounds these films and places them in sharp contrast to many of the other films discussed in this book.

BRITISH SOUNDS AND THE ORGANIZATION OF DISCOMFORT

While *British Sounds* is not officially the first film of the DVG, it was codirected by Godard with the collaboration of Jean-Henri Roger (with whom he would also work on the first DVG film, 1969's *Pravda*); the directors are credited as "Comrades of the Dziga Vertov Group." Given the attention the film pays to issues relevant to May 1968, including "hippie" "flower children" in contrast to workers, as well as its investment in epistemology and use of sexual imagery, it is part and parcel of the more canonical DVG films. While Godard would continue his investigation into "truth" and "reality" within the limits of cinema and television in his films with Anne-Marie Miéville after the collapse of the DVG—the 1976 *Ici et ailleurs*, which used footage from the unrealized film on Palestine, *Jusqu'à la victoire*, is notable in this regard—the DVG films attempt to embody their Marxist-Leninist principles in the fabric of film form. After *Un film comme les autres* (*A Film Like the Others*, 1968), which grappled with the events of May 1968 using techniques of distancing plus footage of the May protests, the 1969 *British Sounds* exemplifies Godard's trajectory of abstraction and unpleasure, while also becoming increasingly concerned with the ethics of documentary film. It also functions alongside the later DVG films because of its focus on *place*: here, Britain, but later, Czechoslovakia (*Pravda*), Italy (*Luttes en Italie*), the United States (*Vladimir et Rosa*), and the aforementioned film on Palestine (*Jusqu'à la victoire*). One might consider them, strangely, Marxist-Leninist travelogues, *Petites planètes* but almost entirely devoid of exotic images.

British Sounds was funded by the BBC, although it was ultimately rejected.[34] It does not have a stable plot structure and instead depicts a series of vignettes, brought together not by their "image" but by their "sound": a man and woman reciting incendiary political statements, as well as a young child reciting historical "lessons" about militant leftism throughout European history (in Tom Luddy's words, "the voice of a little girl memorizing her Marxist catechism").[35] The film is actually quite rigidly organized. Generally, there are six main sequences illustrating the different "British sounds": a factory, women, capitalists, workers, students, and finally, the sound of the Revolution. It also functions as an essentially epistemological exercise by refusing to acknowledge an image as stable or "truthful" and deconstructs the basic premise of conventional documentary.

The bulk of the film is compiled of what appears to be nonacted documentary footage captured in the United Kingdom. For instance, the beginning of the film depicts a factory and incorporates a great deal of the sounds created by the machines within it—hence, *British Sounds*. This scene prioritizes the slow pan, a popular technique in Direct Cinema, and one that Bazin favors as exemplifying a sense of realism. Yet this is complicated by the extremely jarring sound of machinery, also present in earlier Godard films such as *2 ou 3 choses* but here brought to its audial extreme; the seemingly unending sound appears to physically attack the viewer, provoking extreme displeasure. It is an act of violence upon the viewer that is unique and original in the history of documentary.

The film continues its cacophonous take on documentary cinema by including more apparent actuality footage, but with a twist: the next "sound" the film presents is an angered crowd of disgruntled working-class British citizens, arguing for socialism against capitalism and discussing their struggle. The film presents this debate between workers from a "fly-on-the-wall" observational perspective, yet this scene is intercut with scenes in which Godard's voice and politics are made clear: alongside silent actuality footage of British laborers, such as street construction workers, the viewer hears the unmistakable French-accented sound of Godard's voice, whispering "organize!" "unite!" and "strike!" Godard's film uses seemingly conventional observational techniques and subverts them to craft a Marxist-Leninist ideological treatise.

However, the film also uses a significant number of staged or acted scenes. Another "sound" is a television pundit launching into a long tirade against everything leftists hold dear, an explicitly neofascist discourse that reaches such bloodthirsty heights, it exceeds even the rhetoric of ultraconservative pundits. Other scenes in the film defy categorization as fiction or nonfiction; in perhaps its most famous sequence, the film depicts an unapologetic shot of a woman's pubic area for a total of two minutes. The long, single take in medium shot is meant to render the viewer purposefully, and deeply, uncomfortable. Jaudon writes that Godard associated pornography and fascism after 1968, and that *British Sounds* attempts to block the audience's libidinal investment in the naked female

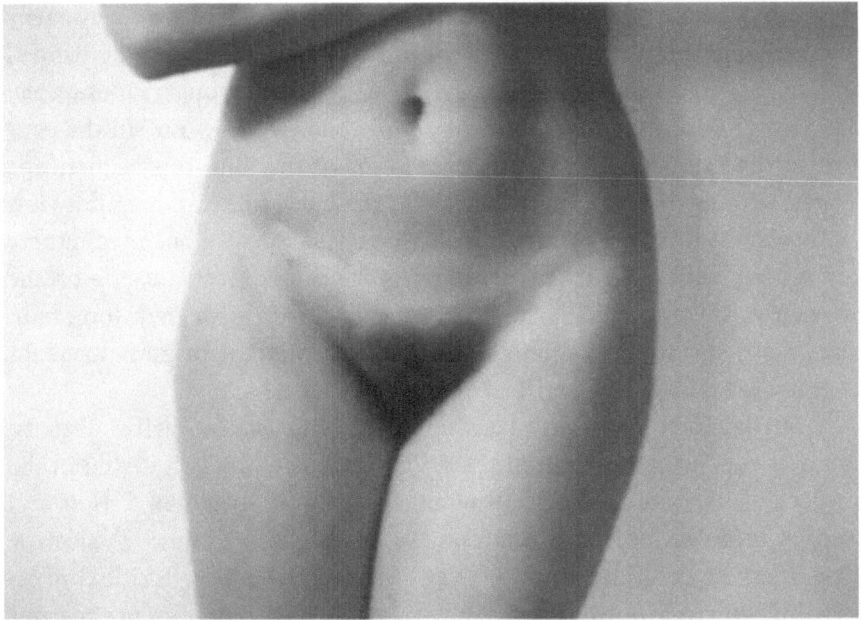

Figure 19. Two-minute-long shot of nude woman's body, in Jean-Luc Godard and Jean-Henri Roger's *British Sounds*, 1969.

body.[36] While the majority of critics note the scene's upending of the erotic gaze, it is worth pointing out that it is not entirely at odds with Linda Williams's analysis of pornography as a "sadistic" body genre, its "being marked, rather, by the prolongation of desire," its emphasis on excess, its "gross" qualities—although "gross" here is more aligned with its form, in its uncomfortable temporal elongation.[37] Likewise, denying the viewer an image of the woman's face might block what John Paul Sadler describes as the view of the woman's pleasure in pornography, but I also do not believe this de facto entails a feminist ethos.[38] While Godard attempted to deplete this shot of eroticism, thus forcing the viewer to confront their own biases, the success of this tactic might conceivably be questioned. Arguably, Godard's persistent use of women to allegorize larger social issues is endemic to not only the DVG period but his filmmaking writ large.

It is therefore important to treat, briefly, the last "sound" of the film, before its iconic concluding scene of a series of fists punching through the Union Jack: the sound of a group of young British hippies, primarily women, listening to Beatles records and working together to transform the lyrics of songs such as "Hello, Goodbye" into leftist songs: for example, "You say Nixon, I say Mao" instead of "You say yes, I say no." In the context of the militancy of the earlier sections of the film, this sequence is tinged with irony and even comedy, and the viewer cannot help but view the decidedly hip young activists from a critical angle. Yet once again there is a misogynistic twist to this critique, as the camera rests its gaze on the women in this sequence, who dominate the frame with their long hair, shag vests, and round Lennon glasses, and become the primary locus for the viewer's questioning, critical, and ironic gaze.

Contributing to this critical gesture is the film's extreme self-reflexivity, another central component of the DVG films: the film is invested in the project of its own making and offers the division between fiction and nonfiction as an object of analysis. As a voice-over states: "Dialectics. Documentary. Fiction. People's War." It is also explicitly critical of its funding source, the BBC, which might have been one of many reasons for the network's rejection. As the voice-over in *British Sounds* intones: "Television and film do not record moments of reality but simply dialectics, areas of contradictions." One might question, however, whether the autonomous, marginal films of the DVG are able to accomplish their "people's war" without access to the very people whose revolution they are proferring, given its rejection by the BBC. Like the uncomfortable pornography (according to Williams's definition) of a naked woman displayed unceremoniously for the audience's gaze, it remains, fundamentally, a contradiction.

DOMESTIC AND POLITICAL STRUGGLES IN *LUTTES EN ITALIE*

In the subsequent two years, the films of the DVG began to skew increasingly in favor of the abstract and auto-critical. *Luttes en Italie*, like all films of the DVG, emphasizes disorientation and Brechtian alienation. I analyze this film as it highlights the role of gender and (un)pleasure more than the previous films of the DVG, *Pravda* and *Le Vent d'est*, although all films of the DVG orient around the concept of epistemological struggle. Like other films of the DVG, *Luttes en Italie* struggled (pun not intended) to find an audience; it was rejected by RAI, despite the Italian television broadcasting company having commissioned and funded its production. In the film, a militant leftist student, Paola, finds work in a garment factory and attempts to radicalize the workers there; upon reflection, and with the film's aid, she slowly realizes how her actions are still tied to bourgeois culture, and she takes steps to correct them (although the film does not show how Paola's new understanding is embodied in radically different forms of behavior). The film does not incorporate much documentary footage aside from B-roll of workers in a factory, but it does appear to document the increasing radicalization of a real-life student.

This access to the "real," however, is persistently questioned, not least by Paola herself, who breaks the fourth wall and addresses the audience: "It wasn't the real me [that you saw], just a reflection." This dichotomy between the real and the reflection, the *réel* and the *reflet*, is the idée fixe of DVG-*Cinéthique* overall. As Comolli, Narboni, and others write in *Cahiers*: "This film produces a political/philosophical critique of 'the innocence of seeing', of the myths of evidence and immediate knowledge, of direct access to the real, which ideologically define empiricism, spontaneism ... and which structure most cinematographic fictions."[39] Like other DVG films, then, the film emphasizes the impossibility "of direct access to the real," criticizing "the innocence of seeing" associated, of course, with conventional reportage and documentary, as well as Direct Cinema. In its denial of "the myths of evidence and immediate knowledge," the film embodies an epistemological struggle—also one that connects the DVG's work to that of Vertov. This struggle is enacted through a dialectic, which is synthesized by Paola's—and the film's—investigation of theory and practice in the latter half of the film. This organization echoes the structure of *Le Vent d'est*, Godard's earlier film *Le Gai Savoir* (1969), and many subsequent DVG films: image/sound organization leads to their criticism and deconstruction, and then finally new images/sounds are created. It also echoes the writing of *Cinéthique*, which carries out its own relentless auto-critique. And *Cinéthique* likewise saw the connection to Vertov: "*Luttes en Italie* [is] no stranger to Vertov's work. ... [T]hese are linked practices, articulated in the same work ... working according to structurally analogous productive processes ... of different materials and sets."[40] According to *Cinéthique*, *Luttes en Italie* is distinguished from Vertov because of their different historical conditions: the dictatorship of the proletariat in the USSR and the state monopoly capitalist regime in France in 1970. These historical differences result in their differences in form.

The film incorporates both French and Italian, which overlap and often remain untranslated. In fact, in contrast to most dubbed films, this DVG film lays bare their difference. The audience hears both delivered at different moments and is thus able to recognize certain inevitable gaps in translation. The voice-over is delivered in a bland, affect-less tone, meant to emotionally distance the viewer from the context to which they have become habituated. Similarly, the film's shot sequences, in which the camera is almost completely static, are often separated by solid black and solid red screens. The second and third sections attempt to "fill the black" with more appropriate revolutionary imagery, such as a factory, to link the film with its own means of production. The brief fourth section is a meta-critique of the film and is almost entirely composed of these red and black frames. Thus the film follows a general DVG-*Cinéthique* dialectical structure: unity (thesis), to critique (anti-thesis), to auto-critique (synthesis), and back to unity.

The film follows the anti-imperialist, antifascist zeitgeist of 1968 by focusing entirely on *personal* transformation as vital to class struggle. As we have seen in the previous chapters, this necessity to integrate revolutionary behavior into the personal is crucial to the political framework of the era and is exemplified in Japanese and French avant-garde documentary production from the period. *Luttes en Italie* is part and parcel of this tendency. As the film describes in its fourth and last section, it aims to allow the viewer to *pensée autrement*—to think otherwise—in order to join the revolution. The revolutionary sphere of the personal necessarily includes self-awareness and self-reflection. As Paola informs the viewer in her concluding remarks, "I had to stop talking about myself."

However, Paola does not seem to be doing much talking about herself at all. The film assigns meaning *to* her character and aligns her with modes of domesticity and capitalist accumulation. In an oft-repeated shot, a hand holds a teacup in the lower left corner of the frame, while the rest of

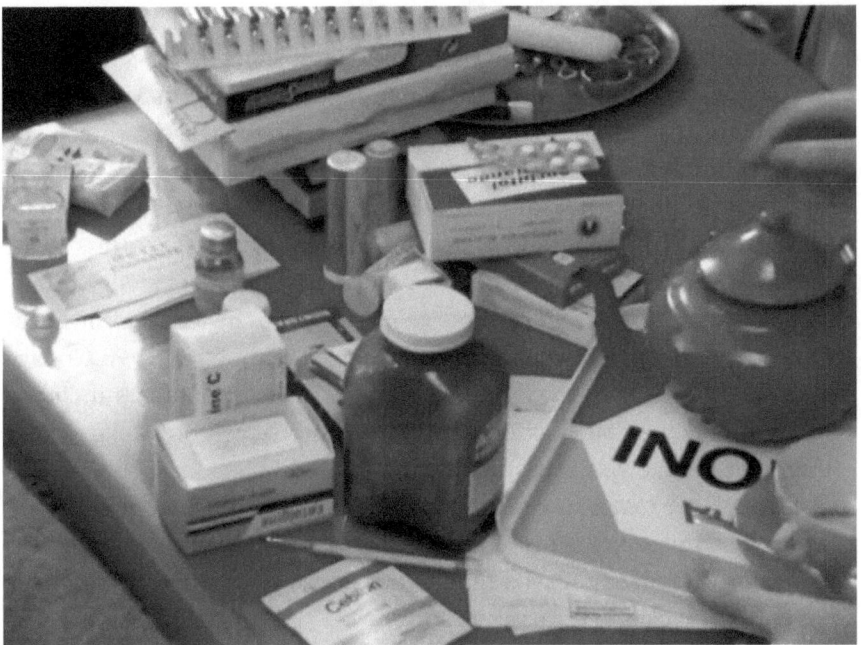

Figure 20. Domestic objects, in the DVG's *Luttes en Italie*, 1970.

the image is a bright red table, upon which various items associated with domesticity are placed: a bright red teapot, matches, cigarettes, books, miscellaneous boxes, and bottles of medicine. Another frequent series of shots shows Paola shopping for dresses in front of a shopkeeper (Anne Wiazemsky). At one point she even argues over the price of a peasant-style dress, stating that the price need not be so high for such a simple and rustic style.

The first section of the film places an emphasis on bourgeois domesticity, and the human element (a hand, a face) is often overshadowed by objects of daily life. This recalls films such as Agnès Varda's *Le Bonheur* (1965), which places images associated with domestic bliss—lush bouquets of flowers, especially, but also teacups, lamps, and other decorative objects—in center frame. Both Varda and Godard share revolutionary politics (as *Le Bonheur*'s tragic ending shows, there is a darkness behind apparent domestic utopia), but in contrast to Varda's elegant portrayals of woman as domesticity, Godard's shots of the same objects feel cluttered and even sinister. They are also juxtaposed with shots of the female Italian protagonist facing the camera directly, repeating militant Marxist propaganda, like the child in *British Sounds* repeating a Marxist catechism. Even in this short section, a contradiction between form and content is already made apparent; a militant reciting quotes from Althusser should not, theoretically, be haggling over the price of a peasant-style dress in the same breath. A rift is formed between her militancy, as evidenced literally *en face* the camera, and the bourgeois existence she leads in the background. The domestic is meant to be criticized and neutralized. Godard shares this criticism of the domestic with militant filmmakers in Japan contemporaneously, such as Adachi Masao and Ogawa Shinsuke, whose gender politics likewise leave much to be desired.

An analysis of *Luttes en Italie* finds that more than 10 percent of the entire film is composed of shots of Paola trying on clothes, paying for clothes, and putting on makeup. Given that an enormous percentage of the film is composed of black and red screens and worker radicalization, this emphasis on dress is substantial. It is also noteworthy that the majority of this 10 percent, comprising 6.5 minutes overall, occurs during the first and second parts of the film, the ones most "criticized" by the directors. That the film aligns Paola's "revisionism" and lack of true revolutionary fervor with the act of *s'habiller* is not an accident; in *2 ou 3 choses*, Godard likewise links fashionable clothing with "neocapitalism" and prostitution through Marina Vlady's/Juliette Janson's engaging in sex work to purchase the latest Paco Rabanne dresses.[41] As noted previously, DVG-*Cinéthique* persistently matched the "decorative" with capitalism, even down to the ascetic and literally iconoclastic layouts of the *Cinéthique* journal in which no images appear (until the late 1970s).

Each time I watch *Luttes en Italie* I cannot help, as a woman-identified viewer, feeling extreme discomfort at the activities the film rejects as unmilitant and bourgeois, such as shopping for clothes. One wonders, indeed, how Godard and Gorin are able to clothe and bathe themselves without at least a temporary foray into the capitalist marketplace. In an interview with Laura Mulvey and Colin MacCabe, Godard compared filmmaking to making a salad, saying "you cannot do both": "I try to make pictures like other people cook. . . . That's why I say to Anne-Marie [Miéville], 'finding the money to make a movie is the same as making a salad for you.'"[42] One wonders whether Miéville would have in fact preferred making a film to making a salad.

The act of sex does not fare much better. In the film, discussions of sex are not avoided but remain relatively puritanical: a shot of a door, slightly ajar, behind which is a couple, off-screen. The voiceover states: "In an attempt to make love better, you do it in the afternoon. Because you have nothing to do you make love in the afternoon. We should ask ourselves why we have time to make love in the afternoon?" Discussions of leisure and pleasure as good in and of themselves are absent. As Jaudon points out, *Luttes en Italie* presents "a question of sex from a social, structural Marxist point of view"; here "no part of a naked body, and *a fortiori* no sexual activity, appears in the film."[43] The film's relative prudishness and asceticism, combined with its criticism of the "bourgeois" and "decorative," was also common in Japan, where the ill-fated Left terrorist organization United Red Army was organizing members. In the Asama Sansō incident perpetrated by the United Red Army—depicted in Wakamatsu Kōji's "docudrama" *Jitsuroku Rengō Sekigun Asama-Sansō e no Dōtei* (*United Red Army*, 2007)—a woman leader of the radical leftist organization tortures other women in their group for wearing makeup, sleeping with other members, and getting pregnant, deeming these actions counterrevolutionary. Although certain pink "eroduction" films such as Wakamatsu's *Tenshi no kōkotsu* (*Ecstasy of the Angels*, 1972), in which glamorous terrorist revolutionaries express their political commitments through sexual coupling, more ambiguously and playfully depict an overlap between sexual and political freedoms, militants in either Godard or the actual United Red Army do not appear to be sexual beings.

It is also worth noting that, like other DVG films, the ending of *Luttes en Italie* does not show significant material change, although Paola claims to think differently. In a notable scene near the end, Paola places a radical newspaper near a coworker's desk at the garment factory. She begins to read it but then angrily throws it aside after understanding its content—similarly, one would imagine, to RAI rejecting the film reels received from the DVG. The film seems to criticize the efficacy of its own approach, since the worker in the factory is no closer to revolutionary ideals, despite Paola's own apparent auto-criticism. One wonders, then, about the efficacy of such filmmaking, despite its dialectical rigor—and in fact Godard and Gorin appear to ask these self-same questions.

LUDIC ABSURDITY IN *VLADIMIR ET ROSA*

Yet not all DVG films are as dry and critical as *Luttes en Italie*. The group's last film, *Vladimir et Rosa*, abandons militant austerity and introduces a more comedic and lighthearted Brechtianism. Brecht had been a constant referent in all DVG productions, especially from *Le Vent d'est* onward, but *Vladimir et Rosa*'s Brechtian inspiration is the most explicit. As we will see, this film is also the most fervently antifascist of the DVG productions. The connection to Brecht had already been noted by many during the period; as the writers of *Cahiers* note: "Brecht's theories have a decisive importance today in the field of cinema, ideologically and politically. The work of the Dziga Vertov Group has revived its full significance."[44] The film follows Brecht's epic theater by joining issues of contemporary relevance with dramatization and techniques of alienation (the *Verfremdungseffekt*).

The film is a loose parody of the trial of the Chicago Eight, in which a group of American activists were prosecuted for crossing state lines and disrupting the Democratic National Convention in Chicago in 1968. Thus, the film dramatizes a major historical event of the 1960s—a trial—from a very recent past in 1969; the film can be considered "artifactual" (to use Furuhata's productive label, drawn from Derrida), as it directly appropriates and "remediates" topical media events.[45] In this way, it mirrors the "cinema of actuality" characteristic of the Japanese political avant-garde cinema during this same period. Here too, Godard presents a highly timely parody of this extremely high-profile event. Characters seem vaguely reminiscent of their real-life counterparts, with a twist: Black Panther Bobby Seale is Bobby X, and the presiding Judge Hoffman is Judge Himmler (evoking a literal Nazi); two are actresses (Godard's then wife Anne Wiazemsky and Juliet Berto, playing themselves); and others are Godard's own fabrications. The film thus blends a nonfiction element—a real-life trial—with explicitly fictional elements.

The film also happens to be quite funny (at least compared to the other DVG films). While the DVG film *Pravda* also included voice-over

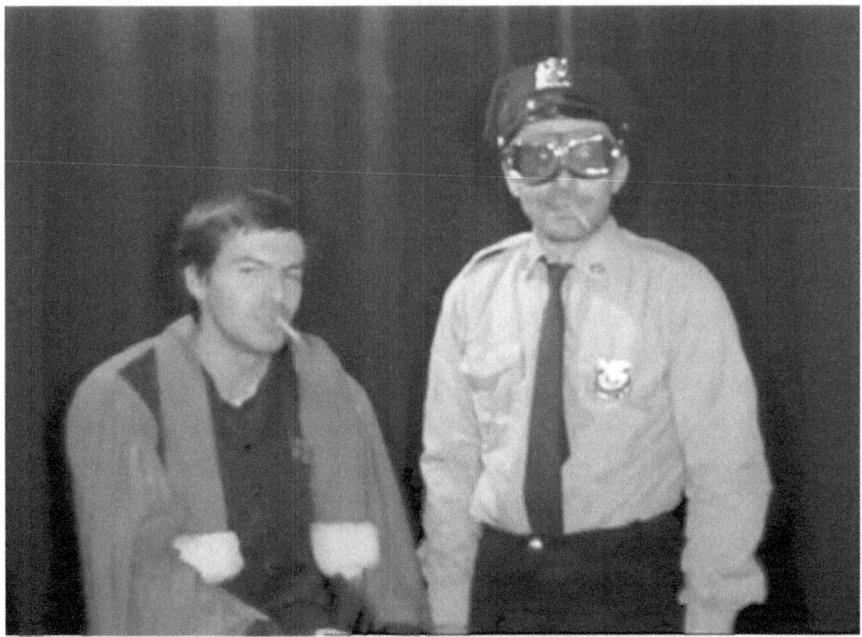

Figure 21. Godard and Gorin as Friedrich Vladimir and Karl Rosa, in the DVG's *Vladimir et Rosa*, 1971.

commentators named Vladimir (after Lenin) and Rosa (after Luxemburg), *Vladimir et Rosa*'s title refers to two fictional characters played by Godard and Gorin: Friedrich Vladimir and Karl Rosa, whose names are an amalgamation of Lenin, Luxemburg, Marx, and Engels. The directors "ham it up" for the camera and are shown (1) stuttering (mostly nonsensically) about political aesthetics, while hovering around the net of a very bourgeois tennis court; (2) jumping and rolling around with an enormous rubber ball; and (3) dressed in either judges' robes (Gorin) or a police uniform with goggles (Godard), while blowing smoke at Judge Himmler.[46] In a moment of almost unbelievably pedestrian humor, Godard unzips his pants, reaches in, and pulls out an enormous wooden police baton. Godard and Gorin even include a brief still of the Marx Brothers, thus supporting the notion that the film is imbued with all kinds of Marxian sensibility, whether Karl's or Groucho's.

The film's ludicrous—thinking through its etymological root, *ludic*—and self-effacing scenes are joined with a firm condemnation of American racism and imperialism as an insidious form of fascism. The term *fascist* and references to Nazis indeed occur in this film more than other DVG films (and possibly, any Godard project save *Histoire(s) du cinéma*). Scenes with "Bobby X," who is mute for the first half of the film and gains his voice in the second, are filled with pathos, and the film demonstrates the unequal treatment Bobby receives compared to the other seven: he is the only figure not released on bail, and his prison sentence is significantly longer. The film also demonstrates Bobby at the receiving end of horrifying police brutality. The film is fiercely and unironically critical of American anti-Blackness, and one is reminded that Godard aimed to platform the Black Panthers while shooting the unrealized documentary collaboration with Direct Cinema pioneers Richard Leacock and D. A. Pennebaker, *One American Movie*, or *One A.M.*, through an interview with Eldridge Cleaver. Sadly, Godard's unwavering support for the Black Panthers contributed to the film's catastrophic result: Godard could not reconcile his persistently auto-critical methodology with the desire to uncritically support the Panthers.[47]

While the film's racial politics are certainly revolutionary for the time, in terms of gender politics, the film remains ambiguous. Wiazemsky's character is a militant feminist, but she is shown in the context of clothing (screenprinting feminist logos on T-shirts) and paramours (blowing kisses to Yves Afonso, also one of the film's Eight). Berto, "a real activist," is praised for her "fighting spirit"—and notably, she is singled out for "being with the Japanese radicals" (referring to the Japanese United Red Army). However, she is shown exhibiting a "free love" lifestyle and living in a collective, demonstrated by a shot of her smoking cigarettes while lying around in a pile of relaxed young activists in hippie clothing. The voice-over asks, "What are the reasons for it?" and directly questions Berto for this choice. Here again we return to a critique of (especially nonmonogamous) "free love" and "feelings" witnessed in the DVG films, for despite the moments of physical comedy witnessed in *Vladimir et Rosa* and a certain Brechtian absurdist affect, its directors are still entirely opposed to "feelings." As Gorin states, "There are no feelings. Absolutely no feelings in Laurel and Hardy, and only a few in Jerry Lewis."[48] To conclude our analysis of the DVG, it is important to return to feelings, to the concept of cinematic pleasure, and to Vertov himself—as indeed it is through the rejection of affect or what Vertov termed "cinematic sensation" (*kinoosh-chushchenie*) that the gap between DVG-*Cinéthique* and the Soviet avant-garde is most evident.

(UN)PLEASURE POLITICS AND THE END OF DVG-*CINÉTHIQUE*

Rodowick notes that Wollen's concept of "counter-cinema," drawn from an exegesis of *Le Vent d'est*, is explicit in its anti-pleasurable provocation. "For Wollen," he writes, "the goal of the modernist text is no longer simply the production of pleasure or narrative entertainment. It equally presents the spectator with contradictions and arguments aimed at unsettling and provoking action in the audience."⁴⁹ This provocation, according to *Cinéthique*, draws from "their multiplicity, their movement, their whirling (*tournoiement*), the films themselves: each shot, each fragment of each film is an object of questioning, study, discussion, knowledge, in its relationship its link to others." This tone of almost breathless infatuation is coupled, mysteriously, with their asceticism: "no more carnal depth of beings" (*plus de profondeur charnelle des êtres*), none of the "bonus of pleasure of the recognition effect" of "dramatic films."⁵⁰

DVG-*Cinéthique* never questioned what Rodowick, referring to Sylvia Harvey's analysis of May 1968 modernist movements, called a "puritanical defense of the 'work' (of reading, of meaning production) ... and an accompanying underestimation of the importance of pleasure and entertainment."⁵¹ *Cinéthique* persistently criticizes audience pleasure and comfort, as evidenced by an early interview between the journal and *cinéma-vérité* pioneer and ethnographer Jean Rouch, in which the two lock horns over the importance of aesthetic dimensions of filmmaking, with *Cinéthique* arguing, exasperatedly, that "aesthetics may simply be the comfort of the spectator."⁵²

What one might call this "ascetic" denial of viewer pleasure would be, I believe, the DVG's downfall. Jean-Luc Godard and Jean-Pierre Gorin disbanded their communist filmmaking collective in 1972, after three tumultuous years of filmmaking. The DVG's contempt for affect (and audience) certainly played a role in the group's disastrous outcome. In the end, aside from a select few American screenings of their films, the public generally ignored them, and the French television studios that helped fund these productions left the many canisters of DVG films unopened. With the exception of those in *Cahiers* and *Cinéthique*, reviews of their films were almost uniformly negative.[53] As David Fresko described in even his generally positive review of a recent retrospective of the films in Brooklyn, "The films ... intimidated audiences with their political modernist aesthetics and doctrinaire hectoring."[54]

As I have shown, this contempt for and denial of pleasure coincided with the DVG's undercurrent of misogyny: their (and *Cinéthique*'s) rejection of all things "decorative" (i.e., feminine), "pleasurable," and "emotional" (de facto associated with the feminine in the DVG works). Jane Fonda, who worked with the two directors for *Tout va bien* (1972), criticized Godard: "To be a revolutionary, you have to be human ... and Godard has contempt for people."[55] Likewise, there is the question of audience: the DVG films continue to be rarely analyzed in the context of Godard's storied career, and perhaps for good reason. The bulk are didactic, difficult, and defined by a Brechtianism striving to alienate the viewer. In fact the works of Bertolt Brecht are exponentially more "fun" than Godard's own work inspired by the German playwright-theorist. As Emmelhainz notes, the DVG films persistently question the representability of political struggle as well as the authorial voice of the filmmaker as the harbinger of political change. In the end, the films leave these questions unanswered, retain a questionable authoritative voice, and appear fundamentally unable to represent political struggle in images that are both cogent and legible for the viewer.[56]

As we have seen, films such as *Luttes en Italie* and *British Sounds* persistently use the female body to allegorize large-scale political problems, often using the figure of the woman to depict largely negative social behaviors. This is in contrast to Japan's problematic use of the woman as an embodiment of national trauma during this period (see 1960s works by Ōshima Nagisa, Imamura Shōhei, and Hani Susumu). Rather, Godard uses the woman to embody the backward and bourgeois. Both Godard and Gorin were notoriously dismissive of what have been unfairly dubbed "women's" concerns, and as Wollen noted, strove to separate the realm of "feelings" from the realm of political militancy. This extreme distaste for "feelings"—especially women's feelings—came to a fore during a Q&A at Berkeley following a rare screening of *British Sounds* in 1970. Tom Luddy notes that when one young woman began a long statement in which she kept returning to her "feelings," Godard yelled: "Fuck your feelings!"[57] One wonders whether Godard would have exclaimed this with such vehemence if its target were male.

Such suspicion of women and women's concerns extends to the last official work affiliated with the DVG, *Letter to Jane* (1972). The film mostly comprises a photographic image of Jane Fonda in Vietnam, with Gorin and Godard supplying fifty-two minutes of oral criticism: a vicious lampooning coupled with visual analysis. The result is nothing short of hateful; in any event, the filmmakers could have chosen both Fonda and Yves Montand, her famous costar in *Tout va bien*, for their scrutiny. Instead, the attacks are leveled at Fonda—a self-proclaimed leftist and humanitarian—and assume her politics are insincere. Unsurprisingly, Fonda is not given a right to respond to these allegations. As Yugoslav filmmaker Dušan Makavejev pithily noted, *Letter to Jane* became "a double rape—two men taking turns assaulting one woman."[58] This treatment of Fonda in *Tout va bien* and *Letter to Jane* reveals a profound misogyny in the DVG and a deeply problematic relation to affective experience.

Although the DVG would give other reasons for splitting—Godard had just spent a year recovering from a serious automobile accident, Jean-Pierre Gorin began making his own films and was burdened by Godard's fame, and Godard appeared to replace his "romance" with Jean-Pierre Gorin with Anne-Marie Melville—the times were simply no longer ripe for their version of militant leftism; the political tide was against them, and the group splintered. Godard and Gorin, having made seven almost entirely invisible works, moved on to other projects and never collaborated again.

More so than the works of other filmmakers described in this book, the DVG films are largely considered failures—not able to be screened nor able to functionally connect with audiences. Baumbach argues that militant "counter-cinema," of which Godard and Gorin's collective is just one example, can only work "within certain situations that are attuned to the nuances of the dominant forms that that they are undermining."[59] In other words, the aesthetic formulas used by the DVG of extreme self-reflexivity, quotation, and audience distancing remain largely illegible even to their most loyal viewers. The "success" of their films was undermined by their explicit rejection of pleasure and the affective mode.

Recent work in queer and Black studies has shown that pleasure need not be disbanded to engage in revolutionary activity. In fact, it requires it. As we will see in the next chapter, other works of the 1960s antifascist avant-garde documentary in Japan embrace a variant of pleasure that engages and activates the spectator. The Japanese example provides an alternative emancipatory politics that mobilizes pleasure rather than rejects it. It is also not a coincidence that many of these works—especially by filmmakers such as Matsumoto Toshio, Terayama Shūji, and Okabe Michio—engage with the late 1960s zeitgeist of sexual liberation, and with queerness in particular. By contrast, Godard does not discuss homosexuality, and pleasure as a potentially revolutionary affect is wholly ignored.

This rejection of pleasure contrasts strongly with what activist and writer adrienne marée brown terms "pleasure activism." Writing on the importance of eroticism (which she carefully separtes from pornography) within the realm of politics, brown exemplifies the careful attention to feeling, affect, and somatization within political organizing in the present day. Their work, which crosses into the realm of conflict mediation through the guidelines of "emergent strategies," aligns with antifascism as this book describes it, and I have personally used their texts in a community-oriented workshop on antifascism. I would argue that brown's work exemplifies a dialectical approach between the psychological and political that continues Mary Watkins and Helene Shulman's earlier work on the "psychologies of liberation."[60]

Such an attention to personal and political liberation has become especially pronounced since the protests against the murder of George Floyd in summer 2020, and in fact Joan Morgan specifically positions "pleasure politics" as "a liberatory, black feminist project."[61] For brown, pleasure activism includes not only the literal erotic but everything from humor to cooking, music and the arts, reading, and even fashion (despite what Godard-Gorin might claim on this particular subject). For brown, "Pleasure activists believe that by tapping into the potential goodness in each of us we can generate justice and liberation, growing a healing abundance where we have been socialized to believe only scarcity exists."[62] Pleasure, then, is an important tool for the revolutionary; for brown, it is the pleasure of those most oppressed by capitalism, racism, and patriarchy that must be prioritized. Here, we might consider that the majority of the DVG-*Cinéthique* audience consisted precisely of those people *least* oppressed in French and North American society at the tail end of the 1960s, despite the connection to the proletariat that the filmmaker-critics so often claim.

In addition, the DVG-*Cinéthique* rejection of the erotic and the pleasurable as mere spectacle or capitalist pornography prevented them from accessing the revolutionary potential of affect. As Audre Lorde writes in "The Uses of the Erotic": "There are frequent attempts to equate pornography and eroticism, two diametrically opposed uses of the sexual. Because of these attempts, it has become fashionable to separate the spiritual (psychic and emotional) from the political, to see them as contradictory or antithetical. 'What do you mean, a poetic revolutionary, a meditating gunrunner?' In the same way, we have attempted to separate the spiritual and the erotic, thereby reducing the spiritual to a world of flattened affect, a world of the ascetic who aspires to feel nothing. But nothing is farther from the truth."[63] Lorde rejects the dichotomy between the political and the erotic and the equation of pornography with eroticism.[64] Her invocation of a poetic revolutionary might remind the reader of Dziga Vertov or Vladimir Mayakovsky, both avant-gardists who did not reject pleasure and the affective and instead mobilized viewer/reader affect. The contrast is between affective liberation and "a world of flattened affect, a world of the ascetic," reminding us of the rejection of "the ascetic" by key philosophical figures of May 1968, including Gilles Deleuze and Herbert Marcuse. As Foucault writes in his preface to Deleuze and Guattari's *Anti-Oedipus*, the first and foremost adversaries for the text are "the political ascetics, the sad militants, the terrorists of theory, those who would preserve the pure order of politics and political discourse. Bureaucrats of the revolution and civil servants of Truth."[65] Deleuze and Guattari equate "internal asceticism and cohesion" with fascism—the "Barbarian Despotic Machine."[66] While DVG-*Cinéthique* would be understandably horrified by the comparison of their antifascist filmmaking and criticism to despotism, it bears repeating that their rejection of "desire"—so integral to 1968 revolutionary movements—removed them from the zeitgeist of the late 1960s, as well as, and as much as, the contemporary moment.

Fundamentally connected to this claim—that the politics of pleasure should not be separated from political agitation—is a recovery of confrontation with what Mark Fisher, in his last, unfinished book on "acid communism," calls "the spectre of a world which could be free." "Instead of seeking to overcome capital," Fisher writes, "we should focus on what capital must always obstruct: the collective capacity to produce, care and enjoy . . . this Red Plenty."[67] As we shall see in the subsequent chapter, films by the Japanese avant-garde of the late 1960s more readily embody such capacities to enjoy and to care—although not without their own ambivalences and contradictions. Their liberatory pleasures are marked by strangeness and disorientation, a late 1960s evolution of Matsumoto's "sadomasochistic aesthetic." Their experimental and reflective take on documentary adopts a more affective, and effective, manner of questioning documentary objectivity and positing a more lucid mode of documentary filmmaking. In no way, however, do these affective aspects negate their antifascist commitment; in fact, they require it. They share with DVG-*Cinéthique*, however, an investment in epistemological rupture, crafting, in cinematographic form, what the journal *Miroir du cinéma* called an "active spectator": *un spectateur agissant*. While Matsumoto, Hani, and Terayama are likewise critics of "truthfulness" in media, as well as a desire to create "new images" and "new sounds," their more *jouissance*-oriented films frame documentary reflection as a space for radical playfulness and affection alongside leftist militancy. They are also, as previously described, resolutely, uncompromisingly queer.

5   1969 Japan

QUEER SELF-REVOLUTIONS
OF THE ART THEATRE GUILD

THE AMBIVALENT QUEER ART OF UN-BECOMING

It is a paradox of film history that the avant-garde documentary films produced in Japan at the end of the 1960s are far more aligned with the aesthetics and politics of Vertov than the French films that claim his influence. I argue elsewhere that this alignment between the Soviet and Japanese avant-garde documentary traditions emerges not *because* of Soviet influence, but due to a vibrant transnational avant-gardist media ecology in the Japanese 1960s that included interest in Soviet and Eastern European filmmaking practices, as well as an already strong tradition of experimental documentary theory in Japan.[1] Yet a comparison between the Soviet 1920s and late Japanese 1960s has its pitfalls. While arguably women fared better in the workplace in 1920s Moscow than 1960s Tokyo, the Soviet Union retreated from a sexually liberated ethos as the 1920s progressed. In this chapter, I argue that the late 1960s Japanese avant-garde documentary films introduce a new kind of emancipatory aesthetics, one that sees sexual liberation and queer politics as inextricable from antifascism and the politics of liberation as a whole. The films I analyze do not see queerness *as* inherently political—identity is resolutely not the point here—but they see self-investigation and experimentation as part and parcel of the living of a revolutionary life.

158   CHAPTER 5

This revolutionary era of filmmaking was largely possible due to the rise of the ATG, an independent international film distributor that became a production company in 1967. Whereas the middle of the decade saw an emergence of allegorical semi-documentary that often worked within the confines of large studios, in the late 1960s there was much more radical formal experimentation at ATG. The films of this era are more exuberantly avant-garde; they are defined by a playful porousness and interpenetration of multifarious forms and genres. Black-and-white film stock blended with color, nonfiction interwove with fiction, irreverent pop culture merged with sophisticated works of high literature and culture, the somber and militant combined with the comically absurd, and theatricality blended with journalistic documentation.

The films from this highly experimental era directly responded to the political protest movements once again gaining ground in Japan in the late 1960s. This time, the films embodied the somewhat anarchistic struggles of youth movements and subcultures. These films demonstrate a prevailing interest in personal expression as part and parcel of revolutionary activity. As we shall see, these films also diegetically represent queerness—both via the centering of noncisgender characters and through the depiction of queer sexualities—as both metaphor and literal embodiment of personal revolution.

In fact, the Shinjuku area of Tokyo was a queer mecca. Not only did a gay district crop up, but gay intellectuals flocked to Tokyo from all over the globe, especially from France: most famously, Roland Barthes, but also Michel Foucault, who likewise visited and even considered moving to Japan.[2] Japanese film historian and filmmaker Donald Richie, a gay man himself, formed a close-knit circle with queer Japanese artists including Terayama Shūji, who is featured in this chapter, iconoclastic countercultural writer (and fascist self-eviscerator) Mishima Yukio, Mishima disciple and writer of homoerotic poetry Takahashi Mutsuo, gay photographer (and long-term-partner of American translator Meredith Weatherby) Yatō Tamotsu, and others.[3] Dutch writer and Japanese film specialist Ian Buruma's *A Tokyo Romance*, an account of 1970s Tokyo life, begins: "The last thing he said to me, before I closed the door of his smartly decorated loft apartment in Amsterdam, was to stay away from Donald Richie's crowd."[4] "He" referred to a dapper stranger, and "Richie's crowd" evidently was comprised of countercultural homosexuals with a penchant for getting into trouble. That Shinjuku in 1969 was an obviously, emphatically *queer space* is well-known but now little discussed; it was evidently understood, behind closed doors, as a place of seemingly unparalleled homosexual freedom for the era, especially for expats, who were already treated as outsiders within their home countries.

Especially intriguing is the role art, literature, and film played in the performance of sexuality and in the creation of queer spaces. I use *queer* here literally, as not a synonym of, but in contrast to, both "heterosexual" *and* "homosexual"; as Andrew Culp reminds us in *Dark Deleuze*, Deleuze and Guattari utilize Marcel Proust's demarcation of three "levels of sexuality" in the fourth novel of *À la recherche du temps perdu* (*In Search of Lost Time*), *Sodom and Gomorrah* (1921–1922): straight, gay, and queer.[5] Where straight and gay are inverses of one another, queerness becomes a space of radical possibility for the creation of other, unforeseen worlds, perhaps nonsensical or strange—embodying a "line of flight" that Deleuze and Guattari describe as deterritorialization. While surely sexual preference varied in the late 1960s among the youthful, radical milieu, including straight and gay alike, using Proust's definition, the (counter)culture was *queer*. And indeed, these spaces did not necessarily exclude heterosexual sex but aimed to disrupt the definitive markers between homo- and heterosexuality. Importantly, in art as in life, the body—its suffering, its pleasures, its animal ferality—became the locus of revolutionary activity and potential.

As KuroDalaiJee writes in *Anarchy of the Body*, the avant-garde performance art of the period was an *embodied* entity. Tokyo was suffused with the arts of "bodily expression" (*shintai hyōgen*)."[6] Performance art "happenings" (to use a more familiar Anglophone term) by groups such as Zero Jigen (Zero Dimension) and Collective Kumo wove through the fabric of everyday life, in turns disturbing and dehabituating, revitalizing and reenchanting it. This was often suffused with an almost orgiastic, unrepentant vulgarity. Artist Asai Masuo, for instance, writes of "the mangy wolves" who "deposited their steaming piles of shit among the flowers in the garden of Art," who "ravenously licked the girls' asses, indulged in homosexual pleasures, and crunched on yellow pickled radish.... Assuredly they perverted vulgar everyday acts into artistic action." Indeed for Asai, art and food and sex were not disparate but were on "the same dimension.... [E]verything relates to living the present moment to the fullest."[7] Indulging in "homosexual pleasures" was part and parcel of the full experience of life, an attempt at radical revisioning of existence that rhymes, I believe, with the surrealist experiments of the 1920s.

From a cultural fascination with Jean Genet to the Sasori-za (Scorpio Theater, a film and live performance space in the basement of the ATG Shinjuku Bunka flagship cinema), there are numerous examples of the overlap between queerness and the countercultural movement in the arts in late 1960s Japan.[8] For example, Ōshima Nagisa's carnivalesque countercultural romp *Shinjuku dorobō nikki* (*Diary of a Shinjuku Thief*, 1968) is an obvious homage to Genet's *Journal de voleur* (*A Thief's Journal*, 1949), in title as in plot; Sasori-za's name derives from *Scorpio Rising* (1963) by Kenneth Anger, one of America's first openly gay filmmakers. I am less interested in detailing specific erotic connections than I am in seeing how queerness is represented in cinema—how queerness is literalized by the characters and narrative of late 1960s avant-garde documentary productions; how the diegetic representation of queerness becomes a metaphor for "self-revolution"; and, most importantly, how the very form of these wildly experimental films embodies this self-revolutionary and self-revolutionizing queerness. Indeed, not only does the content of the films reflect the happenings of the Tokyo antiestablishment underground, but their form enacts this same desire to reject the system, to "pursue fundamental thought" while asserting and transforming the self, society, and the experience of everyday life.

However, analyses of queer filmmaking in East Asia tend to reject many of the late 1960s Japanese productions, either because, with the exception of Mishima and Terayama, their makers were not themselves openly queer, or because their queerness is understood largely on the level of metaphor. Andrew Grossman summarizes this perspective in the introduction to *Queer Asian Cinema*: "The Japanese new-wave, from the late 1950s through its death in the early 1970s, occasionally did address questions of 'aberrant' sexuality, though mostly as a leftist tactic of political shock. Thus, the homosexualities of Matsumoto Toshio's *Funeral Procession of Roses* (1969) or Terayama Shūji's *Throw Away Your Books* (1971) were not homosexual *per se*, but were intended to symbolize positions of radical leftism; thus, they may be not so different from, say, the anarchic sadomasochism of Wakamatsu Kōji, insofar as all portrayals of unconventional sexuality amounted to outspoken liberalism, be they anti-feudal or anti-bourgeois."[9]

Leaving aside the obvious point that fervent communist filmmakers such as Matsumoto would have balked at being compared to liberals, here the queer films of the Japanese new wave are "not homosexual *per se*," but represented "positions of radical leftism." Grossman uses his argument to discuss the "portrayals of unconventional sexuality" in Wakamatsu Kōji's pink films, a uniquely Japanese genre of sexploitation central to Zahlten's analysis of Japanese industrial cinemas, *The End of Japanese Cinema*, and which I discuss elsewhere.[10] I would like, however, to take Terayama's and Matsumoto's films at their word. It is especially important, indeed, that Matsumoto Toshio—*the* central theorist of the antifascist avant-garde documentary—centered his first, and far most important, feature-length production *Bara no sōretsu* (*Funeral Parade of Roses*, 1969) on "gayboy" Shinjuku counterculture, creating the most famous queer Japanese art film ever made. What if films like *Bara no sōretsu* and *Sho o suteyo, machi e deyō* (*Throw Away Your Books, Rally in the Streets*, 1971) were classified as *both* representing "positions of radical leftism" *and* "homosexuality, *per se*"? What would it mean to expand the understanding of queerness in Japanese cinema on both the literal and symbolic registers, without discarding it for being "not queer enough" or "merely symbolic"? It would mean to take seriously the revolutionary potential of queerness, not merely as a "shock value" to viewers but as a striving toward future possibility, as radical Deleuzian deterritorialization.

However, this chapter, and these films, do not see queer sexuality as revolutionary *in itself*. I align with Jonathan M. Hall's reading of Matsumoto's views on queer sexuality when he writes that for Matsumoto, "aberrant" sexuality was not "a subversive, oppositional space associated with individual resistance to state power," nor was sexuality "a privileged space in which the political/social could be brought into relief and altered, as if sexuality was some royal road to socio-political transformation." Queer sexuality was neither "pastoral/utopian" nor "redemptive/political," "but a mode of address that shared with the political, tropes of repetition, claims to authority, as well as the possibility of shattering rupture."[11] Important for all directors discussed in this chapter is the ability of queerness to embody this "shattering rupture"—a rupture of ideas of stable subjecthood and self-knowledge, resulting in the transformative process that Deleuze and Guattari call "Becoming." Yet as Culp argues, "Becoming is really a process of Un-Becoming"—a radical break that is integral to Matsumoto's antifascist revolutionary framework, what he connects to the "masochistic" "scalpel of [self] criticism."[12]

The films in this chapter are usually only uncomfortably slotted in the queer canon because of their fundamental pessimism; all three films discussed here can be considered tragedies, even though each is woven through with ecstatic formal and narrative pleasures, musical interludes, chaotic self-abandonment, the gleefully humorous, and the absurd. They are not films of self-affirming identity; their queerness is ambivalent by nature. And indeed, Matsumoto and Deleuze both "have nothing but scorn for identity politics," as Culp argues about the latter.[13] If anything, these films embrace what family abolitionist Sophie Lewis terms an "affect of queer doom."[14] Yet this pessimism is revolutionary, as it points to the need for other, better futures. As such these films echo José Esteban Muñoz's assertion that "queerness is not here yet.... [It] is that thing that lets us feel that this world is not enough, that indeed something is missing," and moreover, that "engaging the performative as force of and for futurity is queerness's bent."[15] It would mean, fundamentally, to acknowledge queerness in these films as performance and embodiment of futurist radical politics, not despite but *because* of their ambivalence and pessimism, their "affect of queer doom" inextricable from their unapologetic formal experimentation, unforeseen since the 1920s.

This chapter analyzes experimental documentaries of the Japanese late 1960s that combine radical formal experimentation with the "self-revolutionizing" politics of New Left youth. It focuses on films that portray queerness as diegetic and symbolic and in connection with a fervent avant-gardism that not only reflects but enacts and embodies contemporaneous student desires for a radical self-revolution of consciousness. This chapter looks closely at three works produced and distributed by ATG: two aforementioned films, Matsumoto's *Bara no sōretsu* and Terayama's *Sho o suteyo, machi e deyō*, plus the rarely addressed Hani Susumu film *Gozenchū no jikkanwari* (*Morning Schedule*, 1972), a film made with the collaboration of high school students and notable for its portrayal of a genderqueer character. I do not aim to define the complex gender dynamics of figures such as the *gei boi* in postwar Japanese counterculture—great work in sociology, history, and cultural studies already exists by Mark McLelland, Keith Vincent, S. P. F. Dale, and others.[16] My use of the term *queer* is also not meant to map contemporary North American–derived understandings onto a Japanese cultural context. I invoke the term broadly and capaciously, attempting to mirror the playfully exuberant and undefined manner of the films I analyze.

This chapter expands on already existing work on Terayama by Carol Fisher Sorgenfrei and Steven Ridgely; on Matsumoto by Yuriko Furuhata, Jonathan M. Hall, and Miryam Sas; and on Hani Susumu by Takuya Tsunoda and Justin Jesty, by placing these films within the context of a "self-revolution of everydayness." I connect these films, and the "self-revolutions" they embody, to antifascist and anti-imperialist aesthetics as defined in this book: as media literacy via epistemological struggle (the stability of truth is always fervently questioned) and as an emphasis on affective, sensorial liveliness. To these, I add a dimension of self-rupture and self-questioning characteristic of the late 1960s in Japan. I also place the formal configurations of these films within the context of heretofore untranslated writings by these directors gleaned from published interviews, articles, and autobiographies. I explicitly do this not to search for literal examples of queerness within their personal archives, but to show how Terayama, Hani, and Matsumoto conceptualized their filmmaking as a future-oriented antifascist revolutionary phenomenology.

SELF-REVOLUTIONS OF EVERYDAY LIFE

First, however, it is important to lay out the background of politics and protest within late 1960s Japan. The majority of this introductory section is indebted to the important work of Oguma Eiji, Ando Takemasa, Nick Kapur, and Chelsea Szendi Schieder on the history of Japanese protest movements of the 1960s, and I only briefly summarize their work here. In Japan, student uprisings between 1967 and 1969 ultimately forced the closure of university campuses nationwide.[17] As in many parts of the world, including Paris, students did not have a solid plan, and actions emerged spontaneously. Schieder notes that "student activism in Japan in the late 1960s mobilized around two key themes: the violence of the war in Southeast Asia and the rationalization of Japanese society."[18] Japanese students, like their counterparts in France, the United States, West Germany, the United Kingdom, and elsewhere, were enraged by the complicity of their respective conservative governments with oppression and terror, especially in Vietnam, and blamed their country's economic stability on its affiliations with imperialism. Likewise, students saw their new high quality of life as the result of Japan's ties with the American military through ANPO. Because of this sense of economic guilt, much of the exigence behind the students' revolutionary fervor in the late 1960s was not defined by concrete political goals. Instead, these activists sought to highlight the increasing control of mass economic consumption over people's everyday lives and wanted to transform their depoliticized consciousness.

This student movement began even earlier than France's famous university closures, and Japan's protests were loosely tied to the even larger anti-ANPO protests of 1960. However, as Ando Takemasa argues, the ANPO protests of the late 1960s and early 1970s were focused less on repealing ANPO itself, compared with the mass movement of the 1960 protests. These protests were instead focused on the negation and reconstruction of everyday life.[19] As Schieder describes, participating in protest movements "offered an exciting disruption of the everyday cycle of work and common sense and opened up spaces in which students could relate to each other and society in new ways."[20] Oguma writes that this inquiry into everyday-ness, or *nichijōsei*, developed as a critique of liberal democracy in the wake of the high economic growth period in the mid-1960s. Students also criticized their increasingly stringent and overcrowded universities, seeing their authoritarian classrooms as symbolic of an inherently immoral capitalist industrial society.[21]

Ando Takemasa describes these revolutionary goals of late 1960s Japanese student activists as a "self-revolution in 'everydayness.'"[22] The addition of "self" explicitly countered another "revolution": what the government's 1960 White Paper on National Life called a "consumer revolution" and a "revolution of everyday life" (*seikatsu kakumei*).[23] By contrast, the "self-revolution" sought to counter the barrage of consumer goods and complicity with conservative and imperialist regimes. Contra the consumerist *seikatsu kakumei*, this "self-revolution" was profoundly theoretical and abstract by nature. For these student protesters, "self-revolution" through political activism and organizing was key to a meaningful and dignified life; at stake was a complex ethics of selfhood and lived experience. In a 1968 survey that asked University of Tokyo students what they were fighting for on campus, responses stressed this rather abstract "self-revolution in everydayness":

"asserting the self": 41.7 percent

"self-transformation": 31.7 percent

"dismantling the current university structure": 27.2 percent

"pursuing fundamental thought": 25.6 percent

"rejection of the system": 25 percent.[24]

Such beliefs connoted a desire to dismantle current political systems as well as the fundamental transformation of consciousness and life itself. Both were essential to the practice of antifascism, and art was essential in the realization and manifestation of a transformed, revolutionary life. Indeed, youth of the era were known for their passionate support for and interest in experimental art. It may be hard to believe, but many screenings of the avant-garde films described in this chapter, and others of ATG, were filled with eager, engaged youth and intellectuals. For Yomota Inuhiko, the center of underground art and culture was the aforementioned Shinjuku, Tokyo—an area "filled with vulgarity and nihilistic energy... [where] artistic experimentation and political contestation went hand in hand."[25] Yomota's effervescent description of the period evokes descriptions of similar occurrences elsewhere in the world, from Golden Gate Park in San Francisco to New York's Central Park:

> In the square in front of the station *fūtenzoku* (Japanese hippies) from all over Japan, homeless and hungry, sleep on the grass and sing songs. In the café Fugetsudo, self-declared artists with long hair and beards rub shoulders with leftist activists, while American soldiers who are against the Vietnam war and who've gone AWOL from their bases huddle with anti-war groups, plotting escapes to northern Europe. Out in the main street, ten or so men and women form a strange procession. Apart from the gas masks on their

heads they're completely naked. At the other end of the main street a gay bar district has grown up. A French semiotician, not yet famous in Japan, is a furtive regular.[26]

Yomota's description of the Tokyo underground in the late 1960s indicates that art and politics were entirely intertwined in an almost carnivalesque environment, in which the boundary between art and life was increasingly eradicated. Activists and artists rubbed shoulders and engaged with Vietnam War deserters and intellectuals like Roland Barthes in bars and coffeeshops. Outside, performance art interrupted the quotidian, forcing an experience of the unfamiliar in an otherwise familiar space. The performance with gas masks Yomota describes clearly refers to the group Zero Jigen, and this specific performance is also documented in Matsumoto Toshio's *Bara no sōretsu*. The "self-revolution of everydayness" described by Ando was achieved by this porosity between aesthetics and politics, militant activism and playful aestheticization. But this porosity was not without its difficult and ambivalent dimensions.

THE PROBLEMATIC OF SEX AND POLITICS, AND THE PHILOSOPHY OF PLAY

In his analysis of fascism and image culture, Patrick Nathan writes: "There is a reason totalitarian frameworks reject, quarantine, and exterminate what is queer. Queerness is the ultimate protest against fascist binaries, including those established and enriched by capitalism."[27] There is a quintessentially anti-establishment aspect of queerness as protest against the status quo—as true today as in the 1960s. One can argue, however, that Nathan's formulation is overly optimistic about the one-to-one relationship between queerness and liberatory politics. Being queer, unfortunately, does not make a person an antifascist. Mishima Yukio is a famous example of the ways in which counterculture and queerness can align with ultranationalism; in one of the most mediatized and well-documented events in modern Japanese history, the unrepentant fascist writer, countercultural gay icon, and director of *Yūkoku* (*Patriotism*, 1966) attempted to incite a coup d'état while standing on a balcony in a salmon-pink military uniform; when he failed, he committed seppuku. Seemingly paradoxically, a certain kind of Japanese-specific queerness can, in fact, be construed as pronationalist when, as Ayako Kano describes, the history of gender performativity in Japan equated the "opening" of Japan to the West during the Meiji Period with the imposition of sexist Christian-derived heteronormativity (previously, sex was perceived as subordinate to gender).[28]

Likewise, "unconventional sexuality" (Grossman) does not necessarily make someone a feminist. The films of Wakamatsu Kōji, Adachi Masao, Ōshima Nagisa, and others can certainly be criticized for their use of the female body as a canvas for national trauma. As anyone who teaches Japanese films of the 1960s and 1970s can attest, as a whole, the "season of politics" is rife with men in cinema committing egregious acts of sexual violence against women. And women, in fact, are difficult to find in the production sector of Japanese 1960s filmmaking, except as actors. It tends to be a highly masculinist cinema, with virtually no women directors.[29] In the sphere of student organizing, also, despite the calls for a "self-revolution of everydayness," Schieder documents the continued sexism in the student movement, noting: "Young women who were drawn to this expansive call for liberation found new freedoms and also encountered familiar constraints.... [T]he radical student movement... ultimately failed to disrupt the greater social structures against which it battled."[30]

The "self-revolution," then, was not as utopian as one might hope; nor was the world of cinema. The political avant-garde films from this period cannot be placed under the same liberatory umbrella with one fell swoop. Not all of them are explicitly or even implicitly queer; not all of them are sexist, or feminist. Many films from the era depict aberrant sexuality and sadomasochism as a metaphor of national power. Films such as Wakamatsu's *Yuke yuke nidome no shōjo* (*Go, Go Second Time Virgin*, 1969), *Okasareta hakui* (*Violated Angels*, 1967), and *Tenshi no kōkotsu* (*Ecstasy of the Angels*, 1972) depict a metaphorical national impotency that manifests as literal male impotency and conclude with an explosion of terrifying male violence. The films chosen for this chapter exhibit an alternative framework of sexual depiction on screen that is, by contrast, suffused with a tone of pleasure, joy, and play.

The pleasurable and the political joined hands globally in the late 1960s. As Henri Lefebvre argues in the third volume of the *Critique of Everyday*

Life, reflecting on the protests of 1968: "Rejecting, before the ecologists did so, growth, with its brutal implications.... [T]hey counterposed the cult of pleasure to that of work. Against an economism void of values other than those of exchange, protest stood for reuniting the festival and daily life, for transforming daily life into a site of desire and pleasure."[31] Just as the May 1968 protesters in France argued against an inhuman complicity with economic development and growth, Japanese youth in the late 1960s similarly reunited "festival and daily life." The protesters and the hippies did not necessarily coexist in the same person, but both love and politics evinced the rupture of the everyday. The films described in this chapter are characteristic of the students' understanding of antifascism as a practice of personal liberation as well as political engagement.

This does not mean the films do not also incorporate suffering, melancholy, and the abject. They follow Heather Love's formulation, in which "queerness ... is both abject and exalted, a 'mixture of delicious and freak'.... A stigmatizing mark as well as a form of romantic exceptionalism."[32] The films in this chapter thus find themselves joining the ecstatic and exalted with the strange and surreal—and often the abject and horrifying. But more often than not, they are quintessentially fun. Another film that would have served well here is *Kureijī Rabu* (*Crazy Love*, 1968) by Okabe Michio, known for its exuberant "camp" aesthetic, antifascist fervor, kissing cowboys, and au courant psychedelic rock soundtrack. Ōshima's aforementioned *Diary of a Shinjuku Thief*, likewise, would pair well with these in its carnivalesque queer performativity as liberation. These are films that typify a late 1960s zeitgeist linked to the works of Herbert Marcuse as well as of Gilles Deleuze and Félix Guattari and that revel in desire as antiauthoritarian playfulness, with a strong undercurrent of sexual and political ambivalence and even pessimism.

The erotic is closely tied to the revolutionary writings of the period. Countercultural filmmaker Ōe Masanori wrote extensively on this issue. Ōe filmed performances of the Zero Jigen collective in works such as *Inaba no shiro usagi* (*The White Hare of Inaba*, 1970) and created works of experimental filmmaking such as the six-channel work of expanded cinema, *Great Society* (1967). After traveling to the United States in the mid-1960s and meeting Timothy Leary, he later became known for his encomia on psychedelics.[33] Even in the 1960s, his work, according to Ignacio

Adriasola, "drew implicit parallels between altered states of consciousness and the ecstatic experience found in protest."[34]

Ōe described the importance of the erotic in "The Aesthetics of Ecstasy and the Yippie Revolution" in 1969. He writes, almost quoting Marcuse's *Eros and Civilization* (1955) verbatim: "We must discover the civilization of Eros—the essence of life and philosophy of play which is life itself, freed from the reality principle-based oppressive labor of productivity."[35] Ōe joins Freud with Marx in the drive away from productivity and toward "the essence of life." Eros is equated with what he calls the "excellent philosophy of play," and he invites his readers to "drop out" of a capitalist mode of productivity and reengage in "community": "the place for love, the site for communication, the site for living, the site for cultural activity, and indeed, the site for the rite of life."[36] It is notable, indeed, that the films described here engage in a documentation of *communities* of queerness—whether groups of friends or theater troupes.

As KuroDalaiJee recounts, the Zero Jigen collective describes its earlier 1960s experiments as a hodgepodge attempt to "cram as much 'gay and lesbian sex, the destruction of objects, cult dancing, *sadō* [Japanese tea ceremony], poetry reading, eating contest, wedding ceremony, jazz, etc' as possible into a juicer."[37] Ritual joined with anarchy, with delights of the body, and with perversity and destruction. One is reminded immediately of Georges Bataille, a crucial figure alongside Freud for Matsumoto and other intellectuals of the period: for Bataille, festivals as well as political protests and demonstrations open up a space of radical possibility in their circulation of revolutionary energies; they are revolutionary because they are distinct from official parties, whether capitalist or communist, and their functionaries.[38] These festivals of art and/or politics have, for Bataille, a profound antifascist dimension, as well as a sacred one.

This sensibility intertwines with the "self-revolution of everyday life" and manifests in the films described in this chapter: their form is suffused with exuberantly maximalist and disorienting tricks of editing and cinematography, while their content represents queer love and/or queer gender presentation. While the films described here certainly differ—Terayama's film is critical of heterosexual love but does not provide an easy homoerotic or homosexual alternative, and love in Hani's film remains fundamentally tragic and unrequited—they provide varying understandings of gender nonconformity during a highly politicized era. This project therefore attempts to "disorient" (Ahmed) our usual understanding of Japanese political avant-garde productions by emphasizing their ecstatic and playful dimensions: the destabilizing, disorienting, fundamentally queer dynamism of the late 1960s moment.

DISORIENTATION OF "REALITY" IN *BARA NO SŌRETSU*

Matsumoto Toshio's first feature-length film continues the film theorist's longtime interest in a dialectical synthesis of avant-garde and documentary. Like his short neo-documentaries *Nishijin* (1961) and *Ishi no uta* (1963), *Bara no sōretsu* infuses a darkly surreal, and explicitly Freudian, sense into an experimental documentary form. Hall describes Matsumoto's interest in cinema's "purported capability to even fleetingly rupture optic and psychic orders."[39] Correspondingly, Matsumoto believed the avant-garde documentary had a singular ability to inspire such ruptures, necessary for both social and personal transformation. As he wrote in *Kiroku eiga* in 1959, "The creator-subject transforms the tense and dynamic relationship between his/her own inner world and objective reality, or between consciousness and objects, into the transformation of human beings and society."[40] The filmmaker-artist must join the world of "objective reality" with their inner world in order to incite social transformation—of prime importance for the Marxist Matsumoto.

Unlike his more strictly documentarian works from the early 1960s, however, *Bara no sōretsu* revels more fully in the fusion of fiction and nonfiction and dramatic theatricality with documentary technique, which intermix in idiosyncratic and sometimes macabre ways. Notably, compared to his earlier work, *Bara no sōretsu* is far more playful and far more *ecstatic*—a word to which we will return. While the film does have an overarching (hyper-)fictional narrative, it also includes highly reflexive shots of its own production, as well as interviews with the actors and on-the-street interviews with queer people. Half of the interviewees do not act in the film, pointing to the importance of gender as a mode of investigation. The juxtaposition of meta-cinematic reflexivity and an ultra-exaggerated fictionality and performativity create a disorienting experience that constantly draws our attention to the film's creation. As Furuhata describes, "The scripted and unscripted performances are constantly folded onto each other ... giving rise to our awareness of the inseparability of artifice and reality, fiction and nonfiction."[41]

The film loosely adapts Sophocles's Oedipus myth to the queer counterculture of late 1960s Tokyo, with Oedipus rebranded as "Eddy," a trans assigned-male-at-birth woman who unknowingly sleeps with her father, the owner of a transgender nightclub. One should note here that the use of *transgender* is not a direct translation of what occurs in the film, which refers to Eddy as a "gayboy" (*gei boi*)—the most commonly utilized term of the era, and a Japanese-specific phrase that does not directly translate into English despite being derived from it. In fact, the film represents many individuals of fluid gender, some of whom contemporary society might term a transvestite or crossdresser, and others transgender.[42] I use trans more as a placeholder for an overarching sense of gender fluidity.

From its trailer and advertising information, as Taro Nettleton notes, *Bara no sōretsu* advertises itself as "starring 7 real gay boys," sensationalizing this with the ironic question: "Is it a sin or an illness?"[43] Instead of making a specific argument with regard to queer subcultures, the film revels in pop cultural phenomena: Eddy and her friends don the mod and hippie clothing of *fūtenzoku* (literally: "tribe of vagabonds"); they smoke a joint while watching an experimental film—notably, about the student political protesters; and they dance and striptease to jazz and rock 'n' roll. Yet interspersed in these exuberant scenes, politics bubble forth: Eddy cleans up a wounded ANPO protester who stumbles into her doorway; she encounters a political performance art group donning gas masks (the Zero Jigen collective, identical to Yomota's description of Shinjuku quoted earlier); and her filmmaker friend and sometime lover dons a fake beard and mustache and calls himself Guevara. Youthful aesthetics and political form intersect in highly playful ways that are less critical or sardonic than they are joyfully estranging—until horror emerges, with Eddy fainting before surreal images of masks, and before she drives a knife violently through her eyes in the film's dénoument (the resonances with Matsumoto-favorite Luis Buñuel's 1929 *Un chien andalou* are quite explicit). Yet the pathos of dramatic climax is interrupted when, seemingly out of nowhere, TV personality Yodogawa Chogi emerges smiling idiotically, "like a Greek chorus in a suit and tie" (James Phillips).[44] He comments: "Frightening, isn't it? The cursed destiny of man. What a mix of cruelty and laughter it is! Let's look forward to the next program. *Sayonara. Sayonara. Sayonara.*" But then the scene continues.

Cruelty and laughter, indeed. *Bara no sōretsu* is a jumble of media, a frenetic mix of techniques: comic arts are combined with poetry and myth, television is juxtaposed with film, and Eastern setting and characters are juxtaposed with Western literature, philosophy, and music. Hall is correct, I believe, when he labels *Bara no sōretsu* "the most formally complex feature film to emerge from the Japanese new wave."[45] It is unsurprising that the film became an important source of influence for Stanley Kubrick's *A Clockwork Orange*, made two years later. The camerawork in *Bara no sōretsu* is immensely varied, reminiscent of the frenzied editing of Vertov's *Chelovek s kinoapparatom*: for example, fast forward, quick strobe-like shots that appear in rapid succession, warped footage, overexposure, freeze-frame, movie-within-a-movie, stills, advertisement posters, lens flare, curtains on a make-believe stage, cartoon word bubbles with curse words during freeze-frame, and the use of film negatives. Generally, close-ups of the body, especially Eddy's body, take precedence. Matsumoto never provides a long shot portraying Eddy's entire naked body, instead showing fragments. One of these shots is a clear homage to the first shot of Alain Resnais's *Hiroshima mon amour*, beloved by Matsumoto and many Japanese documentarists of the 1960s: "feminine" hands grasp and caress a masculine back and shoulder in soft focus. The erotic body evokes a sense of haptic connection, while also simultaneously estranging this connection and defamiliarizing the human body entirely. This scene dehabituates a common trope in romance cinema, as identities merge into chimeras and truth becomes illusory.

This inquiry into identity and illusion is reflected in a short art film created by Matsumoto in the same year and excerpted in *Bara no sōretsu*, fittingly titled *Ecstasis*. In this film, Eddy rolls her head from side to side in slow motion in a moment of ecstasy, while Guevara holds out his arms as the camera pans toward him, cut with poster advertisements. The imagery is extremely overprocessed and slowed down, creating a cartoonlike high contrast, while a menacing electronic hum drones on the soundtrack. One is reminded again of Muñoz's concept of "queerness as manifestation in and of ecstatic time," in which "the temporal stranglehold" of "straight time is interrupted or stepped out of."[46] For Matsumoto, "straight time" is expanded to mean the capitalist status quo, the temporality of business as usual that film must disrupt. Thus the film represents a certain kind of "ecstasy," yet it is one that is also shocking and unnerving, even painful; one is reminded of the etymology of *ecstasy* or *ekstasis*, which, from the ancient Greek κστασις, means "to be or stand outside oneself, a removal to elsewhere." This also connects to Matsumoto's call for a "sadomasochistic aesthetic consciousness" earlier in the decade: that an artist must perpetually reexamine their own positionality in relation to their subject. Only through such consciousness can an artwork be anti-imperialist and antifascist. As Matsumoto writes, "This process of dismantling the artist's consciousness . . . is nothing less than a daily conversion."[47] This theme of a "removal" outside oneself, of self-dismantling, includes "the temporal stranglehold" of "straight time," the status quo of the everyday.

The filmic trope of mirrors in *Bara no sōretsu* also serve a role of disorientation and self-dismantling. The camera is often fixated on a single baroque mirror in the nightclub, reflecting the bodies of both Leda (the older, more traditional cross-dressing proprietress, who dons kimonos and Kabuki-esque *onna-gata* garb), and Eddy, who slowly transforms into an increasingly glamorous version of herself and becomes the club's "Mama." The film's cine-poetic intertitles—aligning the film with Terayama's intertitle poetics that he wrote for Matsumoto's *Haha-tachi*—constantly quote Snow White ("mirror, mirror on the wall"), and the film becomes a parody of the fairy tale, with Leda as the destroying witch-stepmother and Eddy as the "fairest" new generation of free-spirited youth. The mirror also symbolizes ego and sexuality; in one scene, we see a young teenage version of Eddy (still a boy) discovering her sexuality by putting on her mother's lipstick and erotically kissing her image in the mirror, which Matsumoto films in extreme close-up: the ecstasy of self-discovery, yet one that is darkly Freudian and surrealist. (Eddy, following the inverse Oedipus myth, is shown stabbing her own mother and her mother's lover, so queer identity is not without its significant share of homicide-infused ambivalences.)

This use of mirrors, in relation to gender identity, evokes questions of the virtual and the actual, the "real" and the "artificial." As Matsumoto juxtaposes realism in cinema with surrealist fantasy, he also places this discussion within the realm of gender and sexual identity. Self-investigation here becomes literal (questioning gender) and metaphorical (an "aesthetic sadomasochism" questioning the self, the self's "Un-Becoming"). This relation between the mirrors and virtuality, between the "real" and its image, recalls Gilles Deleuze's concept of the crystal-image in film, of which mirrors are the most familiar example. Mirrors break down the boundaries between fact and fiction, the real and the represented, as the difference between the actual and the virtual becomes indiscernible.[48] The many mirrors of the film disorient the viewer and render the artfulness of the film explicit.

Matsumoto's film refuses to address either politics or sexuality with regard to any kind of objective truth. As such the film might read as "not queer enough" in using gender as a strategy for disorientation. But it is not, I argue, *merely* strategy, or *merely* metaphor. The interviewees are real people, and the film documents their "self-revolution"—albeit through an experimental filmmaking technique that refuses objectification. As Nettleton notes, "Matsumoto pulls a bait-and-switch; if filmgoers really expected the 'truth' of homosexual identity to be revealed in *Funeral*, they would have been very disappointed. Matsumoto's move, however, is strategic. The interviews are necessarily uninformative because Matsumoto does not intend to offer his subjects as objects of knowledge for the viewer's consumption."[49] Taking Nettleton further, I argue that such a refusal to claim or address a "truth" is precisely the point. I also argue against the supposition that the interviews are "necessarily uninformative" because they provide complicated answers that might frustrate contemporary viewers. They do, however, strategically reject a "truth" of gay identity and a stable subjecthood.

This "bait and switch" is also enacted by the film's quasi-documentary quality and its many disorienting scenes that show us the production of the very film we've been watching. We are often presented with erotic close-ups of Eddy only to find that, upon a zoom-out and the word "Cut!," Eddy was simply "acting" for the diegetic camera; in fact, the only time Eddy is not filmed (diegetically) while having sex is when she commits incest.

Ōishi Masahiko attributes these films within a film, an actualization of film's inherently self-analytical nature, to the work of Dziga Vertov. Ōishi notes that *Bara no sōretsu* is the true inheritor of Vertov's techniques, as both entail an "Ouroboros-like" structure and rejuvenate the techniques

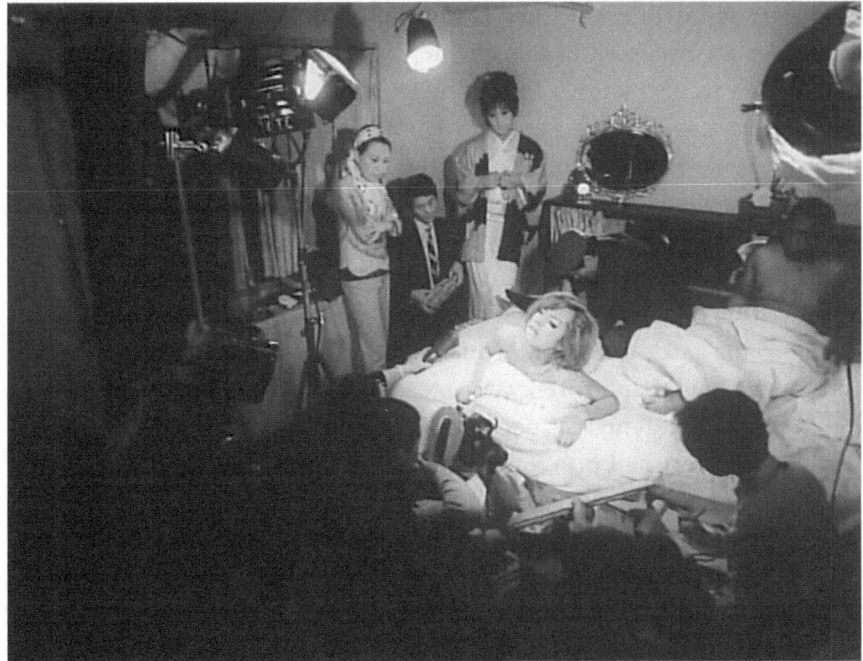

Figure 22. Film set, with Eddy revealed, in Matsumoto Toshio's *Bara no sōretsu*, 1969.

of the avant-garde documentary.[50] Both Vertov's avant-garde documentary and Matsumoto's own retain a clear interest in human perception and argue against the concept of objectivity and the realistic mode. They use the camera as a tool for estrangement and disorientation—what Annette Michelson calls an epistemological struggle that breaks the boundary between an easily conceived reality—but they are also, fundamentally, lively: stimulating, energizing, and even pleasurable in their strangeness.

DREAMING THE DOCUMENTARY IN *SHO O SUTEYO, MACHI E DEYŌ*

The work of Terayama Shūji likewise questions conceptions of truth and reality in cinema and media. His films are commonly acknowledged to be queer; as Garin notes, they always have a "queer gaze," and he is the only director discussed in this chapter who is well-known for his queerness.[51] He was also known for taking care of a large group of young ragtag runaways, an ideal representative of a "family abolitionist" framework (to use Sophie Lewis's provocative title) and far ahead of his time. As Sas writes, Terayama served as a "guarantor" for work and living spaces for more than thirty runaways; some of them lived with him. Many came to sign his *iedenin becchō*, or "runaway book."[52] So far, however, little has been written on the integration between queerness and Terayama's anarchistic avant-garde documentary aesthetic. Indeed, compared to the other directors in this chapter, Terayama steadfastly refuses categorization. Unlike Matsumoto, Terayama seems less obviously aligned with documentary, having launched into the experimental film world from theater and poetry. However, like Matsumoto, his films still remain deeply informed by a playfully documentarian sensibility. Respectful but nevertheless suspicious of observational and scientific documentary formats, Terayama much preferred a "realism" steeped in both fiction and nonfiction. As he claims, "There is a way of thinking that states that fiction is corrupt, and nonfiction is ever-present. But is fiction truly corrupt? . . . One must pay heed that in this relative comparison, in the dynamic between reality and fantasy, 'documentary' (*kiroku*) doesn't quite align with either."[53]

Terayama was less interested in a hard-line "document" and more in a playful reimagining that upsets our perceptual habits. Yet he pushed this distrust of the "documentary" to an extreme; for Terayama, Alain Resnais's *Nuit et brouillard* was far less a "documentary" than *Hiroshima mon amour*, which played out perpetual human conflicts within the film's fictional drama: life and death, love and hate, thought and feeling.[54] As Ridgely argues, Terayama's was not a process of drawing elements of reality into fiction but of seeking a clearer view of reality from the standpoint of fiction. For Terayama, one must exit the real in order to view it from a viable vantage point.[55] And like Matsumoto, Terayama reveled in fictionality by perpetually questioning typical gender roles. Likewise, his larger-than-life persona was affixed to every production, resulting in a uniquely auto-theoretical element. We could conceivably call all of Terayama's oeuvre autofiction. As Terayama defiantly claims, "I am my own documentary" (*Watashi wa jishin no kiroku de aru*).[56]

Terayama, the ultimate jack-of-all-trades—poet, playwright, director, filmmaker, photographer, novelist, cultural critic, and theatrical theorist— was notorious for not following the dogma of any one particular theorist; as such, his work overflows with apparent contradictions, while his artistic output constantly metamorphosed into something else. Terayama's work is a self-conscious, constantly self-evaluating and self-reflecting revolution of forms, distrustful of any alleged claims to objective truth—including the truth of didactic Marxism. As Sas argues, Terayama's work "enact[s] a 'devil-may-care' attitude that itself embraces the challenge to all rigid orthodoxies, to the structure and process of internalizing such orthodoxies (including, one might imagine, even those on the political left)."[57] He therefore follows Viktor Shklovsky in his "Letter to Lev Yakubinsky," who famously wrote: "I am not about to become a hard-and-fast Marxist, and I advise you to follow my example."[58] However, in my estimation, much scholarship tends to prioritize his anarchistic tendencies over his evidently communist ideology. I personally identify Terayama as a romantic and revolutionary anarcho-communist.

Terayama participated in much of the Marxist criticism of the day, although his focus on self-actualization and self-performance was rather idiosyncratic for the time. In a fascinating (and, fittingly, quite poetic) 1961 article in *Kiroku eiga* called "The Old Man and the Fetus"—the meaning of this enigmatic title will soon become clear—he writes that his "destiny is not anti-political," but that his goal and method is the "anti-naturalistic recognition of material." He invokes Matsumoto by emphasizing the importance of the self in art: "The most effective method is the restoration of the 'I'." For Terayama, both the individual and society are trapped within "the dead world and the world that struggles to be born"—a phrase he attributes to British director Lindsay Anderson but that actually derives from Marxist philosopher Antonio Gramsci. Hence the title of his article: art, individual, and society all struggle between the "dead world" of the old man and the "yet unborn" world of the "fetus." As Terayama announces, "We live among many ruins and many seeds," indicating that there are myriad potentials for this "fetus." Echoing Matsumoto's suspicion of the "masses," Terayama claims individuality over all: "It would be futile to appeal to common humanity of all people in order to forcibly give birth to this new world."[59] Even in the early 1960s, Terayama argued powerfully, and viscerally, for the necessity of personal revolution as a precondition of social and political revolution.

It is important, also, that Terayama published this poetic manifesto in a journal devoted to documentary film, given that his films are more often considered experimental and avant-garde than documentarian. Yet his interest in documentary is long-standing, as evidenced by a short film for television he made in 1967, entitled *Americajin, Anata wa?* (*Americans, Who Are You?*). The film, part of a larger series broadcast by the Tokyo Broadcasting System called *Anata wa*, was codirected with Hashimoto Haruhiko and was filmed on the streets of the United States, mostly in New York City. In this forty-minute film, a Japanese woman wields a lightweight sound recorder on her shoulder and asks passersby a series of questions, clearly referring to the first few minutes of Jean Rouch and Edgar Morin's 1961 *cinéma-vérité* film *Chronique d'un été*. At first this appears identical to the conceit of *Chronique*, in which Marceline Loridan and Nadine Ballot conduct a "sociological survey" and ask Parisians: "Are you happy?" However, the questions asked by Terayama and Hashimoto become increasingly political, and then increasingly absurd: "Would you go fight in Vietnam?" "What do you think of Cassius Clay?" (Muhammad Ali's birth name) "Do you kiss with your eyes open or closed?" In contrast to Rouch and Morin's more open-ended questions, Hashimoto and Terayama's questions are meant to sow confusion and disorder. The interview format also dovetails with Terayama's fascination with television and his interest in liveness, shock, and spontaneity. At best, the responses to Terayama's questions result in playful banter and a feeling of goodwill. At worst, they result in fury and contempt. The questions are a destabilizing force meant to produce a radical connection, as well as discord, between Americans and the presence of a single Japanese woman.

In *Anata wa*, the answers do not really matter; it is in the sheer emotional response, and in the radical space between the inquisitor and responder, that Terayama's interests lie. The encounter is meant to disorient, shock, and revive. Terayama's politics yearns to liberate humanity from this burden of everyday life—a term the Soviets called *byt*—as well as from ties to home and country (*furusato*). As epitomized by the title of the film *Sho o suteyo, machi e deyō*, Terayama enjoined Japanese youth to "Throw Away Your Books, Rally in the Streets": to break from obligation to their home and participate in social and political existance, to make their own meaning. Like Vertov, he implored his audience to "come out, please, into life."[60] In a truly countercultural light, Terayama wanted, in his words, to "summon the millions of limping outcasts, blacksmiths, and magicians—to create new chances for encounters."[61] These became integral to Terayama's revolutionary movement: in his words, a *hantaisei undō*, or antiestablishment movement.

Sho o suteyo was one of the "ten million yen" (around US$28,000 in 1971) ATG coproductions, each of which received half of that already rock-bottom budget and were expected to pull together the other five million independently.[62] The film, like Matsumoto's film, engages fully with the carnivalesque youthful landscape of Tokyo. Alongside a largely fictional narrative, it includes documentary footage of *fūten* smoking pot and inhaling paint thinner outside the Shinjuku train station; performance art in which a woman punches a bag in the shape of an enormous penis; long-haired hippies drawing on the pavement and falling over in a drug-induced stupor; a series of video personal ads for gay men; and interviews with a sarcastic and unfazed sex worker ("Which is your favorite book?" "The Bible." "How about Marx's *Das Kapital*?" "Haven't heard of it."). It is resolutely a document of the era, participating in its chaos as well as recording its happenings. As such, Terayama enacts what Yukio Lippit, writing about Shinjuku of the time, describes as "a specific mode of interrelational subjectivity" in which "the resulting subject was not so much a *flâneur*-observer of the streets, but a participant in a dynamic process of becoming through encounters with the fragments of an abstracted, post-industrial landscape."[63] Terayama's camera, itself a participant in this "dynamic process," revels in its playful "encounters" and "fragments" of a modern city, in the midst of self-revolution.

Several critics describe the film as a rock musical due to the importance of its psychedelic soundtrack by J. A. Seazer, Terayama's frequent collaborator, and the tendency of characters to burst into song (this is especially common in the film's "dreamlike" sequences). Indeed, the film is as much an early 1970s rock musical as a political treatise, as much a surrealist, experimental fantasy as a *bildungsroman*. In the film, the teenager Kitagawa Eimei lives at home with an unemployed war criminal father; thief grandmother; and younger sister, Setsuko, who has a sexual attachment to her

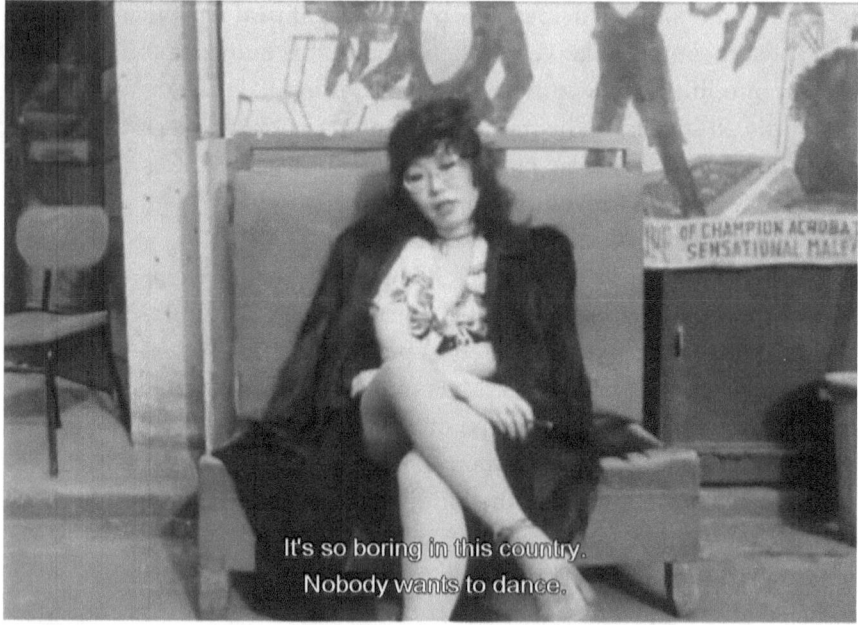

Figure 23. Interview with unfazed sex worker, in Terayama Shūji's *Sho o suteyo, machi e deyō*, 1971.

pet rabbit. The protagonist attempts to join a team of soccer players, but fails; the team's charismatic leader Omi brings Eimei to a prostitute to fulfill the team's initiation rite, but he runs away (rejecting, in a sense, enforced heterosexuality and toxic masculinity). His grandmother asks a Korean neighbor to kill Setsuko's rabbit, and while mourning, Setsuko wanders into the soccer team's changing room, where she is brutally gang-raped. Eventually Setsuko falls in love with Omi and moves in with him and his girlfriend, the grandmother runs away after her son attempts to place her in a Western-style nursing home, and the father is unemployed after the ramen cart Eimei purchased for him ends up being stolen.

Although Terayama's film does include one literally pivotal moment of rape—it bisects the narrative in its center and forms the crux of the film's dramatic arc—it contrasts significantly with the oneiric tone of the rest of the film.[64] *Sho o suteyo* is routinely shot through colored filters, indicating a dreamlike space. A green filter is used to represent Eimei's family, and a magenta filter is typically used for his fantasy of escaping it. Terayama includes a repeated dream sequence with a flying machine motif eerily similar to Soviet avant-garde artist and architect Vladimir Tatlin's unrealized "Letatlin" project, named after the verb meaning "to fly" and Lenin. The Letatlin-like object also appears in the Terayama short film *Seishōnen no tame no eiga nyūmon* (Cinema guide for young people, 1974). In both Terayama's film and Tatlin's original, there is a sense of inherent impossibility: Tatlin, who had drawn the blueprint for the infamous Monument to the Third International, could not realize his modernist masterpiece of architecture, nor can Terayama's protagonist fly away from the burden of his family background and nation-state. Despite its rock operatic sensibility and effervescent humor, the film, like Matsumoto's, is a queer pessimist one.

Besides its oneiric juxtaposition of fantasy and reality, however, *Sho o suteyo* is remarkable in its mixture of text and image; it is what Terayama himself termed a "reading film" due to the graffiti that floods almost every shot. Terayama may have rejected dogmatic Marxism, but nearly all the quotes in the film are communist; citations from Romanian communist Gheorghe Gheorghiu-Dej, poet Vladimir Mayakovsky, novelist André Malraux, and Frankfurt school theorist Erich Fromm cover every possible surface, including brick, cement, grass, and walls. Although the title enjoins the audience to "throw away your books," its meaning is more symbolic: to break with solitary study and join in solidarity with others in the "street." As Terayama notes, "One might say that I, who have thrown out the study of printed material and went out into the city, extended the definition of books."[65] The film is instead a call to arms to bring books out into the streets themselves; in a tone mirroring, and certainly influenced by, Guy Debord and the Situationists in Paris, the graffiti in the film radically alters a homogenous landscape bowed to the submission of capitalism. As one graffito in the film enjoins: "The city is an open book. Write on its infinite margins" (*Machi wa akareta shomotsu de aru. Kakubeki yohaku ga mugen ni aru*).

The film's documentation of city life and its cinematic disruption of the city space echoes city symphonies like Vertov's *Chelovek s kinoapparatom*. But perhaps the film's most Vertovian quality is its reflexivity and breaking of the fourth wall: Eimei addresses the audience directly at both

182   CHAPTER 5

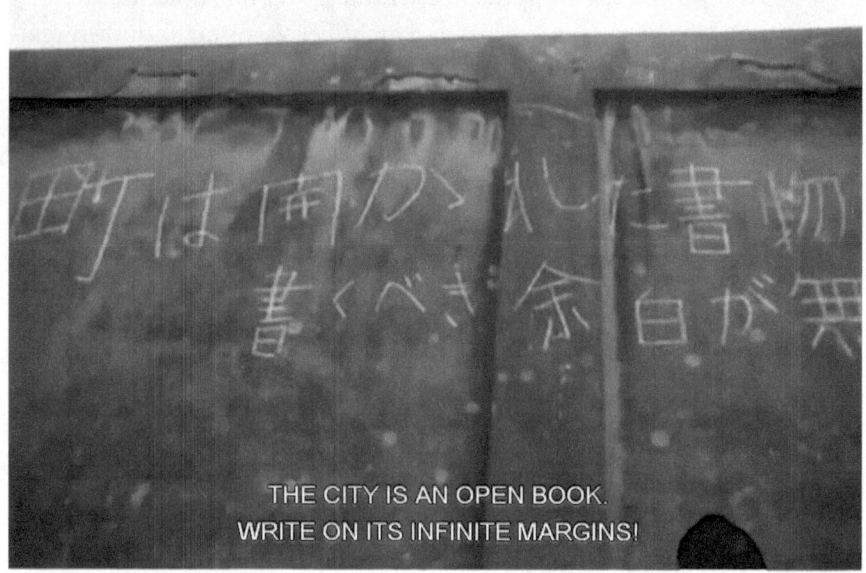

Figure 24. Graffiti in Tokyo, in Terayama Shūji's *Sho o suteyo, machi e deyō*, 1971.

the beginning and end of the film. At the end, he announces: "The film ends here. Now it's my turn to speak. When you think about it, a film can only live in the dark. When the lights go up like that, the world of the film is blotted out. In the film, I dreamed of an airplane. In real life, I also dreamed of a human airplane. And, bit by bit, while that went on, the line between film and reality has disappeared. . . . This fantasy takes hold of me bit by bit." The film exposes itself before us: Eimei reveals himself to be an actor, and the film lays bare its cinematic device. During a moment when Eimei speaks, the film's projector even appears to malfunction, and while Eimei continues his monologue, the film cuts to a shot of its own frame, a device used by Vertov as well as *Bara no sōretsu*, Yoshida Kiju's *Erosu + Gyakusatsu* (*Eros + Massacre*, 1969), and other avant-garde films of the 1960s. The concluding scene, in lieu of ending credits, is a slow pan showing the faces of the actors and crew in close-up: a horizontality with revolutionary purpose in its lack of hierarchical structure. The viewers of *Sho o suteyo, machi e deyō* directly confront the actors involved in its production.

Such filmmaking takes reflexivity and the surreal juxtaposition of the real and oneiric to its furthermost limits. This enfolding of worlds is, I believe, a commitment to queerness—even more so than Terayama's use of actors in drag, who appear in several fantasy sequences near the conclusion of the film. All of these elements, as in Matsumoto's film, symbolize a playfulness and performativity, perpetually critical of any objective "reality." Matsumoto's film reminds us of Ahmed's claim that "to make things queer is certainly to disturb the order of things," a "disorientation" that is "indeed uncanny."[66] Queer, then, in its representation of "aberrant" sexualities, diegetically critical of heteronormativity, queer in its emphasis on unstable subjecthood, and queer in form: the result is a cinematic manifesto, declaring the power of art to revolutionize the way we perceive our own flawed realities.

GENDERQUEER MELANCHOLY IN *GOZENCHŪ NO JIKANWARI*

Like Terayama's work, Hani Susumu's films, especially from the late 1960s and early 1970s, also believe in the power of radical aesthetics, especially art, to change experiences and perceptions. As Satō Tadao claims, for Hani the "main concern was not to project what was in the script but to reflect reality as accurately as he could."[67] This "reality," however, was not necessarily "realistic." According to Justin Jesty, for Hani, who began his career as a renowned documentary filmmaker, documentary was less about being "truthful" or "faithful" to a particular picture of reality; rather, it needed to reanimate the viewer by transporting the affective dynamics of the subjects and their situation into it.[68] Affect, then, is instrumental to the dynamics between filmmaker and subject. The filmmaker's positionality is also key; they must participate, take a position, and adopt a "prejudice" (*henken*). Objectivity is not the answer. As Hani stated in an interview with *Cahiers du cinéma* just prior to the filming of *Gozenchū no jikanwari*: "By 'truth,' I do not mean 'objective truth,' nor 'scientific truth,' but 'human truth.'"[69] Hani was incredibly hostile to claims of neutrality, arguing that they "present nothing more of people... than their subjugation."[70]

And like many other avant-garde documentarists, Hani believed in the potential of truly *intersubjective* film, which one could compare to Matsumoto as well as Jean Rouch and Agnès Varda. Tsunoda notes that Hani conceptualized his filmmaking as "processive" (*purosesshibu na*), highlighting the "three-dimensional" "contact" between the subject of the film, the filmmaker, and the spectator. This is in contrast to "the mirror image-like statis" of the "substantive" (*jittaiteki na*) way of thinking.[71] This complex three-way process overlaps significantly with Matsumoto's theory of filmmaking, also echoed by their comrade, filmmaker Noda Shinkichi, in *Kiroku eiga*, who described their position: "With the artist's subject as the axis, he [the artist] constantly interacts with the real object (the outside world), perceives the real object subjectively, and reconfigures it, subjectively."[72] Hani's "processive" filmmaking follows other avant-garde documentarists of the period in its prioritization of intersubjectivity, although his particular take is suffused with more collaboration, humanism, and tenderness. It is for good reason that Japanese film critic Yamada Koichi called Hani Susumu a *cinéaste de la tendresse* in *Cahiers du cinéma*.[73]

Gozenchū no jikkanwari is Hani Susumu's last film from his avant-garde documentary period and is arguably its most collaborative and intersubjective. The film cedes much control to a group of high school students, who document their lives and craft a semifictional, semi-documentarian film in the process. As expected, as in *Furyō shōnen*, the film is entirely composed of nonprofessional actors. Hani stated that he "prefer[s] non-professional actors on principle.... I hope that each of them feels something new in themselves, something to do with what they haven't yet experienced, but wish to experience, or experiment with."[74] The nonprofessional actors combine with the film's experimental form: the film juxtaposes 8 mm home videos in color with more professional black-and-white film. The jump between film stock is disorienting but not unpleasurable, and the tone is somewhat eulogistic throughout. Hani perceived the film's unconventional editing as an attempt to reject the limitations of the status quo in daily life: "Society tries to impose a certain way of life as normal, getting up in the morning, going to bed at night; I do not reject this society, but it creates a kind of limitation to human life, and what I seek, while remaining within this society, is to try to get out of this framework; each film is an experiment in this sense."[75] Such a critical attitude toward society and civilization (without leaving it wholesale), and the attempt to break out of the framework of business as usual, dovetails with the importance of "self-revolution" for student activists during this period. For activists of the late 1960s and early 1970s, the imposition of rules and routine was stifling, while both students and somewhat older filmmakers such as Hani perceived a strong need for liberation and experiment.

Experimentation in *Gozenchū* applies, also, to gender and sexuality, as the film depicts a character that we would today call "genderfluid." It is a rare instance of a character assigned female at birth who is neither a parody of butch lesbianism (Matsumoto's *Bara no sōretsu* can be criticized for its stereotypical portrayal of a butch lesbian gang sporting rose tattoos) nor a straight fantasy of women lovers as in several Japanese pink "eroductions," but a genuinely unique character experimenting with different modes of gender presentation. This colors the film with a certain softness and malleability compared to earlier works of the Japanese avant-garde— due, I believe, to the collaboration of the film's student actors.

It is impossible to unravel the elements of the film shot by Hani versus his young teenage collaborators, as all are credited as screenwriters as well as actors. It incorporates significant meta-cinematic elements, which play with the interaction between camera and subject. In this, it is reminiscent of Jean Rouch's experimental quasi-documentary ethno-fictions of the late 1950s and 1960s, such as *Moi, un noir* (*I, a Negro*, 1959), *La pyramide humaine* (*The Human Pyramid*, 1961), and *Jaguar* (1967), in which the filmmaker cedes authorship to his subjects, who then control the fate of much of the film's editing and production. In Hani's case, this documentarian aspect did not rely on a process of ethnographic othering. Rather than collaborate with communities far from France but tied to its colonialist history—Mali, Niger, or the Ivory Coast—Hani worked with high-school-age adolescents from Japanese urban centers in the creation of a film about their own lives. Although he was about thirty years older than the subjects of the film, Hani, born in 1928, felt an affinity with the generation born after the war: "My works to date, including my criticism, have actively taken up the opinions of the generation born and raised in postwar Japan."[76]

In the film, three teenage friends make a series of 8 mm films, and the death of one, seventeen-year old Kusako, while camping with her best friend Reiko, leads the remaining two to rewatch Kusako's captured footage to discover clues to her inner life. The footage is also used to reveal a love triangle through the image of another man on their camping trip named Oki, with whom Kusako fell in love. Yet it is also used to reveal Kusako and Reiko's tender, indeed romantic, relationship. Where Reiko tends to follow Japanese gender norms for a young woman—demure, feminine, and calm—the genderfluid Kusako is a ball of chaos. She simply cannot fit in.[77] The film primarily focuses on the playful and flirtatious interactions between Kusako and Reiko. Reiko is a soft-voiced, gentle, long-haired character beloved by the film's milquetoast male protagonist, but the camera especially loves freckled, wild, short-haired Kusako, whose playful antics imbue the film with a joyful whimsy: she prances about pretending to be a cat, swims naked in a stream, places clovers all over her body, films her own bellybutton, pretends to be a bull and toreador, and is sporadically subsumed by *warai-byō*, or "laughing sickness." The film's overall tone is composed of laughter and play, with an undertone of deep melancholy, the singularly "queer affect of doom," as previously noted.

Before Kusako's mysterious disappearance and death, which the viewer assumes to be suicide, footage shows her stealing Oki's pants and newsboy hat and pretending to be Charlie Chaplin on the rocks of a beach, stating, "Chaplin in his movies is sad, somehow" (*nanka kanashisō*). This mention of Chaplin is no accident: Hani, a great admirer of Chaplin, lauded *The Great Dictator* (1940) in an article entitled "The Art and Thought of Chaplin" in 1960. Here, he praises Chaplin's everyman humanism, noting that Chaplin "represents the dictator himself humorously, but conversely does not laugh before nation or power."[78] Such a view of Chaplin would be echoed in the character of Kusako in *Gozenchū*: though filmed twelve years after the article, the seventeen-year old, in all her playful antics and exuberant sense of humor, also reveals a deep sadness and sense of nonbelonging in a society that scorns her innocent behavior. It is, notably, after she draws a mustache on her face that she walks up a cliff and off screen—never to be seen again.

Kusako is more than a tomboy: she is represented as neither man nor woman, at times appearing to court Reiko, at times flirting with Oki. Yet

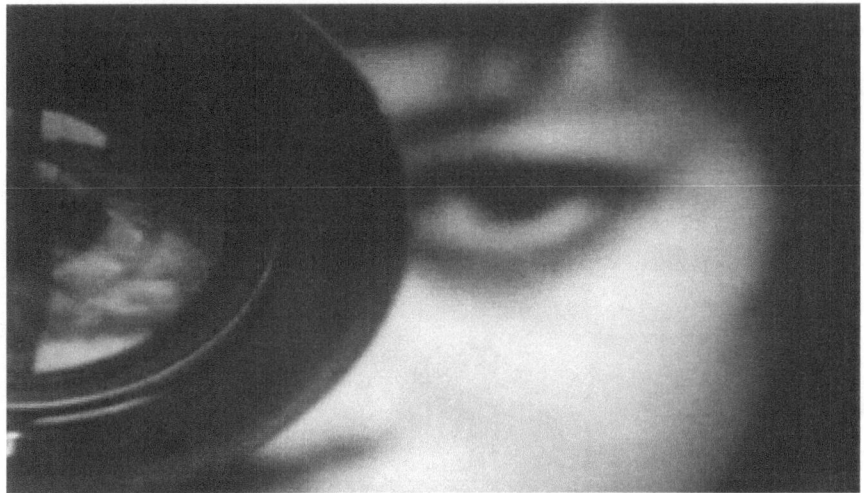

Figure 25. Camera-eye of Kusako, in Hani Susumu's *Gozenchū no jikanwari*, 1972.

it is through the medium of film that this inner, invisible world can be revealed: the film is full of cameras and lenses of all sorts, which serve as a constant source of mediation and self-documentation, as Kusako is frequently seen using the camera to investigate herself, endlessly questioning sexuality and being-in-the-world, without coming to any specific conclusions. She is perpetually in a state of her own (un)becoming. Merging with the subjectivity of its teenage filmmakers and protagonists, the eye of the camera lens is thus equated with the endlessly self-reflective and endlessly self-questioning eye of Tokyo youth in 1972.

Hani's film depicts Kusako as a fully nonconventional character; compared to all others in the film, she embodies a self-revolution by merging boundless creativity (she is diegetically represented as the filmmaker, compared to the other teenagers, who watch her 8 mm footage) with an extraordinary sense of play. In its inclusion of teenage protagonists making films and its meta-cinematic reflexivity, the film echoes Ōshima Nagisa's *Tōkyō sensō sengo hiwa* (*The Man Who Left His Will on Film*, 1970), another film in which the footage of a dead teenager is endlessly pored over and analyzed by his activist-filmmaker friends.[79] In Ōshima's film, (straight) sex between the student filmmakers becomes an allegory of

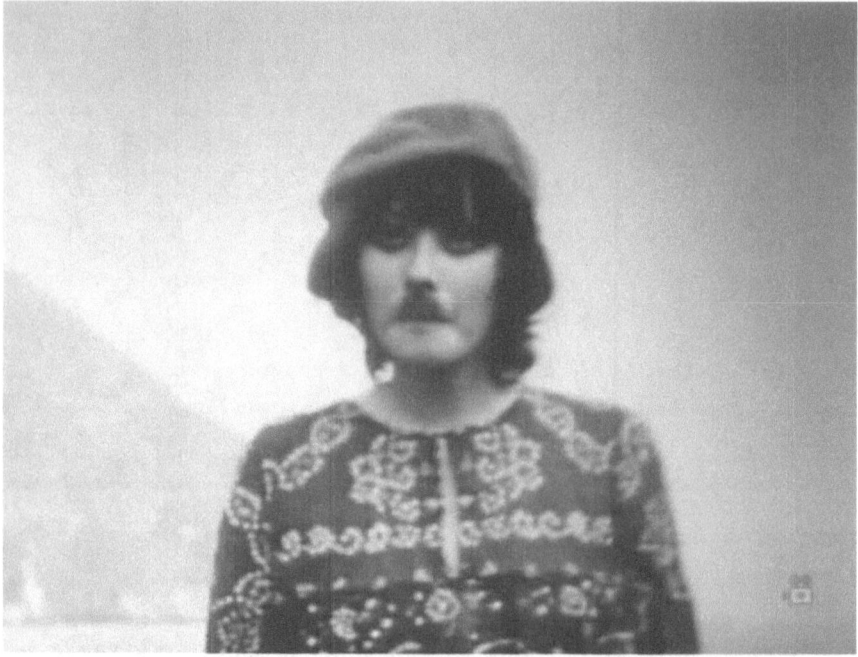

Figure 26. Kusako as Charlie Chaplin, in Hani Susumu's *Gozenchū no jikanwari*, 1972.

national power and impotency. In *Gozenchū*, questions of gender and sex are not merely metaphors but real and embodied, albeit tenderly and subtly portrayed.

In 1970 Hani stated: "I am currently interested in the problems of sex; I believe that in the problem of sexuality, there is something in sex that cannot be made to fit into social norms."[80] Likewise, in the same interview he said, "I cannot believe that the existence of two different sexes, one male and one female, easily determines the sexual act."[81] *Gozenchū* exemplifies this interest in sex and gender, highlighting a character that is notable for her tender ambiguity and inability to "fit into social norms." Fluidity in form, as in gender: *Gozenchū* forms the apex of a career which, through a great variety of genre and style, blends documentary and fiction film, exterior reality and invisible interior worlds. In a colloquium following a retrospective of his films at Harvard in January 2013, Hani emphasized that the distinction between fiction and documentary is in fact quite fluid, and that he meant for his supposedly fiction films to be considered documentaries—echoing the intertitle at the beginning of *Furyō shōnen* and its first intertitle's claim to be a "documentary film," but one in which "its characters and events are fictitious."[82]

When reality could no longer be represented through purely "realistic" modes, Hani crafted a new means to interrogate politics and contemporary Japanese society through a deceptively lighthearted sense of play and through a complex process of intersubjectivity. In Hani's work, reality was less strict journalistic recording than a dialectical relation between camera and subject, which is no less truthful in its engagement with fictionality. In his films, truth is frequently revealed through women and youth—"there is a strong feminism in me," Hani claimed—as in *Gozenchū*, a group of teenage filmmakers searching for meaning and self-revolution within an increasingly deceptive world.[83] Yet it is notable that Kusako's gender fluidity is not utopian and ends tragically—as Mayakovsky would say, with a "love boat smashed against the daily grind." Such an ending recalls Heather Love's notion of "backwardness" as a "feeling and as a model for queer historiography": backwardness as "shyness, ambivalence, failure, melancholia, loneliness, regression, victimhood, heartbreak, antimodernism, immaturity, self-hatred, despair, shame."[84] The character of Kusako embodies much of this backwardness in the complex and ambivalent ending of *Morning Schedule*. Indeed, Hani claimed to "absolutely not believe in 'heroic' sexual stories," and his film does not provide us with a solution.[85] Indeed, by this point he and the Japanese political avant-garde writ large were no longer optimistic about revolutionary possibilities in Japan.

THE END OF THE QUEER POLITICAL AVANT-GARDE

In 1970 Hani stated: "I think that 20 years from now a reaction against democratic politics will take place in the world, and we will come to a choice between two directions: either a politics governed by computers, or the rebirth of a religious politics, of Ancient Empire. Either way will only be a form of fascism."[86] We now know that Hani was more correct than he knew. By the time of his interview, the anarchistic optimism of the political avant-garde period had started to shift into something else.

Japan's fervently antifascist, and unabashedly experimental, era of the avant-garde documentary began to wane in the early 1970s, fully ending around 1973. The passion and political engagement of 1960s cinema in Japan seemed to give way to a more personal documentary mode—one more diaristic and focused on one's own experiences and far less politically engaged. Queerness did not disappear from cinema, but it largely withdrew from an association with vibrant radical leftism. Half a century later Japan continues to lag behind other countries in LGBTQ+ policies, and although certain strides have been made, the country's conservative turn since 1973 does not show much sign of stopping.

This is not to say, however, that the 1960s were necessarily utopian either, despite Shinjuku 1969 being a queer mecca. In fact, despite the evident queerness of these films—Matsumoto's *Bara no sōretsu* and Okabe's *Kureijī Rabu* are obvious examples of films that are nowhere near subtle in their demonstration of "aberrant" sexualities—there remains little work on the era in relation to queerness. There is, in fact, strikingly little in Japanese film archives that speaks to the question of queerness and gender during this period, although much is described about sex as a whole (not surprising, perhaps, given the enormous popularity of the pink film "eroduction" genre). Open discussion of the topic remains quite taboo. Searching for queerness in Japanese archives alongside my research assistant Patrick Carland approximates something like Saidiya Hartman's search for her family's missing archive of the Atlantic slave trade in *Lose Your Mother* (2006); I find myself looking for meaning within gaps and absences. Perhaps unsurprisingly, one is able to find more explicit discussion of gender and sexuality in archives *outside* of Japan than within it; Hani, for example, was much more outspoken in France (where he was a veritable star in the late 1960s) than in Japan when it came to questions of sexuality. Nonetheless the fact remains that many avant-garde documentaries of this era, especially those produced and distributed through ATG, are ardently queer, and not merely as metaphor.

Yet as Eimei states near the conclusion of *Sho o suteyo*, "this film will be over soon." The year of that film's release was already nearing the end of the Japanese political avant-garde; more than a decade of extremely prolific filmmaking would soon be over—or at least, would metamorphose into something else. In 1973 Matsuda Masao, one of the key writers of

Eiga hihyō II, declared that the *kakumei no media*—revolutionary media, the media *of* revolution—gave way to *media no kakumei*, the revolution of media.[87] The post-1973 world saw a massive shift in documentary media practices. Even in France, the DVG, so inspirational for the militant *Eiga hihyō II* journal in Japan, had disbanded by 1972. Nornes notes, "The passion and social commitment of the 1960s cinema seemed to give way to a new kind of documentary centered on the self.... Something happened, the question was what."[88]

Nornes posits that there are many ways to answer the "what happened" question, ranging from the continuing presence of Old Leftist tendencies within the New Left, to the problem of gender (here more connected to the continued misogyny within leftist circles rather than questions of queerness), to the increasing violence and polarization of leftist movements. Although all of these contributed to the demise of radical leftism, I follow Furuhata in believing the latter to be especially important. As she describes in *Cinema of Actuality*, events such as the Asama Sansō incident of 1972, in which the militant leftist United Red Army lynched many of its own members while training in the woods of Nagano and then engaged in a high-profile shoot-out with police, caused the public to shy further away from politics. An astonishing 98.2 percent of viewers in the Tokyo metropolitan area watched live coverage of the event.[89] The incident, as well as a streak of serious and well-documented hijackings of Japan Airlines flights in 1970 by the Red Army Faction of the Japan Communist League and in 1973 by the Japanese Red Army in association with the Palestinian Liberation Front (PLO), effectively ended a period of popular leftism in Japan. As Kimata Kimihiko notes, having lost their goal, and in the wake of countless imprisoned activists, apathy (*shirake*) then spread among the youth.[90]

The filmmakers described in this chapter each experienced their own definitive ending point around 1973. Hani stopped making feature films and settled into the world of shorter animal documentaries created for television (this is what he is best known for in Japan to this day). Matsumoto created only one feature after the Asama Sansō incident (1988's *Dogura magura*), continuing to craft increasingly niche experimental short films, and settled into academia. Terayama was perhaps the most successful of these filmmakers and continued his theater and film productions—although none of his later films would pack the political punch of *Sho o suteyo*; he moved, instead, toward a surrealism and experimentation less focused on documentary, before dying of cirrhosis in 1983.

With all this in mind, it is tempting to think of this strikingly experimental period—in which "self-revolution" was conceptualized as integral to activist activity, in which radical art-making practices questioned truth-telling procedures, and in which ardent and playful queer self-expression incited shock and transformation in the viewer—as a failure. Japan nowadays feels like it is hurtling back blindly toward a fascism these filmmakers vehemently opposed. And yet, I cannot speak for every viewer of these films, but I personally experienced the affective force of these films as a veritable thunderbolt; the term *self-revolution* feels appropriate. I remember the feeling of watching *Sho o suteyo, machi e deyō* with the CinEncounters Japanese film workshop at Harvard, run by Nick Kapur, Franz Prichard, and Alex Zahlten. In that moment, I am twenty-four, sitting in the nondescript, vaguely modernist building called CGIS South, a plate of pad thai balanced precariously on my lap. I remember the breath leaving my body as the credits rolled to Eimei's speech, that terrifying and not-entirely-pleasant moment of perceptual rupture that can only be explained as *ecstatic*. Like Mikhail Koltsov's first review of Vertov's *Kino-Pravda*, "the screen had a terrible quality"—but one that was profoundly energizing, when "suddenly everything starts to move."[91] Someone turns on the lights. I stand up. Everything changes. Within a few weeks I would help start the Harvard Graduate Student Union. Within a month I would end a long-term relationship. Within half a year I would move back to New York City and start drawing the graphic novel that would one day be called *Soviet Daughter*. A decade later I would start writing this book; more changes ensue. I would move to Los Angeles, would end a marriage, and would find a different—queerer—person in the mirror.

Life is an endless struggle of self-transformation. I am reminded of Jean-Pierre Gorin, who described the DVG films as "mad films, love films, political films," and Godard, who claimed in 1968 that "one must give everything up.... One must change one's life.... One must completely change oneself, and that is very difficult."[92] In that moment, watching Eimei's speech, I knew what Godard knew, what Vertov knew, what Hani, Terayama, Imamura, and Matsumoto knew: that everything needed to change, and I must change with it.

Coda

When I first set out to write a conclusion to the first iteration of this project, I had to grasp at straws to find examples of antifascist avant-garde documentary in our contemporary moment. I yearned for films that were the modern-day equivalent of Matsumoto Toshio's *Bara no sōretsu* or Chris Marker and Pierre Lhomme's *Le Joli Mai*, with their singular, peculiar mix of playful affect, epistemological rupture, and anti-imperialist commitment. Donald Trump had just been elected president of the United States; the Bernie Sanders campaign reawakened—or perhaps tapped into—a burgeoning leftism among millennials and Generation Z; and the hubbub surrounding deep fakes, conspiracy theories, and #fakenews created an impetus for radical media literacy in yet another overly mediatized age. As failures of leadership and seemingly endless economic disasters led my peers increasingly to revolutionary thought, and led to a veritable revitalization and flourishing of leftist journalism, I wondered: Shouldn't this be the perfect recipe for a revisitation of the experimental documentary?

Just a few years after filing my dissertation, films appeared, as if magically willed into being. Not just avant-garde documentaries, either, but science fiction films; *Sorry to Bother You* (Boots Riley, 2018) and *Lapsis* (Noah Hutton, 2020) enlist allegory and hyperbole—and even, in the case of the former film, animation—to craft a biting critique of labor and the gig economy in late capitalist North America.[1] Films appeared in mainstream media, too; although it has been denounced for its insufficiently critical portrayal of the Amazon workplace and gig economies, the semi-documentary *Nomadland* (Chloé Zhao, 2020) swept the Academy Awards, winning Best Picture and Best Director—not despite, I believe, but because of its engagement with the documentary medium. The film includes diegetic interviews; many characters play themselves and are credited as such. The film tapped into a national zeitgeist with its sharp lampooning of the "American Dream" in a dying economy and through its portrayal of a protagonist who finds meaning elsewhere—in travel, in community with others of her anti-establishment ilk; there are resonances, indeed, with Agnès Varda's *Sans toit ni loi* (*Vagabond*, 1985), another semi-documentary tracking a woman at the margins of society.

In the field of documentary specifically, experiment is increasingly utilized alongside political critique. In fact, many politically engaged documentary productions from the last few years refer, often quite openly, to the film texts described in this book. Brett Story's thoughtful, effervescent *The Hottest August* (2019) actively engages with *Le Joli Mai* (even Story's title is an echo of Marker's film), as she uses her camera to portray the "hottest august on record" in New York City—a film that, like Marker and Lhomme's, is no less biting in its anti-capitalist and environmentalist commitment despite its gentleness. Ephraim Asili's semi-documentary *The Inheritance* (2020) consciously mobilizes the narrative and unmistakable aesthetics of Godard's *La Chinoise* (1967) to paint a playfully Brechtian portrait of a West Philadelphia collective, the house of Ubuntu; the film not only explicitly quotes *La Chinoise* in a typically Godardian way (including numerous long takes featuring the poster of *La Chinoise* in center frame) but literally repeats the composition and mise-en-scène, with intertitles in Godard's patented font, characters painting political slogans on walls, and piles of books and records serving as a typically Godardian cinematic annotated bibliography.

In addition, Isaac Julien's video installation *Once Again . . .* (*Statues Never Die*, 2022), commissioned for the Barnes Foundation in Philadelphia, is a "quasi-sequel" to *Les statues meurent aussi* (Statues also die, 1953), codirected by Chris Marker and Alain Resnais. As Julien stated,

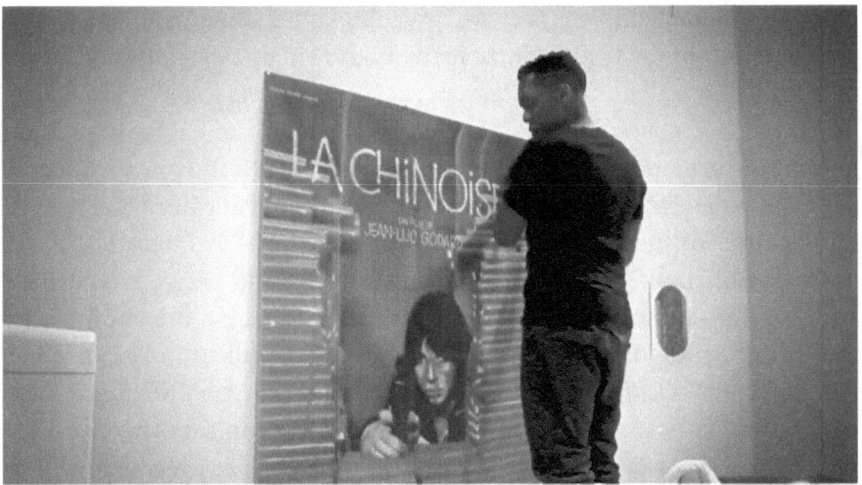

Figure 27. One of many explicit references to Jean-Luc Godard's *La Chinoise* (1967), in Ephraim Asili's *The Inheritance*, 2020.

"I'm calling this the poetics of restitution.... The debates that we're having today that seem contemporaneous were happening 50 years ago, if not before."[2] The many films that not only refer to these antifascist experiments of the postwar period but also explicitly mobilize them as vital predecessors show the continuing power of both the content and form of experimental documentary. The debates, as Julien states, indeed continue to this day.

It is my belief that the lessons of the films and debates featured in this book connect crucially to our contemporary moment in two ways: in their emphasis on media literacy and in their connection to the project of abolition. First, the concern for media literacy is not new; social science disciplines have especially embraced the notion that the media we consume need to be "decoded," "assessed," and "thoughtfully and conscienciously created."[3] Communist experimental documentary filmmakers in the 1960s questioned images as a transparent link to indexical reality. Their models were far more radical and liberation minded than the models of today and more interwoven with debates in philosophy and cultural studies.

This concern with media literacy—which perhaps might be renamed media rupture, or media deterritorialization, in the vein of Deleuze—is crucially connected to the way we are subtly guided by forces that often punish and oppress us. We participate unknowingly, even happily, in our own subjection. Thus media literacy crucially connects to the work of abolition. It is not an accident that the oft-repeated phrase "kill the cop inside your head" originated with the protests of May 1968: the phrase *Chassez le flic de votre tête!* (technically, "get the cop out of your head") appeared on the cover of the January 1969 issue of the short-lived journal *Action*, drawn by Michel Quarez and Georges Wolinski, and became associated with an anti-authoritative leftism.[4] This phrase aligns the abolition of the carceral state directly with antifascism and is linked to Deleuze and Guattari's *Anti-Oedipus*.[5] As Deleuze and Guattari argue, "Repressing desire, not only for others but in oneself, being the cop for others and for oneself—that is what arouses, and it is not ideology, it is economy."[6] For Deleuze and Guattari, capitalism arouses a desire for control "of others and oneself"—what they call asceticism. Modern life is defined by this warped internalized carcerality.

Crucial to my argument is the tie between the formal elements of film and their ability to radically affect the way we perceive reality; film can "condition" us, to use Varda's terminology—it can liberate and reframe what restrains our thinking and feeling. But the stakes of this argument also exceed the confines of film, or even media at large. At heart, this argument is also about the process by which we can counter fascism in our ways of acting, thinking, and feeling, and in the way we treat others. It is fundamentally connected to liberation psychology—to a "liberation" achieved not (just) through military superiority but, in the words of Mary Watkins and Helene Schulman, through "understanding the psychological maiming that affects all involved in oppressive practices. . . . Liberation must involve insight, restoration, and an opening for greater humanity for victims as well as perpetrators, bystanders, and witnesses." Fittingly, they describe liberation as psychological "jailbreak," necessary for the creation of a new commons.[7]

This book did not emerge out of quiet thought and reflection; it is integrally bound to the messy, conflict-ridden work in political organizing. The seeds were sown during my six months working in an official role in conflict resolution with the Democratic Socialists of America. This book was finished in Los Angeles, and its theories were means-tested in a collaboratively led workshop titled "Rethinking Fascism" at the Silver Lake

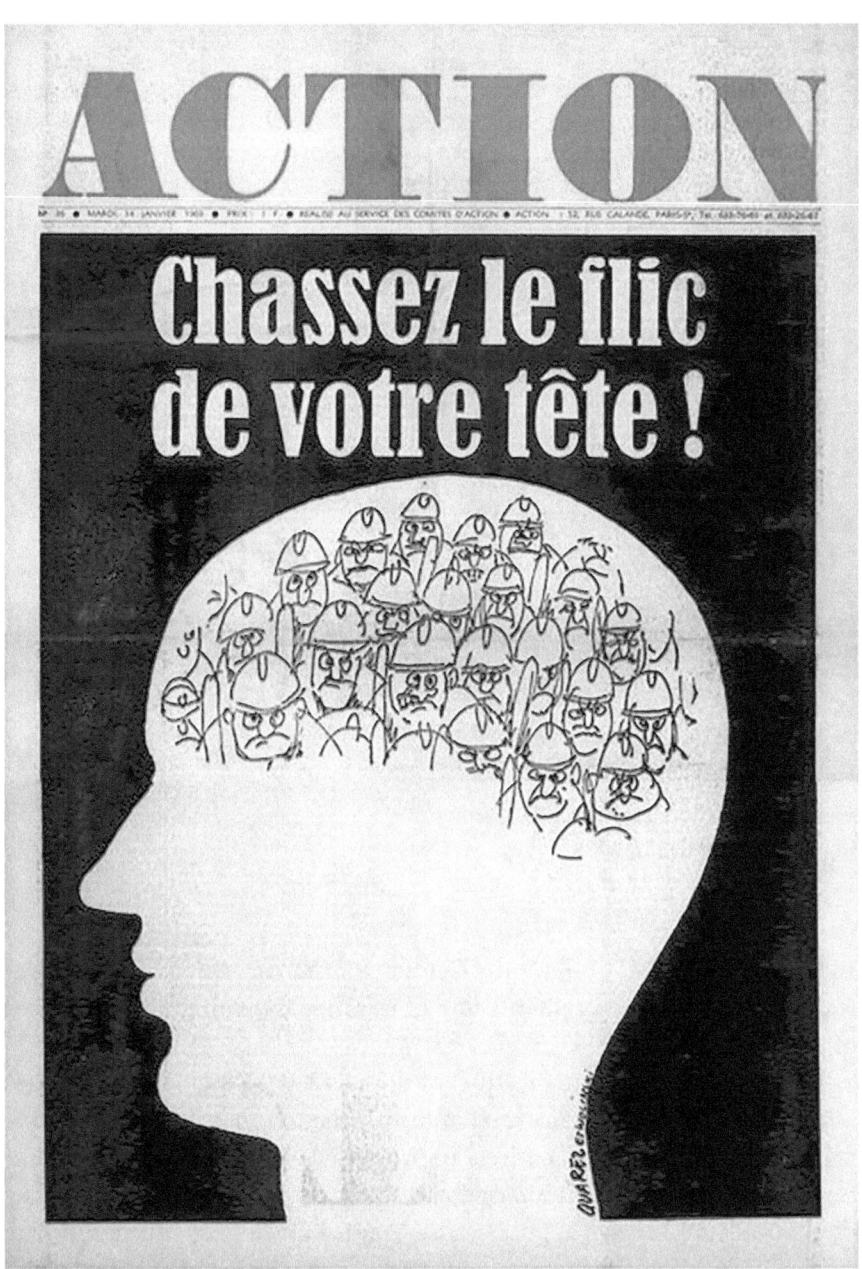

Figure 28. Cover of *Action* magazine, January 1969. Illustration by Michel Quarez and Georges Wolinski.

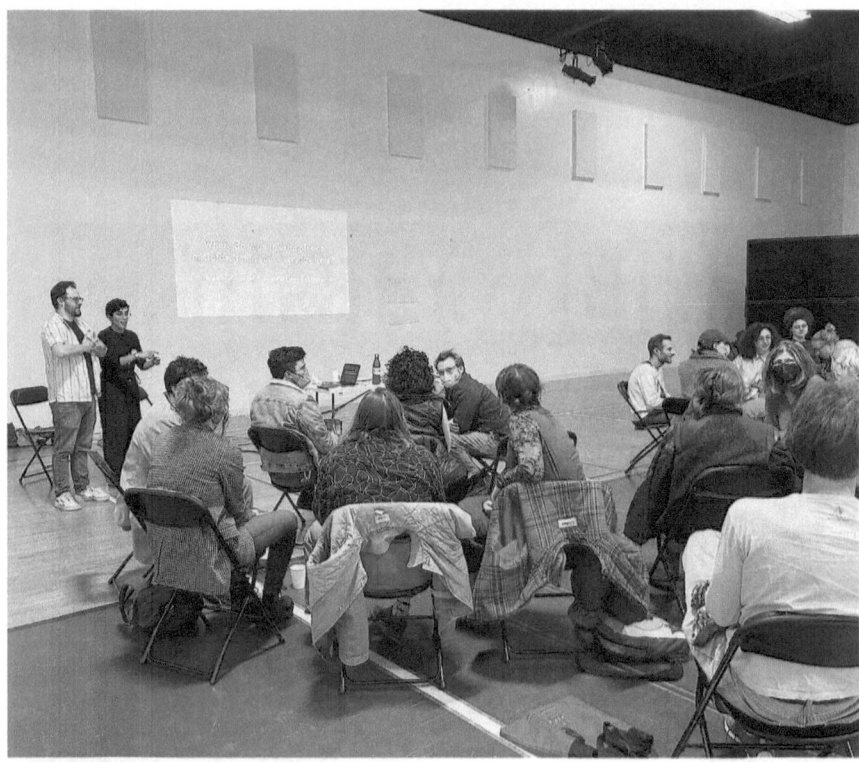

Figure 29. "Rethinking Fascism" workshop at the Silver Lake Independent Jewish Community Center, March 23, 2023.

Independent Jewish Community Center (SIJCC) on March 23, 2023. Co-leading this workshop remains one of the most meaningful experiences of my life.

Participants, who were mostly (but not all) Jewish and mostly (but not all) self-declared leftists, learned and investigated the concept of microfascism. One participant, entirely unprompted, admitted that the idea of microfascism made them worried and uncomfortable—not because they didn't think it was correct, but because they acknowledged the many times in their own life when they had engaged in behaviors that could conceivably be called microfascist: a drive for punishment of others, a fear of acknowledging one's own complicity, a mindset of perpetual victimhood

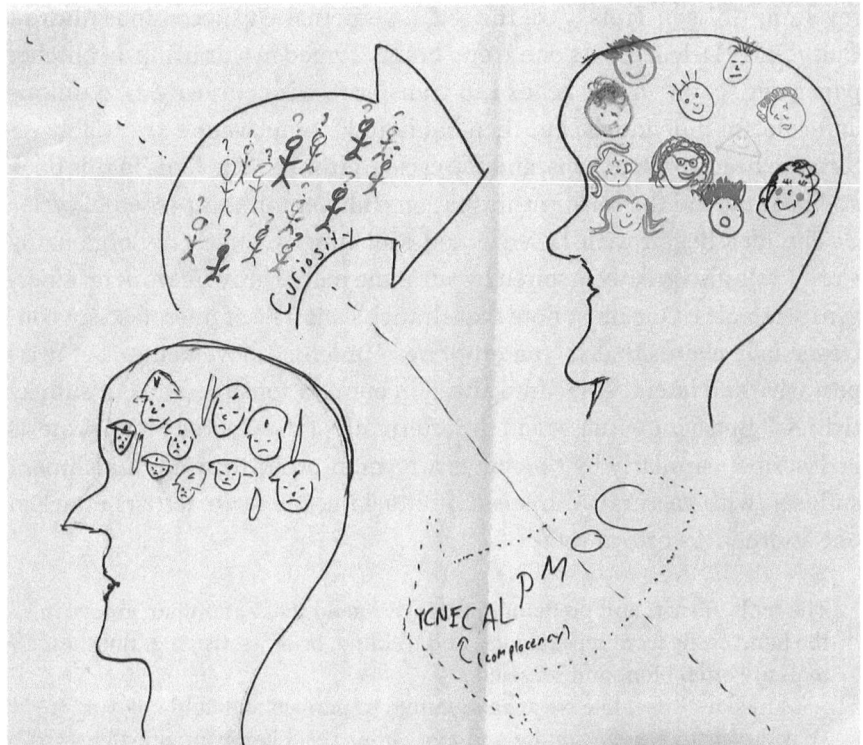

Figure 30. Image from participant brainstorming session at "Rethinking Fascism" workshop at the Silver Lake Independent Jewish Community Center, March 23, 2023.

that might excuse one's own reactive or problematic behavior, a rigidity of thought, a judgmental and domineering "higher than thou" attitude convinced of its own understanding of truth and reality. To this I responded: sitting with this uneasy feeling, this discomfort, and reckoning with it, is, in fact, the point. The battle against fascism is a battle that must be fought daily, perpetually, in the human mind.

When asked to brainstorm methodologies to counter such viewpoints, participants independently arrived at conclusions similar to those of the filmmakers discussed in this book: play, curiosity, combatting rigidity and perfectionism, and the acceptance of ambiguity and contradiction. Importantly, there was no end to this work; it was meant to be a "permanent revolution" (Leon Trotsky) of the self, a perpetual Un-Becoming (Andrew Culp/Gilles Deleuze).[8] As one group brainstormed in a drawing on butcher paper, the "cops" in our heads can transform, with curiosity, into unique and colorful individuals, but then habit and "complacency" invariably return the heads back to cops, and the cycle continues. The films in this book are meant to aid the self-transformations inherent in this perpetual cycle.

The idea began with Deleuze and Matsumoto, but in my organizing work I was also greatly inspired by adrienne marée brown's work on emergent strategies. One must note that Bratich's analysis of microfascism controversially claims that it "can erupt even in leftist movements.... [It is] pervasive and latent, embedding itself in our relationships and our subjectivities."[9] Behavior witnessed in the aftermath of the George Floyd protests is described similarly by brown, as a form of other-focused punishment suffused with carcerality. Instead of attacking the state, leftists attacked one another. As brown writes:

> The tools of swift and predatory justice feel good to use, familiar, groove in the hand easily from repeated use and training, briefly satisfying. But these tools are often blunt and senseless.
>
> Why does it feel like we are committed to punishment, and enjoying it? Why do our movements more and more often feel like we are moving with sharp teeth against ourselves? And what is at stake because of that pattern, that feeling?[10]

Not only are we trained to be our own policemen, but this feeling of carcerality can even feel good, can "groove in the hand easily from repeated use and training," can become a broken record more enjoyable and familiar with each use. Deleuze and Guattari describe this behavior in *Thousand Plateaus:* "Instead of the great, paranoid fear, we are trapped in a thousand little mono-manias, self-evident truths, and clarities that gush from every black hole and no longer form a system, but are only rumble and buzz, blinding lights giving any and everybody the mission of self-appointed judge, dispenser of justice, policeman, neighborhood SS man."[11]

How, then, to do the work of abolition and antifascism when everyone and anyone, leftist or right-wing, can become the cop and "neighborhood SS man"? As Marker's voice-over exclaims at the end of *Le Joli Mai,* an ending that centers on a Parisian prison, "No one is free until we are all free." And we are all, indeed, far less free than we might think.

Common among brown, Deleuze and Guattari, Matsumoto, Watkins and Shulman, and the many theorists of this book is an attempt to recognize that the vast majority of people cannot be slotted into the simple categories of victim, bystander, and abuser. We are all, usually, some combination of the three. The work of antifascism is the work of untangling one's own complicity, of recognizing ambiguity, and of engaging in the vulnerable work of reckoning and auto-critique. Such work recognizes the inseparability of the political and the personal; it understands that liberation must be felt internally before, and alongside, its manifestation externally.

To estrange oneself from the familiar, to shift perspective, becomes a radical act. The films in this book provide the means for undoing "self-evident truths" through an epistemological struggle that can be both painful and pleasurable—a different form of enjoyment from the "briefly satisfying" familiarity described by brown. It is a feeling resolutely unfamiliar, its path unknown and unknowable. But it is a path that brings the viewer, in Vertov's words, "back to life" through "cinematic sensation" (*kinooshchushchenie*). What for Matsumoto are unknown and "unseeable things"—*mienai mono*—must be brought to the surface. The connection, likewise, to surrealism, myth, poetry, and madness is key, for as Bataille argues, fascism is not "rational"; it will not be defeated by reason and argumentation. As Robyn Marasco argues, Bataille claims that "antifascism must stoke a passion for democracy and a delight in its disorders."[12] It is meaningful, also, that contemporary critics like Sylvia Federici and Jackie Wang, abolitionist poet and author of *Carceral Capitalism* (Semiotexte, 2018), are engaged in a project of "reenchantment." Wang's work argues that the very ability to imagine different and better worlds is tied to dreaming, to "Communist Affect," to Freud's "Oceanic Feeling," and to radical acts of imagination.[13]

Radical artmaking can never replace the work of abolitionist organizing and antifascism in the streets, but it necessitates and requires it: to create conditions of liberatory perception—what I call revolutionary phenomenology—and to make our own world liveable in the first place. This is especially important today, when, as Arielle Angel, editor in chief of

Jewish Currents, writes: "These days, I feel the threat of fascism humming in my body like a once-broken bone before the rain."[14] It is a threat I feel, too. It is my belief that this antifascist, communist, fundamentally abolitionist reenchantment is essential to the project of imagining a new and better world.

Notes

INTRODUCTION

1. Andrew Hewitt, *Fascist Modernism: Aesthetics, Politics, and the Avant-Garde* (Palo Alto, CA: Stanford University Press, 1993), 4.

2. Georges Bataille, "The Psychological Structure of Fascism," trans. Carl R. Lovitt, *New German Critique* 16 (Winter 1979): 69.

3. Bataille, "Psychological Structure of Fascism," 70.

4. Matsumoto Toshio, "Geijutsu-teki Sado Mazohisuto no ishiki moshikuwa sōsaku no naiteki katei to geijutsu-teki kyōyō-sei ni tsuite" [Consciousness of the aesthetic sadomasochist: Or, on the internal process of creation and its artistic utility], *Kiroku eiga* 3, no. 2 (February 1960): 8. Translation forthcoming in *Journal of Cinema and Media Studies* 64, no.3 (May 2025).

5. Svetlana Boym, "Estrangement as a Lifestyle: Shklovsky and Brodsky," *Poetics Today* 17, no. 4 (Winter 1996): 515.

6. Jack Z. Bratich, *On Microfascism: Gender, War, and Death* (Brooklyn, NY: Common Notions, 2022), 12.

7. Bratich, *On Microfascism*, 23.

8. Roger Griffin argues that because in Japan "ultimate authority resided in the divinity of the Emperor," the country was not strictly fascist. See Roger Griffin, *Fascism* (Oxford: Oxford University Press, 1995), 238. Griffin's argument, however, is predicated on the origin of fascism in Mussolini's Italy. Although fascism in Germany, Italy, and Japan during World War II had significant

differences, I believe Japan's emphasis on extreme ethnonationalism and its belief in the superiority of the Yamamato race, connected to a divine right to "naturally" rule Asia through the "Greater East Asia Co-Prosperity Sphere," certainly aligns Japan with fascism during the Pacific War. See also Patrick G. Zander, *Fascism through History: Culture, Ideology, and Daily Life* (Santa Barbara, CA: ABC-CLIO, 2020), 255.

9. Robyn Marasco, "Bataille's Anti-fascism," *Contemporary Political Theory* 21, no. 1 (2022): 4.

10. Jennifer Barker, *The Aesthetics of Anti-Fascist Film: Radical Projection* (New York: Routledge, 2013), 32.

11. Although Matsumoto might have been a bit bombastic in his exclamations, he was not wrong. As Japan claimed to turn away from politics after 1973, it also reawakened a latent conservatism and extremely potent racist and classist ideology. Especially when compared with other nations, it might surprise some readers to know that to this day Japan's most left-leaning generation is the elderly (i.e., Matsumoto's generation, who had distant memories of World War II and its aftereffects), while one sees a reawakening of conservatism and neonationalist ideology in youth. On the latter, see Kazuya Fukuoka, "Between Banality and Effervescence? A Study of Japanese Youth Nationalism," *Nations and Nationalism* 23, no. 2 (2017): 346–366.

12. It is important to note that the term Japanese New Wave, or *nūberu bāgu*, was not a reaction to the French; it was applied to films by the Shochiku Studio that shared certain similarities with the French, but it was applied post facto, more of a marketing ploy than a top-down influence. The Japanese term is thus quite problematic and was decried by many of its representative filmmakers, such as Ōshima Nagisa, who declared: "Stop using the term 'New Wave' once and for all! Evaluate each film on its own merits!" See Ōshima Nagisa, *Cinema, Censorship, and the State: The Writings of Ōshima Nagisa, 1956–1978*, ed. Annette Michelson (Cambridge, MA: MIT Press, 1992), 47. Daniel Fairfax, *The Red Years of Cahiers*, vol 1, *Ideology and Politics* (Amsterdam: Amsterdam University Press, 2022), 559.

13. "Les Meilleurs films Français depuis La Libération," *Cahiers du cinéma* 161–162 (January 1965): 130.

14. These films were largely mainstream studio productions, but much of the market—indeed up to half—would turn to "pink films" after 1962. These were sexploitation films that could be made quite cheaply and quickly and served to fill the void left by the crisis in theater attendance. The distinction between these films and arthouse productions after the middle of the decade would become increasingly blurred.

15. Yamada Koichi, "Bilan économique du cinéma japonais," in "Etats Units-Japon," special issue, *Cahiers du cinéma* 166–167 (May-June 1965): 48. One should note that the French numbers are of "authorized" films, so there might be

some that are not counted in these numbers. While this source notes that two or three films were screened to recover numbers, I am grateful to Alex Zahlten for noting that double bills were introduced when the industry was still healthy, and triple bills appeared later.

16. Kristin Ross, *Fast Cars, Clean Bodies: Decolonization and the Reordering of French Culture* (Cambridge, MA: MIT Press, 1995), 4–5.

17. Nick Kapur, *Japan at the Crossroads: Conflict and Compromise after Anpo* (Cambridge, MA: Harvard University Press, 2018), 2.

18. Jonathan M. Hall, "Unwilling Subjects: Psychoanalysis and Japanese Modernity" (PhD diss., University of California–Santa Cruz, 2003), 62.

19. One famous example demonstrates this taboo. When Alain Resnais's Holocaust documentary *Night and Fog* (*Nuit et brouillard*, 1955; its title would inspire Ōshima Nagisa's Japanese New Wave film and biting socialist critique *Night and Fog in Japan* in 1960) screened in French theaters, it removed the highly identifiable rectangular shape of the French *gendarme skepi* (cap with visor), visible in the corner as Jews and other minorities were taken to Auschwitz-Birkenau. See Charles Krantz, "Teaching *Night and Fog*: History and Historiography," *Film & History: An Interdisciplinary Journal of Film and Television Studies* 15, no. 1 (February 1985): 8.

20. See *Les Lettres françaises* 910 (January 18–24, 1962).

21. I have used *cinéma-vérité* in this volume to refer to the originally intended French meaning rather than its contemporary evolution or iteration, instead of the English-language spelling cinema verité, as my research shows that the use of the term in the anglophone context is often profoundly different than its origins in 1960 France. Georges Sadoul, "Un film maudit: 'Octobre à Paris,' long métrage francais, anonyme," *Les Lettres Françaises* 943 (September 13–19 1962): 6

22. Daniel Fairfax lays out the film journalistic ecology of France beautifully in *Red Years of Cahiers*, 12.

23. In this book I use macrons for long vowel sounds in Japanese (i.e., *ou* or *oo* becomes *ō*), *except when a version without a macron has been standardized, as in the city names Tokyo and Kyoto.*

24. Hani Susumu, quoted in Georges Sadoul, "Autour d'une indépendance conversations avec quatres jeunes cinéastes japonaises," , in "Etats Units-Japon," special issue, *Cahiers du cinéma* 166-167 (May–June 1965): 40.

25. Ōishi Masahiko, *Higa tōi : Nihon Modanizumu/Roshia avangyarudo* (Tokyo: Suisei-sha, 2009), 269–270.

26. Yuriko Furuhata, "Refiguring Actuality: Japan's Film Theory and Avant-Garde Documentary Movement, 1950s-1960s" (PhD diss., Brown University, 2009, 23).

27. Aleksandr Pronin, *Bumazhnyi Vertov/Tselluloidnyi Maiakovskii* [Paper Vertov/celluloid Mayakovsky] (Moscow: Novoe literaturnoe obozrenie, 2019), 172.

28. John MacKay, "Dziga Vertov: A Revolution in Film," *Artforum* 49, no. 8 (April 2011): 198; and Annette Michelson, "*The Man with the Movie Camera*: From Magician to Epistemologist," *Artforum*, March 1972, 69. Emphasis in original.

29. D. N. Rodowick, *The Crisis of Political Modernism* (Berkeley: University of California Press, 1994), xiv, xvi.

30. Michelson, "*Man with the Movie Camera*," 72.

31. Joshua Malitsky, *Post-Revolution Nonfiction Film: Building the Soviet and Cuban Nations* (Bloomington: Indiana University Press, 2013), 95.

32. Malitsky, *Post-Revolution Nonfiction Film*, 104. Emphasis in original.

33. For an in-depth analysis of Vertov alongside Shklovsky, see Julia Alekseyeva, "A Stony Stone, a Cinematic Cinema: Shklovskian Estrangement in Dziga Vertov's *Kino-Eye*," *Oxford Research in English* 9 (Autumn 2019).

34. Miriam Hansen, "Benjamin, Cinema and Experience: 'The Blue Flower in the Land of Technology,'" in *New German Critique* 40 (Winter 1987): 204.

35. See Barker, *Aesthetics of Anti-Fascist Film*; Mark Bray, *Antifa: The Anti-Fascist Handbook* (Brooklyn, NY: Melville House, 2017); Bratich, *On Microfascism*; and Patrick Nathan, *Image Control: Art, Fascism, and the Right to Resist* (Berkeley: Counterpoint Press, 2021). Indeed, one can interpret the (increasingly) frequent reliance on the texts of Benjamin—theoretician of fascism and aesthetic experience as well as its tragic victim—as a powerful current cultural drive to reexamine the relationship between politics and art. For an analysis of the contemporary relevance of Benjamin's texts, see Julia Alekseyeva, "Theses on the Philosophy of Walter Benjamin," *Paper Brigade* 2 (2018): 57–64.

36. "Кино-Глаз, оспаривающий зрительное представление о мире у человеческого глаза и предлагающий свое 'вижу!'" See Dziga Vertov, "Postanovlenie Soveta Troikh" [Decree of the Council of Three], in *Iz naslediia*, tom II, *Stat'i i vystupleniia* (Moscow: Eisenstein Center, 2008), 43.

37. Quoted in Michelson, "*Man with Movie Camera*," 66.

38. While there is insufficient space in this book to elucidate on Vertov's concept of *kinooshchushchenie*, or "cinematic sensation," excellent work has recently drawn our attention to the concept, including but not limited to Emma Widdis, *Socialist Senses: Film, Feeling, and the Soviet Subject, 1917–1940* (Bloomington: Indiana University Press, 2017), esp. 127–128; Edward Tyerman, *Internationalist Aesthetics: China and Early Soviet Culture* (New York: Columbia University Press, 2022), 20–21; Lilya Kaganovsky, "'The Threshold of the Visible World': Dziga Vertov's 'A Sixth Part of the World' (1926)," in *Arctic Cinemas and the Documentary Ethos*, ed. Lilya Kaganovsky, Scott MacKenzie, and Anna Westerstahl Stenport (Bloomington: Indiana University Press, 2019), 52; and Malitsky, *Post-Revolution Nonfiction Film*, 92.

39. Michelson, "*Man with Movie Camera*," 69.

40. Dziga Vertov, "O s'emke kinosiuzhetov v khronike," in *Iz naslediia*, tom II, *Stat'i i vystupleniia*, by Dziga Vertov (Moscow: Eisenstein Center, 2008), 22–23.

Translation: Yuri Tsivian, *Lines of Resistance: Dziga Vertov and the Twenties* (Bloomington: Indiana University Press, 2004), 81.

41. While I do not have time to go into *byt* extensively in this monograph, it has been described by writer Anya von Bremzen as "the metaphysical weight of the daily grind, the existentially depleting cares of material living" that the Bolsheviks tried to eliminate. See Anya von Bremzen, *Mastering the Art of Soviet Cooking: A Memoir of Food and Longing* (New York: Broadway Books, 2013), 39. Critic Boris Arvatov also called *byt* "an extra-ordinarily conservative force" in 1925. See Boris Arvatov, "Everyday Life and the Question of the Thing (Toward the Formulation of the Question)," trans. Christina Kaier, *October* 81 (Summer 1997): 121. It was not, however, a new invention of the Soviet period; Soviet cultural identity depended on the heroic opposition to *byt*, but it was also heavily associated with the late nineteenth century. Svetlana Boym notes that everyone from nineteenth-century Westernizers to Slavophiles, Romantics and modernists, and aesthetic and politican utopians, to Bolsheviks and monarchists, all engaged in battles with *byt*. See Svetlana Boym, *Common Places: Mythologies of Everyday Life in Russia* (Cambridge, MA: Harvard University Press, 1994), 3, 31

42. Michel Foucault, preface to *Anti-Oedipus: Capitalism and Schizophrenia*, by Gilles Deleuze and Félix Guattari (Minneapolis: University of Minnesota Press, 1972), xiii.

43. Gilles Deleuze and Félix Guattari, *A Thousand Plateaus: Capitalism and Schizophrenia*, trans. Brian Massumi (Minneapolis: University of Minnesota, 1987), 214.

44. The theorists discussed in this book differ in their treatment of Freud. While many echo the bulk of the arguments of *Anti-Oedipus*, others do not share Deleuze and Guattari's criticisms of Freudian psychoanalysis. Most famously, Matsumoto Toshio and Herbert Marcuse were both extremely influenced by Freud, as were the 1920s surrealists. One can indeed argue that Freud is used as a bit of a straw man in *Anti-Oedipus*, and that the importance of self-criticism and questioning is connected to the internal explorations of psychoanalysis.

45. Eugene Holland, *Deleuze and Guattari's Anti-Oedipus: Introduction to Schizoanalysis* (London: Routledge 1999), 12–13. It is worth pointing out that Marcuse's *Eros and Civilization* (1955) described this as well, alongside *One-Dimensional Man*.

46. Foucault, preface, xiii.

47. Lauren Berlant, *Cruel Optimism* (Durham, NC: Duke University Press, 2011), 15.

48. Brian Massumi, preface to *The Politics of Affect*, ed. Brian Massumi (Cambridge, UK: Polity Press, 2014), x.

49. Miryam Sas, *Feeling Media: Potentiality and the Afterlife of Art* (Durham, NC: Duke University Press, 2022), 7.

50. Sianne Ngai, *Ugly Feelings* (Cambridge, MA: Harvard University Press, 2005), 8.

51. Nathan, *Image Control*, 174.

52. James Phillips, "Anti-Oedipus: The Ethics of Performance and Misrecognition in Matsumoto Toshio's *Funeral Parade of Roses*," *SubStance* 44, no. 141 (2016): 35.

53. This "antinomian spirit" entailed, for Julian Bourg, "the rejection of laws and norms in the name of a liberational ethos. As the critical spirit of the times tuned to the categories of mental health, questions that had been popularly asked earlier in other—notably British—anti-psychiatric milieux were now posed in France with newfound intensity: Was normalcy tantamount to normalization? Was psychiatry merely the furthest reach of an array of social and political institutions whose intention, or at least effective function, was to quiet all kinds of rebellion? Was it not society itself that was mad?" See See Julian Bourg, *From Revolution to Ethics: May 1968 and Contemporary French Thought* (Montreal: McGill University Pres, 2007), 105.

54. Hall, "Unwilling Subjects," 74.

55. Hall, "Unwilling Subjects," 82.

56. Matsumoto, "Geijutsu-teki Sado Mazohisuto," 6. The next several pages are derived entirely from this article.

57. In a somewhat recent and perhaps not entirely unsurprising turn toward right-wing policies, Abe Shinzō, the longest-serving prime minister in Japanese history (2006–2007 and 2012–2020), is the grandson of former class A war criminal Kishi Nobusuke.

58. Kapur, *Japan at the Crossroads*, 1.

59. For an in-depth analysis of this history, see Kapur, *Japan at the Crossroads*, 1–34).

60. See Matsumoto Toshio, *Eizō no hakken (Discovery of the Image): Avant-Garde Documentary* (Tokyo: San'ichi Shobo, 1963), 109–118.

61. Donald LaCross, "Introduction: Surrealism and Romantic Anticapitalism," in *Morning Star: Surrealism, Marxism, Anarchism, Situationism, Utopia*, by Michael Löwy (Austin: University of Texas Press, 2009), vii.

62. Matsumoto Toshio,"Zen'ei kiroku eiga no hōhō ni tsuite" [On the method of avant-garde documentary], *Kiroku eiga* (June 1958): 8. A version of this article appeared in Matsumoto's 1963 collected edition *Eizō no hakken*, translated by Michael Raine. However, this important paragraph was not included in the later version.

63. Matsumoto Toshio, "Taishū toiu no mono kami ni tsuite" [On the fetish called mass], *Kiroku eiga* 5, no. 2 (February 1962): 19.

64. Matsumoto, *Eizō no hakken*, 11–12.

65. Georges Sadoul, *French Film* (New York: Arno Press, 1972), 2 (original language text: Georges Sadoul, *Histoire d'un art: Le cinéma; des origins à nos jours* [Paris: Flammarion, 1949]); Siegfried Kracauer, *Theory of Film: The Redemption of Physical Reality* (Princeton, NJ: Princeton University Press, 1960),

30; Jean-Luc Godard, interview in "Nouvelle Vague," special issue, *Cahiers du cinéma* 23, no. 138 (December 1962): 27; Joris Ivens cited in Nakahara Yūsuke, "Zenei eiga ni tsuite: Vertov no koto nado" [On avant-garde film: Vertov and others], in *Sekai Zenei eigasai* [A retrospective of world avant-garde cinema] (Tokyo: Sōgetsu Art Center,1966), 106; Pascal Bonitzer cited by Sergei Yutkevich, quoted in Louis Marcorelles and Eric Rohmer, "Entretien avec Serge Youtkévitch," *Cahiers* 21, no. 125 (November 1961): 6; and Edgar Morin, *Le Cinéma ou l'homme imaginaire: Essai d'anthropologie sociologique* (Paris: Éditions de minuit, 1956), 58.

66. Fairfax, *Red Years of Cahiers*, 246.

67. I am grateful to Alex Zahlten, who reminded me that the Japanese socialist production *Those Who Make Tomorrow* (*Ashita o tsukuru hitobito*, 1946)—codirected by Kurosawa Akira, Sekigawa Hideo, and Yamamoto Kajiro, produced by Toho filmmakers on strike and created during a short-lived period of Occupation government–supported antifascist and socialist flourishing—shares the synopsis of this Renoir film almost exactly. Given the popularity of Renoir's film, I argue that the influence is direct.

68. Bratich, *On Microfascism*, 9.

69. Pascal Bonitzer, Jean-Louis Comolli, Serge Daney, Jean Narboni, and Jean-Pierre Oudart, "*La Vie est à nous*: Film militant," *Cahiers du cinéma* 218 (March 1970): 48.

70. Bonitzer et al., "*La Vie est à nous*," 49–50.

71. Fairfax, *Red Years of Cahiers*, 250.

72. Bonitzer et al., "*La Vie est à nous*," 48.

73. See Naoki Yamamoto, *Dialectics without Synthesis: Japanese Film Theory and Realism in a Global Frame* (Oakland: University of California Press, 2020).

74. Yuriko Furuhata, *Cinema of Actuality: Japanese Avant-Garde Filmmaking in the Season of Image Politics* (Durham, NC: Duke University Press, 2013), 3.

75. Masha Salazkina, *In Excess: Sergei Eisenstein's Mexico* (Chicago: University of Chicago Press, 2009), 5.

76. Sara Ahmed, *Queer Phenomenology: Orientations, Objects, Others* (Durham, NC: Duke University Press, 2006), 23.

77. Ahmed, *Queer Phenomenology*.

CHAPTER 1. 1960 JAPAN: ANPO AND ANTIFASCISM IN THE NEO-DOCUMENTARY

1. Nagano Chiaki, "Puropaganda eiga no shin no reimei" [The true dawn of propaganda film], *Kiroku eiga* 2, no. 11 (November 1959): 25.

2. Nagano, "Puropaganda eiga no shin no reimei," 24.

3. Yamamoto Naoki, *Dialectics without Synthesis: Japanese Film Theory and Realism in a Global Frame* (Oakland: University of California Press, 2020), 168–169.

4. Sasaki Hajime, "Kiroku eiga to seiji" [Documentary film and politics], *Kiroku eiga* 2, no. 9 (September 1959): 4.

5. Matsumoto Toshio, "Haisen to sengo no fuzai: Shutai-ron no saikentō no tame ni" [Absence of 'defeat and postwar': For a reexamination of subjectivity part II], *Kiroku eiga* 2, no. 8 (August 1959): 35.

6. Thomas Lamarre, "Cartoon Film Theory: Imamura Taihei on Animation, Documentary, and Photography," in *Animating Film Theory*, ed. Karen Redrobe (Durham, NC: Duke University Press, 2014), 231.

7. Lamarre, "Cartoon Film Theory," 235.

8. Iwamoto Kenji, *Roshia avangyarudo no eiga to engeki* [Film and theatre of the Russian avant-garde] (Tokyo: Suisei-sha, 1998), 312.

9. Michael Lucken, "Possibilité et limites d'une philosophie photographique: Une lecture de Nakai Masakazu," *Archives de Philosophie* 1, no. 85 (2022): 74.

10. Aaron Stephen Moore, "Para-existential Forces of Invention: Nakai Masakazu's Theory of Technology and Critique of Capitalism," *positions* 17, no. 1 (2009): 144–145.

11. Lucken, "Possibilité et limites," 77. Original text: Nakai Masakazu, *Nakai Masakazu zenshū* (Tokyo: Nijutsu shuppan, 1981), 3:47.

12. Moore, "Para-existential Forces of Invention," 69.

13. Furuhata Yuriko, *Cinema of Actuality: Japanese Avant-Garde Filmmaking in the Season of Image Politics* (Durham, NC: Duke University Press, 2013), 25.

14. Margaret S. Key, *Truth from a Lie: Documentary Detection, and Reflexivity in Abe Kobo's Realist Project* (Plymouth: Lexington Books, 2011), 10–11.

15. Michael Löwy, *Morning Star: Surrealism, Marxism, Anarchism, Situationism, Utopia* (Austin: University of Texas Press, 2009), 21.

16. Key, *Truth from a Lie*, 9.

17. Key, *Truth from a Lie*, 11.

18. Markus Nornes, *Forest of Pressure: Ogawa Shinsuke and Postwar Japanese Documentary* (Minneapolis: University of Minnesota Press, 2007), 20.

19. Nick Kapur, *Japan at the Crossroads: Conflict and Compromise after Anpo* (Cambridge, MA: Harvard University Press, 2018), 181–182.

20. Matsumoto Toshio, "Geijutsu-teki Sado Mazohisuto no ishiki moshikuwa sōsaku no naiteki katei to geijutsu-teki kyōyō-sei ni tsuite" [Consciousness of the aesthetic sadomasochist: Or, on the internal process of creation and its artistic utility], *Kiroku eiga* 3, no. 2 (February 1960): 6. Translation forthcoming in *Journal of Cinema and Media Studies* 64, no. 3 (May 2025).

21. Miryam Sas, *Feeling Media: Potentiality and the Afterlife of Art* (Durham, NC: Duke University Press, 2022), 9.

22. For an analysis of Matsumoto's interest in *Guernica* as well as an excellent translation of this chapter from *Eizō no hakken*, see Matsumoto Toshio, "A Theory of Avant-Garde Documentary," trans. Michael Raine, *Cinema Journal* 14, no. 4 (Summer 2012): 146.

23. Matsumoto, "Theory of Avant-Garde Documentary," 149.

24. Matsumoto Toshio, *Eizō no hakken (Discovery of the Image): Avant-Garde Documentary* (Tokyo: San'ichi Shobo, 1963), 11–12.

25. Sas, *Feeling Media*, 8–9.

26. Michael Raine, introduction to Matsumoto Toshio, "A Theory of Avant-Garde Documentary," trans. Michael Raine, *Cinema Journal* 14, no. 4 (Summer 2012): 145.

27. Matsumoto Toshio, quoted in Nornes, *Forest of Pressure*, 20.

28. Matsumoto Toshio, "Taishū toiu no mono kami ni tsuite" [On the fetish called mass], *Kiroku eiga* 5, no. 2 (February 1962): 20, 23.

29. Yamamoto, *Dialectics without Synthesis*, 180.

30. Key, *Truth from a Lie*, 3.

31. Furuhata Yuriko, "Refiguring Actuality: Japan's Film Theory and Avant-Garde Documentary Movement, 1950s–1960s" (PhD diss., Brown University, 2009), 71.

32. Satō Tadao, "Matsumoto Toshio's Film-Poem 'Nishijin,'" *Eiga hyōron* 18, no. 8 (1961): 66–68.

33. Ozawa Toshio, "Hihyō-ka to sakka no aida" [Between critics and writers], *Kiroku eiga* 4, no. 9 (September 1961): 16.

34. Watanabe Masami, "Kagaku eiga no shūhen" [On the outskirts of science film], *Kiroku eiga* 4, no. 9 (September 1961): 9–10.

35. Noda Shinkichi, "Sogai no kiroku (1) Danzetsu fuzai" [Record of alienation (1) absence of discontinuity], *Kiroku eiga* 4, no. 9 (September 1961), 7.

36. Georges Sadoul, "Plus de promesses et de diversité que de révélations: Au festival de Tours," *Les Lettres françaises* 1057 (December 3–9, 1964): 8.

37. Miryam Sas, "By Other Hands: Environment and Apparatus in 1960s Intermedia," in *The Oxford Handbook of Japanese Cinema*, ed. Daisuke Miyao (Oxford: Oxford University Press, 2014), 389.

38. Sas, "By Other Hands," 391.

39. Furuhata, *Cinema of Actuality*, 25.

40. Miryam Sas, "Moving the Horizon: Violence and Cinematic Revolution in Ōshima Nagisa's *Ninja bugeichō*," *Mechademia: Second Arc* 7 (1992): 268.

41. Satō, "Matsumoto Toshio's Film-Poem 'Nishijin'," 68.

42. Furuhata, *Cinema of Actuality*, 28.

43. Although Matsumoto does not necessarily exoticize the Ibo tribe, his film might be criticized for evoking a Nigerian tribe as a representation of the "natural" or "primitive." It might be productively compared with Hani Susumu's *Bwana Toshi no uta (The Song of Bwana Toshi)* from 1965, approximately coterminous

with *Haha-tachi*, a fictional film that uses an African man's journey to Africa as a catalyst for his personal change. Therefore, one might criticize this era of Japanese filmmaking as mobilizing Africa merely as metaphor, as a "natural" space that instigates self-analysis and self-critique in the Japanese citizen.

44. Matsumoto Toshio, "Hyōgen keishiki no jikken" [Experiments in forms of expression], in *Gendai eiga jiten* [Contemporary encyclopedia of cinema], ed. Okada Susumu, Sasaki Kiichi, Satō Tadao, and Hani Susumu (Tokyo: Bijutsu Shuppansha, 1967), 155.

45. Dziga Vertov, "O s'yemke kinosyuzhetov v khronike," in *Iz naslediia*, tom II, *Stat'i i vystupleniia* (Moscow: Eisenstein Center, 2008), 22–23.

46. Matsumoto, "Hyogen keishiki no jikken," 155.

47. Nornes, *Forest of Pressure*, 20.

48. Kawachi Kaname, "Ore wa omae ni kajiba no matoi fura renagara mo moeagaru" [Even though you still call me a firefighter, I'm still burning], *Kiroku eiga* 4, no. 9 (September 1961): 19. Emphasis in original.

49. The use of hidden cameras and sound recording equipment generated public outcry at the film's release. While I do not delve into the ethics of Imamura's filmmaking here, his methods can certainly be analyzed as problematic. See Diane Wei Lewis, "Boundary Play: Truth, Fiction, and Performance in *A Man Vanishes*," in *Killers, Clients and Kindred Spirits: The Taboo Cinema of Shōhei Imamura* (Edinburgh: Edinburgh University Press, 2019), 267.

50. Audie Bock, *Japanese Film Directors* (Tokyo: Kodansha International, 1978), 285.

51. Imamura Shōhei, *Eiga wa kyōki no tabi de aru* [Film is a journey in madness] (Tokyo: Tokyo Library Center, 2010), 107.

52. Lewis, "Boundary Play," 276.

53. Imamura Shōhei, "Betwixt Fiction and Documentary," trans. Bill Mihalopoulos, *Asian Cinema* 28, no. 1 (2017): 104. Original essay: Imamura Shōhei, ed., *Toru: Kannu kara yamiichi e* [Shoot: From Cannes to the black market] (Tokyo: Kōsakusha, 2001), 234–238.

54. Quoted in Lewis, "Boundary Play," 273.

CHAPTER 2. 1962 FRANCE: DREAMLIKE COMMUNISM AND THE LEFT BANK IN A DECOLONIZING WORLD

1. Georges Sadoul, *"La Guerre est fini:* La Lutte continue," *Les Lettres françaises* 1132 (May 19–25 1966): 15.

2. Nora M. Alter, *Chris Marker* (Urbana: University of Illinois Press, 2006), 30.

3. Alter, *Chris Marker*, 10.

4. Louis Marcorelles, "Le Mystère Koumiko de Chris Marker," *Cahiers du cinéma* 168 (July 1965): 70.

5. Agnès Varda, "Adieu à Georges Sadoul," *Les Lettres françaises* 1204 (October 18–24, 1967): 15.

6. See Georges Sadoul, "Animation et courts métrages, Cannes 1958: festival moyen," *Les Lettres françaises* 722 (May 15–21, 1958): 9; and Georges Sadoul, "Agnès Varda: Magicienne du réel," *Les Lettres françaises* 777 (June 11–17, 1959): 7.

7. Emphasis in original. Georges Sadoul, "*Cleo de 5 a 7:* Le cœur révélateur," *Les Lettres françaises* 922 (April 12–18, 1962): 12. In his review of the film, Sadoul keeps his very personal reason for his intense reaction to the film private, but in her eulogy for Sadoul Varda tells us that coincidentally Sadoul received news of his first wife's death outside the very same hospital in Paris, Salpêtriére, where Cléo receives news of her cancer diagnosis at the film's dénoument. See Varda, "Adieu à Georges Sadoul," 15.

8. According to Michel Ciment, current head of *Positif:* "The magazine was undoubtedly closer to the Left Bank filmmakers—Chris Marker, Alain Resnais, Agnès Varda, Georges Franju," mostly for their more left-leaning attitudes compared to the "Right Bank" of the nouvelle vague. Indeed, Alain Resnais would become one of the journal's favorite directors. See Michel Ciment, "For Your Pleasure: A Brief Overview of Fifty Years of *Positif*," in *Positif 50 Years: Selections from the French Film Journal*, ed Michel Ciment and Laurence Kardish (New York: Museum of Modern Art, 2002), 10, 19.

9. Armand Gatti, Chris Marker, and Jean-Louis Pays"Des humanistes agissants," *Miroir du cinéma* 2 (May 1962): 5.

10. See Franck Tourret, *Alain Resnais: Le pari de la forme* (Paris: L'Harmattan, 2019), 118–125.

11. Although, in my view, Resnais's film is more succeessful in its disorientation and estrangement than Lanzmann's film.

12. Emily Wilson, *Alain Resnais* (Manchester, UK: Manchester University Press, 2006), 33.

13. Both quotes are from Jean Wagner, "Le Cahier des Autres," *Cahiers du cinéma* 165 (April 1965): 78.

14. Viktor Shklovsky, "Art as Technique," in *Russian Formalist Criticism: Four Essays*, trans. Lee L. Lemon and Marion J. Reis (Lincoln: University of Nebraska Press, 1965), 12.

15. Daniel Fairfax, *The Red Years of Cahiers*, vol. 1, *Ideology and Politics* (Amsterdam: Amsterdam University Press, 2022), 239.

16. Albert Cervoni, "Resnais: Pour un spectateur actif," *Miroir du cinéma* 2 (May 1962): 15.

17. The "drug" in question here is more likely an opioid than the mind-enhancing psychedelic experiments typical of the later 1960s, as Resnais's discussion of "opium cinema" will soon show. It should not be confused with the "Acid Communism" lauded by late cultural critic Mark Fisher. The drug here

more accurately connects to what Fisher termed, reflecting on the contemporary dominance of technological consumerism, "OedIpod consumer bliss, a walling up against the social." See Mark Fisher, *Capitalist Realism: Is There No Alternative?* (Alresford, UK: Zero Books, 2009), 24. For a discussion of this concept see Alexander Billet, *Shake the City: Experiments in Space and Time, Music and Crisis* (London: 1968 Press, 2022), 5.

18. "Au rendez-vous des amis: Ciné-débat; Henri Colpi, Armand Gatti, Alain Resnais, Agnès Varda, Georges Sadoul," *Les Lettres françaises* 903 (November 30–December 6, 1961): 6. Unless otherwise noted, the subsequent few pages derive from the same citation.

19. Because of a scene in which Varda "gleans" heart-shaped potatoes from a field, Varda then began receiving countless heart-shaped potatoes in the mail; this would continue for the rest of her life. Agnès Varda, "The 7th Art and Me" (Norton Lecture presented at Harvard University, February 26, 2018).

20. Antoine de Baecque, *Godard: Biographie* (Paris: Grasset, 2010), 315.

21. See "Le cinéma-vérité," special issue, *Miroir du cinéma* 3 (October 1962).

22. Chris Marker, quoted in Francis Gendron, "Chris Marker ou l'évidence," *Miroir du cinéma* 2 (May 1962): 11. Emphasis in original,

23. Chang-min Yu, "Ciné-méta-vérité: *Le Joli Mai* and the Politics of Fictionality," in "Jacques Rivette and Chris Marker," special issue, *Cine-Files* 12 (Spring 2017): 5, www.thecine-files.com/wp-content/uploads/2017/05/Chang PDFformat.pdf.

24. Georges Sadoul, "Un miroir qui refléchit: *Un Joli Mai*, film français de Chris Marker," *Les Lettres françaises* 977 (May 9–15, 1963): 6. See Edgar Morin, "Pour un nouveau cinéma-vérité," *France Observateur* 11, no. 506 (January 14, 1960): 23.

25. In fact, the only work I've ever seen to approximate its particular style is Brett Story's 2019 documentary *The Hottest August* (a film that refers to Marker's film in title and theme as well as in form).

26. Roger Tailleur, quoted in Yu, "Ciné-méta-vérité," 1.

27. Sadoul, "Un miroir qui refléchit," 6. Sadoul might be wrong here, as there is no definitive account of how much footage Marker actually used; in fact Jean-Louis Pays in *Miroir du cinéma* claims Marker took fifty-five hours of footage. See Jean-Louis Pays, "Le Joli Mai," *Miroir du cinema* 4 (1963): 13.

28. Kristin Ross, *Fast Cars, Clean Bodies: Decolonization and the Reordering of French Culture* (Cambridge, MA: MIT Press, 1995), 154.

29. Ross, *Fast Cars, Clean Bodies*, 154.

30. Sadoul, "Un miroir qui refléchit," 6.

31. This section, however, drew some criticism after the film's release. Marker was occasionally thought to provide a highly partisan presentation of a "documented point of view." Indeed, journalist Françoise Giroud criticized Marker, whom she claims "pinned people down like insects"—referring perhaps to this

exact scene. See Catherine Lupton, *Chris Marker: Memories of the Future* (Chicago: Chicago University Press, 2004), 85.

32. Yu, "Ciné-méta-vérité," 13.

33. Jacques Doniol-Valcroze, "Cannes: Semaine de la Critique," *Cahiers du cinéma* 25, no. 145 (July 1963): 24.

34. Louis Marcorelles and Eric Rohmer, "Interview avec Jean Rouch," *Cahiers du cinéma* 24, no. 144 (June 1963): 16. Eight years later, Rouch would use similar phrasing—"we were playing with fire"—in his preface to Georges Sadoul's posthumously published *Dziga Vertov*.

35. Pays, "Le Joli Mai," 13.

36. Steve MacFarlane, "A Bestiary of Madeleines: On 'Chris Marker: 100' at Peter Blum Gallery," Element X Cinema Substack, February 3, 2022, https://elementxcinema.substack.com/p/a-bestiary-of-madeleines.

37. Armand Gatti in "Au rendez-vous des amis: Ciné-débat; Henri Colpi, Armand Gatti, Alain Resnais, Agnès Varda, Georges Sadoul," *Les Lettres françaises* 903 (November 30–December 6, 1961): 8.

38. Armand Gatti in Gatti, Marker, and Pays, "Des humanistes agissants," 3.

39. Gatti, Marker, and Pays, "Des humanistes agissants," 3.

40. Catherine Roudé, *Le cinéma militant a l'heure des collectifs: Slon et Iskra dans la France de l'apres-1968* (Rennes: Presses universitaires de Rennes, 2017), 31.

41. Sadoul, "*Cleo de 5 a 7*," 12.

42. Claude Beylie, "Le Triomphe de la femme," *Cahiers du cinéma* 22, no. 130 (April 1962): 21.

43. Beylie, "Le Triomphe de la femme," 25–26.

44. Agnès Varda in episode "La nouvelle vague par elle-même," *Cinéastes de notre temps*, aired May 19, 1964, accessed January 2023 on The Criterion Channel.

45. The full reasoning for the ban by the French Ministry of Information was reprinted in full in a review in *Les Lettres françaises*; see Anne Philipe, "*Cuba Si* ou les racines d'une Révolution," *Les Lettres françaises* 910 (January 18–24, 1962): 7.

46. Joshua Malitsky, *Post-Revolution Nonfiction Film: Building the Soviet and Cuban Nations* (Bloomington: Indiana University Press, 2013), 81.

47. Agnès Varda, quoted in Jean-André Fieschi and Claude Ollier, "La grâce laïque," *Cahiers du cinéma* 165 (April 1965): 48.

48. Henri Lefebvre, *The Critique of Everyday Life: The One-Volume Edition* (London: Verso, 2014), 71.

49. Fieschi and Ollier, "La grâce laïque," 48.

50. Fieschi and Ollier, "La grâce laïque," 48.

51. Fieschi and Ollier, "La grâce laïque," 48.

52. Fieschi and Ollier, "La grâce laïque," 48.

53. I am thankful to Josh Malitsky for making this excellent point in an early review of my book.

54. Annie Geng, "One Way or Another," *Screen Slate*, June 17, 2023, www.screenslate.com/articles/one-way-or-another-0?mc_cid=050f41fe5c&mc_eid=0e17485503.

55. Geneviève Van Cauwenberge, "Agnès Varda et le documentaire," *La revue belge du cinéma* (1987): 21.

56. Rebecca J. DeRoo, *Agnès Varda between Film, Photography, and Art* (Oakland: University of California Press, 2018), 103.

57. Sadoul, "Agnès Varda," 7.

58. Varda, "7th Art and Me."

59. Varda, "La nouvelle vague par elle-même."

60. Agnès Varda, "Enquete: Vers un néo-romanticisme au cinéma?," *Les Lettres françaises* 764 (March 12–18, 1959): 7. This survey also included responses from Claude Bernard-Aubert, Claude Chabrol, Louis Malle, Alain Resnais, and Jacques Rivette.

61. Peter Wollen, "Godard and Counter-Cinema: Vent d'Est," in *Film Theory and Criticism: Introductory Readings* (New York: Oxford University Press, 1999)," 500.

62. Fieschi and Ollier, "La grâce laïque," 45.

63. Thomas Elsaesser, "From Anti-Illusionism to Hyper Realism: Bertolt Brecht and Contemporary Film," in *Re-interpreting Brecht: His Influence on Contemporary Drama and Film*, ed. Pia Kleber and Colin Visser (Cambridge: Cambridge University Press, 1990), 172–173.

64. Nelly Kaplan, " Chris Marker: Une lettre d'Israël," *Les Lettres françaises* 851 (November 24–30, 1960): 6.

65. Henri Colpi et al., "Au rendez-vous des amis: Ciné-débat," *Les Lettres françaises* 903 (November 30–December 6, 1961): 8.

66. Agnès Varda, quoted in Michel Capdenac "Agnès Varda: De 5 à 7, l'heure de vérité pour Cléo," *Les Lettres françaises* 922 (April 12–18, 1962): 12.

67. Cervoni, "Resnais," 20.

68. Gendron, "Chris Marker ou l'évidence," 10.

69. Gendron, "Chris Marker ou l'évidence," 11.

CHAPTER 3. 1964 JAPAN: THE ALLEGORICAL SEMI-DOCUMENTARY IN AN AGE OF NEONATIONALISM

1. Marcos P. Centeno Martín, "The Limits of Fiction: Politics and Absent Scenes in Susumu Hani's *Bad Boys* (*Furyō Shōnen*, 1960); A Film Re-reading through Its Script," *Journal of Japanese and Korean Cinema* 10, no. 1 (2018): 2.

2. Hanada Kiyoteru, "Dokyumentarī no kongo no tenbō" [Documentary's future prospects], *Eiga hyōron* 15, no. 2 (February 1958): 17.

3. Yamamoto Naoki, *Dialectics without Synthesis: Japanese Film Theory and Realism in a Global Frame* (Oakland: University of California Press, 2020), 180.

4. Iwasa Hisaya et al., "Eiga ni okeru kiroku-sei" [Documentality in movies], *Kiroku eiga* 3, no. 1 (January 1960): 23.

5. Nakai Masakazu, "Film Theory and the Crisis in Contemporary Aesthetics," trans. Phil Kaffen, in "Decentering Theory: Reconsidering the History of Japanese Film Theory," special issue, *Review of Japanese Culture and Society* 22 (December 2010): 85.

6. Masakazu, "Film Theory," 86.

7. Yamamoto, *Dialectics without Synthesis*, 173–174.

8. Markus Nornes, "Translating Grierson: Japan," in *The Grierson Effect*, ed. Deane Williams and Zoë Druick (London: Palgrave Macmillan, 2014), 59.

9. Haryu Ichiro, "Sengo taiken to dokyumentarī" [Postwar experience and documentary], *Kiroku eiga* 2, no. 10 (October 1959): 5–6.

10. Hani Susumu, "Susumu Hani," interview by Rea Amit and Alexander Jacoby, *Midnight Eye: Visions of Japanese Cinema*, April 22, 2010, http://www.midnighteye.com/interviews/susumu-hani/.

11. Justin Jesty, "Image Pragmatics and Film as a Lived Practice in the Documentary Work of Hani Susumu and Tsuchimoto Noriaki," *Arts* 8, no. 2 (March 2019): 5.

12. Albert Johnson, "The Craft of Cinema," interview with Hani Sasumu [*sic*], audio recording, Berkeley Art Museum Pacific Film Archives (BAMPFA), Berkeley, California, October 28, 1966.

13. Luc Moullet, "Festivals: Berlin," *Cahiers du cinéma* 23, no. 135 (September 1962): 30.

14. Importantly, the representation of Asai and other characters in *Furyō shōnen* is fundamentally collaborative, based on real-life experiences and careful research. Tsunoda describes how Hani used "feedback" (*fīdobakku*) as a practice by "post-recording" (*afureko*) the real-time reactions of the nonprofessional actors and former "bad boys" when showing their filmed performances. Tsunoda compares this with the self-reflexivity of Jean Rouch and Edgar Morin's contemporaneous documentary *Chronique d'un été*, in which the filmmakers screen the in-progress film for its own participants at the film's conclusion. See Takuya Tsunoda, "Hani Susumu, *Nouvelle Vague* in Japan, and Processive Cinema," in *A Companion to Japanese Cinema*, ed. David Desser (Hoboken, NJ: Wiley-Blackwell, 2022), 631.

15. Iwanami produced educational and public relations (PR) films and became, with Hani's help, a hothouse for innovative nonfiction filmmaking in the 1950s and a training ground for directors such as Ogawa Shinsuke, Tsuchimoto Noriaki, Kuroki Kazuo, and several dozen more.

16. Markus Nornes, *Forest of Pressure: Ogawa Shinsuke and Postwar Japanese Documentary* (Minneapolis: University of Minnesota Press, 2007), 14–15.

17. Takuya Tsunoda, "The Dawn of Cinematic Modernism: Iwanami Productions and Postwar Japanese Cinema" (PhD diss., Yale University, 2015), iii; and Tsunoda, "Hani Susumu," 619.

18. Bianca Briciu, "Love and Power: The Objectification of the Adolescent Body in Hani Susumu's *Hatsukoi Jigokuhen/Nanami, Inferno of First Love* (1968)," *Journal of Japanese & Korean Cinema* 5, nos. 1–2 (2013): 68.

19. Matsumoto Toshio, "Zankoku o mitsumeru me geijutsu-teki hitei kōi ni okeru shutai no ichi ni tsuite" [Cruel eyes: On the position of the subject in artistic negation)] *Kiroku eiga* 3, no. 12 (December 1960): 8.

20. See Ōtani Shinpei, "Matsumoto Toshio to Hani Susumu no eiga-ron, soshite avangyarudo geijutsu undō: 1950-nendai kara 1960-nendai shotō made no katsudō kōsatsu" [Toshio Matsumoto and Susumu Hani's film theory and avant-garde art movement: Consideration of activities from the 1950s to the early 1960s], *Eizōgaku* 102 (2019): 94–114.

21. Tsunoda, "Hani Susumu," 614.

22. Hani Susumu, "Ashita no tame no eiga" [A cinema for tomorrow], *Eiga Hyōron* 15, no. 2 (February 1958): 31.

23. Annette Michelson, introduction to Ōshima Nagisa, *Cinema, Censorship, and the State: The Writings of Ōshima Nagisa, 1956–1978*, ed. Annette Michelson (Cambridge, MA: MIT Press, 1992), 5.

24. J. Hillis Miller, "The Two Allegories," *Harvard English Studies*, no. 9 (1981): 256.

25. Hannah Airriess, "White-Collar Comedy and Toho's 'Wholesome Color' in Japan's Era of High Economic Growth," *Journal of Japanese and Korean Cinema* 15, no. 1 (2023): 2.

26. Angus Fletcher, *Allegory: The Theory of a Symbolic Mode* (Princeton, NJ: Princeton University Press, 2012), 22–23.

27. Kyle Peters, "Kyoto School and Totality: Theories of Self-Formation in Modern Japanese Philosophy and Thought" (PhD diss., University of Chicago, 2021), 332–336. For Benjamin reference, see Nezu Masashi, "Shiyakuwai kenkyū zasshi" [Social studies journals], *Bunka Sekai* 21 (1936): 59. I am very grateful to Kyle Peters for this citation and his expertise on this subject.

28. Fletcher, *Allegory*, 7.

29. Margaret S. Key, *Truth from a Lie: Documentary Detection, and Reflexivity in Abe Kobo's Realist Project* (Plymouth: Lexington Books, 2011), 2.

30. Charting the use of allegory in Japanese New Wave film of the 1960s shows a bell curve shape that peaks in 1963 and 1964, with films such as, alongside *Nippon konchūki*, first Kurosawa Akira's *Tengoku to jigoku* (High and Low), Hani Susumu's *Kanojo to Kare* (She and He), and in the early months of 1964, Teshigahara Hiroshi's *Suna no ona* (Woman in the Dunes), Shinoda Masahiro's *Kawaita Hana* (Pale Flower), and Suzuki Seijun's *Nikutai no mon* (Gate of Flesh).

31. Walter Benjamin, *The Work of Art in the Age of Mechanical Reproducibility and Other Writings on Media*, ed. Michael W. Jennings, Brigid Doherty, and Thomas Y. Levin (Cambridge, MA: Harvard University Press, 2008), 168.

32. By the late 1960s, an even newer set of "sacred treasures" appeared: a car, an air conditioner, and a color television. See Shunya Yoshimi, "'Made in Japan':

The Cultural Politics of 'Home Electrification' in Postwar Japan," *Media Culture and Society* 21, no. 2 (1999): 155.

33. Watanabe Hiroshi, *Abe Kobo* (Tokyo: Shinbisha, 1976) 71.

34. Bainard Cowan, "Walter Benjamin's Theory of Allegory," in "Modernism," special issue, *New German Critique* 22 (Winter 1981): 121.

35. Cowan, "Walter Benjamin's Theory of Allegory," 110.

36. Walter Benjamin, "The Ruin," in *Work of Art*, 180.

37. See Miller, "Two Allegories."

38. Matsumoto Toshio, quoted in Matsumoto Toshio et al., "Zadankai: Eiga no mirai wa kanō ka? roku san-nendo no geijutsu shisō jōkyō o megu tsute" [Symposium: Is the future of cinema possible? On the state of art and thought in 1963], *Kiroku eiga* 7, no. 1 (January 1964): 5,13.

39. Matsumoto Toshio, "Undō no henkaku" [Transformation of the movement], *Kiroku eiga* 6, no. 10 (November 1963): 4.

40. Benjamin, quoted in Cowan, "Walter Benjamin's Theory of Allegory," 114.

41. Fredric Jameson, *Signatures of the Visible* (New York: Routledge, 1992), 38.

42. David Desser, *Eros Plus Massacre: An Introduction to the Japanese New Wave Cinema* (Bloomington: University of Indiana Press, 1988), 124.

43. Lindsay Coleman and David Desser, introduction to *Killers, Clients and Kindred Spirits: The Taboo Cinema of Shōhei Imamura* (Edinburgh: Edinburgh University Press, 2019), 4.

44. Diane Wei Lewis, "Boundary Play: Truth, Fiction, and Performance in *A Man Vanishes*," in *Killers, Clients and Kindred Spirits: The Taboo Cinema of Shōhei Imamura* (Edinburgh: Edinburgh University Press, 2019), 282.

45. Walter Benjamin, *Charles Baudelaire: A Lyric Poet in the Era of High Capitalism*, trans. H. Zorn (London: New Left Books, 1973), 171.

46. Imamura Shōhei, *Eiga wa kyōki no tabi de aru* [Film is a journey in madness] (Tokyo: Tokyo Library Center, 2010), 80.

47. Michael Raine, "*The Insect Woman*, or: The Female Act of Failure," in *Killers, Clients and Kindred Spirits: The Taboo Cinema of Shōhei Imamura* (Edinburgh: Edinburgh University Press, 2019), 115.

48. This blend of nationalist pride through capitalist progress was manifested later in the decade and in the 1970s through advertising campaigns such as "Discover Japan." For more on what Tomiko Yoda calls the "mediatized ambience" of this later period in Japanese history, see Tomiko Yoda, "Girlscape: The Marketing of Mediatic Ambience in Japan," in *Media Theory in Japan*, ed. Marc Steinberg and Alexander Zahlten (Durham, NC: Duke University Press, 2017), 177.

49. Raine, "*Insect Woman*," 116.

50. Imamura, *Eiga wa kyōki*, 2.

51. Imamura, *Eiga wa kyōki*, 97.

52. Imamura, *Eiga wa kyōki*, 3.

53. Raine, "*Insect Woman*," 123.

54. Sekine Hiroshi, "Umare kawaru jōkyō" [The situation of being reborn], *Kiroku eiga* 7, no. 1 (January 1974): 28.

55. Raine, *"Insect Woman,"* 117, 128.

56. Matsukawa Yasuo, "Nipponkonchūki ni tsuite no dansei-teki hansei" A masculine reflection on *Insect Woman*], *Kiroku eiga* 7, no. 1 (January 1974), 30.

57. Hani Susumu's *Kanojo to kare* (*She and He*) from 1962 is an allegorical semi-documentary that centers its criticism of capitalism directly on the *danchi* complexes emerging precisely at this time, and it can be productively compared to Jean-Luc Godard's criticism of similar constructions in the rapidly modernizing Paris later in the decade, as in *2 ou 3 choses que je sais d'elle* (*2 or 3 Things I Know about Her*) from 1967.

58. Coleman and Desser, introduction to *Killers, Clients and Kindred Spirits*, 5.

59. Raine, *"Insect Woman,"* 115.

60. Matsukawa, "Masculine Reflection on *Insect Woman*," 30.

61. Michael Raine, Japan Society brochure, New York screening of *Silence Has No Wings*, February 21, 2009.

62. Carol Hayes, "Kuroki Kazuo's Requiem for War," in *Legacies of the Asia-Pacific War: The* Yakeato *Generation*, ed. Roman Rosenbaum and Yasuko Claremont (London: Routledge, 2010), 199.

63. Rio Otomo, "Narratives, the Body, and the 1964 Tokyo Olympics," *Asian Studies Review* 31 (June 2007): 122.

64. Yoshikuni Igarashi, *Bodies of Memory: Narratives of War in Postwar Japanese Culture, 1945–1970* (Princeton, NJ: Princeton University Press, 2000), 153.

65. Kuroki Kazuo, "Bokura no tatte iru tokoro" [Where we stand], *Kiroku eiga* 5, no. 11 (December 1962), 18.

66. Kazuo, "Bokura no tatte iru tokoro," 16–18.

67. Kuroki Kazuo, "'Reporuta-ju, En' wo megutte" [Concerning the "documentary flame"], *Kiroku eiga* 4, no. 4 (April 1961): 23.

68. Nornes, *Forest of Pressure*, 32.

69. Matsumoto Toshio, "*Tobenai Chinmoku* ron nōto" [Notes on the theory of *Silence Has No Wings*], *Eiga hyōron* 23, no. 3 (March 1966): 42.

70. Matsumoto, "*Tobenai Chinmoku* ron nōto," 40.

71. Matsumoto, "*Tobenai Chinmoku* ron nōto," 42.

72. Cowan, "Walter Benjamin's Theory of Allegory," 114.

73. Kuroku Kazuo, "Mu ni tsuite" [On nothingness], *Kiroku eiga* 5, no. 6 (June 1962): 15.

74. Hayes, "Kuroki Kazuo's Requiem for War," 212.

75. Raine, *"Insect Woman,"* 132.

76. Hara Kazuo, introduction to screening of Ogawa Shinsuke's *Magino Village: A Tale* (1983), Light Industry, Brooklyn, New York, July 23, 2018.

77. Matsukawa, "Masculine Reflection on *Insect Woman*," 31.

78. Matsumoto, "Geijutsu-teki Sado Mazohisuto," 8.

79. Yuriko Furuhata, *Cinema of Actuality: Japanese Avant-Garde Filmmaking in the Season of Image Politics* (Durham, NC: Duke University Press, 2013), 98.

CHAPTER 4. 1969 FRANCE: UNPLEASURE AND RADICAL EPISTEMOLOGY IN POST-MAY GODARD

1. Marc Cerisuelo, "Jean-Luc, Community, and Communication," in *A Companion to Jean-Luc Godard*, ed. Tom Conley and T. Jefferson Kline (West Sussex, UK: Wiley and Blackwell, 2014), 302–303.

2. Michael Goodwin, "The Dziga Vertov Film Group in America: An Interview with Jean-Luc Godard and Jean-Pierre Gorin," unpublished manuscript, Pacific Film Archive at the Berkeley Art Museum (BAMPFA), 1970, 3. For the final printed article, see Michael Goodwin, Tom Luddy, and Naomi Wise, "The Dziga Vertov Film Group in America," *Take One: The Film Magazine* II, no. 10 (March/April 1970): 8–27.

3. Raphaël Jaudon, "Réécrire le corps: Érotique et politique dans les films de Godard et Gorin," *French Screen Studies* 22, no. 4 (2022): 232.

4. Jaudon, "Réécrire le corps," 235.

5. Daniel Fairfax, *The Red Years of Cahiers*, vol. 1, *Ideology and Politics* (Amsterdam: Amsterdam University Press, 2022), 49.

6. Paul Douglas Grant, *Cinéma Militant: Political Filmmaking and May 1968* (New York: Columbia University Press, 2016), 152.

7. Sylvia Harvey, *May '68 and Film Culture* (London: British Film Institute, 1978), 45.

8. John MacKay, *Dziga Vertov: Life and Work*, lxxxiii.

9. Jean-Paul Fargier, Gérard Leblanc, et al. "'Ne copies pas sur les yeux' disait Vertov," *Cinéthique* 15 (December 1972): 56.

10. Grant, *Cinéma militant*, 153.

11. Основное и самое главное: КИНООЩУЩЕНИЕ МИРА. Dziga Vertov, *Iz naslediia*, tom II, *Stat'i i vystupleniia* (Moscow: Eisenstein Center, 2008), 38. Emphasis in original. This translation is my own. O'Brien's translation states: "The main and essential thing is: sensory exploration of the world through film" (in "Decree of the Council of Three," 14), but I do not think his translation places as much emphasis on the term as Vertov does in the original document.

12. D. N. Rodowick, *The Crisis of Political Modernism* (Berkeley: University of California Press, 1994), xiv, xvi.

13. Annette Michelson, "*The Man with the Movie Camera*: From Magician to Epistemologist," *Artforum*, March 1972, 69.

14. Gérard Leblanc, "Godard: Valeur d'usage ou valeur d'échange?," *Cinéthique* 5 (September–October 1969): 22.

15. Fairfax, *Red Years of Cahiers*, 303; and Gérard Leblanc, "Quelle avant-garde? (note sur une pratique actuelle du cinéma militant)," *Cinéthique* 7–8 (1970): 73.

16. See Groupe CINEFRONT-Rouen, "Interventions," *Cinéthique* 11–12 (1970–1971): 75.

17. Bertrand Augst, "Jean-Luc Godard," in *Kinopraxis* (pamphlet, Pacific Film Archive of the Berkeley Art Museum [BAMPFA], January 1, 1970), 31.

18. "Du bon usage de la valeur d'echange: Le cahiers du cinéma et le marxisme-leninisme," *Cinéthique* 6 (January 1970): 4.

19. Grant, *Cinéma militant*, 152.

20. Quotation marks in original. "Du bon usage de la valeur d'échange," 4.

21. Jaudon, "Réécrire le corps," 247.

22. Colin MacCabe and Laura Mulvey, "Images of Women, Images of Sexuality," in *Godard: Images, Sounds, Politics* (Bloomington: Indiana University Press, 1980), 89.

23. Peter Wollen, "Godard and Counter-Cinema: Vent d'Est," in *Film Theory and Criticism: Introductory Readings* (New York: Oxford University Press, 1999), 499.

24. Irmgard Emmelhainz, *Jean-Luc Godard's Political Filmmaking* (London: Palgrave Macmillan, 2019), 57.

25. Godard, interview in Michael Goodwin, "The Dziga Vertov Film Group in America: An Interview with Jean-Luc Godard and Jean-Pierre Gorin," unpublished manuscript, Pacific Film Archive at the Berkeley Art Museum (BAMPFA), 1970, 61.

26. Badiou, quoted in Nico Baumbach, *Cinema/Politics/Philosophy* (New York: Columbia University Press, 2018), 147.

27. Jean-Luc Godard, interview in "Nouvelle Vague," special issue, *Cahiers du cinéma* 23, no. 128 (December 1962): 27.

28. Godard, interview, 1962.

29. Michel Delahaye, "Jean-Luc Godard ou l'enfance de l'art," *Cahiers du cinéma* 179 (June 1966): 65.

30. Antoine de Baecque, *Godard: Biographie* (Paris: Grasset, 2010), 315.

31. Fairfax, *Red Years of Cahiers*, 33.

32. Sylvain Godet, "Chemin principal et chemins latéraux," *Cahiers du cinéma* 190 (May 1967): 63.

33. Jean-Louis Comolli, Jean Narboni, et al., "Le groupe Dziga-Vertov (1)," *Cahiers du cinéma* nos. 238–239 (May–June 1972): 34.

34. Comolli, Narboni, et al., "Le groupe Dziga-Vertov," 35.

35. Tom Luddy, "British Sounds," *Take One: The Film Magazine* 2, no. 11 (May/June 1970): 12.

36. Jaudon, "Réécrire le corps," 231, 247.

37. Linda Williams, "Film Bodies: Gender, Genre, and Excess," *Film Quarterly* 44, no. 4 (Summer 1991): 10. It might likewise be worth pointing out that the

production manager of *Deep Throat*, the first contemporary porno, released at the tail end of the DVG period in 1972, "approached those films as if I was Godard," and that the director "claimed[ed] allegiance to the edgy avant-garde." See Linda Williams, "Anatomy of a Skin Flick," *Sight & Sound* 15, no. 6 (June 2005): 25–26.

38. John Paul Sadler, in conversation with Shaka McGlotten and Susanna Paasonen, "The Deep Realness of Deepfake Pornography," in *Deep Mediations: Thinking Space in Cinema and Digital Cultures*, ed. Karen Redrobe and Jeff Scheible (Minneapolis: University of Minnesota Press, 2021), 356.

39. Comolli, Narboni, et al., "Le groupe Dziga-Vertov," 38.

40. Jean-Paul Fargier, Gérard Leblanc, et al., "Le groupe Dziga-Vertov," *Cinéthique* 9–10 (September 1970–March 1971): 91.

41. Bernardo Bertolucci, "Versus Godard," *Cahiers du cinéma* 186 (January 1967): 29.

42. MacCabe and Mulvey, "Images of Women," 103.

43. Jaudon, "Réécrire le corps," 236.

44. Jean-Luc Comilli, Jean Narboni, et al., "Sur les films du 'groupe' (2)," *Cahiers du cinéma* 240 (July–August 1972): 5.

45. Yuriko Furuhata, *Cinema of Actuality: Japanese Avant-Garde Filmmaking in the Season of Image Politics* (Durham, NC: Duke University Press, 2013), 10.

46. The disability politics of the film do not age well.

47. "Cleaver talked to us only because he knew at the time that we were sympathizers. He needed money, so he accepted only for the money." Goodwin, "Dziga Vertov Group in America," 5. The film was eventually finished by D. A. Pennebaker and released as *One P.M.* or *One Parallel Movie* in 1972.

48. Kent E. Carroll, "Film and Revolution: Interview with the Dziga Vertov Group," in *Focus on Godard*, ed. Royal S. Brown (Englewood Cliffs, NJ: Prentice Hall, 1972), 63.

49. Rodowick, *Crisis of Political Modernism*, 54.

50. Comilli, Narboni, et al., "Sur les films du 'groupe' (2)," 6.

51. Rodowick, *Crisis of Political Modernism*, 62.

52. Jean-Paul Fargier, Gérard Leblanc, et al., "Un terrorisme 'economique' entretien avec Jean Rouch," *Cinéthique* 3 (1970): 18.

53. *Cahiers* lays out the various reviews of DVG films in the previously cited two-part analysis by Comilli, Carboni, et al., "Le groupe Dziga-Vertov."

54. David Fresko, "Revolutionary Cinematic Suicide," *Brooklyn Rail*, June 2018, https://brooklynrail.org/2018/06/film/Revolutionary-Cinematic-Suicide.

55. Baecque, *Godard*, 505

56. Emmelhainz, *Godard's Political Filmmaking*, 24.

57. Goodwin, Luddy, and Wise, "Dziga Vertov Film Group in America," 24.

58. Dusan Makavejev, quoted in James Roy Macbean, *Film and Revolution* (Bloomington: Indiana University Press, 1975), 176.

59. Baumbach, *Cinema/Politics/Philosophy*, 183.

60. See Mary Watkins and Helene Shulman, *Toward Psychologies of Liberation* (Hampshire, UK: Palgrave MacMillan, 2008).

61. Joan Morgan, "Why We Get Off: Moving towards a Black Feminist Politics of Pleasure," in *Pleasure Activism: The Politics of Feeling Good*, ed. adrienne marée brown (Edinburgh: AK Press, 2019), 87.

62. adrienne marée brown, introduction to *Pleasure Activism*, 13.

63. Audre Lorde, "Uses of the Erotic: The Erotic as Power," in *Pleasure Activism*, 30.

64. Although this project does not treat pornography at length, it might be useful to consider Lorde's and brown's understanding of pornography as tied to exploitation and the capitalist marketplace, as does Godard. There are, however, works that identify the pornographic as potentially liberatory, such as works by Mari Mikkola and certain texts by Laura Williams.

65. Michel Foucault, preface to *Anti-Oedipus: Capitalism and Schizophrenia*, by Gilles Deleuze and Félix Guattari (Minneapolis: University of Minnesota Press, 1972), xii.

66. Gilles Deleuze and Félix Guattari, *Anti-Oedipus: Capitalism and Schizophrenia* (Minneapolis: University of Minnesota Press, 1972), 193.

67. Mark Fisher, "Acid Communism," April 25, 2019, https://my-blackout.com/2019/04/25/mark-fisher-acid-communism-unfinished-introduction/.

CHAPTER 5. 1969 JAPAN: QUEER SELF-REVOLUTIONS OF THE ART THEATRE GUILD

1. See Julia Alekseyeva, "Vertov and the Avant-Garde Documentary in Japan: Dreaming Reality in the 1960s," *Film History* 35, no. 2 (Spring 2024): 1–25.

2. See Marnia Lazreg, introduction to *Foucault's Orient: The Conundrum of Cultural Difference, from Tunisia to Japan* (Brooklyn, NY: Berghahn Books, 2017), 1–12.

3. I am thankful to my research assistant, Patrick Carland-Echavarria, for this information, which derives from personal papers and correspondence found in the Donald Richie collection at the Howard Gotlieb Archival Research Center, Boston University, Boston, MA.

4. See Ian Buruma, *A Tokyo Romance* (New York: Penguin, 2018), 1.

5. Andrew Culp, *Dark Deleuze* (Minneapolis: University of Minnesota Press, 2016), 45. Original cited section in Gilles Deleuze and Félix Guattari, *Anti-Oedipus: Capitalism and Schizophrenia* (Minneapolis: University of Minnesota Press, 1972), 68–71.

6. KuroDalaiJee, *Anarchy of the Body: Undercurrents of Performance Art in 1960s Japan* (Leuven, Belgium: Leuven University Press, 2023), 43.

7. Asai Masuo, quoted in KuroDalaiJee, *Anarchy of the Body*, 315.

8. Jasper Sharp, "Down the Bunka: Japanese Underground Cinema of the 1960s," *Sight and Sound*, July 11, 2016, www2.bfi.org.uk/news-opinion/sight-sound-magazine/features/down-bunka-japanese-underground-cinema-1960s.

9. Andrew Grossman, "'Beautiful Publicity': An Introduction to Queer Asian Film," in *Queer Asian Cinema: Shadows in the Shade* (Oxfordshire: Routledge, 2001), 2. Copublished simultaneously in *Journal of Homosexuality* 39, nos. 3/4 (2000): 1–29.

10. See Alexander Zahlten, *The End of Japanese Cinema: Industrial Genres, National Times, and Media Ecologies* (Durham, NC: Duke University Press, 2017). I discuss pink films in three publications: "Self-Revolutions of Everyday Life: The Politics of ATG," *The Sixties: A Journal of History, Politics, and Culture* 4, no. 2 (November 22, 2021): 133–150; "Fury and the Landscape Film: Three Men Who Left Their Will on Concrete," *ARTMargins* 10, no. 1 (April 30, 2021): 39–59; and "Nuclear Skin: Hiroshima and the Critique of Embodiment in *Affairs Within Walls*," in , *The Atomic Bomb in Japanese Cinema: Critical Essays*, ed. Matthew Edwards (Jefferson, NC: McFarland, 2015), 99–110.

11. Jonathan M. Hall, "Unwilling Subjects: Psychoanalysis and Japanese Modernity" (PhD diss., University of California-Santa Cruz, 2003), 59–60.

12. Culp, *Dark Deleuze*, 24.

13. Culp, *Dark Deleuze*, 24.

14. Sophie Lewis, "Mermaid Contracts," *Patreon*, published June 11, 2023. https://www.patreon.com/posts/mermaid-84407767

15. José Esteban Muñoz, *Cruising Utopia* (New York: New York University Press, 2009), 1, 32.

16. Mark J. McLelland, "From the Stage to the Clinic: Changing Transgender Identities in Post-war Japan," *Japan Forum* 16, no. 1 (2004): 1–20; and Mark J. McLelland, *Queer Japan from the Pacific War to the Internet Age* (Lanham, MD: Rowman & Littlefield, 2005); Keith Vincent, Kazama Takahashi, and Kawaguchi Kazuya, *Jissensuru sekushuariti: Dōseiai, iseiai no seijigaku* [Practicing sexualities: integrating theory and activism through lesbian/gay/PHA identities] (Tokyo: Ugoku Gei to Rezubian no Kai, 1998); and S. P. F. Dale, "Same-Sex Marriage and the Question of Queerness—Institutional Performativity and Marriage in Japan," *Asian Anthropology* 19, no. 2 (2020): 143–159).

17. Oguma Eiji, "Japan's 1968: A Collective Reaction to Rapid Economic Growth in an Age of Turmoil," trans. Nick Kapur, *Asia Pacific Journal* 13, no. 12 (March 2015): 1.

18. Chelsea Szendi Schieder, *Coed Revolution: The Female Student in the Japanese New Left* (Durham, NC: Duke University Press, 2021), 80.

19. Ando Takemasa, "The Absence of the New Left: The (Un)changing Cultures of Activism in Japan." Lecture delivered at "ANPO Revisited" Workshop, ICC Workshop Series on Youth Activism in Post-War Japan, Sophia University, Tokyo, November 14, 2015.

20. Schieder, *Coed Revolution*, 93.

21. Oguma, "Japan's 1968," 11.

22. Ando Takemasa, "Transforming 'Everydayness': Japanese New Left Movements and the Meaning of their Direct Action," *Japanese Studies* 33, no. 1 (2013): 1.

23. Laura Neitzel, *The Life We Longed For: Danchi Housing and the Middle Class Dream in Postwar Japan* (Portland: MerwinAsia, 2016), 1.

24. Oguma, "Japan's 1968," 11.

25. Yomota Inuhiko, "2 ou 3 choses que je sais d'ATG," in *Art Theatre Guild* (Vienna: Vienna International Film Festival, 2003), 30. It is important, also, that Yomota titles his reflection on ATG after Jean-Luc Godard's avant-garde documentary *2 ou 3 choses que je sais d'elle*, mentioned in the last chapter.

26. Yomota, "2 ou 3 choses que je sais d'ATG."

27. Patrick Nathan, *Image Control: Art, Fascism, and the Right to Resist* (Berkeley: Counterpoint Press, 2021), 78.

28. As Ayako Kano points out, whereas previously sex was perceived as subordinate to gender, in the modern period and after influence from the West, gender began to be perceived as subordinate to sex. See Ayako Kano, *Acting like a Woman in Modern Japan: Theater, Gender, and Nationalism* (London: Palgrave Macmillan, 2001), 28.

29. There are some exceptions: documentarist Hara Kazuo, who continues to make films today, has worked with his producer and wife, Kobayashi Sachiko. They are now usually depicted as a filmmaking duo, although Hara's work began in 1973, at the tail end of the political avant-garde.

30. Schieder, *Coed Revolution*, 93.

31. Henri Lefebvre, *Critique of Everyday Life: The One-Volume Edition* (London: Verso, 2014), 701.

32. Heather Love, *Feeling Backward: Loss and the Politics of Queer History* (Cambridge, MA: Harvard University Press, 2007), 2–3.

33. Ann Adachi-Tasch, Julian Ross, and Go Hirasawa, "Highlighting Masanori Oe—Community of Images," email message to Collaborative Cataloguing Japan, April 16, 2025.

34. Ignacio Adriasola, "Masanori Oe: Filming Ecstasy," screening and talk at the Yale Union, Portland, Oregon, https://yaleunion.org/oe/

35. Ōe Masanori, "The Aesthetics of Ecstasy and the Yippie Revolution," trans. Yuzo Sakuramoto, in *Japanese Expanded Cinema and Intermedia: Critical Texts of the 1960s*, ed. Go Hirasawa, Ann Adachi-Tasch, and Julian Ross (Berlin: Archive Books, 2020), 154. Originally published as "Kōkotsu no bigaku to ippi reborushon," *Eiga hyōron* 26, no. 7 (July 1969: 49–53.

36. Ōe, "Aesthetics of Ecstasy and the Yippie Revolution," 155.

37. Performance artist Katō Yoshihiro on the 1962 Zero Jigen experiment *Ritual by Sound* of 1962, quoted in KuroDalaiJee, *Anarchy of the Body*, 348.

38. Robyn Marasco, "Bataille's Anti-fascism," *Contemporary Political Theory* 21, no. 1 (2022): 18.

39. Hall, "Unwilling Subjects," 85.

40. Matsumoto Toshio, "Haisen to sengo no fuzai: Shutai-ron no saikentō no tame ni" [Absence of "defeat and postwar": For a reexamination of subjectivity part 2], *Kiroku eiga* 2, no. 8 (August 1959): 34.

41. Yuriko Furuhata, *Cinema of Actuality: Japanese Avant-Garde Filmmaking in the Season of Image Politics* (Durham, NC: Duke University Press, 2013), 82.

42. For example, the first interviewee, Mariko, who does not appear in the film, is asked what motivated her to become a *gei boi*. She responds, "Well, I wanted to be like this, a woman. I mean, I like it." The interviewer states, "You like women." She corrects, "No, I like *becoming* one" (*ni naru ita koto wa ne*)

43. Taro Nettleton, "Throw Out the Books, Get Out in the Streets: Subjectivity and Space in Japanese Underground Art of the 1960s" (PhD diss., University of Michigan, 2011), 185–186.

44. James Phillips, "Anti-Oedipus: The Ethics of Performance and Misrecognition in Matsumoto Toshio's *Funeral Parade of Roses*," *SubStance* 44, no. 141 (2016): 40.

45. Hall, "Unwilling Subjects," 101.

46. Muñoz, *Cruising Utopia*, 32.

47. Matsumoto Toshio, "Geijutsu-teki Sado Mazohisuto no ishiki moshikuwa sōsaku no naiteki katei to geijutsu-teki kyōyō-sei ni tsuite" [Artistic sadomasochistic consciousness: Or, about the inner process of creation and its artistic utility], *Kiroku eiga* 3, no. 2 (February 1960): 9.

48. Gilles Deleuze, *Cinema 2: The Time-Image*, trans. Hugh Tomlinson and Robert Galeta (Minneapolis: University of Minnesota Press, 1989), 70.

49. Nettleton, "Throw Out the Books," 186.

50. Ōishi Masahiko, *Higa tōi : Nihon Modanizumu/Roshia avangyarudo* (Tokyo: Suisei-sha, 2009), 269–270, 277–278.

51. Manuel Garin, "Comedies of Resistance: Shūji Terayama and the Politics of Visual Humor," *Sixties* 14, no. 2 (2021): 211.

52. Miryam Sas, *Experimental Arts of Postwar Japan: Moments of Encounter, Engagement, and Imagined Return* (Cambridge, MA: Harvard East Asian Monographs, 2011), 37.

53. Terayama Shūji, *Eiga gishi o ute (Shoot the Projectionist: Collected Writings on Cinema of Terayama Shūji)* (Tokyo: Shinshokan, 1973), 227.

54. Terayama, *Eiga gishi o ute*, 229.

55. Steven C. Ridgely, *Japanese Counterculture: The Antiestablishment Art of Terayama Shūji* (Minneapolis: University of Minnesota Press, 2011), 108.

56. Terayama, *Eiga gishi*, 229.

57. Sas, *Experimental Arts of Postwar Japan*, 55.

58. Viktor Shklovsky, quoted in Richard Sheldon, introduction to *Third Factory*, by Viktor Shklovsky (McLean, IL: Dalkey Archive Press, 2002), xxxv.

59. All quotes in this paragraph are from Terayama Shūji, "Rojin to taiji: Kyōfu no gendai-tekina imi" [The old man and the fetus: The modern meaning of fear," *Kiroku eiga* 4, no. 6 (June 1961): 18–19.

60. Dziga Vertov, *Iz naslediia*, tom II, *Stat'i i vystupleniia* (Moscow: Eisenstein Center, 2008), 42. Translation: Vertov in Tsivian, "The Council of Three," in *Lines of Resistance: Dziga Vertov and the Twenties* (Bloomington: Indiana University Press, 2004), 87–88.

61. Carol Fisher Sorgenfrei, *Unspeakable Acts: The Avant-Garde Theatre of Terayama Shuji and Postwar Japan* (Honolulu: University of Hawaii Press, 2005), 103.

62. Ridgely, *Japanese Counterculture*, 111.

63. Yukio Lippit, "Japan During the *Provoke* Era," in *Provoke: Between Protest and Performance* (Gottingen: Steidl, 2016), 22.

64. The rape sequence in *Sho o suteyo*, however, is the only moment in any Terayama production when a woman is sexually violated. In fact, Terayama's work, in contradistinction to other Japanese filmmakers, is far more likely to involve the humiliation of young men, especially by older, more experienced women. Such controversial scenes exist in both *Sho o suteyo* and *Tomato Kechappu Kōtei* (*Emperor Tomato Ketchup*, 1971), which shows a prepubescent child undressed and fondled by a group of much older women wearing exaggerated drag-like makeup.

65. Terayama, *Eiga gishi*, 218.

66. Sara Ahmed, *Queer Phenomenology: Orientations, Objects, Others* (Durham, NC: Duke University Press, 2006), 161–162.

67. Satō Tadao, *Currents in Japanese Cinema: Essays by Tadao Satō*, trans. Gregory Barrett (Tokyo: Kodansha International, 1982), 209.

68. Justin Jesty, "Image Pragmatics and Film as a Lived Practice in the Documentary Work of Hani Susumu and Tsuchimoto Noriaki," *Arts* 8, no. 2 (March 2019): 10.

69. Hani Susumu, interview by Jacques Aumont, Pascal Bonitzer, and Sylvie Pierre, *Cahiers du cinéma* 224 (October 1970): 27.

70. Hani Susumu (1960), quoted in Jesty, "Image Pragmatics," 9.

71. Takuya Tsunoda, "Hani Susumu, *Nouvelle Vague* in Japan, and Processive Cinema," in *A Companion to Japanese Cinema*, ed. David Desser (Hoboken, NJ: Wiley-Blackwell, 2022), 626.

72. Noda Shinkichi, "Akuchuaritī no sōzō-teki gekika dokyumentarī hōhōron ni suite no nōto" [Creative dramatization of actuality: Notes on documentary methodology, pt. 2], *Kiroku eiga* 1, no. 5 (December 1958): 11.

73. Yamada Koichi, "*La Mariee des Andes* de Hani Susumu," *Cahiers du cinéma* 183 (October 1966): 30.

74. Hani, *Cahiers* interview, 27.

75. Hani, *Cahiers* interview, 28.

76. Hani Susumu, "Watashi no baai" [My situation], *Kiroku eiga* 4, no. 11 (November 1961): 11.

77. I use "she" and "her" in this book because characters generally use "kanojo" to refer to her in the film rather than "kare," but this term doesn't quite sit well either.

78. Hani Susumu with Eto Fumio and Sato Tadao, "Chapurin no gei to shisō" [The art and thought of Charlie Chaplin], *Eiga hyōron* 17, no. 11 (November 1960): 47.

79. I analyze this film in depth in "Fury and the Landscape Film," cited previously.

80. Hani, *Cahiers* interview, 28.

81. Hani, *Cahiers* interview, 33.

82. Hani Susumu, colloquium and Q&A at Harvard University, January 28, 2013.

83. Hani, *Cahiers* interview, 32.

84. Love, *Feeling Backward*, 146.

85. Hani, *Cahiers* interview, 32.

86. Hani, *Cahiers* interview.

87. Matsuda Masao, "Media kakumei no tame no akushisu" [An axis for a media revolution], in *Fukanosei no Media* [Impossible Media] (Tokyo: Tabata Shoten, 1973).

88. Markus Nornes, *Forest of Pressure: Ogawa Shinsuke and Postwar Japanese Documentary* (Minneapolis: University of Minnesota Press, 2007), 128–129.

89. Furuhata, *Cinema of Actuality*, 185–186.

90. Kimata Kimihiko, "Thoughts on the Extremely Private Pink Film of the 1970s," in *The Pink Book: The Japanese Eroduction and Its Contents*, 2nd ed., ed. Mark Nornes, Ann Arbor, MI: Kinema Club, 2014), 52–53.

91. Mikhail Koltsov, "U ekrana," 1, translation in Tsivian, *Lines of Resistance*, 45.

92. Gorin and Godard, quoted in David Fresko, "Revolutionary Cinematic Suicide, Godard + Gorin: Five Films, 1968–1971," *Brooklyn Rail*, June 2018, https://brooklynrail.org/2018/06/film/Revolutionary-Cinematic-Suicide.

CODA

1. I am grateful to my graduate student J. S. Wu, storyboard artist for *Sorry to Bother You*, who draws attention to the animated effects of *Sorry to Bother You* in their dissertation, "The Animating Inbetween: Productions of Race in Contemporary Animation" (University of Pennsylvania, 2024).

2. Isaac Julien, quoted in Arthur Lubow, "Questioning the Place of Black Art in a White Man's Collection,"*New York Times*, August 6, 2022, link.gale.com/apps/doc/A712688230/AONE?u=upenn_main&sid=summon&xid=8b227ae9.

3. "What Is Media Literacy?," Media Literacy Now, accessed June 24, 2023, https://medialiteracynow.org/challenge/what-is-media-literacy/.

4. For an excellent history of this phrase, see Paul Megna, "Juridical Dread and the Self-Disciplining Subject," *Postmedieval: A Journal of Medieval Cultural Studies* 13 (2022): 55.

5. Deleuze and Guattari also critique psychoanalysis by describing the "psychoanalyst-as-cop." See Gilles Deleuze and Félix Guattari, *Anti-Oedipus: Capitalism and Schizophrenia* (Minneapolis: University of Minnesota Press, 1972), 108.

6. Deleuze and Guattari, *Anti-Oedipus*, 346.

7. Mary Watkins and Helene Shulman, *Toward Psychologies of Liberation* (Hampshire, UK: Palgrave Macmillan, 2008), 47–48.

8. See Leon Trotsky, *The Permanent Revolution*, trans. Max Shachtman (New York: Pioneer Publishers, 1931); and Andrew Culp, *Dark Deleuze* (Minneapolis: University of Minnesota Press, 2016), 24.

9. Culp, *Dark Deleuze*, 13.

10. adrienne marée brown, *We Will Not Cancel Us: And Other Dreams of Transformative Justice* (Chico, CA: AK Press, 2020), 44.

11. Gilles Deleuze and Félix Guattari, *A Thousand Plateauss: Capitalism and Schizophrenia*, trans. Brian Massumi (Minneapolis: University of Minnesota, 1987), 228.

12. Robyn Marasco, "Bataille's Anti-fascism," *Contemporary Political Theory* 21, no. 1 (2022): 5.

13. See especially the concluding chapter in Jackie Wang, *Carceral Capitalism* (Cambridge, MA: Semiotext(e), 2018).

14. Arielle Angel, "Responsa: Beyond Grievance," *Jewish Currents* 76, no. 2 (Summer 2022): 16.

Bibliography

Adachi-Tasch, Ann, Julian Ross, and Go Hirasawa. "Highlighting Masanori Oe—Community of Images." Email message to Collaborative Cataloguing Japan, April 16, 2024.
Adriasola, Ignacio. "Masanori Oe: Filming Ecstasy." Screening and talk at Yale Union, Portland, Oregon. https://yaleunion.org/oe/.
Ahmed, Sara. *Queer Phenomenology: Orientations, Objects, Others*. Durham, NC: Duke University Press, 2006.
Airriess, Hannah. "White-Collar Comedy and Toho's 'Wholesome Color' in Japan's Era of High Economic Growth." *Journal of Japanese and Korean Cinema* 15, no. 1, (2023): 1–18.
Alekseyeva, Julia. "Fury and the Landscape Film: Three Men Who Left Their Will on Concrete." *ARTMargins* 10, no. 1 (April 30, 2021): 39–59.
———. "Nuclear Skin: Hiroshima and the Critique of Embodiment in *Affairs Within Walls*." In *The Atomic Bomb in Japanese Cinema: Critical Essays*, edited by Matthew Edwards, 99–110. Jefferson, NC: McFarland, 2015.
———. "Self-Revolutions of Everyday Life: The Politics of ATG." *The Sixties: A Journal of History, Politics, and Culture* 4, no. 2 (November 22, 2021): 133–150.
———. "A Stony Stone, a Cinematic Cinema: Shklovskian Estrangement in Dziga Vertov's *Kino-Eye*." *Oxford Research in English* 9 (Autumn 2019): 9–30.
———. "Theses on the Philosophy of Walter Benjamin." *Paper Brigade* 2 (2018): 57–64.

———. "Vertov and the Avant-Garde Documentary in Japan: Dreaming Reality in the 1960s." *Film History* 35, no. 2 (Spring 2024): 1–25.
Alter, Nora M. *Chris Marker*. Urbana: University of Illinois Press, 2006.
Ando Takemasa. "The Absence of the New Left: The (Un)changing Cultures of Activism in Japan." Lecture presented at ANPO Revisited Workshop in the ICC Workshop Series on Youth Activism in Post-War Japan, Sophia University, Tokyo, November 14, 2015.
———. "'Transforming 'Everydayness': Japanese New Left Movements and the Meaning of Their Direct Action." *Japanese Studies* 33, no. 1 (2013): 1–18.
Angel, Arielle. "Responsa: Beyond Grievance." *Jewish Currents* 76, no. 2 (Summer 2022): 7–16.
Arvatov, Boris. "Everyday Life and the Question of the Thing (Toward the Formulation of the Question)." Translated by Christina Kaier. *October* 81 (Summer 1997): 119–128.
Augst, Bertrand ["Jack Flash"]. "Jean-Luc Godard." In *Kinopraxis* (pamphlet). Pacific Film Archive of the Berkeley Art Museum (BAMPFA), January 1, 1970.
Baecque, Antoine de. *Godard: Biographie*. Paris: Grasset, 2010.
Barker, Jennifer. *The Aesthetics of Anti-Fascist Film: Radical Projection*. New York: Routledge, 2013.
Bataille, Georges. "The Psychological Structure of Fascism." Translated by Carl R. Lovitt. *New German Critique* 16 (Winter 1979): 64–87.
Baumbach, Nico. *Cinema/Politics/Philosophy*. New York: Columbia University Press, 2018.
Benjamin, Walter. *Charles Baudelaire: A Lyric Poet in the Era of High Capitalism*. Translated by H. Zorn. London: New Left Books, 1973.
———. *The Work of Art in the Age of Mechanical Reproducibility and Other Writings on Media*. Edited by Michael W. Jennings, Brigid Doherty, and Thomas Y. Levin. Cambridge, MA: Harvard University Press, 2008.
Berlant, Lauren. *Cruel Optimism*. Durham. NC: Duke University Press, 2011.
Bertolucci, Bernardo. "Versus Godard." *Cahiers du cinéma* 186 (January 1967): 28–31.
Beylie, Claude. "Le Triomphe de la femme." *Cahiers du cinéma* 22, no. 130 (April 1962): 19–28.
Billet, Alexander. *Shake the City: Experiments in Space and Time, Music and Crisis*. London: 1968 Press, 2022.
Bock, Audie. *Japanese Film Directors*. Tokyo: Kodansha International, 1978.
Bonitzer, Pascal, Jean-Louis Comolli, Serge Daney, Jean Narboni, and Jean-Pierre Oudart. *"La Vie est à nous:* Film militant." *Cahiers du cinéma* 218 (March 1970): 44–51.
Bourg, Julian. *From Revolution to Ethics: May 1968 and Contemporary French Thought*. Montreal: McGill University Pres, 2007.

Boym, Svetlana. *Common Places: Mythologies of Everyday Life in Russia*. Cambridge, MA: Harvard University Press, 1994.

———. "Estrangement as a Lifestyle: Shklovsky and Brodsky." *Poetics Today* 17, no. 4 (Winter 1996): 513–530.

Bratich, Jack Z. *On Microfascism: Gender, War, and Death*. Brooklyn, NY: Common Notions, 2022.

Bray, Mark. *Antifa: The Anti-Fascist Handbook*. Brooklyn, NY: Melville House, 2017.

Bremzen, Anya von. *Mastering the Art of Soviet Cooking: A Memoir of Food and Longing*. New York: Broadway Books, 2013.

Briciu, Bianca. "Love and Power: The Objectification of the Adolescent Body in Hani Susumu's *Hatsukoi Jigokuhen/Nanami, Inferno of First Love* (1968)." *Journal of Japanese & Korean Cinema* 5, nos. 1–2 (2013): 59–76..

brown, adrienne marée. *Pleasure Activism: The Politics of Feeling Good*. Edinburgh: AK Press: 2019.

———. *We Will Not Cancel Us: And Other Dreams of Transformative Justice*. Chico, CA: AK Press, 2020.

Buruma, Ian. *A Tokyo Romance*. New York: Penguin, 2018.

Capdenac, Michel. "Agnès Varda: De 5 à 7, l'heure de vérité pour Cléo." *Les Lettres françaises* 922 (April 12–18, 1962): 1, 12.

Carroll, Kent E. "Film and Revolution: Interview with the Dziga Vertov Group." In *Focus on Godard*, edited by Royal S. Brown, 50–64. Englewood Cliffs, NJ: Prentice Hall, 1972.

Cerisuelo, Marc. "Jean-Luc, Community, and Communication." In *A Companion to Jean-Luc Godard*, Edited by Tom Conley and T. Jefferson Kline, 296–317. West Sussex, UK: Wiley and Blackwell, 2014.

Cervoni, Albert. "Resnais: Pour un spectateur actif." *Miroir du cinéma* 2 (May 1962): 15.

Ciment, Michel. "For Your Pleasure: A Brief Overview of Fifty Years of *Positif*." In *Positif 50 Years: Selections from the French Film Journal*. edited by Michel Ciment and Laurence Kardish, 9–14. New York: Museum of Modern Art, 2002.

Coleman, Lindsay, and David Desser. Introduction to *Killers, Clients and Kindred Spirits: The Taboo Cinema of Shōhei Imamura*, 1–20. Edinburgh: Edinburgh University Press, 2019.

Colpi, Henri, Armand Gatti, Alain Resnais, Agnès Varda, and Georges Sadoul. "Au rendez-vous des amis: Ciné-débat." *Les Lettres françaises* 903 (November 30–December 6, 1961): 6.

Comolli, Jean-Louis, Jean Narboni, et al. "Le groupe Dziga-Vertov (1)." *Cahiers du cinéma* 238–239 (May–June 1972): pp34–39.

———. "Sur les films du 'groupe' (2)." *Cahiers du cinéma* 240 (July–August 1972): 4–9.

Cowan, Bainard. "Walter Benjamin's Theory of Allegory." In "Modernism," special issue, *New German Critique* 22 (Winter 1981): 109–122.

Culp, Andrew. *Dark Deleuze*. Minneapolis: University of Minnesota Press, 2016.

Dale, S. P. F. "Same-Sex Marriage and the Question of Queerness—Institutional Performativity and Marriage in Japan." *Asian Anthropology* 19, no. 2 (2020): 143–159.

Delahaye, Michel "Jean-Luc Godard ou l'enfance de l'art." *Cahiers du cinéma* 179 (June 1966): 64–73.

Deleuze, Gilles. *Cinema 2: The Time-Image*. Translated by Hugh Tomlinson and Robert Galeta. Minneapolis: University of Minnesota Press, 1989.

Deleuze, Gilles, and Félix Guattari. *Anti-Oedipus: Capitalism and Schizophrenia*. Minneapolis: University of Minnesota Press, 1972.

———. *A Thousand Plateaus: Capitalism and Schizophrenia*. Translated by Brian Massumi. Minneapolis: University of Minnesota, 1987.

DeRoo, Rebecca J. *Agnès Varda between Film, Photography, and Art*. Oakland: University of California Press, 2018.

Desser, David. *Eros Plus Massacre: An Introduction to the Japanese New Wave Cinema*. Bloomington: University of Indiana Press, 1988.

Doniol-Valcroze, Jacques. "Cannes: Semaine de la Critique." *Cahiers du cinéma* 25, no. 145 (July 1963): 23–37.

"Du bon usage de la valeur d'echange: le cahiers du cinéma et le marxisme-leninisme." *Cinéthique* 6 (January 1970): 1–12.

Elsaesser, Thomas. "From Anti-Illusionism to Hyper Realism: Bertolt Brecht and Contemporary Film." In *Re-interpreting Brecht: his Influence on Contemporary Drama and Film*, edited by Pia Kleber and Colin Visser, 170–185. Cambridge: Cambridge University Press, 1990.

Emmelhainz, Irmgard. *Jean-Luc Godard's Political Filmmaking*. London: Palgrave Macmillan, 2019.

"Enquete: Vers un néo-romanticisme au cinéma ?" *Les Lettres françaises* 764 (March 12–18, 1959): 7.

Fairfax, Daniel. *The Red Years of Cahiers*. Vol. 1, *Ideology and Politics*. Amsterdam: Amsterdam University Press, 2022.

Fargier, Jean-Paul, Gérard Leblanc, et al. "Le groupe Dziga-Vertov." *Cinéthique* 9–10 (September 1970–March 1971): 91–94.

———. "'Ne copies pas sur les yeux' disait Vertov." *Cinéthique* 15 (December 1972): 55–57.

———. "Un terrorisme 'economique' entretien avec Jean Rouch." *Cinéthique* 3 (1970): 15–21.

Fieschi, Jean-André, and Claude Ollier. "La grâce laïque." *Cahiers du cinéma* 165 (April 1965): 42–51.

Fisher, Mark. "Acid Communism." April 25, 2019. https://my-blackout.com/2019/04/25/mark-fisher-acid-communism-unfinished-introduction/

———. *Capitalist Realism: Is There No Alternative?* Alresford, UK: Zero Books, 2009.
Fletcher, Angus. *Allegory: The Theory of a Symbolic Mode.* Princeton, NJ: Princeton University Press, 2012.
Fresko, David. "Revolutionary Cinematic Suicide." *Brooklyn Rail*, June 2018. https://brooklynrail.org/2018/06/film/Revolutionary-Cinematic-Suicide.
Fukuoka, Kazuya. "Between Banality and Effervescence? A Study of Japanese Youth Nationalism." *Nations and Nationalism* 23, no. 2 (2017): 346–366.
Furuhata, Yuriko. *Cinema of Actuality: Japanese Avant-Garde Filmmaking in the Season of Image Politics.* Durham, NC: Duke University Press, 2013.
———. "Refiguring Actuality: Japan's Film Theory and Avant-Garde Documentary Movement, 1950s–1960s." PhD diss., Brown University, 2009.
Garin, Manuel. "Comedies of Resistance: Shūji Terayama and the Politics of Visual Humor." *The Sixties* 14, no. 2 (2021): 197–219.
Gatti, Armand, Chris Marker, and Jean-Louis Pays. "Des humanistes agissants." *Miroir du cinéma* 2 (May 1962): 2–7.
Gendron, Francis. "Chris Marker ou l'évidence." *Miroir du cinéma* 2 (May 1962): 10–11.
Geng, Annie. "One Way or Another." *Screen Slate.* June 17, 2023. www.screenslate.com/articles/one-way-or-another-0?mc_cid=050f41fe5c&mc_eid=0e17485503.
Godard, Jean-Luc. Interview in "Nouvelle Vague," special issue, *Cahiers du cinéma* 23, no. 138 (December 1962); 21–39.
Godet, Sylvain. "Chemin principal et chemins latéraux." *Cahiers du cinéma* 190 (May 1967): 63–64.
Goodwin, Michael. "The Dziga Vertov Film Group in America, an Interview with Jean-Luc Godard and Jean-Pierre Gorin." Unpublished manuscript, 1970. Pacific Film Archive at the Berkeley Art Museum (BAMPFA), Berkeley, California.
Goodwin, Michael, Tom Luddy, and Naomi Wise. "The Dziga Vertov Film Group in America." *Take One: The Film Magazine* 2, no.10 (March/April 1970): 8–27.
Grant, Paul Douglas. *Cinéma Militant: Political Filmmaking and May 1968.* New York: Columbia University Press, 2016.
Griffin, Roger. *Fascism.* Oxford: Oxford University Press, 1995.
Grossman, Andrew. "'Beautiful Publicity': An Introduction to Queer Asian Film." In *Queer Asian Cinema: Shadows in the Shade*, 1–29. Oxfordshire: Routledge, 2001.
Groupe CINEFRONT-Rouen. "Interventions." *Cinéthique* 11–12 (1970–1971): 72–76.
Hall, Jonathan M. "Unwilling Subjects: Psychoanalysis and Japanese Modernity." PhD diss., University of California-Santa Cruz, 2003.

Hanada Kiyoteru, "Dokyumentarī no kongo no tenbō" [Documentary's future prospects]. *Eiga hyōron* 15, no. 2 (February 1958): 16–19.

Hani Susumu. "Ashita no tame no eiga" [A cinema for tomorrow]. *Eiga Hyōron* 15, no. 2 (February 1958): 28–31.

———. Colloquium and Q&A at Harvard University, January 28, 2013.

———. Interview by Jacques Aumont, Pascal Bonitzer, and Sylvie Pierre. *Cahiers du cinéma* 224 (October 1970): 27–33.

———. "Susumu Hani." Interview by Rea Amit and Alexander Jacoby. *Midnight Eye: Visions of Japanese Cinema*, April 22, 2010. www.midnighteye.com/interviews/susumu-hani/.

———. "Watashi no baai" [My situation]. *Kiroku eiga* 4, no. 11 (November 1961): 11.

Hani Susumu with Eto Fumio and Sato Tadao. "Chapurin no gei to shisō" [The art and thought of Charlie Chaplin]. *Eiga hyōron* 17, no. 11 (November 1960): 46–52.

Hansen, Miriam. "Benjamin, Cinema and Experience: 'The Blue Flower in the Land of Technology.'" *New German Critique* 40 (Winter 1987): 179–224.

Hara Kazuo. Introduction to screening of Ogawa Shinsuke's *Magino Village: A Tale* (1983), Light Industry, Brooklyn, NY, July 23, 2018.

Harvey, Sylvia. *May '68 and Film Culture*. London: British Film Institute, 1978.

Haryu Ichiro. "Sengo taiken to dokyumentarī" [Postwar experience and documentary]. *Kiroku eiga* 2, no. 10 (October 1959): 4–6.

Hayes, Carol. "Kuroki Kazuo's Requiem for War." In *Legacies of the Asia-Pacific War: The* Yakeato *Generation*, edited by Roman Rosenbaum and Yasuko Claremont, 198–215. London: Routledge, 2010.

Hewitt, Andrew. *Fascist Modernism: Aesthetics, Politics, and the Avant-Garde*. Palo Alto, CA: Stanford University Press, 1993.

Holland, Eugene. *Deleuze and Guattari's Anti-Oedipus: Introduction to Schizoanalysis*. London: Routledge 1999.

Igarashi, Yoshikuni. *Bodies of Memory: Narratives of War in Postwar Japanese Culture, 1945–1970*. Princeton, NJ: Princeton University Press, 2000.

Imamura Shōhei. "Betwixt Fiction and Documentary." Translated by Bill Mihalopoulos. *Asian Cinema* 28, no. 1 (2017): 101–105.

———. *Eiga wa kyōki no tabi de aru* [Film is a journey in madness]. Tokyo: Tokyo Library Center, 2010.

———. *Toru: Kannu kara yamiichi e* [Shoot: From Cannes to the black market]. Tokyo: Kōsakusha, 2001.

Iwamoto Kenji. *Roshia avangyarudo no eiga to engeki* [Film and theatre of the Russian avant-garde]. Tokyo: Suisei-sha, 1998.

Iwasa Hisaya, Matsumoto Toshio, Noda Shinkichi, Ōshima Nagisa, and Terayama Shūji (Roundtable). "Eiga ni okeru kiroku-sei" [Documentality in movies]. *Kiroku eiga* 3, no. 1 (January 1960): 23–27.

Jameson, Fredric. *Signatures of the Visible*. New York: Routledge, 1992.
Jaudon, Raphaël. "Réécrire le corps: Érotique et politique dans les films de Godard et Gorin." *French Screen Studies* 22, no. 4 (2022): 229–250.
Jesty, Justin. "Image Pragmatics and Film as a Lived Practice in the Documentary Work of Hani Susumu and Tsuchimoto Noriaki." *Arts* 8, no. 2 (March 2019): 41.
Johnson, Albert. "The Craft of Cinema." Interview with Hani Sasumu [sic]. Audio recording, Berkeley Art Museum Pacific Film Archives (BAMPFA), Berkeley, California, October 28, 1966.
Kaganovsky, Lilya. "'The Threshold of the Visible World': Dziga Vertov's A Sixth Part of the World (1926)." In *Arctic Cinemas and the Documentary Ethos*, edited by Lilya Kaganovsky, Scott MacKenzie, and Anna Westerstahl Stenport, 46–67. Bloomington: Indiana University Press, 2019.
Kano, Ayako. *Acting like a Woman in Modern Japan: Theater, Gender, and Nationalism*. London: Palgrave Macmillan, 2001.
Kaplan, Nelly. "Chris Marker: Une lettre d'Israël." *Les Lettres françaises* 851 (November 24–30, 1960): 6.
Kapur, Nick. *Japan at the Crossroads: Conflict and Compromise after Anpo*. Cambridge, MA: Harvard University Press, 2018.
Kawachi Kaname. "Ore wa omae ni kajiba no matoi fura renagara mo moeagaru" [Even though you still call me a firefighter, I'm still burning]. *Kiroku eiga* 4, no. 9 (September 1961): 19–20.
Key, Margaret S. *Truth from a Lie: Documentary Detection, and Reflexivity in Abe Kobo's Realist Project*. Plymouth: Lexington Books, 2011.
Kimata Kimihiko. "Thoughts on the Extremely Private Pink Film of the 1970s." In *The Pink Book: The Japanese Eroduction and Its Contents*, edited by Mark Nornes, 49–92. 2nd ed. Ann Arbor, MI: Kinema Club, 2014.
Kracauer, Siegfried. *Theory of Film: The Redemption of Physical Reality*. Princeton, NJ: Princeton University Press, 1960.
Krantz, Charles. "Teaching *Night and Fog*: History and Historiography." *Film & History: An Interdisciplinary Journal of Film and Television Studies* 15, no. 1 (February 1985): 1–11.
KuroDalaiJee. *Anarchy of the Body: Undercurrents of Performance Art in 1960s Japan*. Leuven, Belgium: Leuven University Press, 2023.
Kuroki Kazuo. "Bokura no tatte iru tokoro" [Where we stand]. *Kiroku eiga* 5, no. 11 (December 1962): 16–18.
———. "Mu ni tsuite" [On nothingness]. *Kiroku eiga* 5, no. 6 (June 1962): 14–15.
———. "'Reporuta-ju, En' wo megutte" [Concerning the "documentary flame"]. *Kiroku eiga* 4, no. 4 (April 1961): 23–24.
LaCross, Donald. "Introduction: Surrealism and Romantic Anticapitalism." In *Morning Star: Surrealism, Marxism, Anarchism, Situationism, Utopia*, by Michael Löwy, vii–xxx. Austin: University of Texas Press, 2009.

Lamarre, Thomas. "Cartoon Film Theory: Imamura Taihei on Animation, Documentary, and Photography." In *Animating Film Theory*, edited by Karen Redrobe, 221–251. Durham, NC: Duke University Press, 2014.

Lazreg, Marnia. Introduction to *Foucault's Orient: The Conundrum of Cultural Difference, From Tunisia to Japan*, 1–12. Brooklyn, NY: Berghahn Books, 2017.

"Le cinéma-vérité." Special issue, *Miroir du cinéma* 3 (October 1962).

Leblanc, Gérard. "Godard: Valeur d'usage ou valeur d'échange?" *Cinéthique* 5 (September–October 1969): 22.

———. "Quelle avant-garde? (note sur une pratique actuelle du cinéma militant)." *Cinéthique* 7–8 (1970): 72–92.

Lefebvre, Henri. *The Critique of Everyday Life: The One-Volume Edition*. London: Verso, 2014.

"Les Meilleurs films Français depuis La Libération." *Cahiers du cinéma* 161–162 (January 1965): 130.

Lewis, Diane Wei. "Boundary Play: Truth, Fiction, and Performance in *A Man Vanishes*." In *Killers, Clients and Kindred Spirits: The Taboo Cinema of Shōhei Imamura*, 267–286. Edinburgh: Edinburgh University Press, 2019.

Lewis, Sophie. "Mermaid Contracts." *Patreon*. June 11, 2023. www.patreon.com/posts/mermaid-84407767.

Lippit, Yukio. "Japan During the *Provoke* Era." In *Provoke: Between Protest and Performance*, 19–22. Göttingen: Steidl, 2016.

Lorde, Audre. "Uses of the Erotic: The Erotic as Power." In *Pleasure Activism: The Politics of Feeling Good*, by adrienne marée brown, 12–15. Edinburgh: AK Press: 2019.

Love, Heather. *Feeling Backward: Loss and the Politics of Queer History*. Cambridge, MA: Harvard University Press, 2007.

Löwy, Michael, *Morning Star: Surrealism, Marxism, Anarchism, Situationism, Utopia*. Austin: University of Texas Press, 2009.

Lubow, Arthur. "Questioning the Place of Black Art in a White Man's Collection." *New York Times*, August 6, 2022. link.gale.com/apps/doc/A712688230/AONE?u=upenn_main&sid=summon&xid=8b227ae9.

Lucken, Michael. "Possibilité et limites d'une philosophie photographique: Une lecture de Nakai Masakazu." *Archives de Philosophie* 1, no. 85 (2022): 67–84.

Luddy, Tom. "British Sounds." *Take One: The Film Magazine* 2, no. 11 (May/June 1970): 12.

Lupton, Catherine. *Chris Marker: Memories of the Future*. Chicago: Chicago University Press, 2004.

Macbean, James Roy. *Film and Revolution*. Bloomington: Indiana University Press, 1975.

MacCabe, Colin, and Laura Mulvey. "Images of Women, Images of Sexuality." In *Godard: Images, Sounds, Politics*, 79–104. Bloomington: Indiana University Press, 1980.

MacFarlane, Steve. "A Bestiary of Madeleines on 'Chris Marker: 100' at Peter Blum Gallery." Element X Cinema Substack. February 3, 2022. https://elementxcinema.substack.com/p/a-bestiary-of-madeleines.
MacKay, John. "Dziga Vertov: A Revolution in Film." *Artforum* 49, no. 8 (April 2011): 196–238.
Malitsky, Joshua. *Post-Revolution Nonfiction Film: Building the Soviet and Cuban Nations*. Bloomington: Indiana University Press, 2013.
Marasco, Robyn. "Bataille's Anti-fascism." *Contemporary Political Theory* 21, no. 1 (2022): 3–23.
Marcorelles, Louis. "Le Mystère Koumiko de Chris Marker." *Cahiers du cinéma* 168 (July 1965): 70.
Marcorelles, Louis, and Eric Rohmer. "Entretien avec Serge Youtkévitch." *Cahiers* 21, no. 125 (November 1961): 1–27.
———. "Interview avec Jean Rouch." *Cahiers du cinéma* 24, no. 144 (June 1963): 1–22.
Martín, Marcos P. Centeno. "The Limits of Fiction: Politics and Absent Scenes in Susumu Hani's *Bad Boys* (*Furyō Shōnen*, 1960): A film Re-reading through Its Script." *Journal of Japanese and Korean Cinema* 10, no. 1 (2018): 1–15.
Massumi, Brian. Preface to *The Politics of Affect*, edited by Brian Massumi, vii–xii. Cambridge, UK: Polity Press, 2014.
Matsuda Masao. "Media kakumei no tame no akushisu" [An axis for a media revolution]. In *Fukanosei no Media* [Impossible media], 210–228. Tokyo: Tabata Shoten, 1973.
Matsukawa Yasuo. "Nipponkonchūki ni tsuite no dansei-teki hansei" [A masculine reflection on *Insect Woman*]. *Kiroku eiga* 7, no. 1 (January 1974): 30–31.
Matsumoto Toshio. *Eizō no hakken* (*Discovery of the Image*): *Avant-Garde Documentary*. Tokyo: San'ichi Shobo, 1963.
———. "Geijutsu-teki Sado Mazohisuto no ishiki moshikuwa sōsaku no naiteki katei to geijutsu-teki kyōyō-sei ni tsuite" [Consciousness of the aesthetic sadomasochist: Or, on the internal process of creation and its artistic utility]. *Kiroku eiga* 3, no. 2 (February 1960): 6–9.
———. "Haisen to sengo no fuzai: Shutai-ron no saikentō no tame ni" [Absence of "defeat and postwar": For a reexamination of subjectivity part 2]. *Kiroku eiga* 2, no. 8 (August 1959): 34–36.
———. "Hyōgen keishiki no jikken" [Experiments in forms of expression]. In *Gendai eiga jiten* [Contemporary encyclopedia of cinema], edited by Okada Susumu, Sasaki Kiichi, Sato Tadao, and Hani Susumu, 154–157. Tokyo: Bijutsu Shuppansha, 1967.
———. "Taishū toiu no mono kami ni tsuite" [On the fetish called mass]. *Kiroku eiga* 5, no. 2 (February 1962): 19–23.
———. "A Theory of Avant-Garde Documentary." Translated by Michael Raine. *Cinema Journal* 14, no. 4 (Summer 2012): 144–148.

———. "Tobenai Chinmoku ron nōto" [Notes on the theory of *Silence Has No Wings*]. *Eiga hyōron* 23, no. 3 (March 1966): 40–41.

———. "Undō no henkaku" [Transformation of the movement]. *Kiroku eiga* 6, no. 10 (November 1963): 7–9.

———. "Zankoku o mitsumeru me geijutsu-teki hitei kōi ni okeru shutai no ichi ni tsuite" [Cruel eyes: On the position of the subject in artistic negation]. *Kiroku eiga* 3, no. 12 (December 1960): 6–10.

———. "Zen'ei kiroku eiga no hōhō ni tsuite" [On the method of avant-garde documentary]. *Kiroku eiga* (June 1958): 6–11.

Matsumoto Toshio, Takei Akio, Ogawa Toru, and Ōshima Nagisa. "Zadankai: Eiga no mirai wa kanō ka? roku san-nendo no geijutsu shisō jōkyō o megu tsute" [Symposium: Is the future of cinema possible? On the state of art and thought in 1963]. *Kiroku eiga* 7, no. 1 (January 1964): 4–13.

McGlotten, Shaka, and Susanna Paasonen. "The Deep Realness of Deepfake Pornography." In *Deep Mediations: Thinking Space in Cinema and Digital Cultures*, edited by Karen Redrobe and Jeff Scheible, 351–360. Minneapolis: University of Minnesota Press, 2021.

McLelland, Mark J. "From the Stage to the Clinic: Changing Transgender Identities in Post-war Japan." *Japan Forum* 16, no. 1 (2004): 1–20.

———. *Queer Japan from the Pacific War to the Internet Age*. Lanham, MD: Rowman & Littlefield, 2005.

Megna, Paul. "Juridical Dread and the Self-Disciplining Subject." *Postmedieval: A Journal of Medieval Cultural Studies* 13 (2022): 55–79.

Michelson, Annette. Introduction to Oshima Nagisa, *Cinema, Censorship, and the State: The Writings of Ōshima Nagisa, 1956–1978*, edited by Annette Michelson, 1–5. Cambridge, MA: MIT Press, 1992.

———. "*The Man with the Movie Camera*: From Magician to Epistemologist." *Artforum*, March 1972.

Miller, J. Hillis. "The Two Allegories." *Harvard English Studies* 9 (1981): 355.

Moore, Aaron Stephen. "Para-existential Forces of Invention: Nakai Masakazu's Theory of Technology and Critique of Capitalism." *positions* 17, no. 1 (2009): 127–157.

Morgan, Joan. "Why We Get Off: Moving towards a Black Feminist Politics of Pleasure." In *Pleasure Activism: The Politics of Feeling Good*, edited by adrienne marée brown, 32–37. Edinburgh, AK Press: 2019.

Morin, Edgar. *Le Cinéma ou l'homme imaginaire: Essai d'anthropologie sociologique*. Paris: Éditions de minuit, 1956.

———. "Pour un nouveau cinéma-vérité." *France Observateur* 11, no. 506 (January 14, 1960): 23.

Moullet, Luc. "Festivals: Berlin." *Cahiers du cinéma* 23, no. 135 (September 1962): 26–32.

Muñoz, José Esteban. *Cruising Utopia*. New York: New York University Press, 2009.

Nagano Chiaki. "Puropaganda eiga no shin no reimei" [The true dawn of propaganda film]. *Kiroku eiga* 2, no. 11 (November 1959): 24–25.

Nakahara Yūsuke. "Zenei eiga ni tsuite: Vertov no koto nado" [On avant-garde film: Vertov and others]. In *Sekai Zenei eigasai* [A retrospective of world avant-garde cinema], 106–107. Tokyo: Sōgetsu Art Center, 1966.

Nakai Masakazu. "Film Theory and the Crisis in Contemporary Aesthetics." Translated by Phil Kaffen. In "Decentering Theory: Reconsidering the History of Japanese Film Theory," special issue, *Review of Japanese Culture and Society* 22 (December 2010): 80–87.

———. *Nakai Masakazu zenshū*. vol. 3. Tokyo: Nijutsu shuppan, 1981.

Nathan, Patrick. *Image Control: Art, Fascism, and the Right to Resist*. Berkeley: Counterpoint Press, 2021.

Neitzel, Laura. *The Life We Longed For: Danchi Housing and the Middle Class Dream in Postwar Japan*. Portland: MerwinAsia, 2016.

Nettleton, Taro. "Throw Out the Books, Get Out in the Streets: Subjectivity and Space in Japanese Underground Art of the 1960s." PhD diss., University of Michigan, 2011.

Nezu Masashi. "Shiyakuwai kenkyū zasshi" [Social studies journals]. *Bunka Sekai* 21 (1936.

Ngai, Sianne. *Ugly Feelings*. Cambridge, MA: Harvard University Press, 2005.

Noda Shinkichi, "Akuchuaritī no sōzō-teki gekika dokyumentarī hōhō-ron ni suite no nōto" [Creative dramatization of actuality: Notes on documentary methodology, pt. 2]. *Kiroku eiga* 1, no. 5 (December 1958): 11–14.

———. "Sogai no kiroku (1) Danzetsu fuzai" [Record of alienation (1) absence of discontinuity]. *Kiroku eiga* 4, no. 9 (September 1961): 4–7.

Nornes, Markus. *Forest of Pressure: Ogawa Shinsuke and Postwar Japanese Documentary*. Minneapolis: University of Minnesota Press, 2007.

———. "Translating Grierson: Japan." In *The Grierson Effect*, edited by Deane Williams and Zoë Druick, 59–78. London: Palgrave Macmillan, 2014.

Ōe Masanori. "The Aesthetics of Ecstasy and the Yippie Revolution." Translated by Yuzo Sakuramoto. In *Japanese Expanded Cinema and Intermedia: Critical Texts of the 1960s*, edited by Go Hirasawa, Ann Adachi-Tasch, and Julian Ross, 153–168. Berlin: Archive Books, 2020.

Oguma Eiji. "Japan's 1968: A Collective Reaction to Rapid Economic Growth in an Age of Turmoil." Translated by Nick Kapur. *Asia Pacific Journal* 13, no. 12 (March 2015): 1–24.

Ōishi Masahiko. *Higa tōi: Nihon Modanizumu/ Roshia avangyarudo*. Tokyo: Suisei-sha, 2009.

Ōshima Nagisa. *Cinema, Censorship, and the State: The Writings of Ōshima Nagisa, 1956–1978*. Edited by Annette Michelson. Cambridge, MA: MIT Press, 1992.

Ōtani Shinpei. "Matsumoto Toshio to Hani Susumu no eiga-ron, soshite avangyarudo geijutsu undō: 1950-nendai kara 1960-nendai shotō made no katsudō kōsatsu" [Toshio Matsumoto and Susumu Hani's film theory and avant-garde art movement: Consideration of activities from the 1950s to the early 1960s]. *Eizōgaku* 102 (2019): 94–114.

Otomo Rio. "Narratives, the Body, and the 1964 Tokyo Olympics." *Asian Studies Review* 31 (June 2007): 117–132.

Ozawa Toshio. "Hihyō-ka to sakka no aida" [Between critics and writers]. *Kiroku eiga* 4, no. 9 (September 1961): 16.

Pays, Jean-Louis. "Le Joli Mai." *Miroir du cinema* 4 (1963): 13.

Peters, Kyle. "Kyoto School and Totality: Theories of Self-Formation in Modern Japanese Philosophy and Thought." PhD diss., University of Chicago, 2021.

Philipe, Anne. "*Cuba Si* ou les racines d'une Révolution." *Les Lettres françaises* 910 (January 18–24, 1962): 7.

Phillips, James. "Anti-Oedipus: The Ethics of Performance and Misrecognition in Matsumoto Toshio's *Funeral Parade of Roses*." *SubStance* 44, no. 141 (2016): 33–48.

Pronin, Aleksandr. *Bumazhnyi Vertov/Tselluloidnyi Maiakovskii* [Paper Vertov/celluloid Mayakovsky]. Moscow: Novoe literaturnoe obozrenie, 2019.

Raine, Michael. "*The Insect Woman*, or: The Female Act of Failure." In *Killers, Clients and Kindred Spirits: The Taboo Cinema of Shōhei Imamura*, 115–138. Edinburgh: Edinburgh University Press, 2019.

———. Introduction to Matsumoto Toshio, "A Theory of Avant-Garde Documentary." Translated by Michael Raine. *Cinema Journal* 14, no. 4 (Summer 2012): 144–148.

———. Japan Society brochure, New York screening of *Silence Has No Wings*. February 21, 2009.

Ridgely, Steven C. *Japanese Counterculture: The Antiestablishment Art of Terayama Shūji*. Minneapolis: University of Minnesota Press, 2011.

Rodowick, D. N. *The Crisis of Political Modernism*. Berkeley: University of California Press, 1994.

Ross, Kristin. *Fast Cars, Clean Bodies: Decolonization and the Reordering of French Culture*. Cambridge, MA: MIT Press, 1995.

Roudé, Catherine. *Le cinéma militant a l'heure des collectifs: Slon et Iskra dans la France de l'apres-1968*. Rennes: Presses universitaires de Rennes, 2017.

Sadler, John Paul, in conversation with Shaka McGlotten and Susanna Paasonen. "The Deep Realness of Deepfake Pornography." In *Deep Mediations: Thinking Space in Cinema and Digital Cultures*, edited by Karen Redrobe and Jeff Scheible, 351–360. Minneapolis: University of Minnesota Press, 2021.

Sadoul, Georges. "Agnès Varda: Magicienne du réel." *Les Lettres françaises* 777 (June 11–17 1959): 7.

———. "Animation et courts métrages, Cannes 1958: Festival moyen." *Les Lettres françaises* 722 (May 15–21, 1958): 8–9.

———. "Autour d'une indépendance conversations avec quatres jeunes cinéastes japonaises." In "Etats Unis-Japon," special issue, *Cahiers du cinéma* 166–167 (May–June 1965): 35–42.
———. *"Cleo de 5 a 7:* Le Cœur Révélateur." *Les Lettres françaises* 922 (April 12–18, 1962): 6.
———. *French Film.* New York: Arno Press, 1972.
———. *Histoire d'un art: Le cinéma; des origins à nos jours.* Paris: Flammarion, 1949.
———. *"La Guerre est fini:* La Lutte continue." *Les Lettres françaises* 1132 (May 19–25, 1966): 14–15.
———. "Plus de promesses et de diversité que de révélations: Au festival de Tours." *Les Lettres françaises* 1057 (December 3–9, 1964): 8.
———. "Un film maudit: *Octobre à Paris,* long métrage francais, anonyme." *Les Lettres françaises* 943 (September 13–19, 1962): 6.
———. "Un miroir qui refléchit: *Un Joli Mai,* film français de Chris Marker." *Les Lettres françaises* 977 (May 9–15, 1963): 6.
Salazkina, Masha. *In Excess: Sergei Eisenstein's Mexico.* Chicago: University of Chicago Press, 2009.
Sas, Miryam. "By Other Hands: Environment and Apparatus in 1960s Intermedia." In *The Oxford Handbook of Japanese Cinema,* edited by Daisuke Miyao, 1–34. Oxford: Oxford University Press, 2014.
———. *Experimental Arts of Postwar Japan: Moments of Encounter, Engagement, and Imagined Return.* Cambridge, MA: Harvard East Asian Monographs, 2011.
———. *Feeling Media: Potentiality and the Afterlife of Art.* Durham, NC: Duke University Press, 2022.
———. "Moving the Horizon: Violence and Cinematic Revolution in Ōshima Nagisa's *Ninja bugeichō.*" *Mechademia: Second Arc* 7 (1992): 264–280,.
Sasaki Hajime. "Kiroku eiga to seiji" [Documentary film and politics]. *Kiroku eiga* 2, no. 9 (September 1959): 4–5.
Satō Tadao. *Currents in Japanese Cinema: Essays by Tadao Sato.* Translated by Gregory Barrett. Tokyo: Kodansha International, 1982.
———. "Matsumoto Toshio's Film-Poem 'Nishijin.'" *Eiga hyōron* 18, no. 8 (1961): 66–68.
Schieder, Chelsea Szendi. *Coed Revolution: The Female Student in the Japanese New Left.* Durham, NC: Duke University Press, 2021.
Sekine Hiroshi. "Umare kawaru jōkyō" [The situation of being reborn]. *Kiroku eiga* 7, no. 1 (January 1974): 28–29.
Sharp, Jasper. "Down the Bunka: Japanese Underground Cinema of the 1960s." *Sight and Sound,* July 11, 2016.
Sheldon, Richard. Introduction to *Third Factory,* by Viktor Shklovsky. McLean, IL: Dalkey Archive Press, 2002.

Shklovsky, Viktor. "Art as Technique." In *Russian Formalist Criticism: Four Essays*, translated by Lee L. Lemon and Marion J. Reis, 3–24. Lincoln: University of Nebraska Press, 1965.
———. *Third Factory*. McLean, IL: Dalkey Archive Press, 2002.
Sorgenfrei, Carol Fisher. *Unspeakable Acts: The Avant-Garde Theatre of Terayama Shuji and Postwar Japan*. Honolulu: University of Hawaii Press, 2005.
Takuya Tsunoda. "The Dawn of Cinematic Modernism: Iwanami Productions and Postwar Japanese Cinema." PhD diss., Yale University, 2015.
———. "Hani Susumu, *Nouvelle Vague* in Japan, and Processive Cinema." In *A Companion to Japanese Cinema*, edited by David Desser, 612–638. Hoboken, NJ: Wiley-Blackwell, 2022.
Terayama Shūji. *Eiga gishi o ute (Shoot the Projectionist: Collected Writings on Cinema of Terayama Shūji)*. Tokyo: Shinshokan, 1973.
———. "Rojin to taiji: Kyōfu no gendai-tekina imi" [The old man and the fetus: The modern meaning of fear.] *Kiroku eiga* 4, no. 6 (June 1961): 18–19.
Tourret, Franck. *Alain Resnais: Le pari de la forme*. Paris: L'Harmattan, 2019.
Trotsky, Leon. *The Permanent Revolution*. Translated by Max Shachtman. New York: Pioneer Publishers, 1931.
Tsivian, Yuri. *Lines of Resistance: Dziga Vertov and the Twenties*. Bloomington: Indiana University Press, 2004.
Tyerman, Edward. *Internationalist Aesthetics: China and Early Soviet Culture*. New York: Columbia University Press, 2022.
Van Cauwenberge, Geneviève. "Agnès Varda et le documentaire." *La revue belge du cinéma* (Summer 1987): 19–23.
Varda, Agnès. "Adieu à Georges Sadoul." *Les Lettres françaises* 1204 (October 18–24, 1967): 15.
———. *Cinéastes de notre temps*. Episode "La nouvelle vague par elle-même." Aired May 19, 1964, on ORTF. Accessed January 2023 on The Criterion Channel.
———. "Enquete: Vers un néo-romanticisme au cinéma?" *Les Lettres françaises* 764 (March 12–18, 1959): 7.
———. "The 7th Art and Me." Norton Lecture at Harvard University, February 26, 2018.
Vertov, Dziga. *Iz naslediia*. Tom II, *Stat'i i vystupleniia*. Moscow: Eisenstein Center, 2008.
Vincent, Keith, Kazama Takahashi, and Kawaguchi Kazuya. *Jissensuru sekushuariti: Dōseiai, iseiai no seijigaku* [Practicing sexualities: Integrating theory and activism through lesbian/gay/PHA identities]. Tokyo: Ugoku Gei to Rezubian no Kai, 1998.
Wagner, Jean. "Le Cahier des Autres." *Cahiers du cinéma* 165 (April 1965): 78.
Wang, Jackie. *Carceral Capitalism*. Cambridge, MA: Semiotext(e), 2018.

Watanabe Hiroshi. *Abe Kōbō*. Tokyo: Shinbisha, 1976.
Watanabe Masami. "Kagaku eiga no shūhen" [On the outskirts of science film]. *Kiroku eiga* 4, no. 9 (September 1961): 7–10.
Watkins, Mary, and Helene Shulman. *Toward Psychologies of Liberation*. Hampshire, UK: Palgrave Macmillan, 2008.
"What Is Media Literacy?" Media Literacy Now. Accessed June 24, 2023. https://medialiteracynow.org/challenge/what-is-media-literacy/.
Widdis, Emma. *Socialist Senses: Film, Feeling, and the Soviet Subject, 1917–1940*. Bloomington: Indiana University Press, 2017.
Williams, Linda. "Anatomy of a Skin Flick." *Sight & Sound* 15, no. 6 (June 2005): 25–26.
———. "Film Bodies: Gender, Genre, and Excess." *Film Quarterly* 44, no. 4 (Summer 1991): 2–13.
Wilson, Emily. *Alain Resnais*. Manchester, UK: Manchester University Press, 2006.
Wollen, Peter. "Godard and Counter-Cinema: Vent d'Est." In *Film Theory and Criticism: Introductory Readings*. New York: Oxford University Press, 1999.
Wu, J. S. "The Animating Inbetween: Productions of Race in Contemporary Animation." PhD diss., University of Pennsylvania, 2024.
Yamada Koichi. "Bilan économique du cinéma japonais." In "Etats Units-Japon," special issue, *Cahiers du cinéma* 166–167 (May–June 1965): 48–49.
———. "*La Mariee des Andes* de Hani Susumu." *Cahiers du cinéma* 183 (October 1966): 29–30.
Yamamoto, Naoki. *Dialectics without Synthesis: Japanese Film Theory and Realism in a Global Frame*. Oakland: University of California Press, 2020.
Yoda, Tomiko. "Girlscape: The Marketing of Mediatic Ambience in Japan." In *Media Theory in Japan*, edited by Marc Steinberg and Alexander Zahlten, 173–199. Durham, NC: Duke University Press, 2017.
Yomota Inuhiko. "2 ou 3 choses que je sais d'ATG." In *Art Theatre Guild*, 30–35. Vienna: Vienna International Film Festival, 2003.
Yoshimi, Shunya. "'Made in Japan': The Cultural Politics of 'Home Electrification' in Postwar Japan." *Media Culture and Society* 21, no. 2 (1999): 149–171.
Yu, Chang-min. "Ciné-méta-vérité: *Le Joli Mai* and the Politics of Fictionality." In "Jacques Rivette and Chris Marker," special issue, *Cine-Files* 12 (Spring 2017): 1–20.
Zahlten, Alexander. *The End of Japanese Cinema: Industrial Genres, National Times, and Media Ecologies*. Durham, NC: Duke University Press, 2017.
Zander, Patrick G. *Fascism through History: Culture, Ideology, and Daily Life*. Santa Barbara, CA: ABC-CLIO, 2020.

Index

1920s: avant-gardes, 4, 28; French, 43, 171; general, 32, 162; Japanese, 112; Soviet, 11–17; 26–27, 60, 157; Soviet film, 35, 42; surrealism, 43, 97–98, 160
1973: Cuba, 91; Japan, 8; 190–192
2 ou 3 choses que je sais d'elle (*2 or 3 Things I Know About Her*), 138, 140, 146

Abe Kōbō, 42, 49, 107
abolition: family abolition, 162, 176; general, 70, 82, 195–202. *See also* police
Adachi Masao, 10, 146, 167
Africa, 59–60, 70, 211–212
agitational propaganda (agitprop), 36–38, 67, 87, 108. *See also* propaganda
Ahmed, Sara, 19, 32, 170, 183
Algerian War, 6, 9, 28, 38, 66, 70, 76–78, 83, 95, 137
Ali, Muhammad, 178
alienation from one's labor, 18, 44, 50, 54–55, 106, 108, 117, 120, 126
Alienation Effect. *See* Verfremdungseffekt
allegory: allegorical semi-documentary, 29–30, 97–98, 102, 107, 110–113, 118–121, 127–128, 158; general, 98–99, 105–110, 118–127, 141, 152, 187, 193
Allende, Salvador, 26
Álvarez, Santiago, 86

America. *See* United States of America
Americajin, Anata wa? (*Americans, Who Are You?*), 178
anarchism, 158–159, 161, 169, 176–177, 189
Anderson, Lindsay, 177
Ando Takemasa, 163–166
Anger, Kenneth, 160
animation, 1–3, 41, 55–56, 87, 194. *See also* stop-motion
ANPO: ANPO struggle (1960 protest movement), 28–30, 38–40, 48–49, 61, 111–115, 123; general history, 21, 58, 124, 164; late-1960s ANPO struggle, 164, 171; post-ANPO 1960, 48, 105. See also *ANPO Jōyaku* (film)
ANPO Jōyaku (film), 34–40, 48, 54–55, 108
anthropology, 111–114
anti-Americanism: contemporary Russian, 3, in international cinema, 10–11, 58, 105, 113, 135, 148–150, 194; in relation to complicity question, 7–9, 21, 34–38, 108, 164–165
anti-capitalism: in contemporary film, 194–196; contemporary politics, 3; in DVG, 131–132, 140–146, 155–156; in European philosophy, 18, 22, 27, 108; in Imamura, 98, 112–113; in Kuroki, 125–127 in late 1960s Japan, 164–169, 181; in Matsumoto, 21–23, 35–37, 55–57, 173; in Marker, 83

247

anti-cinema. *See* counter-cinema. *See also* Wollen, Peter
anti-colonialism. *See* decolonialism
anti-communism, 35
antifascism: in aesthetic practice, 5–6, 12, 17, 24–33, 60; in allegorical semi-documentary, 110, 127; in anti-Nazi function, 14–15; in connection with abolition, 196–202; in contemporary films, 193; definition, 2–4, 19; in DVG, 135–136, 138, 144, 148, 154–156; in everyday life, 17, 22; in French history, 38; in Marker and Varda, 76, 79, 82–84, 91–95, 98–99, 195; in Matsumoto Toshio's work, 34–39, 45, 54–62, in philosophy, 16, 106; in queer ATG films: 157, 161–169, 173, 190
anti-imperialism: in aesthetics, 30, 70, 84, 86, 135–136, 163, 173, 193; in general, 3, 66, 144
Anti-Oedipus: Capitalism and Schizophrenia, 18, 20, 155, 196, 207
anti-psychiatric, 20, 208
anti-racism, 70, 134–135, 150. *See also* racism
antisemitism, 3, 14
anti-war, 35, 45, 165. *See also* Vietnam War
Antonioni, Michelangelo, 83
Ao no Kai (Blue Group), 121
Aragon, Louis, 9, 65, 67–69, 107
Art Theatre Guild (ATG), 30, 105, 119, 124, 158–165, 179, 190
Article IX, 21
Asai Masuo, 159–160
Asama Sansō incident, 147, 191
asceticism, 27–28, 69, 138, 146–147, 151, 155, 196
authoritarianism and anti-authoritarianism, 43, 61, 164, 168
auto-critique: in general, 5, 201, 207; Matsumoto's concept, 20, 22, 35, 39–40, 47, 54, 61, 64, 104, 212; in post-May France, 133–137, 142–144, 147, 150
avant-folk, 1–2

Badiou, Alain, 136
Ballot, Nadine, 178
Bara no sōretsu (Funeral Parade of Roses), 11, 19–20, 58, 160–162, 166, 170–175, 182, 185, 190, 193
Barker, Jennifer, 6, 16
Barthes, Roland, 158, 166
bases. *See* military bases (American)
Bataille, Georges, 3, 6, 18, 169, 201
Bazin, André, 67–68, 103, 140

Beauvoir, Simone de, 128
Benjamin, Walter, 11, 16, 42, 99, 106–111, 125–126, 132, 206
Berlant, Lauren, 19
Berto, Juliet, 148, 150
bidonville, 78
Black Panthers, 135, 148, 150
blackness, Black Studies, 30, 87, 135, 150, 154
Le Bonheur, 145
Bonitzer, Pascal, 24, 26
bourgeois, 16, 26, 129–137, 143–152, 161
Boym, Svetlana, xi, 4, 207
Bratich, Jack Z., 5, 16, 25, 27, 200
Bray, Mark, 16
Brecht, Bertolt, 15, 26, 93–94, 132, 136, 142, 148–152, 194
Breton, André, 28, 73
British Sounds, 133, 138–142, 146, 152–153
Buck-Morss, Susan, 4
Buddhism, 50, 52, 56
Buñuel, Luis, 70, 97–104, 125, 171. *See also Los Olvidados*
Buruma, Ian, 158
byt, 17, 178, 207

Cahiers du cinéma: journal history, 9–10, 24–26, 32, 67–70, 130–134, 137–137; quote cited in, 83, 85, 88, 103, 143, 148, 152, 183–184
caméra-vivante, 80, 84
capitalism. *See* anti-capitalism
carcerality. *See* abolition
censorship, 9, 72–73
Chabrol, Claude, 7
Chaplin, Charlie, 186, 188
Chelovek s kinoapparatom (Man with a Movie Camera), 12–14, 42, 55, 135, 172, 181
Chronique d'un été (Chronicle of a Summer), 9, 76–81, 137, 178, 217
chuvstvennost', 16
cinéma-vérité: connection to Japan: 103; connection to Vertov: 16–17, 132; history of genre, 9, 76–78, 83, 137, 178, 205
cinematic sensation. *See kinooshchushchenie*
Cinéthique, 10, 30, 132–134, 143–146, 151–156
Ciné-tracts, 85
Clay, Cassius. *See* Ali, Muhammad
Cleaver, Eldridge, 150, 223
Cléo de 5 à 7, 9, 68, 76, 85–86, 213. *See also* Varda, Agnès
Cold War, 7, 21, 35. *See also* anti-Americanism
Collective Kumo, 159
Colpi, Henri, 72–74, 94

INDEX 249

communism: acid communism, 156; affect, 201; artists, 11, 107; Cold War geopolitics, 21, 99; communist presses, 66–69; connection to Soviet Union, 16, 36, 181; film, 26–28, 65–67, 79–81, 86–95, 151, 177, 195; French intellectuals, 9, 32, 68, 78, 93, 132; French political party, 25, 30, 136; Japan Communist League, 191; Japanese intellectuals, 6, 8, 126, 161, 169; Marxist-Leninists, 130, 132, 138; New Left, 5; Old Left, 22, 44. *See also* anti-communism; PCF (Parti communiste français); Union de la Jeunesse Communiste Marxiste-Léniniste
Comolli, Jean-Louis, 24, 143
complicity: with American military aggression, 7, 35, 108, 164–165, 168; of documentary medium, 39, as documentary technique, 71; with fascism in France, 8–9, 66, 76, 87; with fascism in general, 2–5, 198, 201; with fascism in Japan, 30, 39, 98; in Imamura, 110, 112; in Matsumoto, 40, 49–51
consciousness: altered states, 169; artist's consciousness, 126, 170, 173; as choice, 95; development of, 15–16, 20–23, 54, 60; fascist, 5; political consciousness, 109–110; rupture of, 4, 38, 57, 101; self-consciousness, 64, 90, 110, 177; self-revolution of, 162–165. *See also* surrealism; unconscious
constitution (Japanese), 21
consumerism, 30, 78, 86, 105, 108, 164–165, 214
counter-cinema, 30, 135, 151, 153. *See also* Wollen, Peter
counterculture: in France, 10, 131; in Japan, 30, 158–163, 166–168, 171, 179
Coutant-Malthot-Éclaire, 77, 80
Cuba, 29, 32, 72, 76, 85–92, 95. *See also* ¡*Cuba Sí!*; *Salut les Cubains*
¡*Cuba Sí!*, 86–88, 90
Culp, Andrew, 159, 162, 200
Czechoslovakia, 139

Dakhabrakha, 1–3
danchi, 117, 220
Daney, Serge, 24
Dassin, Jules, 99
Dasté, Jean, 25–26
De cierta manera (One Way or Another), 91–92
de Gaulle, Charles, 6
Debord, Guy, 181. *See also dépaysement*
decolonialism, 29–30, 66, 70–72, 76, 86
Delahaye, Michel, 137

Deleuze, Gilles, 155, 162, 174, 195, 200
Deleuze, Gilles and Félix Guattari, 5, 17–19, 22, 27, 155, 159, 162, 168, 196, 200–201. *See also Anti-Oedipus: Capitalism and Schizophrenia*; *A Thousand Plateaus*
dépaysement, 44
deterritorialization, 159, 161, 195. *See also* Deleuze, Gilles
dialectic: dialectical montage, 27; of film history, 23–26, 42–47, 100–101, 124–125, 137, 170; general structure, 40, 50, 54, 70, 81, 118, 142, 144, 148, 154, 189; Hegelo-Marxist, 22, 142; without synthesis (Hanada), 31, 42
Diet (Japanese Parliament), 124
Direct Cinema, 77, 140, 143, 150
discomfort: audience, 4, 88, 139, 146; of auto-critique, 5, 135, 198; general, 17, 133
disorientation: aesthetic strategy, 12, 15, 39, 62, 88, 111, 142, 156, 169–170, 173–175, 183–184; Ahmed's concept, 170
domesticity, 138, 142, 144–145
dream: American dream, 52, 194; general, 22, 201; in Left Bank filmmakers, 65–67; quality of filmmaking, 48–49, 103, 125; sequence in *Los Olvidados*, 100–101; sequence in *Sho o suteyo*, 175, 179–182. *See also Los Olvidados*; Terayama Shūji
Drew, Robert, 77
Drobashenko, Sergei, 132
drug (cinema as), 71–72
Dziga Vertov Group (DVG), 10, 16, 28, 30, 69, 84, 89, 93, 130–156, 191–192. *See also* Godard, Jean-Luc

economic growth: in France, 168; in general, 7–8; in Japan, 8, 30, 35, 52, 55, 106–112, 117, 126, 164
Ecstasis (film), 172
ecstasy: in film form, 30, 55, 162; in general, 5, 168–169, 172–173, 192. *See also Ecstasis* (film); *Tenshi no kōkotsu*
editing (film): in general, 169; in Hani, 184–185; in Imamura, 116; in Kuroki, 124; in Marker, 78, 84; in Matsumoto, 35–39, 48, 54–55, 58–61, 138; in Resnais, 45; in Varda, 85–87, 91; in Vertov, 13–17, 42, 172
education, 15, 20, 25, 136
Eiga hihyō II, 10, 191
Eiga hyōron, 10, 24, 40, 50, 64, 105
Eisenstein, Sergei, 26–27
ekphrasis, 45, 70, 88, 125
Elsa la rose, 68, 85, 88, 107

Elsaesser, Thomas, 94
engagement: with antifascism, 40; of audience through affect, 16, 28, 88–89, 94–95, 136, 154; between director and subject, 104; with fictionality, 189; with the political, 33, 66–73, 79, 93, 108, 114, 138, 154, 165–169, 190, 194; with youth subculture, 179
enlightenment, 20
epistemology: break/rupture/struggle of, 4, 25–26, 133, 136, 143, 156, 163, 175, 193, 201; method (of liberation), 14–15, 19, 69, 139
eroticism. See sexuality
estrangement, 4–5, 15, 43, 58, 64, 83, 175, 213
ethics: ambiguity of, 111; in filmmaking, 15, 30, 39–40; 43, 103, 139; lack of, 128, 212; of self-revolution, 165
ethnonationalism, 2, 5–6, 28, 50–51, 110–113, 204
everydayness, everyday life: burden of, 178, 207; dehabituation of, 16, 22, 38, 60, 101, 159; joy in, 87–92, 168; as sphere of struggle, 17–18, 30, 76, 160–169; stagnancy of, 55, 83, 173; usefulness of, 73. See also *byt*; Lefebvre, Henri; surrealism

Fairfax, Daniel, 7, 25–26, 32, 133, 137
Fanon, Frantz, 112
fantasy: in documentary theory, 41; in film content, 20, 46, 62, 65, 68, 111, 125, 174, 181–183
Far Right, 5, 18, 113
feminism: as character in film, 150; feminist studies, 30, 128, 134–135, 154; as filmmaker's ethics, 141, 167, 189; as topic of conversation, 80
fetish, fetishization, 20, 22–23, 48
Un film comme les autres, 27, 139
Fisher, Mark, 156, 213–214
folklore, 1–2, 20, 98, 111–112, 116
Foucault, Michel, 18–19, 155, 158
Frankfurt School, 106, 181
Freud, Sigmund: concepts from, 52, 88, 118, 169, 201; connected to aesthetic technique, 53, 100, 170, 173; critique of, 18; philosophers' influence from, 20, 57, 88, 207. See also psychoanalysis; uncanny
Funeral Parade of Roses. See *Bara no sōretsu*
Furuhata, Yuriko, 31, 40, 49, 55–59, 128, 148, 163, 171, 191
Furusato, 178
Furyō shōnen (*Bad Boys*), 53, 97–98, 102–105, 184, 189, 217

fūten, fūtenzoku, 165, 171, 179
Futurism, 3, 162

Gance, Abel, 60
Gatti, Armand, 66–67, 71–75, 84, 86, 95
gayboy, 20, 161–163, 171, 227
gayness. See homosexuality
Gei boi. See *gayboy*
gender: in French film, 138, 142, 145, 150; in Japanese culture, 167, 191, 226; in Japanese film, 30, 127–129, 158, 163, 169–173, 176, 185–186, 189–190. See also *gayboy*; homosexuality; queerness
genderfluid. See genderqueer
genderqueer, 163, 183–186
Genet, Jean, 160
Germany: fascism in, 6, 39, 203; West Germany, 8, 164
ghost. See fantasy; folklore; supernatural
Godard, Jean-Luc: connection to DVG, 10, 16, 27–31, 84, 93, 130–154; connection to French new wave, 69, 85, 89; films by, 7, 9, 77, 127–129, 194–195; politics/theory of, 19, 24, 110, 192
Gómez, Sara, 91–92
Goodwin, Michael, 131, 133
Gorin, Jean-Pierre, 130–132, 138, 146–154, 192
Gozenchū no jikkanwari (*Morning Schedule*), 162, 183–189
graffiti, 27–28, 103, 181–182
Gramsci, Antonio, 177
Great Patriotic War. See World War II
Greater East Asia Co-Prosperity Sphere, 8, 37–38, 204
Grierson, John, 100
Guattari, Félix. See Deleuze, Gilles and Félix Guattari
Guernica, 45–46, 57, 70, 73, 211
La guerre est finie (*The War Is Over*), 25, 65
Guevara, Che, 171–172
gutai, 42

Hall, Jonathan M., 20, 161, 163, 170, 172
Hanada Kiyoteru, 11, 29–31, 40–49, 61, 64, 99, 112, 118
Hani Susumu: films by, 53, 97, 102–106, 162–163, 169, 183–192; as Japanese political avant-garde, 42, 49, 111, 119, 125, 128, 137, 152, 156; theory of, 10, 110, 217
Hansen, Miriam, 16
happenings (performance art), 159–160, 179. See also theater; Zero Jigen

Hara Kazuo, 128, 226
Hariu Ichiro, 6, 100–101
haunting. *See* supernatural
Hegel, Georg Wilhelm Friedrich, 22–23, 46, 109
hibakusha, 112
hippies, 139, 142, 150, 165, 168, 171, 179. See also *fūten*
Hirohito, 34–35, 115
Hiroshima, 118, 121, 122, 125. See also *Hiroshima mon amour*
Hiroshima mon amour, 54, 72–73, 125, 172, 176
Hitler, Adolf, 18, 35
Hokkaido, 117–118, 121, 126
Holocaust, 14, 38, 70, 205
homosexuality: in France, 154; in Japan, 20, 30, 158–161, 166, 169–171, 174, 179
La hora de los ornos (*Hour of the Furnaces*), 9
humanism, 11, 44, 84, 99, 103–104, 184–186
humor: in French film, 25, 73, 80, 148–149; in general, 154; in Japanese film, 162, 181, 186

ICAIC (Instituto Cubano del Arte e Industria Cinematográficos), 86, 91
iconoclasm, 10, 30, 135, 146, 158
iedenin becchō ("runaway book"), 176
Igarashi, Yoshikuni, 120
Imamura Shōhei: film analysis of, 28, 61–64, 98, 106–119, 122–128; as part of Japanese political avant-garde, 49, 137, 152, 192
Imamura Taihei, 41, 99
imperialism: American, 8, 37–39, 105, 164; global, 2, 33, 66, 88, 98, 108, 150; in Japan, 22, 37–39. *See also* anti-imperialism; United States of America
indigeneity, 111–112, 117
individualism, 15, 48, 80, 132, 177
intersubjectivity. *See* subjectivity
Ishi no uta (*Song of the Stone*), 50, 55–57, 60, 88, 170
Israel, 79
Ivens, Joris, 24, 86, 209
Iwanami Productions, 103, 119, 121, 217
Iwasaki Akira, 39, 47, 61

Japanese Communist Party (JCP), 22, 44, 47, 99, 126
Japanese New Wave. *See* New Wave
japonisme, 10
Jews, 2–3, 13–14, 198, 202, 205
Jew's harp. See *mukkuri*
Jikken Kōbō, 56
Jizo statue, 55, 116

Le Joli Mai, 76–85, 90, 137, 193–194, 200
journals: in both France and Japan, 9–10, 24, 29–30; connection to documentation, 5, 31, 158, 189; connection to leftism generally, 7, 32, 95, 106, 193; in France, 25, 65–71, 130–134, 137, 146, 151, 156, 196, 213–214; in Japan, 35, 40, 64, 70, 100, 108, 110, 118, 178, 191; in USA, 131; in USSR, 70, 75. See also *Cahiers du cinéma*; *Kiroku eiga*
jump cut, 3, 31, 60, 91
Jusqu'à la victoire (*Until Victory*), 139

kabuki, 173
Kalatozov, Mikhail, 86
Kanba Michiko, 48
Kapur, Nick, ix, 8, 21, 44, 163, 192
Karatani Kōjin, 4
Karmen, Roman, 86
Kaufman, Boris, 132. *See also* Vertov, Dziga
Kaufman, David. *See* Vertov, Dziga
Kaufman, Mikhail, 42. *See also* Vertov, Dziga
Kinema junpō, 10, 64, 105, 118
Kino-Glaz (*Kino-Eye*): concept, 13, 90; film, 17, 89
kinoks, 42
kinooshchushchenie, 16, 133, 151, 201, 206
Kino-Pravda, 16, 132, 192
Kiroku eiga: in general, 10, 70; quotes from, 20–24, 35, 39–40, 43, 53–54, 61, 100, 104, 108–110, 120, 125–126, 170, 177, 184
Kishi Nobusuke, 21, 35–36, 124, 208
Kobayashi Sachiko, 226
Kracauer, Siegfried, 24
Kubrick, Stanley, 172
Kureijī Rabu (*Crazy Love*), 168
KuroDalaiJee, 159, 169
Kuroki Kazuo, 6, 28, 98, 107, 110–111, 117–128, 217
Kurosawa, Akira, 105, 209, 218
Kyoto, 50, 121, 124

Lamarre, Thomas, 41
Latin America, 5, 9, 24, 26, 29, 32, 72, 76, 85–92, 100–102
Leacock, Richard, 77, 85, 150
Lefebvre, Henri, 76, 167
leftism: of 1960s in general, 5–8, 11, 30; contemporary movements, x, 2–3, 196–200; in France, 9–10, 66–69, 75–77, 83, 94–95, 107, 131–147, 153; general films of, 29, 86; global culture of, 26, 32, 44, 72, 193; in Japan, 20–21, 35, 42, 47, 70, 99, 104–106,

leftism (*continued*)
  108–113, 128, 156, 160–165, 177, 190–191, 204; militancy of, 25–30, 72–73, 84, 89, 130, 155–156, 191. *See also* New Left; Old Left
Left Bank, 64–69, 94, 107, 136, 213
Lenin, Vladimir: person, 12, 42, 149, 181; theory of, 89, 130–140
lesbianism, 169, 185
Lettre de Sibérie (*Letter from Siberia*), 72, 83–84
Les Lettres françaises: history of, 9, 24, 30, 66–67; publication from, 65, 68–72, 94
Letter to Jane, 153
Lewis, Sophie, 162, 176
Lhomme, Pierre, 79–80, 193–194
life caught unawares. *See zhizn' v rasplokh*
life (return to), liveliness, 4–5, 16, 24–28, 87, 93, 99, 157, 160–169, 179, 201
Loin du Vietnam (*Far from Vietnam*), 85
Loridan, Marceline, 178
love: free love, 131, 147, 150, maternal, 59–60; revolutionary, 192; romantic, 68, 168–169, 171, 173, 176
Love, Heather, x, 168, 189
Löwy, Michael, 22, 43
Lukács, György, 42
Lumière, Brothers, 23, 46, 124, 137
Lumpenproletariat, 78, 112
Luttes en Italie (*Struggle in Italy*), 127, 133, 138–139, 142–148, 152

MacArthur, Douglas, 35
Mackay, John, x, 14, 32, 132
magic, 12, 15, 93, 179, 193
Makavejev, Dušan, 153
Malitsky, Joshua, 15, 32, 86
Malraux, André, 181
Mao Zedong, 18, 133, 138, 142
Marcuse, Herbert, 18, 155, 168–169, 207
Marker, Chris: comparison to Godard, 136–137; comparison to Japanese filmmakers, 54, 57; connection to Left Bank filmmakers, 64–76, 86–95; film analysis of, 9, 30–31, 50, 76–86, 193–194, 200, 214
Marx, Karl, 18, 42, 179
Marxism: in aesthetics, 4; connection to Freud, 18, 57, 169; connection to Nietzsche, 18; ideology of filmmakers, 22–23, 50–56, 67, 75–76, 110, 130–140, 147–149, 170, 177, 181; ideology of theorists, 39–44, 177; in politics, 15, 89, 146

masks, 51–52, 106, 165–166, 171
masochism: as framework, 51, 162. *See also* sadomasochism
Massumi, Brian, 19
Matsuda Masao, 10, 190
Matsukawa Yasuo, 6, 117–118, 128
Matsumoto Toshio: analysis of *Bara no sōretsu*, 11, 156, 160–163, 166, 170–175; analysis of short films, 34–39, 50–62, 108, 211; connection to French New Wave, 66, 70, 83, 88, 138, 154, 193, 200; connection to Japanese political avant-garde, 10, 97, 101, 104–105, 109–110, 113, 115–118, 121–125, 128, 176–185, 190–192; theory of, 4–6, 19–24, 26, 29–33, 40–49, 64, 137, 169, 201, 207. *See also Bara no sōretsu*
May 1968: culture of, 24, 151; film of, 16, 27, 84–85, 129–134, 137; philosophy of, 18, 20, 155, 208; protests of, 48, 67, 168, 196
Mayakovsky, Vladimir, 68, 155, 181, 189
media: film and television, 2–4, 9, 105, 136–139, 156–157, 175, 194; journalism, 7, 48, 112, 166; media literacy, 15, 24–25, 64, 94, 136, 163, 193–196; media theory in general, 5, 31, 106; media theory in Japan, 42, 45, 191; mediation, 115, 148, 187; mixed media, 172; representation in, 87
Méliès, Georges, 23–24, 46, 93, 124, 137
Melville, Anne-Marie, 153
Michelson, Annette, 4, 14, 17, 105, 133, 175
middle-classification: France, 78; in Japan, 8, 30
migrants, 78, 87
militarism, 6, 119–120
military bases (American), 21, 165
Miroir du cinéma, 10, 24, 30, 66–71, 77, 84, 156
Mishima Yukio, 113, 158, 160, 166
misogyny. *See* sexism
Mizoguchi Kenji, 10
modernism: aesthetic, 51, 103, 151, 181, 207; antimodernism, 189; political, 14, 69, 133, 152
modernity, 32, 52, 111–112
Montand, Yves, 65, 82, 153
Morin, Edgar, 9, 11, 24, 76–77, 80–81, 132, 137, 178, 217. *See also Chronique d'un été*; *cinéma-vérité*; Rouch, Jean
mukkuri (Jew's harp), 117–118
Muñoz, José Esteban, 162, 172
music: in film analysis, 56–58, 82, 88–93, 116, 162, 172, 179; in general, 87–88, 154

INDEX   253

Mussolini, Benito, 6, 18, 203
myth: in general, 201; in Imamura, 30, 111, 116, 118; mythic couple, 68; myth of evidence, 143; Oedipus myth, 20, 171–173. *See also* Oedipus

Nagano (place), 191
Nagano Chiaki, 6, 35–36, 38–40
Nagasaki, 123–125
Nakahara Yūsuke, 24
Nakai Masakazu, 11, 41–42, 59, 99–100, 106
nakedness. *See* nudity
Narboni, Jean, 24, 143
Nathan, Patrick, 16, 19, 166
National Socialism. *See* Nazi
nationalism, 2, 5–7, 26–30, 50–51, 96–98, 105–113, 166–167, 204, 219. *See also* ethnonationalism
Nazi, 3, 14, 18, 25, 39, 148–150
neo-documentary, 23, 39–40, 45–49, 57–66, 70, 97, 101, 104, 115, 137, 170
neofascist, 140
neorealism, 99, 103
New Left, 30, 106, 128, 162, 191
New Wave: French Left Bank, 29, 64–65, 107; French Right Bank, 130; global new waves, 7, 91–92; Japanese, 10, 160–161, 172, 204–205, 218
Ngai, Sianne, 19
Nietzsche, Friedrich, 18, 27
nihilism, 18, 126 165
nihonjinron, 111–113
Ningen jōhatsu (*A Man Vanishes*), 61–64
Nippon konchūki (*Insect Woman*), 28, 98, 107, 110–119, 122, 128, 218
Nishijin (*Weavers of Nishijin*), 50–57, 61–62, 83, 104, 110, 115, 170
Nixon, Richard, 142
Noda Shinkichi, 40, 54, 184
Noh, 32, 52, 62
Nornes, Markus, 31, 40, 60, 100, 103, 121, 191
nūberu bāgu. *See* New Wave
nuclear radiation, 123
nuclear weapons, 38, 122
nudity, 140–142, 147, 166, 172, 186
Nuit et brouillard (*Night and Fog*), 38, 70, 72–73, 176, 205

objectivity: Abe's challenge of, 49; in documentation, 83, 85; Matsumoto's rejection of, 41–44, 53–54, 169–170, 174–177, 183; reality, 95; rejection of, 63, 69, 80, 121, 133, 136, 183; vs. subjectivity, 16, 19, 52, 57, 85, 101. *See also* subjectivity
Octobre à Paris (*October in Paris*), 9
Ōe Masanori, 168–169
Oedipus: in Deleuze and Guattari, 18, 155, 196, 207, in Matsumoto, 19–20, 171–173. See also *Anti-Oedipus*
Ogawa Productions, 128
Ogawa Shinsuke, 121, 128, 146, 217
Oguma Eiji, 163–164
Ōishi Masahiko, 174
Okabe Michio, 154, 168, 190
Okamoto Tarō, 42
Old Left, 44
Los Olvidados (*The Young and the Damned*), 97–102, 104, 125. *See also* Buñuel, Luis
Olympics (Tokyo), 28, 30, 96, 105, 107–108
Oncle Yanco (*Uncle Yanco*), 86, 88, 92
One American Movie (*One A.M.*), 150
One-Dimensional Man, 18, 207
Ōshima Nagisa, 10, 42, 57, 99, 109, 113, 152, 160, 167–168, 187, 204–205
ostranenie. *See* estrangement
El otro cristóbal (*The Other Christopher*), 72
Oudart, Jean-Pierre, 24
Ozu Yasujirō, 58, 113

Pacific War. *See* World War II
PCF (Parti communiste français), 25, 65, 68, 71
PCMLF (Parti communiste marxiste-léniniste de France), 138,
pain. *See* discomfort
Palestine, 79, 139
Paris, protests in, 27, 48, 164; subject of film, 58, 68, 76–83, 178, 201, 220; theory of, 181; university location, 132
Pays, Jean-Louis, 84
pedagogy. *See* education
perception: faculty of sight, 175, 183; liberatory perception, 201; public perception, 135; renewal/transformation of, 4, 17, 60, 115
performance art, 159, 166, 171, 179
Le Petit Soldat, 9, 137
phenomenology, revolutionary, 17, 163, 201
photography: methods, 41, 134; profession, 55, 158, 177; use in film, 1, 34–35, 57–60, 87–90, 153
Picasso, Pablo, 45
Piccoli, Michel, 89
pink film, 128, 147, 161, 185, 190, 204, 225
play: act of, 186–187, 199; affect of, 4–5, 17, 30, 66, 73–75, 84–86, 91–94, 121, 147, 189,

play (*continued*)
  193–194; relation to queerness/queer film, 156–159, 163, 166–171, 176–180, 183, 192
pleasure: connection to bodily sensuality, 159–162, 168; critique of, 28, 30, 129–142, 147, 150–156; feeling of, 4–5, 12, 19, 37, 66, 69, 85, 88–89, 93, 162, 167; use of, 26,
pogrom. *See* antisemitism
La Pointe Courte, 68, 74–75
police, 149–150, 191
political modernism, 14, 69, 133
pornography: critique of, 131, 140, 155; genre, 141–142, 154, 224; *The Pornographers* (film), 111
Positif, 9, 68, 71, 213
positivism, 4, 20, 22, 45
postwar: in general, 7, 94, 195; period in France, 9, 32, 78; period in Japan, 23–24, 31, 34–48, 61, 99–103, 108, 111–114, 118–120, 127, 163, 185
PR films, 22, 47–48, 119–212
Pravda (film), 139, 142, 148. See also Kino-Pravda
prewar, 31, 36, 41, 79, 106, 120
prison, 82–83, 150, 191, 201. *See also* abolition
processive filmmaking, 184
Proletarian Film League of Japan (Prokino), 36
Pronin, Aleksandr, 14
propaganda, 20, 22, 26, 35–39, 45–47, 86, 95, 119, 124, 146, 155. *See also* agitational propaganda
protest: act in general, 2, 40; ANPO 1960, 21, 30, 34, 40, 48–49, 61, 111–115, 124; of late 1960s, 10, 67, 139, 164–171, 196; other protests, 123, 154, 158, 163, 200
protofascism, 3, 23
protopolitics, 19
Proust, Marcel, 159
psychedelics, 168, 179, 213
psychiatry and the anti-psychiatric, 20, 208
psychoanalysis: critique of, 18, 207, 230; method of, 40, 45
psychology: combined with politics, 5, 154; film interest in, 104; inner world, 40, 43–44; liberation psychology, 154, 196; philosophical interest in, 20
public relations films. *See* PR films

queer studies, 135, 154
queerness: in film content, 19; in Japanese ATG films, 30, 156–163, 166–176, 181–183, 186–192

racism, 6, 8, 78, 91, 135, 150, 155, 204. *See also* anti-racism
Raine, Michael, 2, 40, 47, 107, 111, 113, 115, 119, 127–128
realism, 10, 31, 41–44, 49, 61, 85, 99, 107, 122, 124, 140, 174–176, 183, 189. *See also* socialist realism
reenchantment, 4–5, 17, 159, 201–202
religion. *See* spirituality
Renoir, Jean, 24–27, 209
repetition, 54–55, 58, 60, 124, 136, 161
reportage, 8, 44, 86, 115, 133, 143
Resnais, Alain: connection to Marker/Varda, 64–75, 213; contemporary influence from, 194; films by, 9, 25, 29–31, 38, 85, 88, 90, 95, 205, 213; Japanese influence from, 45, 54, 57, 125, 136, 172, 176
responsibility (postwar), 21, 39–40, 71
reverse-reel/reverse-motion, 12, 60
Revolution, 1868, 122; 1960s, 28, 130–132, 155; Bolshevik, 14–16, 32; Cuban, 29, 32, 86–92; Haitian, 87; Yippie, 169. *See also* self-revolution
Richie, Donald, 158
Riefenstahl, Leni, 3
Right (the), 5, 18, 113, 200, 208
Right Bank, 213
ritual, 116–117, 169
Rodowick, D.N., 4, 14, 133, 151
romantic anti-capitalism, 22, 177, 207
Ross, Kristin, 8, 78–79
Rossellini, Roberto, 99
Rotha, Paul, 100
Rouch, Jean, 9, 76–77, 80–85, 132, 137, 151, 178, 184–185, 217
runaway book. See *iedenin becchō*

sadism, 22, 141
sadomasochism, 5, 58, 161, 167; sadomasochistic aesthetic, 4, 19–22, 40, 55, 64–66, 88, 104, 138, 156, 173–174
Sadoul, Georges, 9–11, 15, 24, 29, 55, 64–68, 72–79, 84–85, 93, 132, 213–215
Salazkina, Masha, x, 32
Salut les Cubains, 76, 86–92
Sas, Miryam, x, 19, 31, 40, 45–48, 52, 55–57, 70, 163, 176–177
Sasaki Hajime, 6, 39–40
Sasori-za (Scorpio Theater), 160
Satō Tadao, 50–52, 57, 183
Schieder, Chelsea Szendi, x, 163–164, 167
Scorpio Rising, 160

Seazer, J.A., 179
self-criticism. *See* auto-critique
Self-Defense Forces (Japanese), 34, 124
self-revolution, 30, 157, 160–169, 174, 179, 185–189, 192,
semi-documentary: adjective, 184; connections to non-Japanese film, 76, 91, 137; contemporary examples, 194; genre in Japan, 42, 46, 61, 66, 97–111, 118–128, 158, 220
sexism: in culture generally, 167; in film, 89, 127–128, 134, 142, 152–153, 167; in journalism, 128; in Left spaces, 91, 191
sexuality: heterosexuality, 91, 180; queer sexuality, 30, 154, 157–161, 167–169, 174, 183–190; sexploitation, 128, 204; sexual imagery in film, 139, 147; sexual/romantic interest/sexual leasure, 89, 117, 129, 133–134, 147, 155, 173, 179, 189; sexual violence/rape, 35, 114, 153, 167, 180, 228; sex work, 114, 124, 146, 179–180; vs. gender, 167, 226
Shinjuku, Tokyo, 158–161, 165, 171, 179, 190
Shinjuku dorobō nikki, 160, 168
Shinto, 52
Shklovsky, Viktor, 15–16, 59, 70–71, 93, 177
Sho o suteyo, machi e deyō, 161–162, 175, 180–183, 190, 192, 228
Showa Era, 6, 34, 107
shutai (subject), 10, 44, 47
shutaiseiron, 10, 44. *See also* subjectivity
sight. *See* vision
Situationism, 134, 136, 181
SLON (Société pour le lancement des ouvres Nouvelles), 84–85
socialism: against fascism, 3; connection to USSR, 11, 37; contemporary movements, 196; global socialism, 26, 87; ideology of film, 67, 79, 87–88, 107, 140, 205, 209. *See also* socialist realism
socialist realism, 22, 43–44, 47–48, 70
Southeast Asia, 5, 35, 58–60, 153, 164–166, 178
Soviet Union. *See* USSR
spirituality: connection to political, 98; contrast to political, 155; religious, 50–52, 114, 118, 189
Stachka (Strike), 26–27
Stalin, Joseph: post-Stalin, 11, 15, 48
Stalinism, 41, 44, 48
stop-motion, 12, 60, 88, 91
strike (labor movement), 25, 140, 209. See also *Stachka (Strike)*
student: character in film, 25, 91, 139, 143, 163, 184, 187; personal experience, ix, 192;

radicals during protest movements, 18, 48, 105, 111–113, 162–168, 171, 185
Les Statues meurent aussi (Statues Also Die), 70, 72–73, 194
subconscious, 52, 58, 104
subjectivity: consciousness, 198; debates in Japan, 10; emphasis in documentary, 23, 42, 64, 66, 76–77, 81–85, 90; intersubjectivity, 102–104, 110, 179, 184, 187, 189; subjective expression, 41, 48, 60; suppression of, 49, 61; vs objectivity, 16, 19, 44, 47, 52–53, 57, 101. *See also* objectivity
supernatural: feeling of, 2, 56–57; Japanese folklore in film, 39, 48–49, 61, 111; as metaphor, 16, 40. *See also* folklore
sur-documentary, 43, 45–46, 49, 64, 118
surrealism: aesthetic, 4, 22, 39–51, 60–68, 72, 81, 86, 97–107, 116–118, 160, 173, 179, 192, 201; person(s), 9, 28, 65, 68, 107, 207
Svilova, Elizaveta, 15, 132

taboo, 9, 125, 127, 190, 205
taikyoku shugi (bipolarism), 42
taishō (subject), 38, 44. See also *shutaiseiron*; subjectivity
Takahashi Mutsuo, 158
Take One (journal), 131
Tatlin, Vladimir, 181
television: funding source, 143, 152; people appearing on, 74, 140, 171; topic of discourse, 8, 142, 178, 218; use by filmmakers, 49–50, 55, 58, 139, 172, 178, 191
Tenshi no kōkotsu (Ecstasy of the Angels), 147, 167
Terayama Shūji: collaboration with Matsumoto, 58, 173; connection with Japanese political avant-garde, 49, 62, 113, 154–163, 183, 191–192; film analysis, 169, 175–183, 228
Teshigahara Hiroshi, 42, 218
theater: art form, 69, 169, 176–177, 191; Art Theatre Guild (ATG), 30, 157–158; epic theater (Brecht), 148; space, 74, 160, 204–205; theatrical quality, 70, 105, 124, 170. *See also* performance art
A Thousand Plateaus, 18, 200
Tobenai chinmoku (Silence Has No Wings), 28, 98, 107, 117–127
Tōhō studios, 105, 119, 209
Tokyo: counterculture of, 20, 158–160, 165–166, 171, 179; filming/studio location, 112, 178; postwar history, 61, 100, 102, 120,

Tokyo (*continued*)
  126, 156, 191; relation to Olympics, 28, 30, 105–108, 119; setting of film, 114–115, 119, 121, 182, 187. *See also* Olympics
Tokyo Olympics. *See* Olympics
Tōkyō sensō sengo hiwa (*The Man Who Left His Will on Film*), 187
Tomato Kechappu Kōtei (*Emperor Tomato Ketchup*), 228
Tout va bien, 152–153
Treaty of Mutual Cooperation and Security. *See* ANPO
tricks, 13–17, 35, 39, 60, 82, 118, 169
Triolet, Elsa, 68, 88
triuki. *See* tricks
Truffaut, François, 69, 102–103, 130
truth: approved/official, 4, 8, 20, 74, 136, 155; as artifice, 77, 121; from lies, 97, 107, 137, 189; personal, 78; revealing/telling, 40, 57, 82, 109, 111, 125, 133, 136, 139, 155, 183; thwarting/refusal of, 11, 16, 20, 62–64, 133, 140, 156, 163, 172–177, 183, 192, 198–201; truthfulness, 49
Tsuchimoto Noriaki, 121, 125–126, 217

Ukraine, 1–3, 12
ultraright. *See* Far Right
uncanny: in aesthetic form, 46–53, 61, 64, 87–88, 116–118, 123, 125; in language, 39; in relation to queerness, 183. *See also* Freud, Sigmund; surrealism
unconscious, 46, 49, 52, 134
Union de la Jeunesse Communiste Marxiste-Léniniste (UJCML), 130, 138
United Red Army, 147, 150, 191
United States of America (USA): culture of, 10–11, 24, 77, 163; imperialism/militarism of, 7–8, 11, 21, 34–38, 58, 105, 108, 113, 164, 194; nationality of, 158, 160, 178; oppression/racism in, 135, 149–150, 155; radicals in, 148, 196; screenings in, 152; soldiers of, 165. *See also* anti-Americanism; Cold War
unveiling: atrocities, 8, 38, 49, 64, 66, 70, 78, 118; connection to epistemological break, 16, 26, 34, 39, 62–64, 136; revealing the hidden in general, 4, 30, 54, 60–61, 95, 131; veiling, 61, 98
USSR: country/location, 2, 5, 11, 13, 15, 32, 35, 41, 75, 144, 157; influence from, 11, 32, 36, 132
utopia, 110, 145, 161, 167, 189–190, 207

Varda, Agnès: connection to Left Bank, 9, 29–31, 64–69, 72–76, 136, 213; connection to other filmmakers, 184; films by, 3, 9, 53–54, 85–95, 107, 145, 194; other discussion of, 196, 213–214
veiling. *See* unveiling
Le Vent d'est (*Wind from the East*), 135, 138, 142–143, 148, 151
Verfremdungseffekt (Alienation Effect), 15, 142, 148, 152
Vertov, Dziga: analysis of films, 3–4, 11–17, 55, 172; connection to DVG, 132–135, 143–144, 150; connection to Japanese film, 60, 70, 98, 157, 174–175, 179, 181–182, 192; connection to Latin American film, 86; connection to other French film, 26, 32, 83, 89, 93; film theory, 133, 151, 201, 206, 221; personality of, 155. *See also Chelovek s kinoapparatom*; DVG
Vichy France, 6, 8
victimhood: of atomic bomb, 123; connection to queerness, 189; liberation for, 196; perpetual victimhood/criticism of category, 198, 201; of radical theorists during WWII, 42, 206; of Vietnam War, 58
La vie est à nous (*Life Belongs to Us*), 25–26
Vietnam, esp. Vietnam War, 58–60, 153, 164–166, 178
vision, 16, 46, 49, 50, 108, 121
Vladimir et Rosa, 135, 138–139, 148–151
voice-over, 25–26, 34–39, 48–55, 76–83, 89–90, 103, 118, 142–150, 200

Wakamatsu Kōji, 10, 128, 147, 161, 167
Watanabe Hiroshi, 108
Weatherby, Meredith, 158
West Germany. *See* Germany
Wiazemsky, Anne, 145, 148, 150
Williams, Linda, 141–142, 222–223
Williams, Raymond, 19
Wollen, Peter, 93, 135, 151–152
World War II: in France, 7–8, 66, 72; in Japan, 6–8, 21, 35–40, 61, 64, 115, 119, 122, 127, 203–204; postwar, 100, 118; in USSR, 13, 35. *See also* complicity

Yamamoto, Naoki, 31, 39–40, 48, 99–100
Yamamoto Satsuo, 22
Yamato (race), 38, 117
Yanagita Kunio, 111–112, 116
Yatō Tamotsu, 158
Yomota Inuhiko, 165–166, 171, 226

Yoru no Kai (The Night Society), 42
Yoshida Kiju, 182
youth: as baby boomer generation, 11; collaborators with Hani, 185–189; in contemporary Japan, 204; in French film, 78, 83–85, 91–92; in Japanese film, 51, 100–103, 121, 139; members of counterculture, 142, 150, 158–159, 165, 168, 173, 176–181; members of student movement, 162, 167, 191; youthful aesthetics, 94, 171. See also *fūten*; hippies

Yūkoku (*Patriotism*), 166
Yutkevich, Sergei, 24, 132

Zahlten, Alex, ix, 161, 192, 205, 209
zasetsu-kan (disappointment), 105
Zero Jigen (Zero Dimension), 159, 166, 168–169, 171
zhizn' v rasplokh (Life caught unawares), 17, 77

Founded in 1893,
UNIVERSITY OF CALIFORNIA PRESS
publishes bold, progressive books and journals
on topics in the arts, humanities, social sciences,
and natural sciences—with a focus on social
justice issues—that inspire thought and action
among readers worldwide.

The UC PRESS FOUNDATION
raises funds to uphold the press's vital role
as an independent, nonprofit publisher, and
receives philanthropic support from a wide
range of individuals and institutions—and from
committed readers like you. To learn more, visit
ucpress.edu/supportus.

www.ingramcontent.com/pod-product-compliance
Lightning Source LLC
Chambersburg PA
CBHW021342230426
43666CB00006B/382